NEO-ASSYRIAN HISTORICAL INSCRIPTIONS AND SYRIA-PALESTINE

Israelite/Judean-Tyrian-Damascene Political and Commercial Relations in the Ninth–Eighth Centuries BCE

JEFFREY KAH-JIN KUAN

WIPF & STOCK • Eugene, Oregon

NEO-ASSYRIAN HISTORICAL INSCRIPTIONS AND SYRIA-PALESTINE:

Israelite/Judean-Tyrian-Damascene Political and Commercial Relations in the Ninth–Eighth Centuries BCE

Jeffrey Kah-jin Kuan

Ph.D., 1994
Emory University

Advisor:
John H. Hayes

Wipf and Stock Publishers
199 W 8th Ave, Suite 3
Eugene, OR 97401

Neo-Assyrian Historical Inscriptions and Syria-Palestine
Israelite/Judean-Tyrian-Damascene Political and Commercial
Relations in the Ninth-Eighth Centuries BCE
By Kuan, Jeffrey Kah-Jin

ISBN 13: 978-1-4982-8143-0
Publication date 2/19/2016
Previously published by Alliance Bible Seminary, 1995

To Valentine Toh

TABLE OF CONTENTS

Abbreviations xi
Series Foreword xv
Foreword xvii
Preface xix
Abstract xxi

Introduction 1

Chapter One: The Reign of Shalmaneser III 5
- I. Introduction 5
- II. Assyrian Inscriptions 7
  - A. The Eponym Chronicle 7
  - B. The "Bronze Gates of Balâwât" 22
  - C. The Monolith Inscription 27
  - D. The "Baghdad Text" 47
  - E. III R 5, 6 51
  - F. The Marble-Slab Inscription 61
  - G. The Black Obelisk Inscription 62
- III. Synopsis 66

Chapter Two: The Reign of Adad-nirari III 69
- I. Introduction 69
- II. Assyrian Inscriptions 71
  - A. The Eponym Chronicle 71
  - B. The Antakya Stela 75
  - C. The el-Rimah Stela 78
  - D. The Calah (Nimrud) Slab 81
  - E. The Saba'a Stela 84
  - F. The Sheikh Hammad Stela 87
  - G. The Scheil and Millard Fragment 88
  - H. The Pazarcik (Kahramanmaraş) Stela 89

III. Synopsis 93
A. History of Interpretation 93
B. Critique 97
C. Reconstruction 99

Chapter Three: The Reigns of Shalmaneser IV, Ashur-dan III, and Ashur-nirari V 107
I. Introduction 107
II. Assyrian Inscriptions 112
A. The Eponym Chronicle 112
B. The Pazarcik Stela 115
III. Šamši-ilu and Syro-Palestinian Politics 120
IV. Synopsis 133

Chapter Four: The Reign of Tiglath-pileser III 135
I. Introduction 135
II. Assyrian Inscriptions 136
A. The Eponym Chronicle 136
B. Layard 45b + III R 9, 1 138
C. The Iran Stela 146
D. Layard 50a + 50b + 67a 153
E. Layard $69a_1$ + $69b_2$ 157
F. II R 67 161
G. ND 400 164
H. Layard 29b 167
I. Layard 72b + 73a 171
J. Layard 66 173
K. III R 10, 2 176
L. ND 4301 + 4305 182
III. Synopsis 186

Chapter Five: The Reign of Shalmaneser V 193
I. Introduction 193
II. Assyrian (Babylonian) Sources 193
A. The Eponym Chronicle 193
B. Babylonian Chronicle 1 194
III. Non-Cuneiform Sources 197
A. Josephus's *Antiquities* 9.14.2 §§283–287 197
B. 2 Kings 17:1–6; 18:9–12 200
C. Hosea 9:10–14 204

ABBREVIATIONS

AB	Anchor Bible
ABC	A. K. Grayson, *Assyrian and Babylonian Chronicles*
ABD	D. N. Freedman (ed.), *Anchor Bible Dictionary*
ABRL	Anchor Bible Reference Library
AfO	*Archiv für Orientforschung*
Ag.Ap.	Josephus, *Against Apion*
AION	*Annali del'Istituto Universitario Orientale de Napoli*
AJA	*American Journal of Archaeology*
AJSL	*American Journal of Semitic Languages and Literature*
ANEP	J. B. Pritchard (ed.), *The Ancient Near Eastern in Pictures Relating to the Old Testament*
ANET	J. B. Pritchard (ed.), *Ancient Near Eastern Texts Relating to the Old Testament*
AnOr	Analecta orientalia
AnSt	*Anatolian Studies*
Ant.	Josephus, *Jewish Antiquities*
AOAT	Alter Orient und Altes Testament
AOS	American Oriental Series
ARAB	D. D. Luckenbill, *Ancient Records of Assyria and Babylonia*
ARI	A. K. Grayson, *Assyrian Royal Inscriptions*
AzTh	Arbeiten zur Theologie
ATD	Das Alte Testament Deutsch
AW	*Antike Welt*
AUSS	*Andrews University Seminary Studies*
BA	*Biblical Archaeologist*
BAR	*Biblical Archaeologist Reader*
BARev	*Biblical Archaeology Review*

BASOR	*Bulletin of the American Schools of Oriental Research*
BAT	Die Botschaft des Alten Testaments
Bib	*Biblica*
BKAT	Biblischer Kommentar: Altes Testament
BN	*Biblische Notizen*
BO	*Bibliotheca orientalis*
BZAW	Beihefte zur Zeitschrift für die alttestamentliche Wissenschaft
CAD	*The Assyrian Dictionary of the Oriental Institute of the University of Chicago*
CAH	*Cambridge Ancient History*
CBQ	*Catholic Biblical Quarterly*
CBQMS	Catholic Biblical Quarterly—Monograph Series
CBSC	Cambridge Bible for Schools and Colleges
CRAIBL	*Comptes rendus de l'Académie des inscriptions et belles-lettres*
DOTT	D. W. Thomas (ed.), *Documents from Old Testament Times*
EHAT	Exegetisches Handbuch zum Alten Testament
ErIsr	Eretz Israel
FOTL	Forms of Old Testament Literature
FRLANT	Forschungen zur Religion und Literatur des Alten und Neuen Testaments
GTA	Göttinger theologische Arbeiten
HAIJ	J. M. Miller and J. H. Hayes, *A History of Ancient Israel and Judah*
HAT	Handbuch zum Alten Testament
HKAT	Handkommentar zum Alten Testament
HSM	Harvard Semitic Monographs
HSS	Harvard Semitic Studies
ICC	International Critical Commentary
IEJ	*Israel Exploration Journal*
JANESCU	*Journal of the Ancient Near Eastern Society of Columbia University*
JAOS	*Journal of the American Oriental Society*
JBL	*Journal of Biblical Literature*
JCS	*Journal of Cuneiform Studies*

JESHO	*Journal of (the) Economic and Social History of the Orient*
JJS	*Journal of Jewish Studies*
JNES	*Journal of Near Eastern Studies*
JNSL	*Journal of Northwest Semitic Languages*
JPOS	*Journal of Palestine Oriental Society*
JQR	*Jewish Quarterly Review*
JRAS	*Journal of the Royal Asiatic Society*
JSOT	*Journal for the Study of the Old Testament*
JSOTSup	Journal for the Study of the Old Testament—Supplement Series
JSS	*Journal of Semitic Studies*
JTS	*Journal of Theological Studies*
KAT	Kommentar zum Alten Testament
KHC	Kurzer Hand-Commentar zum Alten Testament
LCL	Loeb Classical Library
MIO	*Mitteilungen des Instituts für Orientforschung*
MVAG	Mitteilungen der vorderasiatisch-ägyptischen Gesellschaft
NCBC	New Century Bible Commentary
OLP	*Orientalia Lovaniensia Periodica*
OLZ	*Orientalische Literaturzeitung*
Or	*Orientalia* (Rome)
OrAnt	*Oriens Antiquus*
OTL	Old Testament Library
OTS	*Oudtestamentische Studiën*
PEQ	*Palestine Exploration Quarterly*
PJ	*Palästina-Jahrbuch*
RA	*Revue d'assyriologie et d'archéologie orientale*
RB	*Revue biblique*
RLA	E. Ebeling and B. Meissner (eds.), *Reallexikon der Assyriologie*
RSO	*Rivista degli Studi orientali*
SAA	State Archives of Assyria
SAOC	Studies in Ancient Oriental Civilization
SBLDS	Society of Biblical Literature Dissertation Series
ScrHier	Scripta hierosolymitana

SHANE	Studies in the History of the Ancient Near East
SOTSMS	Society for Old Testament Study Monograph Series
ST	*Studia theologica*
StudOr	Studia orientalia
TSBA	*Transactions of the Society of Biblical Archaeology*
TSSI	J. C. L. Gibson, *Textbook of Syrian Semitic Inscriptions*
UF	*Ugarit-Forschungen*
VT	*Vetus Testamentum*
VTSup	Vetus Testamentum, Supplements
WBC	Word Biblical Commentary
WHJP	World History of the Jewish People
WMANT	Wissenschraftliche Monographien zum Alten und Neuen Testament
WO	*Die Welt des Orients*
ZA	*Zeitschrift für Assyriologie*
ZAW	*Zeitschrift für die alttestamentliche Wissenschaft*
ZDMG	*Zeitschrift der deutschen morgenländischen Gesellschaft*
ZDPV	*Zeitschrift des deutschen Palästina-Vereins*

FOREWORD

This work provides a thorough and comprehensive treatment of all the Assyrian inscriptions related to Syro-Palestinian history during the ninth and eighth centuries. It is up-to-date, incorporating materials only recently published. Interesting and important new insights on the politics of Israel, Judah, Damascus, and Phoenicia are found throughout the volume which must be taken into consideration by all historians of biblical times.

John H. Hayes
Professor of Old Testament
Emory University
Atlanta, Georgia
USA

PREFACE

My interest in historical studies began while I was doing coursework in the graduate program. Prof. J. Maxwell Miller introduced me to ancient Israelite history and Syro-Palestinian archaeology. Prof. John H. Hayes helped me see the importance of ancient Near Eastern historical texts for the study of the history of ancient Palestine. In a reading course I took with him, we once talked about the lack of comprehensive and systematic work on Israelite/Judean-Phoenician relations. We talked about the value of the Assyrian historical inscriptions in shedding light on the nature of such relations. Thus began my journey into the past, into the ancient world of the Phoenicians and the Israelites.[1]

In the course of working on the dissertation, it became apparent to me that Israelite-Phoenician relations must be set against the backdrop of the Syro-Palestinian world (of which Aram-Damascus was a key player) and the involvement and influence of Assyria in the region. Therefore, the dissertation was expanded to include Aram-Damascus. I am convinced that Assyrian involvement in the west had a major impact on the relations between Syro-Palestinian states.

It is beyond the scope of this dissertation to cover the entire period of ancient history; hence the focus on the ninth and eighth centuries BCE. Moreover, it is not possible to treat every aspect of relationships; hence the attention on the political and commercial relations.

Through the years of my graduate education and involvement in this project, I have been supported by many individuals and institutions. Emory University awarded me a George W. Woodruff Graduate Fellowship that made my graduate studies possible. Pacific School of Religion provided me a summer grant to assist me in the completion of my dissertation. My fellow students at

---

[1]See my articles "Third Kingdoms 5:1 and Israelite-Tyrian Relations During the Reign of Solomon," *JSOT* 46 (1990), 31–46; "Hosea 9:13 and Josephus's *Antiquities* IX, 277–287," *PEQ* 123 (1991), 103–108; and "Was Omri a Phoenician?," *History and Interpretation: Essays in Honour of John H. Hayes*, eds. M. P. Graham, W. P. Brown, and J. K. Kuan (JSOTSup 173; Sheffield: JSOT, 1993), 231–44.

Emory—in particular, Bill Brown, Brian Jones, Paul Hooker, and Ehud Ben-Zvi—and colleagues at Pacific School of Religion gave me their unselfish support and encouragement. My dissertation committee—Dr. M. Patrick Graham, Dr. Theodore J. Lewis, Dr. Carol A. Newsom, and Dr. J. Maxwell Miller—took much time to read a draft of the dissertation and to make many helpful comments and suggestions. To all of these individuals and institutions, I am grateful.

A special word of thanks and appreciation goes to Dr. John H. Hayes, my dissertation director, mentor, and friend. It was he who pointed me to the wealth of this area of study and guided me throughout the project with his insightful comments and suggestions. His constant support and affirmation of my work helped carry me through difficult periods of writing and revising.

I would also like to acknowledge the help I received from a few individuals in the preparation of the manuscript for publication. Thanks are due to Dr. Philip P. Chia and Dr. K. K. Yeo of *Jian Dao* for their continuing efforts to promote the scholarship of Asian scholars and for their decision to include this work in the Jian Dao Dissertation Series, Dr. Jo Ann Hackett of Harvard University for the use of the diacritical font (*MyFont*) for the Akkadian texts, and Therese DesCamp, my graduate assistant, for her help in editing and proofreading.

Finally, I must express my sincere thanks and gratitude to my parents, Kuan Choon Hock and Ong Geok Luen, for their unending support from half the globe away; to my daughter, Valene, for being a bundle of joy even when I faced difficult moments of the project; and, most of all, to my spouse, Valentine Toh, for believing in me, for encouraging me onward, and for all the sacrifices she had to make for my graduate education. It is to her that I dedicate this dissertation.

Jeffrey Kah-jin Kuan

ABSTRACT

This dissertation investigates the political and commercial relations among Israel/Judah, Aram-Damascus, and Tyre/Sidon in the ninth and eighth centuries BCE. The work focuses primarily on Assyrian historical inscriptions from the period, while non-Assyrian sources, including biblical material, is treated where it supplements the Assyrian sources.

The work consists of five chapters, organized according to the reigns of the Assyrian kings prior to the capture of Samaria by Argon II in 720-719 BCE. The first chapter deals with the reign of Shalmaneser III. It offers a new reading of the eponym chronicle, one that has broad implications for the interpretation of historical events. Attention is given to the anti-Assyrian coalition of the 850s, where Assyrian inscriptions provide evidence that Israel and Aram-Damascus were in close cooperation. In interpreting the relationship between Assyria and Tyre/Sidon in the Assyrian texts, it is suggested that Tyre/Sidon may have been involved in the anti-Assyrian coalition. The break-up of the coalition in the 840s was triggered primarily by the dynastic change in Aram-Damascus, leading Jehu to inaugurate a new pro-Assyrian policy for Israel that was to last until the time of Pekah.

The second chapter treats the reign of Adad-nirari III. Through a new reading of the eponym chronicle, it is suggested that Adad-nirari attacked Damascus sometime between 805 and 802 BCE. During these years, Joash of Israel paid tribute to the Assyrian king. Moreover, the payment of tribute by Israel, Tyre/Sidon, Edom, and Philistia was an anti-Damascene move.

The third chapter takes up the period of the reigns of Shalmaneser IV, Ashur-dan III, and Ashur-nirari V. This was a period in which the turtanu, Samsi-ilu, an important but generally overlooked figure, played a prominent role in the politics of Syria-Palestine. Samsi-ilu's presence in the west curtailed anti-Assyrian activities and helped pro-Assyrian states such as Israel and Judah to regain territorial holding lost to Aram-Damascus at the height of its expansion. Tyre Amy have severed relations with Israel late in the reign of Jeroboam II and cooperated with Aram-Damascus.

The fourth chapter is devoted to the reign of Tiglath-pileser III. Close attention is given to dating and offering new dates for the different tribute lists found in Tiglath-pileser's inscriptions. In light of a new understanding of the eponym chronicle, Tiglath-pileser could have been in Israel between 743 and 740 BCE to assist Menahem in securing the throne. In the 730s, a strong anti-Assyrian coalition-headed by Rezin of Aram-Damascus and participated in by Pekah of Israel and Hiram of Tyre-was in existence, precipitating a major western campaign of Tiglath-pileser that led to the provincialization of several provinces in Syria-Palestine, including Damascus, Megiddo, Dor, and Gilead.

The fifth and final chapter deals with the reign of Shalmaneser V, a period that saw the collaboration of Israel and Tyre in revolting against Assyria. This revolt resulted in Shalmaneser's campaign that led to the end of Israel as an independent state.

The conclusion summarizes nine different phases of relations which Israel/Judah, Tyre/Sidon, and Aram-Damascus underwent during the two centuries of history under investigation. Assyrian involvement in the west had a major impact on the relations between Syro-Palestinian states.

It is beyond the scope of this dissertation to cover the entire period of ancient history; hence the focus on the ninth and eighth centuries BCE. Moreover, it is not possible to treat every aspect of relationships; hence the attention on the political and commercial relations.

Through the years of my graduate education and involvement in this project, I have been supported by many individuals and institutions. Emory University awarded me a George W. Woodruff Graduate Fellowship that made my graduate studies possible. Pacific School of Religion provided me a summer grant to assist me in the completion of my dissertation. My fellow students at Emory--in particular, Bill Brown, Brian Jones, Paul Hooker, and Ehud Ben-Zvi--colleagues at Pacific School of Religion gave me their unselfish support and encouragement. My dissertation committee--Dr. M. Patrick Graham, Dr. Theodore J. Lewis, Dr. Carol A. Newsom, and Dr. J. Maxwell Miller--took much time to read a draft of the dissertation and to make many helpful comments and suggestions. To all of these individuals and institutions, I am grateful.

A special word of thanks and appreciation goes to Dr. John H. Hayes, my dissertation director, mentor, and friend. It was he who pointed me to the wealth of this area of study and guided me throughout the project with his insightful comments and suggestions. His constant support and affirmation of my work helped carry me through difficult periods of writing and revising.

Finally, I must express my sincere thanks and gratitude to my parents, Kuan Choon Hock and Ong Geok Luen, for their unending support from half the globe away; to my daughter, Valene, for being a bundle of joy even when I faced difficult moments of the project; and, most of all, to my spouse, Valentine Toh, for believing in me, for encouraging me onward, and for all the sacrifices she had to make for my graduate education. It is to her that I dedicate this dissertation.

INTRODUCTION

The history of ancient Israel and Judah is integrally related not only with the history of the major ancient near eastern power centers of Egypt and Mesopotamia but also with the smaller kingdoms of Syria-Palestine. Israel and Judah's relationships with both the more remote great kingdoms of Egypt and Mesopotamia and the nearer smaller powers of Syria-Palestine were reciprocally interrelated. That is, relationships with regional states were influenced by the relationships that existed with the major powers and vice versa.

Israelite and Judean relationships with Phoenicia and Aram-Damascus were probably more influential in their history than those with any other Syro-Palestinian states.[1] This was especially the case during the period of Neo-Assyrian expansion into and dominance over Syria-Palestine. The primary sources for studying the relationships that Israel and Judah had with Phoenicia and Aram-Damascus are the Hebrew scriptures and Assyrian sources.[2] The biblical materials are skimpy, inconsistent, and often tendentious. For example, the accounts of the reign of Jeroboam II hint at but do not fill out the picture of Syro-Palestinian relations during his reign. In addition, the "history" of the northern kingdom of Israel in the Hebrew scriptures is written from a

---

[1]The study of these relationships has been the subject of some recent works on Syro-Palestinian history. See, especially, F. Briquel-Chatonnet (*Les relations entre les cités de la côte Phénicienne et les royaumes d'Israël et de Juda* [Studia Phoenicia 12; Leuven: Peeters, 1992]), G. G. G. Reinhold (*Die Beziehungen Altisraels zu den aramäischen Staaten in der israelitisch-judäischen Königszeit* [Europäische Hochschulschriften 23; Frankfurt am Main: Peter Lang, 1989]), as well as W. T. Pitard (*Ancient Damascus: A Historical Study of the Syrian City-State from Earliest Times until its Fall to the Assyrians in 732 B.C.E.* [Winona Lake, IN: Eisenbrauns, 1987]).

[2]Contemporary records from Phoenicia and Aram-Damascus are absent. Moreover, secondhand sources like Josephus and his sources present an historian with great difficulties (see, e.g., the critiques of S. Timm, *Die Dynastie Omri: Quellen und Untersuchungen zur Geschichte Israels im 9. Jahrhundert vor Christus* [FRLANT 124. Göttingen: Vandenhoeck & Ruprecht, 1982], 200–224; D. Mendels, *The Land of Israel as a Political Concept in Hasmonean Literature: Recourse to History in Second Century B.C. Claims to the Holy Land* [Texte und Studien zum Antiken Judentum 15; Tübingen: J. C. B. Mohr (Paul Siebeck), 1987], 131–43). Texts from Egypt directly relative to the topic are lacking as well.

Judean perspective that is biased and condemnatory of all Israelite kings. The relative strength of Israel in certain periods is thereby obscured by the pen of the ancient historian.

The Assyrian inscriptions provide an invaluable contemporaneous source for examining the relationships among Israel/Judah and Phoenicia and Aram-Damascus. The present dissertation focuses on these inscriptions and what may be drawn from them concerning Israel and Judah's political and commercial involvements with Phoenicia and Aram-Damascus. Such an investigation is warranted for three reasons. First, although many of these inscriptions have been known for over a century, many of them have not been reexamined in recent years.[3] New insights, as this study will demonstrate, can be gained from a fresh examination. Second, previous scholarship shows incomplete comprehension of several Assyrian inscriptions. This is especially the case with the eponym chronicle, which remains the primary source for Assyrian history and chronology and for Assyrian relations with foreign powers. Third, new texts recently discovered or published (as, for example, the Antakya and Pazarcik Stelae) provide new data for Syro-Palestinian history. This is especially the case for the first half of the eighth century BCE.

This dissertation consists of five chapters, organized according to the reigns of the Assyrian kings prior to the capture of Samaria by Sargon II in 720–719 BCE. The first chapter deals with the reign of Shalmaneser III, the second with the reign of Adad-nirari III, the third with the reigns of Shalmaneser IV, Ashur-dan III, and Ashur-nirari V—a period in which the turtānu, Šamši-ilu, played a prominent role in the politics of Syria-Palestine. The fourth chapter is devoted to the reign of Tiglath-pileser III; the fifth and final chapter to the reign of Shalmaneser V, a period that saw the end of Israel as an independent state.

The conclusion will summarize the different phases of relations which Israel/Judah, Phoenicia, and Aram-Damascus underwent during the ninth and eighth centuries BCE as the inscriptions can shed light on them.

---

[3]The exceptions to this are the works of H. Tadmor on Sargon II ("The Campaigns of Sargon II of Assur: A Chronological-Historical Study," *JCS* 12 [1958], 22–40; 77–100) and of T. J. Schneider on Shalmaneser III (*A New Analysis of the Royal Annals of Shalmaneser III* [diss., University of Pennsylvania, 1991] and *Form and Context in the Royal Inscriptions of Shalmaneser III* [Occasional Papers of the Institute for Antiquity and Christianity 26; Claremont: Institute for Antiquity and Christianity, 1993]).

The main focus of the dissertation is on the Assyrian historical inscriptions. Each chapter will begin with a brief introduction to the reign(s) of the Assyrian king(s) with whom the inscriptional material is historically related. Each Assyrian text will be analyzed thoroughly and systematically for information relating to the political and commercial relations between Israel/Judah, Aram-Damascus, and Phoenicia. Non-Assyrian sources, including biblical material, will be dealt with where it supplements the Assyrian sources. A synopsis at the end of the chapter will summarize the findings of the chapter and draw conclusions about the relationships between the three entities—Israel/Judah, Aram-Damascus, and Phoenicia.

CHAPTER ONE

THE REIGN OF SHALMANESER III

I. INTRODUCTION

Ashurnasirpal II (883–859 BCE) was the first "great" king and the real founder of the Neo-Assyrian empire.[1] During his reign, he conducted at least fourteen major campaigns, but most of these were undertaken in neighboring regions: east in the Zagros mountains, north in the areas south of Lake Van, and south as far as the middle Euphrates. His first western campaign was conducted against Bit-Adini. In a subsequent campaign Ashurnasirpal crossed the Orontes and made his way down to the Lebanon without much resistance. He received *maddattu*[2] from the coastal cities of Tyre, Sidon, Byblos, and Arwad.[3] The part of the annals describing this western campaign, unfortunately, is undated but falls between the *limmu* years of Dagan-bēlu-nāṣir and Šamaš-nūri, that is, the sixth and eighteenth regnal years of Ashurnasirpal.[4]

When Shalmaneser III (858–824 BCE) succeeded his father on the Assyrian throne, he focused his attention on the west and north. Apparently, he conducted his first western campaign as early as his first regnal year. In a number of successive campaigns in his early years, Shalmaneser was able to crush Bit-Adini and annex it to the Assyrian empire. Presumably, his campaigns west of the Euphrates were carried out to establish dominance over the

---

[1]For treatment of the Assyrian history for this period, namely, the reigns of Ashurnasirpal II and Shalmaneser III, see A. K. Grayson, "Assyria: Ashur-dan II to Ashur-nirari V (934–745 B.C.)," in CAH^2 III/1, 253–69; *idem*, "Mesopotamia, History of (Assyria)," *ABD*, 4. 741–43; and H. W. F. Saggs, *The Might That Was Assyria* (London: Sidgwick & Jackson, 1984), 72–78.

[2]On *maddattu*, see n. 53 below.

[3]An English translation of Ashurnasirpal's annals may be found in Luckenbill, *ARAB*, 1. §§436–84; and A. K. Grayson, *ARI*, 2. 117–47.

[4]*ARAB*, 1. §§469–80; *ARI*, 2. 137–45. Cf. the eponym list in A. Ungnad, "Eponymen," *RLA*, 2. 418. For the dating of the *limmu* years, see below (pp. 7–8).

trade routes and perhaps to set up trade colonies as well.[5] None of the regions west of the Euphrates was transformed into an Assyrian province. In several of his western campaigns, Shalmaneser was confronted by western coalitions, not only small coalitions, but also the formidable Syro-Palestinian coalition headed by Adad-idri of Aram-Damascus and Irḫuleni of Hamath. Ahab of Israel was also an important participant in the coalition. According to his annals, Shalmaneser fought this coalition in his sixth, tenth, eleventh, and fourteenth *palê*.[6] Although he claims to have defeated the coalition on each of these occasions, this is not likely, since he never seems to have pushed farther westward than just beyond the Orontes. He never mentions the taking of the cities of the coalition partners nor their submission. The Assyrian king subsequently conducted two more campaigns, in his eighteenth and twenty-first *palê* (841 and 838 BCE), during which he was finally able to establish a strong Assyrian presence in Syria-Palestine, campaigning against Damascus and collecting *maddattu* from numerous states, including from Jehu of Israel as well as from Tyre and Sidon.

The politico-economic relations between Damascus, Israel, and Phoenicia during this period must be seen against the background of a struggle between Assyria and a western anti-Assyrian coalition which was powerful during the first half of the reign of Shalmaneser but subsequently, disintegrated and collapsed. A comprehensive treatment of the Assyrian texts pertaining to Shalmaneser's relations with the west forms the primary basis for understanding Damascene-Israelite-Phoenician relations during this period since the biblical texts are highly tendentious and other non-biblical texts are nonexistent. The inscriptions relevant to this discussion include the eponym chronicle, the "Bronze Gates of Balâwât," the Monolith Inscription, the "Baghdad Text," III R 5, 6, the Marble-Slab Inscription, and the Black Obelisk Inscription. These texts provide important data on Shalmaneser's contacts and involvement—predominantly through battles and the collection of gifts and tributes—in the west, especially those contacts that relate to Aram-Damascus, Israel, and the Phoenician states.

---

[5]For discussions of the economic interests of Assyria's expansion to the west, see H. Tadmor, "Assyria and the West: The Ninth Century and its Aftermath," in *Unity and Diversity: Essays in the History, Literature and Religion of the Ancient Near East*, ed. H. Goedicke and J. J. M. Roberts (Baltimore: Johns Hopkins University Press, 1975), 36–48; A. K. Grayson, "Studies in Neo-Assyrian History: The Ninth Century B.C.," *BO* 33 (1976), 134–38.

[6]On the meaning of *palû*, see below n. 46.

Something of the relations between these western kingdoms may be deduced from an analysis of the texts. These will be dealt with in the order of the historical events mentioned in the texts. Some of the texts are datable, while others—usually because of their fragmentary state—are not. Since the eponym chronicle is indispensable for establishing dates and sequence of events, not only for this period, but also for the whole of Neo-Assyrian history, it is appropriate to begin with the chronicle.

II. ASSYRIAN INSCRIPTIONS

A. The Eponym Chronicle

The value of the Assyrian eponym (*limmu*) chronicle as a source for the reconstruction of Assyrian history and international relations has long been recognized.[7] The Assyrians adopted a system of naming their years after *limmus*. The *limmu* was the title assumed by a different high governmental official for each year and documents drawn up during the year of his tenure were dated giving the month and day of the particular *limmu*. For example, the colophon of Esarhaddon's Succession Treaty provides the following information:

> 18th day of Iyyar, limmu of Nabû-bēlu-uṣur, governor of Dur-Šar-rukku. The treaty of Esarhaddon, king of Assyria, conclu[ded] on behalf of Ashurbanipal, the great crown prince designate of Assyria, and Šamaš-šumu-ukin, the crown prince designate of Babylon.[8]

The main duties of the *limmu* were to preside over state cultic functions in the city of Aššur for the given year and to care for the needs of the temples of Aššur and other deities.[9] Personnel functioning as *limmus* included the king, high ranking royal officials, and governors of provinces. Originally, it seems, the order of the

[7]See, e.g., G. Smith, *The Assyrian Eponym Canon* (London: S. Bagster & Sons, 1875); and A. T. Olmstead, "The Assyrian Chronicle," *JAOS* 34 (1915), 344–68. For a detailed discussion of the Assyrian eponym lists, see Ungnad, "Eponymen," 412–57; see also E. F. Weidner, "Die assyrischen Eponymen," *AfO* 13 (1939–40), 308–18 and Tadmor, "Campaigns of Sargon," 28 and nn. 53 and 57. With the exception of the work of Tadmor for the reign of Sargon II, there are no recent studies that examine the eponym chronicle in detail.

[8]See S. Parpola and K. Watanabe, *Neo-Assyrian Treaties and Loyalty Oaths* (SAA 2; Helsinki: Helsinki University Press, 1988), 58.

[9]A. Poebel, "The Assyrian King List from Khorsabad," *JNES* 2 (1943), 76; A. L. Oppenheim, *Ancient Mesopotamia: Portrait of a Dead Civilization* (Chicago: University of Chicago Press, 1964), 99–100; Saggs, *Assyria*, 273–74.

limmus was determined by lot; later, it was determined by rank and tradition.[10] The year was officially named after the *limmu*.[11]

Two major chronicle types have survived; one lists only the names of the *limmus* (or eponyms), while the other notes the names of the *limmus* and their positions as well as some significant event or condition occurring during the period of the *limmu*'s tenure. The most comprehensive list is Canon C^{a}, which belongs to the first category and lists the *limmus* from the last decade of the tenth century to the middle of the seventh century BCE.[12] Canon C^{a}'s usefulness for historical reconstruction is limited since it provides only a list of the *limmus*. Canon C^{b},[13] belonging to the second category, is more valuable for the historian. Canon C^{b} is divided into four columns. The first column has the words *ina lime* written after every sectional dividing-line, which, in most cases,[14] marks the year of the monarch as *limmu*. The second column gives the name of the *limmu*, and the third column his title. The final column notes some significant event that occurred or condition that existed during the year, most often related to campaigns. (Sometimes the notation in the final column is written across both the third and fourth columns.) While the notation "*ana* GN" occurs most often, other significant factors were also occasionally noted. The entries in the final column(s) from the tenth to the fifteenth year (712–707 BCE) of Sargon II provide good examples of the variety of notations in the chronicle.[15]

712–711 BCE	*i-na* KUR in the land
711–710 BCE	*a-na* ^{URU}*mar-qa-sa*

---

[10]So, e.g., Weidner, "Die assyrischen Eponymen," 308; Oppenheim, *Ancient Mesopotamia*, 99-100; Saggs, *Assyria*, 273.

[11]In the Monolith Inscription, for example, the campaigns of Shalmaneser III are dated according to *limmu* rather than regnal years (cf. *ARAB*, 2. §§594–611).

[12]For a discussion of all the different canons and fragments of the *limmu* lists, see Ungnad, "Eponymen."

[13]At least eight fragments belonging to this canon have been found. The longest fragment is Canon C^{b} 1 (tablet number K 51), first published in H. C. Rawlinson, *Cuneiform Inscriptions of Western Asia* (5 vols.; London: British Museum, 1861–1909), 2. plate 52. The best edition in cuneiform is that by F. Delitzsch, *Assyrische Lesestücke* (2d ed.; Leipzig: J. C. Hinrichs, 1878), 92–94, while the best transliteration is that by Ungnad, "Eponymen," 428–31. D. D. Luckenbill, *ARAB*, 2. §§431–38, provides a widely used English translation, although the translation contains numerous mistakes especially for the reigns of Adad-nirari III and Shalmaneser IV but also elsewhere.

[14]Exceptional cases of sectional dividing lines, not followed by *ina li-me* include the *limmu* year of Bur-sagale (763–762 BCE) when an eclipse of the sun occurred and the *limmu* year of Nabû-bēlu-uṣur (745–744 BCE) when Tiglath-pileser III ascended the throne of Assyria. Notably, these were considered significant events in the life of Assyria.

[15]So Eponym Canon C^{b} 4; Ungnad, "Eponymen," 433.

	at Marqasa
710–709 BCE	*a-na* URUÉ-IKUL-*i* LUGAL AŠ KIŠKI *bi-e-di* at Bit-Zeri. The king stayed overnight in Kiš.
709–708 BCE	I10-GI.NA ŠU.II dEN *iṣ-ṣa-bat* Sargon took the hand of Bêl.
708–707 BCE	URU*ku-mu-ḫa ka-šid* LÚNAM *šá-kin* Kummuḫ was captured. A governor was appointed.
707–706 BCE	LUGAL TA KÁ.DINGIR.RAKI *is-su-uḫ-ra* The king returned from Babylon.

From all the existing fragments of the canon, the Canon Cb chronicle from the accession of Shalmaneser III to the first few years of the reign of Sennacherib can be reconstructed.

Although this chronicle material has been known and used for a long time, some significant issues concerning its nature and interpretation remain unsolved. One issue concerns the question of the first regnal year of the king in relationship to the year of the king's service as *limmu*. E. Forrer argued that the king served as *limmu* during his first regnal year, basing his position on the fact that sectional dividing-lines are placed before the *limmu* years of the kings from Adad-nirari III (810–783 BCE) to Ashur-nirari V (754–745 BCE).[16] A. Poebel correctly criticized Forrer's argument as without any foundation and proposed that the lines were placed indiscriminately.[17] He argued that the last *limmu* before the king's own *limmu* was the first regnal year of the king and concluded that kings from Shalmaneser III (858–824 BCE) to Tiglath-pileser III (744–727 BCE) served as *limmus* in their second regnal year.[18] He further pointed to other inscriptional evidence from the reigns of Ashurnasirpal II (883–859 BCE) and Shalmaneser III indicating that their second regnal years coincided with their *limmu* years.[19] As a general rule, Poebel's position that the king served as the *limmu* during his second regnal year is correct; however, as we shall see, the pattern was broken beginning with the reign of Shalmaneser V. The proper correlation of the king's first regnal year in relationship to his *limmu* year is, of course, strategic in establishing chronology for the Assyrian kings and their activities.

---

[16]E. Forrer, *Zur Chronologie der neuassyrischen Zeit* (MVAG 20/3; Leipzig: J. C. Hinrichs, 1916), 15. So, also, Olmstead, "Assyrian Chronicle," 346, 349; Oppenheim, *Ancient Mesopotamia*, 99; Saggs, *Assyria*, 273.

[17]Poebel, "Assyrian King List," 77.

[18]*Ibid.*, 76–78; so, also, Tadmor, "Campaigns of Sargon," 28, n. 53.

[19]Poebel, "Assyrian King List," 76.

A second issue in the interpretation of the canons concerns the nature of the eponym notations themselves. Scholars have utilized these notations unsystematically, generally failing to ask significant questions about their nature and function. Several questions need to be raised.

(1) At what point in the year were the name and the event officially recorded in the eponym chronicle? On the basis of the formula "*ana* GN," it has been almost universally assumed that these notations were recorded at the beginning of the year. This interpretation thus sees the formula "*ana* GN" as futuristic, as a statement about the king's anticipated and planned military campaign for the coming year. Thus *a-na* ^{URU}*mar-qa-sa* would indicate that Sargon II anticipated a campaign to Marqasa in the coming year. Other notations (for example, the capture of cities, references to the accession of kings, and the repair of temples), however, immediately contradict this interpretation, since notations about these events had to be recorded after the events had occurred, that is, during or at the end of the year. That the formula "*ana* GN" would be written at the beginning of the year and the other items written at a different point in time is unlikely. Each notation recorded some significant matter of the year, and whatever the formulas or statements used, they would most logically have been written at a similar point in time. The notation for the year 710–709 BCE, *ana* ^{URU}*bît-*^{I}*zêrî šarru ina kîš*^{KI} *biedi* ("at Bit-Zeri. The king stayed overnight in Kiš"), further implies that the recording was made on some specific day. This implication, however, cannot be proven conclusively.

(2) What then does the formula "*ana* GN" signify? Tadmor has argued that

> the specific historical entry [i.e. *ana* GN] indicates neither the main military target, nor the main city conquered, but the actual location of the king and his camp at the turn of the year, when such a report (probably in the form of a letter to the god Aššur) was sent home. Such a location could have been a strategically placed fortress and not necessarily the enemy's capital. Once the notation had been recorded it was not modified, even if a major victory was achieved later in the course of the very same year.[20]

---

[20]A. R. Millard and H. Tadmor, "Adad-nirari III in Syria: Another Stele Fragment and the Dates of His Campaigns," *Iraq* 35 (1973), 62. Tadmor's conjecture that the report sent home was "probably in the form of a letter to the god Aššur" is purely speculative. While it is true that the "Letter to God" genre exists among Assyrian inscriptions, they are few in number. N. Na'aman notes that only a single "Letter to God" has survived for each of the Assyrian kings Shalmaneser IV, Sargon II, Sennacherib, Esarhaddon, and Ashurbanipal ("Sennacherib's 'Letter to God' on His Campaign to Judah," *BASOR* 214 [1974], 31, n. 25). Since the earliest letter belonged to Shalmaneser IV, it appears that the genre may

Tadmor's suggestion that the historical notation relates to the "actual location of the king and his camp at the turn of the year" is improbable. Even if the king had been on campaign near the end of the year, he would have returned to the capital to preside over the annual Akîtu festival.[21] Thus, the notation could refer *only* to the location of the main army. The whereabouts of the king, if other than at Aššur, would be made specific. For example, the eponym notation for the year 710–709 BCE reads, *ana* ^{URU}*bît-*^{I}*zêrî šarru ina kîš*^{KI} *biedi.* While the first part of the notation refers to Bit-Zeri as the location of the army, the second specifies that the king was in Kiš.

Tadmor is right, however, in arguing that the most logical time for a report to have been recorded regarding the location of the main Assyrian army would have been in conjunction with the spring new year festival in Nisan. Statements such as *ana* GN would then give the location of the main army on a campaign already underway rather than refer to an anticipated campaign. Likewise, the other kinds of notation recorded certainly refer to events that had already taken place.

(3) What was the relationship of the *limmu*'s tenure of office to the notations assigned to the particular *limmu*'s year? At the close of the new year festival the name and position of the *limmu* for the preceding year were noted as well as some significant event of the year, be it the accession of the king, some significant battle, the present location of the Assyrian army, the inactivity of the king, or temple repairs. The following entry may be used to illustrate the case.

[AŠ *li-me*	^{Id}PA.EN.PAB	*ša*] ^{URU}4-*ḫa*	AŠ ^{ITI}GU$_4$ UD 13.KÁM
		$^{\text{I.GIŠ}}$TUKUL]-*ti*-DUMU.UŠ. É-*šár-ra*	AŠ ^{GIŠ}GU.ZA *it-tu-šib*

have been a late development in the literary history of Assyria. Na'aman surmises too that "a 'Letter to God' was a sort of personal report of the king to Ashur the god on his activities during campaigns carried out in the god's name, and such texts were composed for only the most outstanding of the campaigns conducted by the king" (30). It is thus difficult to maintain with Tadmor that a "Letter to God" was written and sent home at the end of the year when a campaign was underway.

Tadmor's final remark in the above quote assumes that the notation was recorded at the beginning of the year. While it is true that the writing of the notation most probably took place in the month of Nisan, in conjunction with the Akîtu festival, it is too simplistic to assume that to be the beginning of a year. Rather, it will be argued that events up to the conclusion of the Akîtu festival were reckoned as belonging to the preceding year (see below, pp. 11–15).

[21] Saggs, *Assyria*, 208–9; cf. S. A. Pallis, *The Babylonian Akîtu Festival* (Copenhagen: A. F. Høst & Son, 1926), 139–43.

| | AŠ ^{ITI}]DU$_6$ *a-na bi-rit* ÍD | *it-ta-lak*

In the *limmu* of Nabû-bēlu-uṣur (governor) of Arapḫa. On the 13th day of Aiaru Tiglath-pileser sat on the throne. In the month of Tašritu he marched to the territory between the rivers.

This example illustrates that when Nabû-bēlu-uṣur ended his tenure as *limmu*, the accession of Tiglath-pileser and his campaign to "the territory between the rivers" had already occurred. The conclusion can be drawn that the notations in Canon C^b were all made simultaneously at the time of the new year (or Akîtu) festival, during which festival the official concluded his tenure in office as *limmu*.

Tiglath-pileser III's final two years can serve as a test case for the accuracy of this approach to reading the eponym chronicle. Evidence regarding Tiglath-pileser's final two years appears in both the eponym canon and the Babylonian Chronicles.[22] Babylonian Chronicle 1.i, lines 19–26 reads as follows:

The third year of (Nabu)-mukin-zeri: When Tiglath-pileser (III) had gone down to Akkad he ravaged Bit-Amukkanu and captured (Nabu)-mukin-zeri. For three years (Nabu)-mukin-zeri ruled Babylon. Tiglath-pileser (III) ascended the throne in Babylon.

The second year: Tiglath-pileser (III) died in the month of Tebet. For <*eighteen*> years Tiglath-pileser (III) ruled Akkad and Assyria. For two of these years he ruled in Akkad.[23]

The Babylonian Chronicles make clear that Tiglath-pileser ruled as king over Babylon during his final two regnal years (728–727 and 727–726 BCE). In the eponym chronicle, the following entries are found regarding the very end of his reign:

[„ ^{I}*lip-ḫur*-DIN]GIR *ša* ^{KUR}*kìr-ru-ri* LUGAL ŠU.II ^{d}EN DAB^{bat}

[„ ^{I}BÁD-*aš-š*]*ur ša* ^{URU}*tuš-ḫa-an* LUGAL ŠU ^{d}EN DAB^{bat} ^{URU}*di*[. . .][24]

[In the *limmu* of Lipḫur-i]lu (governor) of Kirruri. The king took the hand of Bêl.

[In the *limmu* of Dūr-Ašš]ur (governor) of Tušḫan. The king took the hand of Bêl. The city of Di[. . .].

---

[22]The best edition of the Babylonian Chronicles is that by A. K. Grayson, *ABC*. See also the latest study on the subject by J. A. Brinkman, "The Babylonian Chronicle Revisited," in *Lingering Over Words: Studies in Ancient Near Eastern Literature in Honor of William L. Moran*, ed. T. Abusch, J. Huehnergard, and P. Steinkeller (Atlanta: Scholars Press, 1990), 73–104.

[23]Grayson, *ABC*, 72–73.

[24]Eponym Canon C^b 3. So G. Smith, "On a New Fragment of the Assyrian Canon Belonging to the Reigns of Tiglath-pileser and Shalmaneser," *TSBA* 2 (1873), 330–31; cf. F. Delitzsch, *Assyrische Lesestücke*, 94; Ungnad, "Eponymen," 431–32.

Scholars have observed that the notation *šarru qâtā*^{II} ^{d}*bêl iṣṣabat*^{bat} ("the king took the hand of Bêl") implies that Tiglath-pileser escorted the deity, that is Marduk, "in the New Year (Akîtu) ceremony at Babylon."[25] It follows then that at the conclusion of the tenures of Lip-ḫur-ilu and Dūr-Aššur as *limmu* respectively, Tiglath-pileser escorted the statue of Marduk in the Akîtu festival in Babylon. These two years must be correlated with the two years of the Babylonian Chronicles in which he is specifically noted to have ruled over Babylon as well as Assyria.

A problem might appear to arise when one considers the events of the final year of Tiglath-pileser. Tiglath-pileser's taking of Bêl's hand in Nisan was followed by his death and the succession of Shalmaneser V (726–722 BCE) in Tebet nine months later. Tiglath-pileser's taking of Bêl's hand was recorded for one year, in the *limmu* of Dūr-Aššur, while Shalmaneser's accession for another, in the *limmu* of Bēl-ḫarrān-bēlu-uṣur, although both events would have occurred between 1 Nisan 727 and 1 Nisan 726, that is, what appears to have been the same year.

> [„ ^{I}BÁD-*aš-š*]*ur ša* ^{URU}*tuš-ḫa-an* LUGAL ŠU ^{d}EN DAB^{bat} ^{URU}*di*[. . .]
>
> [In the *limmu* of Dūr-Ašš]ur (governor) of Tušḫan. The king took the hand of Bêl. The city of Di[. . .].

> [AŠ *li-me* ^{I}EN.KAS.EN.PAB] *ša* [^{URU}*gu*]*-za-na a-na* ^{URU}[. . .] [^{Id}SILIM.MA-*n*]*u*-MAŠ AŠ ^{GIŠ}GU.[ZA *it-tu-šib*][26]
>
> [In the *limmu* of Bēl-ḫarrān-bēlu-uṣur] (governor) of Guzana. At the city of [. . .]. [Shalman]eser [sat on] the throne.

How is this situation to be explained? The Babylonian Chronicles' notations about the beginning of the reign of Nebuchadnezzar point toward a solution. Chronicle 5, obverse lines 12–15 reads as follows:

---

[25]Saggs, *Assyria*, 91. On the Akîtu festival in general and "the hand ceremony" in particular, see Pallis, *Babylonian Akîtu Festival*, 174–83; J. A. Black, "The New Year Ceremonies in Ancient Babylon: 'Taking Bel by the Hand' and a Cultic Picnic," *Religion* 11 (1981), 39–59; K. van der Toorn, "The Babylonian New Year Festival: New Insights from the Cuneiform Texts and Their Bearing on Old Testament Study," *Congress Volume: Leuven, 1989*, ed. J. A. Emerton (VTSup 43; Leiden: E. J. Brill, 1991), 331–39; J. Klein, "Akitu," *ABD*, 1. 138–40; and M. E. Cohen, *The Cultic Calendars of the Ancient Near East* (Bethesda, MD: CDL Press, 1993), 400–453.

Another Assyrian king whom the eponym chronicle also noted as taking Bêl's hand was Sargon II (721–705 BCE) (so Eponym Canon C^{b} 4; Ungnad, "Eponymen," 433). This event is also noted in the Babylonian Chronicles (Grayson, *ABC*, 75).

[26]So Eponym Canon C^{b} 3; cf. Delitzsch, *Assyrische Lesestücke*, 94; Ungnad, "Eponymen," 432. See also G. Smith, "New Fragment ," 330–31.

In (his) accession year Nebuchadnezzar (II) returned to Hattu. Until the month Shebat he marched about victoriously in Hattu. In the month Shebat he took the vast booty of Hattu to Babylon. In the month Nisan he took the hand of Bel and the son of Bel (and) and celebrated the Akîtu festival.

The first year of Nebuchadnezzar: . . . .[27]

Since in the Babylonian Chronicle, the notations following a line denoting a new year describe events of the new year, this text indicates that the first regnal year of Nebuchadnezzar was preceded by his "taking the hand of Bêl," that is, his participation in the celebration of the Akîtu festival, an event which fell in his accession year. Although the festival obviously fell in the first days of the month Nisan of the new year already begun, the official regnal year of the king did not begin until after the king had taken the hand of Bêl, that is, until after his participation in the Akîtu festival.[28] Thus the *limmu* served from the conclusion of one Akîtu festival to the conclusion of the following festival and a regnal year of the king extended from the completion of one Akîtu festival to the completion of the following Akîtu festival. Just as the conclusion of the Akîtu festival of Nebuchadnezzar's accession year ushered in his first regnal year, so also the celebration of the Akîtu festival at the conclusion of Tiglath-pileser's sixteenth and seventeenth years ushered in his seventeenth and eighteenth regnal years. Thus, according to the Assyrian and Babylonian reckoning, events of the preceding year included all events occurring until the conclusion of the festival.[29] Thus, although Tiglath-pileser took Bêl's hand in Nisan of 727 BCE, it was considered part of his preceding seventeenth year, that is 728–727 BCE. Only after the conclusion of the Akîtu festival did the king's eighteenth year commence. The fact that Tiglath-pileser took the hand of Bêl would have been officially recorded in the eponym chronicle as soon as the new year festival ended. It follows also that the festival represented the *limmu*'s final official function. The new *limmu* for the coming year would have been proclaimed, but he

---

[27]Grayson, *ABC*, 100.

[28]Van der Toorn notes that only with Marduk's safe return to Esagil, his temple, may the "new year" begin ("Babylonian New Year Festival," 338–39), but does not deal with the chronological issues, however.

[29]There is some uncertainty regarding when the Akîtu festival was celebrated. Black conjectures that it was celebrated from the 1st to the 12th Nisan ("New Year Ceremonies," 42), while van der Toorn argues that the festival does not begin until the 4th Nisan and concluded on the 11th ("Babylonian New Year Festival," 332–34; cf. also Grayson, *ABC*, 111). Most recently, Cohen suggests that the Nisan Akîtu festival probably lasted from the 2nd to the 12th of Nisan (*Cultic Calendars*, 433–40).

would have assumed office only after the completion of the new year festival, and his name, office, and any significant event of his *limmu* year would have been officially recorded in the *limmu* chronicle at the end of his tenure in association with the new year festival. Therefore, Tiglath-pileser began his eighteenth year following the celebration of the Akîtu festival in Nisan 727 and died nine months later. That was also the year that Bēl-ḫarrān-bēlu-uṣur served his tenure as *limmu*. Shalmaneser's accession was recorded in the eponym chronicle at the following new year festival when the *limmu* of Bēl-ḫarrān-bēlu-uṣur officially terminated.

As is well known, the issue of the absolute dating of the reigns of the Assyrian kings is confirmed by the notation about an eclipse of the sun that occurred in the month of Simanu during the *limmu* of Bur-sagale. This eclipse can be dated to June 15, 763 BCE by astronomical calculation. This reading confirms the above approach to interpreting the eponym chronicle.

AŠ *li-me*	^{I}*bur-*^{d}*sa-gal-e*	*ša* ^{URU}*gu-za-na si-ḫu* AŠ ^{URU}ŠÀ.URU	*i-na*^{ITI}SIG$_4$ ^{d}UTU AN.MI GAR^{an}

In the *limmu* of Bur-sagale (governor) of Guzana. Revolt in the city of Aššur. In the month of Simanu an eclipse of the sun took place.

The eclipse could only have been noted after its occurrence and would have been recorded at the end of the *limmu* of Bur-sagale, at the conclusion of the new year festival.

From the preceding analysis, two conclusions may be drawn about how the eponym chronicle should be read and the implications of this reading for the understanding of Assyrian history and Assyrian relations with the west.

First, there was a specific time when the annual notations in eponym canon C^b were all concurrently recorded. The time of recording was, most probably, at the conclusion of the new year (or Akîtu) festival. Once the notations were inscribed, they were not modified, since they accounted for events that had taken place up until the completion of the festival.[30]

Second, since all the notations must be read as relating to past events, the formula "*ana* GN" should be interpreted as indicating the location of main army at the time of the recording, and not as

---

[30]For example, there was an apparent error in recording during the *limmu* of Ulūlāyu (832–831 BCE), where the notation *a-na* ^{KUR}*qu-e* was wrongly inscribed in column III. Although the notation was subsequently inscribed in column IV, it was left uncorrected in column III.

an indication of an intended campaign. Moreover, the formula *ina māti*[31] should not be understood as referring to the king being "in the land"—for under normal circumstances at the new year the king would be in Assyria to preside over the Akîtu festival—but should be interpreted as an indication that at the time of the recording of the notations, the main army was "in the land" and not on campaign elsewhere.

The notations from the years 756–755 to 753–752 BCE can serve as an illustration of how the expression *ina māti* should be read and interpreted. The notation for 756–755 BCE, the next to last year of the reign of Ashur-dan III, reads *ina māti*, that is, at the time of the new year festival the main Assyrian army was not away on campaign. It is not certain whether or not any campaign was conducted *during* the year; it is more likely that none was conducted as the notation for the previous year (757–756 BCE) also reads *ina māti*. However, for the year 755–754 BCE, the last of Ashur-dan's reign, the notation for the eponym chronicle reads *ana* ^{URU}*ḫatarikka*.[32] That campaign probably began during the spring of 755–754 BCE. Toward the end of that year, the campaign had not concluded since the army was noted as encamped in the vicinity of Ḫatarikka/Hadrach. This year saw a change of kingship in Assyria, since 754–753 BCE was Ashur-nirari V's first regnal year.[33] The eponym notation for 754–753 BCE reads *ana* ^{URU}*arpadda ištu* ^{URU}*aššur taʾʾartu*.[34] While the first part refers to the location of the main army at Arpad, the meaning of the second part is not clear. The word *taʾʾartu* is a nominal form meaning "return"; the phrase may be translated, "Return from the city of Aššur." Whose "return" is meant? It is submitted that it was the king's return from the capital to the battlefield that was meant. The king had gone back to Aššur to preside over the new year's festival, and it is likely that as soon as his official function in the Akîtu festival was concluded, he hurried back to the battlefield,

---

[31]Tadmor has suggested that *ina māti* is an abbreviated form of *šarru ina māti* ("Adad-nirari III in Syria," 62, n. 19). There is, however, no occurrence of *šarru ina māti* in the eponym chronicle; Tadmor's reconstruction of the phrase for the *limmu* year of Mutakkil-Aššur (706–705 BCE) in Eponym Canon C^b 6 (K 4446 = II R 69, 6) is purely conjectural (see his "Campaigns of Sargon," 85). The fragmentary text of II R 69, no. 6 reads *šarru mu-ma*(?)-[. . .]; cf. Ungnad, "Eponymen," 435.

[32]So Eponym Canon C^b 2 (Ungnad, "Eponymen," 432). The determinative in Eponym Canon C^b 1 reads KUR instead of URU.

[33]See Grayson, "Ashur-dan II to Ashur-nirari V," 276.

[34]Following Eponym Canon C^b 2 (Ungnad, "Eponymen," 432). The determinative before *arpadda* in Eponym Canon C^b 1 reads KUR instead of URU.

perhaps before the conclusion of the festival itself, and thus his return was placed in his first regnal year. This campaign against Arpad must also be seen as an extension of the campaign against Hadrach. Although these were the only two states mentioned for those years, it would be wrong to assume that the Assyrian army dealt only with them. It should be remembered that the notations recorded only the location of the main army at the time of the festival. It is more likely that a revolt of Syrian states had broken out and the army was in the region for some time quelling the rebellion. At some point during the year 754–753 BCE, the army must have completed its campaign in southern Syria where Ḫatarikka was located—it is not known whether the campaign was successful—and returned from the region. But it then had to deal with a rebellion of north Syrian states, headed most probably by Arpad. This was almost certainly the campaign which concluded with a vassal treaty with Matiʾ-ilu of Arpad,[35] because there is no evidence of another campaign in the vicinity of Arpad during the reign of Ashur-nirari V.

The results of this study of the eponym chronicle may be summarized in six points.

(1) The notations in the eponym chronicle of a given *limmu* year must be read as a record of the year just concluded, namely, as notations written down at the end of the new year festival. These notations, thus, refer to past events.

(2) The official regnal year of an Assyrian king began after the conclusion of the festival, that is, near the middle of the month of Nisan.

(3) The formula *ana* GN refers to the location of the main Assyrian army at the time of the Akîtu festival.

(4) While an Assyrian king, such as Shalmaneser III, speaks in his annals of leaving the capital city to go on campaign, this does not necessarily mean that the main Assyrian army had returned home and was then required to march from the capital city to the place of military engagement. The army could already have been in the field on campaign.

(5) A statement about the location of the army at the end of the year does not mean that the Assyrian army was present or fought only at that one locale during the year. Neither is it neces-

[35] For the text, see Parpola and Watanabe, *Neo-Assyrian Treaties*, 8–13; *ARAB*, 1. §§749–60.

sarily a notation about the main battle the Assyrian army was engaged in for the year.

(6) On chronological issues, the eponym chronicle is probably the most reliable historical source we possess for Assyrian history since the notations about events were written almost contemporaneously with the events.

The date of the eclipse in 763 BCE and the length of reigns given in the Assyrian King List help to establish 858–857 BCE as Shalmaneser III's first regnal year. The previous year, 859–858 BCE, would have been Shalmaneser's accession year. The *limmu* for that year was Ṭāb-bēlu and the event recorded was the accession of Shalmaneser.[36]

The eponym chronicle from the reign of Shalmaneser III is not well preserved. Eponym Canon C^b 5 contains notations from the years 859–858 to 847–846 BCE. Unfortunately, the important fourth column, which provides information on the location of the army and other significant events, is broken. D. D. Luckenbill's translation in *ARAB*[37] is dependent on A. T. Olmstead,[38] who in turn had filled in the fourth column with information derived from the annals of the Assyrian king. In addition, nothing is preserved in any texts of Canon C^b for the years 846–845 to 841–840 BCE, although again Olmstead restored them. Olmstead's reconstruction must, however, be viewed with caution. Moreover, the years given by Luckenbill from the *limmu* of Ṭāb-bēlu in the accession year of Shalmaneser III to the *limmu* of Iluma-lēʾi in the first regnal year of Shalmaneser IV are a year off and must be reduced accordingly by one year. Luckenbill's notations in column IV from the *limmu* of Bēl-abūa (840–839 BCE) to the *limmu* of Šamaš-ilāya (818–817 BCE) are misplaced and wrong.[39]

The following is the restorable eponym chronicle for the period of the reign of Shalmaneser III. It is of particular importance in establishing the absolute chronology of the period and provides a chronological framework for understanding Assyria's relations with western powers. It covers the period beginning with the

---

36So Eponym Canon C^b 5; Ungnad, "Eponymen," 434. Although only Shalmaneser's name and his patronym can be read, it is almost certain that the notation would have referred to his accession.

37*ARAB*, 2. 431.

38Olmstead, "Assyrian Chronicle," 360.

39Luckenbill's Eponym Lists are fraught with errors and should no longer be used as a reliable source.

king's nineteenth regnal year (840–839 BCE) and extends to the end of his reign in 824–823 BCE:

Regnal Year	*Dates*	*Reported Event*[40]
19	840–839 BCE	[*a-na* KUR] *e-re-na* at the Cedar Mountain
20	839–838 BCE	*a-na* URU*qu-u-e* at Que
21	838–837 BCE	*a-na* KUR*m*[*a-la*]*-ḫi*[41] at Malaḫu
22	837–836 BCE	*a-na* KUR*da-na-bi* at Danabu
23	836–835 BCE	*a-na* KUR*ta-ba-li* at Tabalu
24	835–834 BCE	*a-na* KUR*me-li-di* at Melid
25	834–833 BCE	*a-na* KUR*nam-ri* at Namri
26	833–832 BCE	*a-na* KUR*qu-e* at Que
27	832–831 BCE	*a-na* KUR*qu-e* *ilu rabû ištu* URU*di-ri it-tal-ka*[42] at Que The great god went out from Der
28	831–830 BCE	*a-na* KUR*ur-ar-ṭi* at Urartu
29	830–829 BCE	*a-na* KUR*un-qi* at Unqi
30	829–828 BCE	*a-na* KUR*ul-lu-ba* at Ulluba

40Information for this column is derived from Eponym Canon C^{b} 4 (Ungnad, "Eponymen," 433) and STT 46 + 348 (O. R. Gurney and J. J. Finkelstein, *The Sultantepe Tablets I* [London: British Institute of Archaeology at Ankara, 1957], #46; and O. R. Gurney and P. Hulin, *The Sultantepe Tablets II* [London: British Institute of Archaeology at Ankara, 1957], #348). For the sake of presentation, the *limmus* for the years are omitted. The numbers for the regnal years and modern dating have been supplied.

41Restored as KUR*m[a-la]-ḫi* by J. E. Reade, "Assyrian Campaigns, 804–811 B.C., and the Babylonian Frontier," *ZA* 68 (1978), 251–52, 254. He is followed by Pitard (*Ancient Damascus*, 150), who notes a cylinder seal referring to Malaḫu as a royal city of Hazael. Ungnad's reconstruction reads KUR*s[u(?)-ú(?)]-ḫi*.

42According to Reade, the eponym list for the years 833–832 to 831–830 reads as follows:

833–832 BCE	Que
832–831 BCE	Que
831–830 BCE	Que, Der (?)

Reade's attribution of an additional year to the campaign at Que is a misreading of the notations in Eponym Canon C^{b} 4. The additional *a-na* KUR*qu-e* in column III is most probably a scribal error (see n. 30 above). Thus the reference to the deity going out from Der should be dated to 832–831 BCE (cf. Ungnad, "Eponymen," 433).

31	828–827 BCE	*a-na* ^{KUR}*man-na-a-a* at Mannai
32	827–826 BCE	*si-ḫu* revolt
33	826–825 BCE	*si-ḫu* revolt
34	825–824 BCE	*si-ḫu* revolt
35	824–823 BCE	*si-ḫu* revolt

The eponym chronicle essentially shows that the Assyrian army was busy campaigning from one region to another until 828–827 BCE, at which time a major revolt broke out in Assyria that continued even after the death of Shalmaneser. Important for the purposes of this study are the notations for the years 840–839, 838–837, and 837–836 BCE. The first of these notations pertains to the Cedar Mountain. It is not possible to determine whether the notation is to be understood as a reference to an expedition of the Assyrian king to the mountain—which the Black Obelisk specified as Mt. Amanus—to "cut cedar timbers,"[43] or whether it is a description of the location of the main army on a military campaign. Additionally, it is not clear whether the army had returned to Assyria following the campaign against Hazael of Aram-Damascus (about which we know from other texts) or whether the campaign lasted beyond the king's eighteenth regnal year, thereby accounting for the presence of the army in northern Syria in the nineteenth regnal year. The latter is a possibility that should not be ruled out.

The second and third of these notations, namely, for the years 838–837 and 837–836 BCE, depict the Assyrian army as stationed at Malaḫu and Danabu, both cities in Aram-Damascus.[44] Reade has dealt with the issue of the discrepancy between the eponym notations and the accounts in the annals beginning with Shalmaneser's twenty-second *palû*, when the eponym list and the annals differ by one year.[45] Specifically, while the eponym chronicle noted that Assyrians were in Aram-Damascus in 838–837 and 837–836 BCE, the annals recorded the Assyrian-Aramean conflict

---

[43]E. Michel, "Die Assur-Texte Salmanassars III. (858–824)," *WO* 2 (1954–59), 154–55; *ARAB*, 1. §576.

[44]See Pitard, *Ancient Damascus*, 150.

[45]Reade, "Assyrian Campaigns," 254–55. Reade's obvervation that after the Que campaign in 833–832 and 832–831 BCE, "the year-numbers are two too low" cannot be sustained (see nn. 30 and 42 above).

as having lasted only a year, that is, during Shalmaneser's twenty-first *palû*.[46] Pitard, following Reade, suggests that

> it is difficult to determine whether the eponym canon has accidentally used the names of two towns from a single campaign to the Damascus region in forming the list, or whether the author of the annals has conflated two campaigns to the same area into one.[47]

While Pitard has correctly recognized the problem, his suggestion about the origin of the error is flawed. First, he assumes that the names of the two towns were officially recorded at the same time, which clearly cannot be the case. The names of the two towns are associated with two different *limmus*, meaning that they were inscribed on different occasions. Second, a campaign in the same geographical region that lasted more than a year (even if separately recorded in the annals) should be treated as a single campaign. The version of the annals in which this campaign against Hazael of Aram-Damascus is noted is already a late one, inscribed in the 820s; it extends into the thirty-first *palû* (thirty-second regnal year?) of Shalmaneser. It is still uncertain if *palû* was being used unequivocally for regnal years during the reign of Shalmaneser. If it is used definitely for regnal years, one of two things may have occurred in the transmission of the annals. First, in the recopying of the events of earlier years, the author of the annals may have skipped an almost parallel account of the twenty-second *palû* and instead copied the account of the twenty-third *palû* as the twenty-second. Second, in an attempt to gloss over the difficulty Shalmaneser might have had with Hazael, the author conflated a campaign that had lasted two years into one. In any case, the evidence of the eponym chronicle is arguably more reliable than that

---

[46]See Tadmor, "Campaigns of Sargon," 22–33. Tadmor states that the method of dating every year of a king's reign by *palû*, beginning with the first regnal year, began sometime after the tenth year of Shalmaneser III's reign (30, n. 70) and presupposes that the king carried out a campaign every single year. Even with Shalmaneser, however, the use of *palû* to date the years of reign is not consistent. It may be more appropriate to translate *palû* as "campaign year" even for the reign of Shalmaneser. Thus, questions remain concerning *palû* dating and therefore cannot be uncritically treated as equilavent to regnal years. This method of dating by *palû* fell out of use in the reign of Šamši-Adad V and was not revived until the reign of Tiglath-pileser III, who seems to have counted his accession year as his first *palû*. Since Tiglath-pileser ascended the throne only a month after the beginning of the new year, this must have been an attempt to claim his accession year as his full year of reign. With that as the probable reason, it may be assumed that *palû* refers to Tiglath-pileser's regnal years (cf. M. Ford, "The Contradictory Records of Sargon II of Assyria and the Meaning of *palû*," *JCS* 22 [1969], 83–84, who argues for the retention of the meaning of *palû* as regnal year for the reign of Sargon II).

[47]Pitard, *Ancient Damascus*, 150.

of the annals.[48] The eponym chronicle indicates that the Assyrian army was already in Aram-Damascus at the time of the Akîtu festival in Nisan 838 BCE and campaigned there until after the Akîtu festival in 837 BCE.

B. The "Bronze Gates of Balâwât"

A second source for the reign of Shalmaneser III are the so-called "Bronze Gates of Balâwât" which refers to the inscribed bronze bands employed as part of the decoration of a monumental pair of gates at the entrance to a palace of Shalmaneser III. These bands were discovered by an Arab in 1876 at Balâwât, a village about nine miles north-east of Nimrûd. Besides the thirteen almost complete bands which are housed in the British Museum, there are additional fragments in the possession of others.[49] The bands were nailed across the doors and around massive doorposts. They depict the activities and military expeditions of Shalmaneser in relief. On each band is engraved a short inscription related to the relief. At the edge of the doors were bronze edgings engraved with the so-called "Gate Inscription," which contains a brief account of the Assyrian king's activities in his first four years of reign as well as a more detailed description of his campaigns in Babylonia during his eighth and ninth regnal years.[50] The first serious study of these materials was done by A. Billerbeck and F. Delitzsch in 1908.[51]

---

[48]The relative reliability of the eponym lists was already affirmed by Reade ("Assyrian Campaigns," 255).

[49]See Michel, "Die Assur-Texte," *WO* 2, 408–9 for a listing of these fragments.

[50]G. G. Cameron ("The Annals of Shalmaneser III, King of Assyria," *Sumer* 6 [1950], 7) suggests that the excerpts of this inscription were probably drawn from what must have been a second edition of Shalmaneser's annals (the earliest, it was alleged, being the Monolith Inscription), prepared at the conclusion of the king's Babylonian campaigns. This, however, can no longer be true since the discovery of another annals text of Shalmaneser III in the Temple of Nabu at Nimrûd. This text was written at the end of Shalmaneser's first regnal year, 858–857 BCE (see M. Mahmud and J. Black, "Recent Work in the Nabu Temple, Nimrud," *Sumer* 44 [1985–86], 135–55). Given the present inscriptional evidence, the excerpts of the "Bronze Gates" should be classified as a third edition. The scenes and inscriptions on the bands, however, include campaigns that were conducted through probably the fourteenth *palû* (contra Luckenbill, *ARAB*, 1. §615). In view of the disparity in the inclusion of the content between the "Gate Inscription" and the bands, one can only speculate on the issue of the dating of the engraving and the setting up of these bronze gates.

[51]A. Billerbeck and F. Delitzsch, "Die Palasttore Salmanassars III. aus Balawat," in *Beiträge zur Assyriologie und semitischen Sprachwissenschaft*, IV/1 (Leipzig: J. C. Hinrichs, 1908), 1–144; pl. I–IV. L. W. King reproduced better pictures of the bands with his study in 1915 (*Bronze Reliefs from the Gates of Shalmaneser, King of Assyria B.C. 860–825* [London: British Museum, 1915]). A transliteration of the "Gate Inscription" and

Important for this discussion is the relief[52]—showing the Phoenicians bearing *maddattu*[53] to the Assyrian king—with an accompanying inscription on the upper register of Band III. King describes the depiction on the relief as follows:

> On the left . . . is the fortified city of Tyre, on its rocky island off the Syrian coast. Tribute is being carried across to the mainland in boats, which, as they near the shore, are drawn in with ropes attached to the prow. They are

---

the inscriptions on the bands may be found in Michel, "Die Assur-Texte," *WO* 2, 408–15; *idem*, "Die Assur-Texte Salmanassars III. (858–824)," *WO* 4 (1967–68), 29–37. See *ARAB*, 1. §§612–25 for an English translation of the texts.

[52]See *ANEP*, nos. 356–58.

[53]There are three Akkadian terms used to denote tribute or gifts—*biltu*, *maddattu*, and *nāmurtu*. The first word, *biltu*, has a broad range of meaning although it is the basic word for "tribute paid by subject rulers" from as early as the reign of Šamši-Adad I (1813–1781 BCE) (*CAD*, 2. 234–36; cf. C. C. Smith, "Jehu and the Black Obelisk of Shalmaneser III," in *Scripture in History and Theology: Essays in Honor of J. Coert Rylaarsdam*, ed. A. L. Merrill and T. W. Overholt [Pittsburgh: Pickwick, 1977], 87). The second word, *maddattu*, appears to be commonly used for "tribute" during the Middle Assyrian and Neo-Assyrian periods (*CAD*, 10/1. 13–14). Note, for example, the following statement from the reign of Tiglath-pileser I (1114–1076 BCE): *ma-da-at-ta šattišamma ana la šuparkê elišunu ukīn* "I imposed upon them as tribute (to be paid) every year without exception" (*AKA*, 72 v 40; *CAD*, 10/1. 13). The combination *biltu u maddattu* occurs quite frequently without any distinction in meaning, as in, for example, *šattišamma bilta u maddatta ana ālija . . . maḫrija littarrūni* "let them bring every year tribute and gifts to me" (*AKA*, 47 ii 94; *CAD*, 2. 235). The third word, *nāmurtu*, is generally defined as a "gift" (*CAD*, 11/1. 254–55). J. N. Postgate defines *nāmurtu* (or *tāmartu* in Babylonian) as "a subsidiary gift to accompany tribute" (*Taxation and Conscription in the Assyrian Empire* [Studia Pohl 3; Rome: Biblical Institute, 1974], 154). He further makes a clear distinction between *nāmurtu* and *maddattu*; the latter he alleges "is applied strictly only to compulsory payments, and not to gifts freely offered" (119). C. C. Smith challenges this assumption, arguing instead that "*nāmurtu* appears almost exclusively in the annals of TN [Tukulti-Ninurta] II (890–884), quite obviously with meanings going well beyond 'subsidiary gift' to include full tribute." He adds that "from the more 'propagandistic' annals . . . either *madattu* or *nāmurtu* might comprehend both ends of Postgate's contrasting spectrum, and probably several shades of verbal coloration in between" ("Jehu and the Black Obelisk," 87). Smith's latter statement is of particular import. Precisely because of the propagandistic nature of the Assyrian royal inscriptions, one should not jump to the conclusion that every time *maddattu* is mentioned, it implies an imposed or mandatory tribute the Assyrian king was exacting from a subject ruler or state. It could very well have been a one time gift a certain state was offering to pacify the Assyrian monarch, to remain on non-belligerent terms, or to express a desire for friendly relations (cf. D. B. Redford, *Egypt, Canaan, and Israel in Ancient Times* [Princeton: Princeton University Press, 1992], 338–39, who views these as "diplomatic gifts.").

The exacting of yearly tribute and the taking of booty were important aspects of the economy of the Assyrian empire (see, e.g., J. N. Postgate, "The Economic Structure of the Assyrian Empire," in *Power and Propaganda: A Symposium on Ancient Empires*, ed. M. T. Larsen [Copenhagen: Akademisk Forlag, 1979], 193–221; E. Moshe, "The Impact of Tribute and Booty on Countries and Peoples within the Assyrian Empire," in *Vorträge gehalten auf der 28. Rencontre Assyriologique Internationale in Wien 6.–10. Juli 1981*, ed. H. Hirsch [AfO Beiheft 19; Horn: Berger, 1982], 244–51). Assyrian annals are full of texts describing the imposition and reception of tribute as well as the taking of booty following the capture of cities. It must be noted, particularly, that the payment of yearly tribute by subject states often goes unmentioned in Assyrian texts. When references to payments appear in texts, such payments were generally made in contexts where the king received the tribute personally outside Assyria and under extraordinary circumstances, usually during or following major campaigns.

> being unloaded by porters, who wade up to their knees into the sea, and wear shoulder pads .... Bales of goods, bronze cauldrons, trays perhaps containing ivory, and other objects of value are being carried in procession before the king. All the Phoenicians wear pointed skull-caps, those of the better class having turban-cloths rolled tightly round them. Behind the king chariots, calvary, and infantry are advancing from an Assyrian camp.[54]

The inscription that accompanies the relief reads:

ma-da-tú šá ^{GIŠ}MÁ.MEŠ *šá* ^{URU}*ṣu-ra-a-a* ^{URU}*ṣi-du-na-a-a am-ḫu-ur*[55]

The *maddattu* of the ships of the Tyrians and Sidonians I received.

The presentation by the Tyrians and Sidonians can be related to the account of Shalmaneser's first year in the Monolith Inscription (to be dealt with below) for 858–857 BCE.[56] In correlating the events depicted on the Bronze Gates with Shalmaneser's annals, it is evident that the bands are arranged in chronological order. The first and second bands depict the king's campaign against Naʾiri and Urartu in his accession year (859–858 BCE).[57] Bands IV, V, and VI depict Shalmaneser's campaign to northern Syria in his second regnal year (857–856 BCE).[58] Thus, the dating of Band III to 858–857 BCE is certain. Shalmaneser must have regarded the payment of *maddattu* by the Tyrians and Sidonians early in his reign as a significant occasion and as another step in his political and economic expansion in the west.[59] Nevertheless, it is less certain that the payment indicates that Tyre was subjecting itself to a pro-Assyrian stance or had accepted Assyrian hegemony.[60] It is more likely that the *maddattu* represented gifts offered to the visiting monarch, Shalmaneser III, early in his reign in recognition of Assyria's emerging significance in the region. In the annals of Shalmaneser's predecessor, Ashurnasirpal, there is only one record of Tyre and Sidon together with other Phoenician coastal cities offering *maddattu* to the Assyrian king. This event

---

[54]King, *Bronze Reliefs*, 28.

[55]Michel, "Die Assur-Texte," *WO* 4, 34.

[56]So already King, *Bronze Reliefs*, 23; cf. Monolith Inscription, col. II, lines 5–12 (*ARAB*, 1. §600); Black Obelisk, lines 26–31 (*ARAB*, 1. §558). King's dates for all the campaigns, however, have to be lowered by one year.

[57]Cf. Monolith Inscription, col. I, lines 23–27 (*ARAB*, 1. §598).

[58]Cf. Monolith Inscription, col. II, lines 13–30 (*ARAB*, 1. §601).

[59]See Tadmor ("Assyria and the West") for a discussion of the economic interests of Assyria in the west in the ninth century BCE.

[60]H. J. Katzenstein points out that the Tyrian king is not depicted in the relief as leading the delegation of tribute-bearers, but rather as remaining behind in his city (*The History of Tyre from the Beginning of the Second Millenium B.C.E. until the Fall of the Neo-Babylonian Empire in 586 B.C.E.* [Jerusalem: Schocken Institute for Jewish Research, 1973], 164, n. 187).

took place sometime between the king's seventh and seventeenth regnal years (877–876 to 867–866 BCE).[61] Ashurnasirpal was the first Neo-Assyrian king to penetrate Phoenician territory and thus to inaugurate direct relationships with western kingdoms. Olmstead suggests that the payments of *maddattu* made on this occasion by the Phoenician rulers originated from commercial interests rather than fear of conquest. The Phoenicians saw the occasion as an opportunity to expand their commerce and trade through friendly relations with Assyria.[62] Such a gesture to ensure good relations would have been appropriate.

In the Balâwât materials, a contrast may be made between the depiction of the Phoenicians delivering *maddattu* on Band III with that on Band VI where Sangara king of Carchemish is depicted as delivering his *maddattu* in person.[63] Similarly, on the Black Obelisk, panel B, Jehu is presumably represented as bowing before Shalmaneser when he offered his *maddattu*.[64] Therefore, it is likely that from the perspective of the Tyrians, their *maddattu* did not represent so much a political gesture as a commercial one.

Thus, the relief and inscription of Band III, although depicting the giving of *maddattu* by the Tyrians and Sidonians, do not necessarily indicate that Tyre was pro-Assyrian nor that it submitted to Assyrian hegemony in the first year of Shalmaneser's reign. Rather, it was more probably an act to establish good relations with the new Assyrian monarch.

In addition to Band III, a fragment mentioning the Phoenicians has been identified as part of the lower register of Band XIV.[65] The inscription reads:

> [*ma-da-*]*tú šá* ^{URU}*ṣu-ra-a-a* ^{URU}*ṣi-du-na-a-a* KÙ.BABBAR.MEŠ KÙ.GI.MEŠ AN.NA.MEŠ UD.KA.BAR.MEŠ SÍK ZÁ.GÌN ZÁ.GUG *am-ḫur*[66]
>
> [The *madda*]*ttu* of the Tyrians and Sidonians—silver, gold, tin, copper, and red-purple wool—I received.

---

[61]*ARAB*, 1. §479.

[62]A. T. Olmstead, *History of Assyria* (New York/London: C. Scribner's Sons, 1923), 95; cf. also Katzenstein, *History of Tyre*, 141, 166.

[63]King, *Bronze Reliefs*, pl. XXXIV.

[64]*ANEP*, no. 355.

[65]This fragment, N^{a}, belongs to the Rassam Collection (so W. G. Birch and T. G. Pinches, *The Bronze Ornaments of the Palace Gates of Balawat (Shalmaneser II, B.C. 859–825)* [2 vols.; London: Society of Biblical Archaeology, 1880–1902], 1. 14 and plate N; E. Unger, *Zum Bronzetor von Balawat* [Leipzig: Eduard Pfeiffer, 1913], 8 and table 1, plate N).

[66]Michel, "Die Assur-Texte," *WO* 4, 36.

It is not entirely clear whether the event depicted on this band is the same as that of Band III. Given the fact that the bands are arranged in chronological order, however, it is not likely that Band XIV refers to the same event as Band III. Since Band XIII—relating to the capture of Aštamaku, the royal city of Irḫuleni of Hamath, and other cities—can be safely dated to Shalmaneser's eleventh regnal year (848–847 BCE)[67] and Band XVI—relating to a battle against Hamath—should probably be dated to the fourteenth regnal year (845–844 BCE),[68] the event of Band XIV must have occurred sometime between 848–847 and 845–844 BCE. It is likely that during either of these two Assyrian campaigns in southern Syria Shalmaneser received *maddattu* from Tyre and Sidon. Nothing more specific can be said beyond this approximate dating.

Again, as with Band III, the issue is whether or not this payment of *maddattu* represents the Tyrians and Sidonians' military or political submission to Assyrian hegemony and thus a pro-Assyrian stance. It is true that the items listed—silver, gold, tin, copper, and red-purple wool—are generally associated with the yearly tribute exacted by the Assyrians from vassal states,[69] yet because the word *maddattu* was used as an inclusive word for gifts and tribute either imposed or mandatory, it cannot be simply assumed that the reference is to yearly tribute and hence that Tyre and Sidon were under the hegemony of Assyria during this period. This may, again, have been a gift to appease or buy favor from the Assyrian monarch in order to protect Phoenician commercial interests without necessarily indicating either a pro-Assyrian posture or submission to Assyria.

In summary, two facts can be noted from this analysis of the "Bronze Gates of Balâwât." (1) There is no evidence of any political coalition in southern Syria-Palestine early in the reign of Shalmaneser. The kingdoms seem to have been operating independently of one another militarily. Commercial and economic cooperation may have existed but about this we have no evidence. (2) The Phoenicians chose to establish cordial relations with Assyria early in the reign of Shalmaneser.

---

[67]Cf. the Black Obelisk Inscription, lines 87–98 (*ARAB*, 1. §568) and the Bull Inscription, lines 90–96 (*ARAB*, 1. §653).

[68]Cf. the Bull Inscription, lines 99–102 (*ARAB*, 1. §658–59).

[69]See N. B. Jankowska, "Some Problems of the Economy of the Assyrian Empire," in *Ancient Mesopotamia: Socio-Economic History* (Moscow: "Nauka" Publishing House, 1969), 253–76.

C. Monolith Inscription

The Monolith Inscription is an annalistic text discovered at Kurkh. The 156 lines of text are inscribed on a stela that contains a figure of Shalmaneser III in relief. As well as giving the name of the king, his titles, and genealogy, the text provides a detailed description of Shalmaneser's military expeditions from his accession year through the *limmu* year of Dayān-Aššur (853–852 BCE). This text is the second edition of the annals of Shalmaneser III, and unlike later editions is dated by *limmu* instead of *palû*.[70] The text was first published by H. C. Rawlinson.[71] Before turning attention to the text's account of the battle of Qarqar with which biblical scholars have been primarily concerned, two matters in the text should be noted. First, col. I, line 29–col. II, line 13 describe a campaign which probably took place in Shalmaneser's first regnal year. Although only the month and the day the campaign commenced is given, it is clear from the sequence of the annals that the campaign occurred in the king's first regnal year. Bit-Adini seems to have been the major object of this campaign, although some north Syrian states were dealt with as well. After the date appears the following remark: "I received the *maddattu* of the kings of the seacoast and I marched along the shore of the wide sea, straightaway and victorious."[72] It is obvious that the "wide sea" is used here as a reference to the Mediterranean Sea and the "seacoast" to the Phoenician coast. The king of Tyre and Sidon was probably among those who paid *maddattu*.[73]

---

[70]That the "Gate Inscription" of the Gates of Balâwât represents a third edition of the annals has already been noted (see n. 50 above). A fourth edition is the "Baghdad Text" published by Cameron ("Annals of Shalmaneser III," 6–26) and includes the first sixteen *palê* of Shalmaneser. The Bull Inscription closely resembles this "fourth edition," although it was written at least two years later. A fifth edition is probably the Marble-Slab Inscription published by F. Safar ("A Further Text of Shalmaneser III. From Assur," *Sumer* 7 [1951], 3–21), which includes campaigns through the twentieth *palû*. A final (sixth) edition of the annals is the Black Obelisk, which includes expeditions through the thirty-first *palû*.

[71]H. C. Rawlinson, *Cuneiform Inscriptions*, 3. pls. 7 and 8.

[72]Cf. *ARAB*, 1. §600.

[73]Cf. Band III of the "Bronze Gates of Balâwât" (see above, p. 24). Katzenstein (*History of Tyre*, 130–34) has argued that during this period in their history, Tyre and Sidon were ruled by a single king. The following are given as evidence:

(1) In the "Bronze Gates of Balâwât" (Bands III and XIV) Tyre and Sidon are mentioned together. Of particular significance is Band III. While the accompanying inscription mentions both city-states, the relief depicts only a single monarch standing on the island city of Tyre (*ANEP*, no. 356).

(2) In III R 5, 6, lines 24–26 (*ARAB*, 1. §672), along with Jehu, the Bit-Ḫumrite, the Tyrians and the Sidonians were mentioned as having paid tribute to the Assyrian king. However, in a parallel text, the Marble-Slab Inscription, col. IV, lines 10–12 (Safar,

The second matter concerns a campaign that took place in the *limmu* of Aššur-bēlu-kaʾʾin, the third regnal year of Shalmaneser (856–855 BCE). Again the campaign for that year was directed principally at Bit-Adini where the important city of Til-Barsip was captured and renamed Kar-Shalmaneser and the region provincialized. The following piece of information is pertinent to the Assyrian-Phoenician relations during this period: "When I (Shalmaneser III) was staying in Kar-Shalmaneser I received the *maddattu* of the kings of the seacoast and the kings of the banks of the Euphrates—silver, gold, tin, copper, copper vessels, cattle, sheep, brightly colored woolen and linen garments."[74] Exactly who these "kings of the seacoast" were remains uncertain, but this text does indicate that there is no evidence of a south Syrian-Palestinian coalition organized against the Assyrians by 856–855 BCE. Thus the military alliance of western states that encountered Shalmaneser at Qarqar in 853–852 BCE must have come into existence after and perhaps as a response to the events of 856–855 BCE in the vicinity of Bit-Adini. Since Ashurnasirpal had already received *maddattu* from Phoenician rulers, Phoenician payments in 856–855 BCE probably reflect the continuing efforts of the Phoenicians to remain in good economic and political relations with Assyria. That no openly anti-Assyrian coalition seems to have existed in 856–855 BCE would indicate that it was not Omri of Israel who inaugurated participation in a western anti-Assyrian coalition.

The two preceding matters suggest that harmonious relations were established between Tyre and Assyria early in the reign of Shalmaneser for commercial reasons. There is nothing in the inscriptional material that suggests hostility between the two states, military encounters, or a forced submission.

In the *limmu* year of Dayān-Aššur (853–852 BCE), Shalmaneser crossed the Euphrates and encountered a coalition led by Adad-idri of Aram-Damascus and Irḫuleni of Hamath. The following is a transliteration of col. II, lines 78–101 of the Monolith Inscription which describes this episode.[75]

"Further Text of Shalmaneser III," 11–12), the name of the monarch, Baʿli-ma-AN-zēr the Tyrian, is given in place of Tyre and Sidon along with a reference to Jehu, the Bit-Ḫumrite.

74 *ARAB*, 1. §603.

75 Other transliterations of the text may be found in E. Schrader, *Keilinschriftliche Bibliothek* (2 vols.; Berlin: H. Reuther, 1889–90), 1. 172–74; and N. Rasmussen, *Salmanasser den II's Indskrifter* (Kjobenhavn: Nielsen and Lydiches, 1897), 2–30. English translations may be found in *ARAB*, 1. §§594–611; and *ANET*, 277–78.

78) . . . AŠ *li-me* ^{Id}DI-KUD-*aš-šur* AŠ ^{ITI}GU$_{4}$ UD.14.KÁM TA ^{URU}N-INA *at-tu-muš* ^{ÍD}ḪAL.ḪAL *e-te-bir a-na* URU.MEŠ-*ni*

79) *ša* ^{I}*gi-am-mu* ^{ÍD}KASKAL.KUR.A *aq-tí-rib púl-ḫa-at* EN-*ti-ia na-mur-rat* ^{GIŠ}TUKUL.MEŠ *iz-zu-te ip-la-ḫu-ma* AŠ ^{GIŠ}TUKUL *ra-ma-ni-šú-nu* ^{I}*gi-am-mu* EN-*šú-nu*

80) *i-du-ku a-na* ^{URU}*saḫ-la-la u* ^{URU}*tíl-ša-tur-a-ḫi lu* KU$_{4}$-*ub* DINGIR. MEŠ-*ia* DIŠ É.GAL.MEŠ-*šú lu ú-še-ri-ib ta-ši-il-tu* AŠ É.GAL.MEŠ-*šú lu áš-kun*

81) *na-kám-te lu ap-ti ni-ṣir-tú-šu lu a-mur* NÍG.GA-*šú* NÍG.ŠU-*šú áš-lu-la a-na* URU-*ia aš-šur ub-la* TA ^{URU}*saḫ-la-la at-tu-muš a-na* ^{URU}*kar-*SILIM.MA-*nu*-MAŠ

82) *aq-tí-rib* AŠ ^{GIŠ}MÁ.MEŠ ^{KUŠ}*táḫ-ši-e šá* 2-*te-šú* ^{ÍD}A.RAT AŠ *mi-li-šá e-bir ma-da-tu ša* XX.MEŠ *šá* GÌR *am-ma-te ša* ^{ÍD}A.RAT *ša* ^{I}*sa-an-gar*

83) ^{URU}*gar-ga-miš-a-a šá* ^{I}*ku-un-da-ás-pi* ^{URU}*ku-mu-ḫa-a-a šá* ^{I}*a-ra-me* DUMU *gu-si ša* ^{I}*lal-li* ^{URU}*me-li-da-a-a ša* ^{I}*ḫa-ia-ni* DUMU *ga-ba-ri*

84) *ša* ^{I}*qàl-pa-ru-da* ^{KUR}*pa-ti-na-a-a ša* ^{I}*qàl-pa-ru-da* ^{KUR}*gam-gu-ma-a-a* KÙ.BABBAR KÙ.GI AN.NA.MEŠ UD.KA.BAR TU$_{7}$.MEŠ UD.KA.BAR

85) ^{URU}*aš-šur-ut-tir-aṣ-bat šá* GÌR *am-ma-te šá* ^{ÍD}A.RAT *šá* UGU ^{ÍD}*sa-gu-ri šá* LÚ.MEŠ-*e* ^{KUR}*ḫat-ta-a-a* ^{URU}*pi-it-ru*

86) *i-qa-bu-šú-ni* AŠ *lìb-bi am-ḫur* TA UGU ^{ÍD}A.RAT *at-tu-muš a-na* ^{URU}*ḫal-man aq-tí-rib* MÈ *e-du-ru* GÌR.II *iṣ-bu-tú*

87) KÙ.BABBAR KÙ.GI *ma-da-ta-šú-nu am-ḫur* ^{UDU}SISKIR.MEŠ DIŠ ^{d}IŠKUR *ša* ^{URU}*ḫal-man* DÙ-*uš* TA ^{URU}*ḫal-man at-tu-muš a-na* 2 URU.MEŠ-*ni*

88) *ša* ^{I}*ir-ḫu-le-e-ni* ^{KUR}*a-mat-ai aq-tí-rib* ^{URU}*a-di-in$_{4}$-nu* ^{URU}*bar-ga-a* ^{URU}*ar-ga-na-a* URU *šar$_{4}$-ti-šú* KUR-*ud šal-la-su* NÍG.ŠU-*šú*

89) NÍG.GA É.GAL.MEŠ-*šú ú-še-ṣa-a a-na* É.GAL.MEŠ-*šú* IZI.MEŠ ŠUB-*du* TA ^{URU}*ar-ga-na-a at-tu-muš a-na* ^{URU}*qar-qa-ra aq-tí-rib*

90) ^{URU}*qar-qa-ra* URU *šar$_{4}$-ti-ia ab-búl aq-qur* AŠ IZI.MEŠ *áš-ru-up* 1 LIM 2 ME ^{GIŠ}GIGIR.MEŠ 1 LIM 2 ME *pit-ḫal-lu* 20 LIM ÉRIN.MEŠ *ša* ^{Id}IM-*id-ri*

91) [^{KUR}]ANŠE-*šú* 7 ME ^{GIŠ}GIGIR.MEŠ 7 ME *pit-ḫal-lu* 10 LIM ÉRIN.MEŠ *šá* ^{I}*ir-ḫu-le-e-ni* ^{KUR}*a-mat-ai* 2 LIM ^{GIŠ}GIGIR.MEŠ 10 LIM ÉRIN.MEŠ *šá* ^{I}*a-ḫa-ab-bu*

92) ^{KUR}*sir-ʾi-la-a-a* 5 ME ÉRIN.MEŠ *ša* KUR *gu-a-a* 1 LIM ÉRIN.MEŠ *šá* ^{KUR}*mu-uṣ-ra-a-a* 10 ^{GIŠ}GIGIR.MEŠ 10 LIM ÉRIN.MEŠ *šá* ^{KUR}*ir-qa-na-ta-a-a*

93) 2 ME ÉRIN.MEŠ *šá* ^{I}*ma-ti-nu-ba-ʾa-li* ^{URU}*ar-wa$_{4}$-da-a-a* 2 ME ÉRIN.MEŠ *šá* ^{KUR}*ú-sa-na-ta-a-a* 30 ^{GIŠ}GIGIR.MEŠ 10 LIM ÉRIN.MEŠ

94) *ša* ^{I}*a-du-nu-ba-ʾa-li* ^{KUR}*ši-a-na-a-a* 1 LIM ^{ANŠE}*gam-ma-lu šá* ^{I}*gi-in-di-bu-ʾu* ^{KUR}*ar-ba-a-a* [ ] LIM ÉRIN.MEŠ

95) *šá* ^{I}*ba-ʾa-sa* DUMU *ru-ḫu-bi* ^{KUR}*a-ma-na-a-a* 12 XX.MEŠ-*ni an-nu-ti* [*a-na*] ÉRIN.TÁḪ-*ti-šú il-qa-a a*[-*na e-piš*]

96) MURUB$_4$ *u* MÈ DÌŠ GAB-*ia it-bu-ni* AŠ Á.MEŠ MAḪ.MEŠ *ša aš-šur* EN SÌ-*na* AŠ ^{GIŠ}TUKUL.MEŠ KAL.MEŠ *šá* ÙRI.GAL *a-lik* IGI-*ia*

97) *iš-ru-ka it-ti-šú-nu am-daḫ-ḫi-iṣ* TA ^{URU}*qar-qa-ra a-di* ^{URU}*gíl-za-ú* BAD$_5$.BAD$_5$-*šú-nu lu áš-kun* 14 LIM ÉRIN.MEŠ

98) *ti-du-ki-šú-nu* AŠ ^{GIŠ}TUKUL.MEŠ *ú-šam-qit kīma* ^{d}IŠKUR UGU-*šú-nu ri-ḫi-il-ta ú-ša-az-nin u-má-ṣi*[76] *šal*-GAM[77]-*šú-nu*

99) *pa-an na-me-e ú-šam-li* DAGAL.MEŠ ÉRIN.ḪI.MEŠ-*šú-nu* AŠ ^{GIŠ}TUKUL.MEŠ *u-šar-di* ÚŠ.MEŠ-*šú-nu ḫur-pa-lu šá na-gu*

100) *i-me-eṣ* EDIN *a-na šúm-pùl* ZI.MEŠ-*šú nap-ra-ru-ú rap-šu a-na qub-bu-ri-šú-nu iḫ-li-iq* AŠ LÚ.MEŠ-*šú*

101) ^{GIŠ}*a-ra-an-tu lam ti-i-ri ak-šud* AŠ *ki-rib tam-ḫa-ri šu-a-ti* ^{GIŠ}GIGIR.MEŠ-*šú-nu pit-ḫal-la-šú-nu*

102) ANŠE.KUR.RA.MEŠ-*šú-nu* LAL-*at* ^{GIŠ}*ni-ri-šú-nu e-kim-šú-nu*

In the *limmu* of Dayān-Aššur, in the month of Airu, the fourteenth day, I departed from Nineveh, crossed the Tigris, and approached the cities of Giammu on the river Baliḫ. They became afraid of the terror of my sovereignty and the splendor of my fierce weapons, and killed Giammu their master with their own weapons. $^{(80)}$I entered the towns Saḫlala and Til-ša-Turaḫi, brought my gods into his palaces, and established the *tašiltu*-festival in his palaces. I opened the treasury and saw his wealth. I took as booty his possessions and his property and brought to my city Aššur. I departed from Saḫlala and approached Kar-Shalmaneser. I crossed the Euphrates at its flood for the second time in goat-skin boats. The *maddattu* of the kings on the other side of the Euphrates—of Sangara the Carchemishite, of Kundaspi the Kummuḫite, of Arame the (A)gusite, of Lalli the Melidean, of Hayani the Gabarite,[78] of Qalparuda the Pattinean, and of Qalparuda the Gurgumite—silver, gold, tin, copper, and copper vessels, $^{(85)}$at Aššur-uttir-aṣbat, on the other side of the Euphrates, on the river Sagur, which the people of Ḫatti call Pitru, I received. I departed from the Euphrates and approached Ḫalman (Aleppo). They were afraid to fight and seized my feet. I received silver and gold as their *maddattu* and offered sacrifices before the god Adad of Ḫalman.

I departed from Ḫalman and approached the two cities of Irḫuleni the Hamathite and captured the cities of Adinnu and Barga, and Argana his

---

[76]The word *u-má-ṣi* is probably a scribal error for the unintelligible *u-ta-ṣi* (cf. Schrader, *Keilinschriftliche Bibliothek*, 1. 172). H. Tadmor has observed that this text, copied rather carelessly by a local scribe, contains over fifty scribal errors, omissions, and misspellings ("Que and Muṣri," *IEJ* 11 [1961], 144–45). The verb *maṣû* means "to be sufficient for" (cf. *CAD* 10/1, 344–45).

[77]Restoring GAM for the illegible sign and taking it as *mâtu* (cf. R. Borger, *Assyrisch-babylonische Zeichenlist* [2d ed.; Neukirchen-Vluyn: Neukirchener Verlag, 1981], 148). The whole word *šalmātešúnu* means "their corpses."

[78]Neither of the terms DUMU *gu-si* and DUMU *ga-ba-ri* is a patronym. DUMU (= *māru*) is used here as a reference to a citizen or native of a city or a country (*CAD* 10/1. 315–16) and would be used synonymously with gentilics. S. Parpola (*Neo-Assyrian Toponyms* [AOAT 6; Neukirchen-Vluyn: Neukirchener Verlag, 1970], 75–92) notes that the rulers of Bit-(A)gusi, Bit-Adini, and Bit-Dakuri are designated *mār Agūsi*, *mār Adīni* and *mār Dakūri*. The same gentilic sense applies to the phrase ^{I}*ia-ú-a mâr ḫu-um-ri-i*. Cf. similar usage of בן, e.g., in בן־יבש (2 Kgs 15:10). Contra Briquel-Chatonnet, who suggests that DUMU is the equivalent of *Bit* (*Les relations*, 107, n. 35).

royal city. I brought out his spoil, his property, and the possessions of his palaces and set fire to his palaces. I departed from Argana and approached Qarqar. (90)I destroyed, devastated, and burned with fire Qarqar his royal city. 1,200 chariots, 1,200 calvary, and 20,000 soldiers of Adad-idri of the land of Imērišu,[79] 700 chariots, 700 calvary, and 10,000 soldiers of Irḫuleni the Hamathite, 2,000 chariots and 10,000 soldiers of Ahab the Israelite, 500 soldiers of the Gueans [or Byblians], 1,000 soldiers of the Muṣreans [or Egyptians], 10 chariots and 10,000 soldiers of the Irqanateans, 200 soldiers of Matinu-baʾil the Arwadite, 200 soldiers of the Usanateans, 30 chariots and 10,000 soldiers of Adunu-baʾil the Šianean, 1,000 camels of Gindibuʾ the Arabian, [ ],000 soldiers (95)of Baʾsa the (Bit-)Ruḫu-bite,[80] the Ammonite—these twelve kings he brought to his help. They marched against me for battle and combat. I fought with them with the mighty forces which Aššur, my lord, gave me, and the powerful weapons which Nergal, my leader, presented me. I accomplished their defeat from Qarqar to Gilzau. I slew 14,000 of their soldiers with the sword. Like Adad, I rained destruction upon them. I made their corpses sufficient and filled the entire plain with their wide spreading armies. I made their blood flow down the *ḫur-pa-lu* of the district with weapons. (100)The plain was too small to let their bodies fall, the vast field was used up in burying them. I spanned the Orontes with their bodies as with a bridge. In that battle I took away from them their chariots, their calvary, and their horses broken to the yoke.

The preceding account is dated to the *limmu* of Dayān-Aššur. From the eponym canon[81] it can be established that Dayān-Aššur served as the *limmu* in the sixth regnal year (853–852 BCE) of Shalmaneser's reign. This account in the Monolith Inscription is the most detailed description of this particular campaign of Shalmaneser.[82] Shalmaneser appears to have encountered military opposition of varying degrees throughout the region west of the Euphrates. In his march to the west in his first regnal year (858–857 BCE), Shalmaneser had encountered a north Syrian coalition of states that included Bit-Adini, Carchemish, Samaʾl, Que, and Pattin (Unqi).[83] By his second regnal year (857–856 BCE), most of these states were defeated or had submitted and subsequently paid *maddattu* (*ARAB*, 1. §601), with the exception of Bit-Adini. Shalmaneser's warfare with Ahuni of Bit-Adini continued into his

---

[79]For a discussion of the Assyrian usage of Imērišu and Ša-imērišu as designations for Aram-Damascus, see Pitard, *Ancient Damascus*, 14–17.

[80]Cf. n. 78 for this usage of DUMU.

[81]See Ungnad, "Eponymen," 420.

[82]Shorter accounts of this campaign may be found in the "Baghdad Text" (see Cameron, "Annals of Shalmaneser III," 13, 21), the Bull Inscription (see Billerbeck and Delitzsch, "Palasttore Salmanassars," 144–51; *ARAB*, 1. §§646–47), the Marble-Slab Inscription (see Safar, "Further Text of Shalmaneser III," 7–8, 16), and the Black Obelisk (see Michel, "Die Assur-Texte," *WO* 2, 148; *ARAB*, 1. §563).

[83]*ARAB*, 1. §600. Cf. G. W. Ahlström, *The History of Ancient Palestine from the Palaeolithic Period to Alexander's Conquest* (JSOTSup 146; Sheffield: JSOT, 1993), 577; Briquel-Chatonnet, *Les relations*, 77–79; and the Appendix at the end of the dissertation.

third regnal year (856–855 BCE); Bit-Adini was defeated and its territory provincialized. By this time, western kingdoms must have become aware that Shalmaneser was moving to dominate the area. The need to form defensive alliances against Assyrian encroachment must have become more and more obvious. By 853 BCE, a major coalition had formed in central and southern Syria and Palestine. The 853 BCE campaign began early in the year, in the second month (April/May), with the Assyrian army first advancing against a state on the river Baliḫ forcing it into submission. The king and his army then crossed the Euphrates at its flood and received *maddattu* from several north Syrian states—Carchemish, Kummuḫ, Bit-Agusi, Melid, Gabari, Pattin, and Gurgum—at (Ana-)Aššur-uttir-aṣbat (Pitru), a city captured in Shalmaneser's third regnal year.[84] These north Syrian states had paid *maddattu* very early in Shalmaneser's reign and had probably remained loyal to the Assyrian king. Shalmaneser continued his campaign by moving to Ḫalman (Aleppo), which submitted voluntarily. With northern Syria under firm Assyrian control, Shalmaneser turned his attention to central Syria, where he plundered and burned three cities of Irḫuleni of Hamath. He then advanced against the royal city of Qarqar on the Orontes. Following the destruction of Qarqar, the Assyrian army was confronted by a strong coalition of central and southern Syrian and Palestinian states, headed by Adad-idri of Aram-Damascus. Although it is said in the account that there were twelve kings, it has often been assumed that only eleven states were named.[85] The phrase ^{I}*ba-ʾa-sa* DUMU *ru-ḫu-bi* ^{KUR}*a-ma-na-a-a* is usually translated "Ba'sa, son of Ruḫubi, the Ammonite."[86] However, DUMU *ru-ḫu-bi* should be treated as a gentilic rather than a patronym.[87] Therefore ^{I}*ba-ʾa-sa* DUMU *ru-ḫu-bi* should be translated "Ba'sa the Bit-Ruḫubite" which refers most probably to the Aramean state of Beth-Rehob, the "missing twelfth state."[88] ^{KUR}*a-ma-na-a-a* must refer to a separate state, the "missing twelfth state." Due to scribal mistakes the contingent (and perhaps also the name of the ruler) of this state has been omitted. While it has often been assumed

[84] See *ARAB*, 1. §603.

[85] Tadmor surmises that the name and country of the twelfth state was erroneously omitted by the scribe ("Que and Muṣri," 144–45). Reinhold, on the other hand, suggests "das angegriffene Karkar" as the twelfth state (*Die Beziehungen Altisraels*, 125).

[86] So, e.g., *ARAB*, 1. §611; cf. *ANET*, 278.

[87] See n. 78 above.

[88] Cf. Pitard, *Ancient Damascus*, 130, n. 87.

that ^{KUR}*a-ma-na-a-a* is to be identified with Ammon, some scholars prefer to identify it with a small country, ᶜAmmana, in northern Syria.[89] Na'aman, however, has argued quite convincingly that it should be identified with Ammon.[90] He notes that ᶜAmmana is normally rendered in Assyrian sources as *KUR* (= *šadû) am-ma-na-na* and identified as a mountain rather than a kingdom.[91] He further suggests that the name is here simply written without the element *bīt*.[92] Of the other states, Irqanata, Šianu, and Usanata are lesser known, but are presumably located along the northern Phoenician coast,[93] in the general vicinity of ancient Ugarit.[94] The identity of Gua and Muṣri, on the other hand, is disputed. While they have been traditionally identified with Anatolian Que and Muṣri,[95] these Anatolian states would more likely have been partners in a north Syrian coalition but there is no evidence that Shalmaneser was met by any united front in the north where states apparently submitted voluntarily. Tadmor has put forth a case to identify them with Byblos and Egypt instead.[96] Tadmor argues that the gentilic *gu-a-a* is probably a scribal mistake for *gu-<bal>-a-a*. Given the numerous scribal errors and omissions in the document, that omission is not unlikely. Moreover, because of its location in southern Syria, it is logical to assume that Byblos would be involved in the coalition. Egypt's participation in the coalition is also understandable. With its strong ties to Byblos and its interest in eastern Mediterranean trade, Egypt's interests were served in any effort to prevent Assyrian advance into Syria-Palestine.[97] Assyrian domination would have eroded Egypt's trade in the region, and Egypt's participation in the alliance was a means of lending support to "its clients and

---

[89]So, e.g., Pitard, *Ancient Damascus*, 130, n. 86.

[90]N. Na'aman, "Two Notes on the Monolith Inscription of Shalmaneser III from Kurkh," *Tel Aviv* 3 (1976), 98 and n. 20.

[91]Cf. also F. M. Cross, *Canaanite Myth and Hebrew Epic* (Cambridge: Harvard University Press, 1973), 26–28.

[92]Another instance where this is done is II R 53, 1, col. II., line 12 (cf. Parpola, *Neo-Assyrian Toponyms*, 16).

[93]Cf. W. Culican, "Phoenicia and Phoenician Colonization," in *CAH*^{2} III/2, 467; Pitard, *Ancient Damascus*, 130.

[94]For their location, see H. Klengel, *Geschichte Syriens im 2, Jahrtausend v.u.Z.* (3 vols.; Deutsche Akademie der Wissenschaften zu Berlin, Institut für Orientforschung 40; Berlin: Akademie-Verlag, 1965–70), 3. 6–7, 11–12, 36–37.

[95]See, e.g., P. Garelli, "Nouveau coup d'œil sur Muṣur," in *Hommages à André Dupont-Sommer*, ed. A. Caquot and M. Philonenko (Paris: Librairie Adrien Maisonneuve, 1971), 37–48.

[96]Tadmor, "Que and Muṣri," 143–50.

[97]See Tadmor, "Assyria and the West," 39.

neighbors in the Levant."[98] The influence of the outside power—Egypt—may explain why a south Syrian coalition came into being at the time. The military contingents of the coalition partners are as follows:

States	*Chariots*	*Calvary*	*Soldiers*	*Camels*
Aram-Damascus	1,200	1,200	20,000	
Hamath	700	700	10,000	
Israel	2,000		10,000	
Byblos			500	
Egypt			1,000	
Irqanata	10		10,000	
Arwad			200	
Usanata			200	
Šianu	30		10,000	
Arabia				1,000
Beth-Rehob			[ ],000	
Ammon				

Besides Adad-idri of Aram-Damascus, the leader of the anti-Assyrian coalition, Irḫuleni of Hamath and Ahab of Israel appear to have been the major participants.[99] Adad-idri supplied 1,200 chariots, 1,200 calvary, and 20,000 soldiers; Irḫuleni furnished 700 chariots, 700 calvary, and 10,000 soldiers; and Ahab dispensed 2,000 chariots and 10,000 soldiers. The rest of the contingent provided 40 chariots, 1,000 camels, and more than 22,000 soldiers. The total military force of the coalition may have exceeded that of the Assyrians. The annals for the sixteenth year of Shalmaneser (843–842 BCE) describe the Assyrian army as consisting of 2,002 chariots and 5,542 calvary,[100] while that of the twentieth year (839–838 BCE) sets the numbers at 2,001 chariots and 5,242 calvary.[101] There is no reason to assume that in 853 BCE Shalmaneser's military force was any larger.[102]

The size of the military contingent assigned Ahab, especially the chariot force, has been questioned. Na'aman, particularly, ar-

---

[98]Redford, *Egypt, Canaan, and Israel*, 339.

[99]In later editions of the annals, only Adad-idri of Aram-Damascus and Irḫuleni of Hamath are mentioned among the members of the coalition (for these texts, see n. 70 above). ^{KUR}*sir-ʾi-la-a-a* in line 92 represents the only occurrence of the name Israel in Assyrian texts. Earlier scholars understood this reading to refer to Ahab "of Israel (or *Jezreel*)" (see Rawlinson, *Cuneiform Inscriptions*, 3. 6).

[100]Cameron, "Annals of Shalmaneser III," 18, 47–48.

[101]Safar, "Further Text of Shalmaneser III," 14, 20.

[102]See M. Elat, "The Campaigns of Shalmaneser III against Aram and Israel," *IEJ* 25 (1975), 29.

gues that Israel could have afforded neither to purchase nor to maintain such a force.[103] He suggests instead that 2,000 is probably a scribal error for 200. Although all the figures given in the Assyrian annals may have been exaggerated, there is no reason to single out the size of the contingent assigned Ahab as any more exaggerated than the others.[104]

The Monolith Inscription provides evidence of close cooperation between Syro-Palestinian states in general and between Israel and Aram-Damascus in particular during the reign of Ahab. However, the biblical texts of 1 Kings 20 and 22:1–38, which do not refer to Qarqar, provide a completely different view, vis-à-vis a series of three battles fought between the Israelites and the Arameans.[105] 1 Kings 20 begins by describing a siege that the king of Aram, identified as Ben-Hadad, and his allies laid against Samaria. The king of Israel, identified as Ahab, was utterly dominated by the king of Aram. Subsequently, Ahab refused to comply with the excessive demands of the king of Aram and rebelled against him. This led to a battle in which Ahab was able to defeat Ben-Hadad with a considerably smaller army. The following year, Ben-Hadad and his forces again mounted an offensive against Ahab and the Israelites. At the battle at Aphek, the smaller Israelite force soundly defeated the massive Aramean army. Ahab spared the life of Ben-Hadad after he made the following agreement: "The cities which my father took from your father I will restore; and you may establish bazaars for yourself in Damascus, as my father did in Samaria" (1 Kgs 20:34). 1 Kings 22:1–38 reports a third battle between the Arameans and the Israelites. After a period of three years of relative peace, the king of Judah, identified as Jehoshaphat, instigated the king of Israel to take the offensive

---

[103]Na'aman, "Two Notes on the Monolith Inscription," 97–102.

[104]For a discussion of the issue, see Pitard, *Ancient Damascus*, 128, n. 81. That Israel was a chariot power is supported by evidence from the Calah/Nimrud Prism inscription of Sargon II (see C. J. Gadd, "Inscribed Prisms of Sargon II from Nimrud," *Iraq* 16 [1954], 179–82; cf. S. Dalley, "Foreign Chariotry and Calvary in the Armies of Tiglath-pileser III and Sargon II," *Iraq* 47 [1985], 31–38). Lines 25–49 of the inscription describe a rebellion in Samaria at the beginning of Sargon's reign (on the last decade of Israel's history, see J. H. Hayes and J. K. Kuan, "The Final Years of Samaria [730–720 BC]," *Bib* 72 [1991], 153–81). A campaign against Samaria was undertaken by the Assyrian king, who recaptured Samaria and conscripted two hundred chariots into the royal Assyrian army. If 200 chariots had survived the warfare with Assyria and the capture of Samaria by Sargon, then surely the kingdom of Israel at a time of prosperity and at the zenith of its military strength during the reign of Ahab could have maintained a chariot force many times larger. Cf. also Briquel-Chatonnet (*Les relations*, 80–81), who argues for the number of 2,000 for Ahab's chariot force.

[105]Pitard addresses the issue in detail in his *Ancient Damascus*, 114–25.

against the Arameans and win Ramoth-gilead back from their hands. At the battle at Ramoth-gilead, Ahab met his fateful death.

How are such contrasting positions between the Assyrian inscription and the biblical texts to be viewed? How is the historian to depict the relationship between Israel and Aram-Damascus during the reign of Ahab? Presented with obvious incongruity between the Assyrian and biblical materials, at least three possible solutions have been proposed by scholars. The first solution treats the battles in 1 Kings 20 between the Israelites and the Arameans as having taken place during the early rather than the latter years of Ahab's reign.[106] The second solution seeks to minimize the difficulties and argue that the battles could have occurred near the end of Ahab's reign.[107] The third solution asserts that the three battles belonged to the period of the Jehu dynasty and initially had nothing to do with Ahab. This last solution was initially proposed by A. Jepsen[108] and followed with modifications by C. F. Whitley,[109] J. M. Miller,[110] and, most recently, W. T. Pitard.[111] The arguments in favor of this solution may be summarized as follows.[112]

(1) The animosity between the Israelites and the Arameans reflected in 1 Kings 20 and 22:1–38 contradicts what is known from Assyrian sources. Evidently, their cooperation in the anti-Assyrian coalition extended beyond the sixth regnal year of Shalmaneser, as Assyrian inscriptions recorded the Assyrian king's encounter with

---

[106]So J. Morgenstern, "Chronological Data of the Dynasty of Omri," *JBL* 59 (1940), 385–92.

[107]See, e.g., M. F. Unger, *Israel and the Arameans of Damascus* (Grand Rapids: Zondervan, 1957), 70–74. J. Bright combines the first and second solutions, locating 1 Kings 20 early in Ahab's reign and 1 Kgs 22:1–40 at the end of his reign (*A History of Israel* [3d ed.; Philadelphia: Westminster, 1981], 243–47).

[108]A. Jepsen, "Israel und Damaskus," *AfO* 14 (1941–45), 153–59. M. Noth, while agreeing that these texts do not concern Ahab, nonetheless rejected Jepsen's suggestion to date them to the period of the Jehu dynasty. Instead, the texts present a general picture of conflict between Israel and Aram-Damascus during the Omride dynasty (*The History of Israel* [2d ed.; New York: Harper & Row, 1960], 243–44).

[109]C. F. Whitley, "The Deuteronomic Presentation of the House of Omri," *VT* 2 (1952), 137–52.

[110]J. M. Miller, *The Omride Dynasty in the Light of Recent Literary and Archaeological Research* (diss.; Emory University, 1964), 78–86; idem, "The Elisha Cycle and the Accounts of the Omride Wars," *JBL* 85 (1966), 441–54; idem, "The Fall of the House of Ahab," *VT* 17 (1967), 307–24; idem, "The Rest of the Acts of Jehoahaz (I Kings 20, 22:1–38)," *ZAW* 80 (1968), 337–42.

[111]Pitard, *Ancient Damascus*, 114–25.

[112]See S. L. McKenzie, *The Trouble with Kings: The Composition of the Book of Kings in the Deuteronomistic History* (VTSup 42; Leiden: E. J. Brill, 1991), 88–93 for a review of the discussion.

the coalition in his tenth, eleventh, and fourteenth regnal years (849–848, 848–847, and 845–844 BCE). While the picture of antagonism does not fit the era of the Omride dynasty, it conforms to what is known of Israelite-Aramean relations during the post-Omride period of the Jehu dynasty. Specifically, 2 Kings 13 describes a period of hostility between Israel and Aram—during the reigns of Jehoahaz and Joash of Israel—and alludes to three battles fought between them. These three battles can be related to those recounted in 1 Kings 20 and 22:1–38. Noteworthy is the fact that in both 2 Kings 13 and 1 Kings 20 Ben-Hadad was the king of Aram-Damascus. Moreover, Elisha predicted that the Israelites would do battle with and defeat the Arameans at Aphek (2 Kgs 13:17), which was precisely where the second battle occurred (1 Kgs 20:26).

(2) 1 Kings 20 and 22:1–38 presents the king of Israel as weak and completely under the domination of the king of Aram. The king of Israel is noted as having said to the king of Aram: "As you say, my lord, O king, I am yours, and all that I have" (1 Kgs 20:4). The Israelite monarch was able to muster an army of seven thousand men to fight the Arameans (1 Kgs 20:15). In addition, the Arameans intended to fight the Israelites in the plains, unafraid of Israel's chariot force which was presumably weak (1 Kgs 20:23–25). This picture of a weak Ahab clashes with what is known from the Monolith Inscription as well as other biblical and non-biblical material. In the Monolith Inscription, Ahab's military force is equal to that of both Adad-idri and Irḫuleni. In fact, his chariot force far exceeds that of the Arameans. The Mesha Inscription and the biblical text (2 Kgs 1:1; 3:5), in addition, reveal that Moab was under the control of Israel during the period of the Omride dynasty. Judah was a subordinate of Israel as well. The strength of Israel during this period is further attested by its wealth, evident in the artifactual remains of several key sites including Samaria,[113] Megiddo,[114] Hazor,[115] and Dan.[116]

---

[113]See J. W. Crowfoot, K. M. Kenyon, and E. L. Sukenik, *Samaria–Sebaste I. The Buildings at Samaria* (London: Palestine Exploration Fund, 1942), 5–20, 94–100; K. M. Kenyon, *Royal Cities of the Old Testament* (New York: Schocken, 1971), 71–89; cf. R. E. Tappy, *The Archaeology of Israelite Samaria* (HSS 44; Atlanta: Scholars Press, 1992).

[114]Y. Yadin, "New Light on Solomon's Megiddo," *BA* 23 (1960), 62–68.

[115]Y. Yadin, *Hazor: The Head of All the Those Kingdoms* (Schweich Lectures, 1970; London: Oxford University Press, 1972), 165–78; *idem*, *Hazor: The Rediscovery of a Great Citadel of the Bible* (New York: Random House, 1975), 158–70.

[116]A. Biran, "Tell Dan—Five Years Later," *BA* 43 (1980), 172–77; J. C. H. Laughlin, "The Remarkable Discoveries at Tel Dan," *BAR* 7/5 (1981), 33–34.

The portrait of a weak Israelite king again fits better with what is known to have been the situation during the Jehu dynasty. It was during this period that Israelite territory in Transjordan was lost to the Arameans under Hazael (2 Kgs 10:32–33). It is in the context of the reign of a weak king of the Jehu dynasty that 1 Kgs 20:34 makes sense. Ben-Hadad, after his defeat by the Israelite king, said, "I will restore the towns my father took from your father." This can be correlated with 2 Kgs 13:25 which notes, "Then Joash son of Jehoahaz took again from Ben-Hadad son of Hazael the towns that he had taken from his father Jehoahaz in war."

(3) The third battle at Ramoth-gilead (1 Kgs 22:3) implies that the city was under the control of the Arameans during the Omride dynasty. Other biblical texts, however, contradict this claim. Ramoth-gilead was still in Israelite hands at the end of Joram's reign (2 Kgs 8:28–29), and it was there that Jehu began his rebellion (2 Kgs 9:1, 4, 14). Furthermore, 2 Kgs 10:32–33 indicates that Gilead was lost to the Arameans only during the reign of Jehu.

(4) There are a number of literary clues that suggest that 1 Kings 20 and 22:1–38 do not belong to the reign of Ahab. First, the DtrH in his concluding formula notes that "Ahab slept with his fathers" (1 Kgs 22:40). This formula is used elsewhere in Kings for rulers who died a natural death. The DtrH is thus unaware of a violent death for Ahab.

Second, the name Ahab occurs only three times in 1 Kings 20 (vv. 2, 13, 14) and once in 1 Kgs 22:1–38 (v. 20) in the MT. Other than these few occurrences, the king is referred to only as מלך ישראל. In LXX^{B} and Lucianic recensions, the name Ahab appears slightly more often and not always in the same locations. This suggests that the identification of מלך ישראל with Ahab is secondary.

Third, there is a difference in the order of the texts between the MT and LXX. In the MT, 1 Kings 20 and 22 are separated by the story of Naboth's vineyard (chap. 21). In the LXX, however, the narratives of the three battles are kept together, following the story of Naboth's vineyard. Again, the difference in the order of these chapters further illustrates that the placement of these stories in their present narrative context is secondary.

At this juncture, it is important to note that the Monolith Inscription reflects a western anti-Assyrian coalition of states determined to block Shalmaneser's advance into central Syria and beyond. The coalition was made up of states in central Syria (Hamath), south Syria (Aram-Damascus and Beth-Rehob), Palestine (Israel and Ammon), the northern Phoenician coast (Byblos, Irqanata, Arwad, Usanata, and Šianu) as well as Egypt and Arabia. There were no north Syrian states involved, as they had already submitted to Shalmaneser in his earlier campaigns in the west. It is difficult to ascertain the date for the formation of this south-Syrian anti-Assyrian coalition. In 858–857 and 856–855 BCE, when Shalmaneser was in the west, he claimed to have "received the *maddattu* of the kings of the seacoast," probably including some of the states who were now participants in the coalition. It is likely that these states were willing to send gifts to the Assyrian king to placate him as long as they could deal with him from a safe distance and their territories had not been threatened with conquest or submission. With the loss of the north Syrian states to the Assyrians in 856–855 BCE, states to the south could no longer feel safe from the advance of the Assyrians into their territories. Hence, it must have been sometime between 856–855 and 853–852 BCE that the anti-Assyrian coalition was formed in response to the changing political situation. It was a military cooperation aimed at protecting not only their own autonomy but also their economic and commercial interests in the region. Thus, by the time Shalmaneser and his army marched against them in 853–852 BCE, the coalition was ready and able to battle the Assyrian onslaught.

Noticeably missing from this list of anti-Assyrian coalition members are states like Judah, Moab, and Edom. The Mesha Inscription indicates that Moab was subject to Israel at this point in its history and thus its absence is not surprising.[117] Of Judah and Edom, Miller suggests that the two states "were so closely aligned with Israel at the time that their soldiers were simply counted as belonging to Ahab."[118] Judah's close ties with Israel are attested by the marriage of Athaliah daughter of Ahab to Jehoram son of Jehoshaphat. Also the sentence וישלם יהושפט עם־מלך ישראל in 1 Kgs 22:45 is better understood as indicative of Jehoshaphat's subordinate status to Ahab. S. Parpola has recently pointed out that the Akkadian verb *salāmu*, equivalent to the Hebrew שלם, does not necessarily denote parity relations but "could equally well

[117]Cf. the Mesha Inscription (see J. A. Dearman, ed., *Studies in the Mesha Inscription and Moab* [Archaeology and Biblical Studies 2; Atlanta: Scholars Press, 1989], esp. 155–210) and 2 Kgs 1:1; 3:5.

[118]See *HAIJ*, 270.

connote 'to seek détente'" or "'to surrender.'"[119] Thus, וישלם in the Kings text most probably implied a relationship of a superior Ahab with a subordinate Jehoshaphat. This is supported by 1 Kgs 22:4, which remembers Jehoshaphat as saying to the king of Israel, "I am as you are, my people as your people, my horses as your horses," indicating his subordinate status. Edom, on the other hand, was probably subject to Judah at the time (cf. 1 Kgs 22:48).[120] Therefore, it is not unreasonable to suppose that Ahab's large military contingent also included Judean, Edomite, and Moabite forces.

That the Monolith Inscription indicates a situation of close cooperation between Israel and Aram-Damascus during this period of history is quite clear. Less evident, however, is the role the Phoenician cities of Tyre and Sidon played in the regional coalition. While Arwad and possibly also Byblos participated in the coalition, Tyre and Sidon are not mentioned in the text. What then might have been the posture of Tyre and Sidon in the international affairs, with regard to Assyria on the one hand and to Israel and Aram-Damascus on the other?

The absence of Tyre and Sidon in the Monolith Inscription has been explained as the Phoenician cities' inclination towards non-intervention in the wars outside their territories.[121] However, it is difficult to imagine that Tyre and Sidon would stay away from regional politics or follow a policy different from other Syro-Palestinian states at a time when they were so closely aligned with Israel and when the anti-Assyrian coalition included states to their north, south, and east, as well as Egypt. Evidence of this close alignment between Israel and Tyre and Sidon comes from two sources. First, 1 Kgs 16:31 reports the marriage of Ahab and Jezebel, the daughter of Ethbaal, king of the Sidonians. Although it is true that this verse is now part of the DtrH's theological evaluation of Ahab, the specific mention that Jezebel was the

---

[119]S. Parpola, "Neo-Assyrian Treaties from the Royal Archives of Nineveh," *JCS* 39 (1987), 182.

[120]Cf. G. H. Jones, *1 and 2 Kings* (2 vols.; NCBC; Grand Rapids: Eerdmans, 1984), 2. 374.

[121]B. Oded, "The Phoenician Cities and the Assyrian Empire in the Time of Tiglath-pileser III," *ZDPV* 90 (1974), 40–41. Cf. also Briquel-Chatonnet, *Les relations*, 86–88; G. Kestemont, "Les Phéniciens en Syrie du Nord," *Phoenicia and Its Neighbours*, ed. E. Gubel and E. Lipiński (Studia Phoenicia 3; Leuven: Peeters, 1985), 143, n. 33; *idem*, "Tyr et les Assyriens," *Redt Tyrus/Sauvons Tyr: Histoire phénicienne/Fenicische geschiedenis*, ed. E. Lipiński and B. Servais-Soyez (Studia Phoenicia 1–2; Leuven: Katholieke Universiteit Leuven, 1983), 57–59.

daughter of Ethbaal, king of the Sidonians, probably goes back to a historical record. Ethbaal is to be identified with Ἰθόβαλος (= Ittobaal) mentioned in Josephus's quotation of material from the Tyrian King List reported by Menander of Ephesus.[122] According to Menander, Ethbaal was a priest of Astarte, who murdered his predecessor, Phelles, and reigned in his place. Ethbaal is identified as "king of the Sidonians." Since he appeared as a king in the Tyrian King List,[123] he must have ruled over Tyre. Josephus, however, calls him "the king of the Tyrians and Sidonians."[124] These references are best understood on the assumption that Ethbaal ruled over both Tyre and Sidon during this period (c. 887 to 856 BCE).[125] It has also been mentioned earlier that while the inscription on Band III of the "Bronze Gates of Balâwât" notes that Shalmaneser received *maddattu* from the Tyrians and Sidonians, only one king was represented in the relief. S. Timm has questioned the reliability of Menander's source for the Tyrian King List. He argues that Ethbaal was only the king of Sidon and had nothing to do with Tyre.[126] One must note that in its context, the DtrH was most probably using the term "Sidonians" as a generic term for Phoenicians (cf. 1 Kgs 5:20). If so, then Timm's identification of Ethbaal as "king of Sidon" based solely on the biblical text is without strong foundation. The marriage alliance between the Israelites and the Tyrians must have been made for both political and commercial reasons and profited both states.

In addition to relating the marriage of Ahab and Jezebel, 1 Kgs 16:31 contains the condemnation that Ahab patronized Baalism. The DtrH adds that Ahab "erected an altar for Baal in the house of Baal, which he built in Samaria" (v. 32). It is true that this condemnation is deuteronomistic in character and that other biblical materials that linked the Omrides to Baalism were written from a Yahwistic and pro-Judean perspective. Such references are confined basically to the Elijah stories, which were probably included in the DtrH late and had their origins in some prophetic circle. Yet because of the strong relationship that the Omrides had

---

[122]Josephus, *Ag. Ap.*, 1.18 §123.

[123]For a study of the Tyrian King List, see W. H. Barnes, *Studies in the Chronology of the Divided Monarchy of Israel* [HSM 48; Atlanta: Scholars Press, 1991], 29–55. This dissertation, however, does not follow his [or Cross's] dates for the Tyrian kings.

[124]*Ant.*, 8.13.1 §317; 9.6.6 §138. In *Ant.*, 8.13.2 §324, Ethbaal is called "king of the Tyrians."

[125]For the chronology of the rulers of Tyre, this dissertation follows the approximate dates given by Katzenstein in *History of Tyre*, 349.

[126]Timm, *Die Dynastie Omri*, 224–31.

with the Phoenicians, baalistic presence in Israel, particularly in the capital city of Samaria, cannot be ruled out. It is very likely that Baalism was present because of the metropolitan nature of Samaria and the "ecumenical" politics in Syria-Palestine at the time. The Baal temple could have been built to accommodate the Phoenician segment of the population resident in Samaria for commercial or emissarial purposes. The Omrides' patronage of the Baal cult finds its parallel in the Melqart Stela,[127] which indicates the worship of Phoenician deities by Bar-Hadad,[128] a Syrian king. Thus the deuteronomistic attack may not be without a kernel of truth.

The second source of evidence comes from archaeological data. Most notable are the artifactual remains in Building Periods I and II of Samaria.[129] In Period I, probably from the reign of Omri, "a fine ashlar masonry wall . . . built in the 'headers and stretchers' technique"[130] surrounds the acropolis. This type of masonry regularly used bossed and well-hewn ashlar blocks. It was executed meticulously and used both for the foundation of buildings and for the outer walls of defenses. Dressed stones were carefully fitted and joined together. Stones that are chipped in the corner were patched to a degree of exactness.[131] This type of masonry shows up in Ugarit and in the harbor survey of Tyre by A. Poidebard[132] as well as at the Phoenician city of Sarepta.[133] J. W. Crowfoot has suggested that this type of masonry is

---

[127]On the Melqart Stela, see *KAI*, no. 201; *TSSI*, 2. 1–4; and bibliography in J. A. Fitzmyer and S. A. Kaufman, *An Aramaic Bibliography, Part I: Old, Official, and Biblical Aramaic* (Baltimore: Johns Hopkins University Press, 1992), 11.

[128]The identity of Bar-Hadad of the Melqart Stela has long been an issue of dispute. Pitard has argued quite convincingly that he was not a king of Aram-Damascus (*Ancient Damascus*, 138–44; "The Identity of the Bir-Hadad of the Melqart Stela," *BASOR* 272 [1988], 3–21). Most recently, É. Puech identifies Bar-Hadad as the son of Ataršumki, the Arpadite king mentioned in the inscriptions of Adad-nirari III ("La Stèle de Bar-Hadad à Melqart et les Rois d'Arpad," *RB* 99 [1992], 311–34).

[129]Most recently, Tappy (*Archaeology of Israelite Samaria*, 1–11) has renewed a call to distinguish more carefully between the pottery periods and the building periods in describing the material culture of Samaria.

[130] A. Mazar, *Archaeology of the Land of the Bible, 10,000–586 B.C.E.* (ABRL; New York: Doubleday, 1990), 408.

[131] Kenyon, *Royal Cities*, 76.

[132]Cf. A. Poidebard, *Un grand port disparu-Tyr* (Paris: Librarie Orientaliste Paul Geuthner, 1939).

[133]See J. B. Pritchard, *Sarepta: A Preliminary Report on the Iron Age: Excavations of the University Museum of the University of Pennsylvania, 1970–1972* (Philadelphia: University Museum, University of Pennsylvania, 1975), 15; *idem*, *Recovering Sarepta, a Phoenician City* (Princeton: Princeton University Press, 1978), figs. 91 and 92.

Phoenician[134] and archaeologists are almost unanimous in identifying the masonry and construction technique as Phoenician.[135] According to Y. Shiloh, however, since all the examples of ashlar masonry found outside Israel are later than the time of Solomon and Ahab, it should be regarded as an original Israelite innovation.[136] Mazar points out that ashlar masonry was widespread not only in late Iron Age Phoenician architecture, but also in the succeeding period in Phoenicia, Cyprus, and Phoenician colonies in the Mediterranean. He notes in particular that "the fact that its earliest known examples are Israelite may be due to the fact that Israelite sites have been more extensively excavated than those in Phoenicia."[137]

In Building Period II, ascribed to Ahab, a similar type of masonry is evident in the enclosure casemate walls.[138] Although headers and stretchers were used, they were not set in any regularity. In the three top courses, the stones are dressed smoothly all over.

In addition to ashlar masonry, seven Proto-Aeolic capitals[139] have been found at Samaria, in the eastern side of the acropolis. Although they were all found in secondary use, they belong to Building Periods I and II. Mazar observes that "the volutes decorating these capitals are a stylized form of the palmette, one of the best-known motifs in Canaanite and Phoenician art."[140] J. M. Miller has suggested that these Proto-Aeolic capitals are further evidence of Phoenician influence.[141] While no such capitals have been found in Phoenicia proper, Miller claims that "their Phoenician character is confirmed by the fact that the Greeks of Cyprus and Ionia borrowed them from Phoenicia about the eighth

---

[134]Crowfoot *et al.*, *Buildings at Samaria*, 5–9.

[135]See the important studies by G. Van Beek and O. Van Beek, "Canaanite-Phoenician Architecture: The Development and Distribution of Two Styles," in *Y. Aharoni Memorial Volume*, ed. B. Mazar (EI 15; Jerusalem: Israel Exploration Society, 1981), 70*–77*; pls. V–VII; I. Sharon, "Phoenician and Greek Ashlar Construction Techniques at Tel Dor, Israel," *BASOR* 267 (1987), 21–42. Cf. also Mazar, *Archaeology*, 471–75.

[136]Y. Shiloh, *The Proto-Aeolic Capital and Israelite Ashlar Masonry* (Qedem 11; Jerusalem: Hebrew University, 1979), 82–87.

[137]Mazar, *Archaeology*, 474.

[138]Crowfoot *et al.*, *Buildings at Samaria*, 97–100.

[139]These capitals are sometimes referred to as Proto-Ionic or volute capitals. For an extensive study of these capitals, see Shiloh, *Proto-Aeolic Capital*, 1–49.

[140]Mazar, *Archaeology*, 475.

[141]Miller, *Omride Dynasty*, 134–36.

century, B.C."[142] Most scholars would agree that these capitals are Phoenician in origin.[143] Shiloh, noting the close connection between ashlar masonry and Proto-Aeolic capitals, challenges this assumption. Again, he argues that no such capitals have been found on sites in Phoenicia proper and suggests instead that they were an Israelite innovation based on Phoenician wooden prototypes and should properly be called "Israelite capitals."[144] Mazar, similarly, has countered Shiloh's conclusion, commenting that "the lack of evidence from Phoenicia cannot be taken as proof that such stone capitals were not in use there as early as the tenth century B.C.E."[145]

De Geus has recently noted that "it is hardly possible to distinguish between 'Phoenician' and 'Israelite/Judean' architecture in the tenth and ninth centuries B.C."[146] The similarity of architecture styles in Israel/Judah and Phoenicia makes it difficult to ascribe its origin to one ethnic group or the other. It is therefore more appropriate to say that Phoenicia and Israel/Judah shared a common culture, although with differences as well. This commonality in material culture is illustrative of the cooperation and exchange between the Phoenicians and Israel/Judah.

Now we return to the question: Why is there no reference to Tyre and Sidon in the Monolith Inscription's account of the battle of Qarqar either in the description of the membership list of the coalition or as paying *maddattu* to Assyria? If Tyre and Sidon had not been members of the coalition and had paid *maddattu* in 853 BCE when Shalmaneser was in the vicinity, this would most probably have been recorded in the royal inscriptions. Note, particularly, that on lines 82–85 of the Monolith Inscription, Shalmaneser mentions receiving *maddattu* from various north Syrian states. Moreover, the Phoenician states of Tyre, Sidon, Byblos, and Arwad had paid *maddattu* to Shalmaneser's predecessor, Ashurnasirpal sometime between the sixth and the

---

[142]*Ibid.*, 134. Cf. W. F. Albright, *The Archaeology of Palestine* (4th ed.; London: Penguin, 1960), 126.

[143]See, e.g., Crowfoot *et al.*, *Buildings at Samaria*, 14–15; Y. Aharoni, "Beth-Haccherem," in *Archaeology and Old Testament Study*, ed. D. W. Thomas (Oxford: Clarendon, 1967), 179; Mazar, *Archaeology*, 474–75.

[144]Shiloh, *Proto-Aeolic Capital*, 88–91. While his study included a capital found on the surface of the ruins of a royal citadel at Medeibiyeh in Moab (see pp. 11, 14, 19, 21), Shiloh did not deal with the issue of the origin of that capital.

[145]Mazar, *Archaeology*, 475.

[146]C. J. H. de Geus, "The Material Culture of Israel and Phoenicia," in *Phoenicia and the Bible*, ed. E. Lipiński (Studia Phoenicia 11; Leuven: Peeters, 1991), 11–16, esp. 13.

eighteenth regnal years.[147] There are, in addition, five documentations of *maddattu* that Shalmaneser personally received from Tyre and Sidon, all reported in inscriptions that note his suppression of opposition in the region. First, as has been mentioned earlier in the study of the bronze reliefs from the "Bronze Gates of Balâwât," Tyre and Sidon are depicted as bringing *maddattu* to Shalmaneser while he was on his first western campaign in 858–857 BCE. The accompanying inscription reads: "I received the *maddattu* (brought) on ships from the inhabitants of Tyre and Sidon."[148] The same event is reported in the Monolith Inscription, where in the campaign of his first regnal year, Shalmaneser claimed: "I received the *maddattu* of the kings of the seacoast and I marched along the shore of the wide sea, straightaway and victorious."[149] The "seacoast" is a reference to the Phoenician coast, which would have included Tyre and Sidon among others. Second, again in the Monolith Inscription in the *limmu* of Aššur-bēlu-kaʾʾin (856–855 BCE), Shalmaneser is said to have "received the *maddattu* of the kings of the seacoast when he was at Kar-Shalmaneser (Til-Barsip)."[150] Third, in Band XIV of the "Bronze Gates of Balâwât," which we have dated to the period of 847–845 BCE, the Assyrian king notes the receipt of *maddattu* from Tyre and Sidon.[151] Fourth, in the Marble-Slab Inscription, Shalmaneser records that in his eighteenth year (841–840 BCE) "the *maddattu* of Baᶜli-ma-AN-zēr the Tyrian and Jehu the Bit-Ḫumrite, I received."[152] In a fragment of the annals from Calah, the account reads "I received the *maddattu* of the inhabitants of Tyre, Sidon, and Jehu the Bit-Ḫumrite."[153] Finally, the Black Obelisk of Shalmaneser again notes that he "received *maddattu* from the countries of the inhabitants of Tyre, Sidon, and Byblos" in his twenty-first year (838–837 BCE).[154] Thus, if Tyre and Sidon had paid *maddattu* in 853–852 BCE while the anti-Assyrian coalition, of which Ahab of Israel was a strong participant, was fighting Shalmaneser at Qar-

---

[147] *ARAB*, 1. §479; *ARI*, 2. 143

[148] *ANEP*, #356–58; *ANET*, 281; *ARAB*, 1. §§612–14.

[149] Cf. *ARAB*, 1. §600.

[150] *ARAB*, 1. §603.

[151] See above, pp. 25–26.

[152] Safar, "Further Text of Shalmaneser III," 11–12, 19.

[153] E. Michel, "Die Assur-Texte Salmanassars III. (858–824)," *WO* 1 (1947–52), 265–67; *ARAB*, 1. §672; *ANET*, 280.

[154] Michel, "Die Assur-Texte," *WO* 2, 154–55; *ARAB*, 1. §578; *ANET*, 280.

qar, and if Shalmaneser had followed his normal pattern, one would expect that such a *maddattu* would have been recorded in the Assyrian inscriptions. Therefore, it is reasonable to assume that Tyre and Sidon were somehow involved in the anti-Assyrian coalition. One could argue that Tyre and Sidon participated by contributing money to the allies' war chest.[155] If the size of Ahab's military contingent was not an exaggeration[156] but was made up of more than just Israelites, it is conceivable that Phoenician participation in the coalition may have been represented by more than monetary contribution; because of their close alliance with Israel, their troops may have fought under Ahab's leadership, just as did, in all probability, the troops of Moab, Judah, and Edom.

When he discusses the outcome of the battle at Qarqar, Shalmaneser claims to have defeated the coalition and carried out a great slaughter of 14,000 warriors. The claim, however, is doubtful since there is no mention of the Assyrian army moving southward, nor the capture of the cities of the coalition participants, nor the taking of booty, nor the exaction of *maddattu* from them. The number of coalition warriors killed by the Assyrian army is also probably exaggerated. This number became even more preposterous in later editions of the campaign. In the later "Baghdad Text" and the Marble-Slab Inscription the number is given as 25,000 and in the Black Obelisk as 20,500. Shalmaneser's lack of success against the coalition is evidenced also by the fact that he did not return to the region until his tenth regnal year.

Several conclusions about the relationships among Assyria, Aram-Damascus, Israel, and the Phoenicians in the mid-ninth century may be drawn from the preceding analysis of the Monolith Inscription, supplemented by the biblical traditions.

(1) Shalmaneser III took the offensive against Syro-Palestinian states in his sixth regnal year in an attempt to dominate the region. The coalition of states that confronted the Assyrian king at the battle of Qarqar was clearly anti-Assyrian and refused to submit.

(2) Regional cooperation (with Egyptian participation in Syro-Palestinian politics) was a consequence of an anti-Assyrian stance based on protecting local autonomy and economic and commercial interests.

155So, e.g., Katzenstein, *History of Tyre*, 169.

156See, e.g., M. Elat, "Campaigns of Shalmaneser III," 25–35.

(3) Israel's anti-Assyrian stance at the time and her participation as a full member in the regional coalition were unambiguous. Israelite actions were probably based on economic factors. Moreover, Israel at the time was itself strong enough to dominate other Palestinian states like Judah, Edom, and Moab.

(4) Aram-Damascus at the time was the dominant power in Syria-Palestine and related to some smaller states in the region as sovereign.[157] It was not about to hand over its political domination and control of commerce in the region to the Assyrians. Thus, it is understandable why it was an important leader of the coalition for as long as the coalition was in place.

(5) Although Tyre and Sidon were not mentioned as participants in the coalition, it is likely that they shared in the anti-Assyrian coalition along with their neighbors, although perhaps only indirectly.

(6) Israelite Baalism reported in the Bible was reflective of the political conditions at the time. Major centers of politics and commerce were therefore metropolitan and ecumenical in religious matters, accommodating the residents of other states.

D. The "Baghdad Text"

That the anti-Assyrian coalition continued in existence for sometime is indicated by the so-called "Baghdad Text,"[158] which was presumably discovered in the ruins of the city of Aššur. The text is inscribed on a baked clay tablet and consists of 256 lines in four columns with a colophon at the end that dates the writing of the inscription to the 22nd day of Tašritu (Tishri) in the *limmu* of Taklāk-ana-šarri, which according to the eponym chronicle would have been the seventeenth regnal year of Shalmaneser (842–841 BCE). The inscription contains descriptions of the first sixteen years of Shalmaneser's reign, including a detailed account of the king's campaigns in his fifteenth and sixteenth *palê*. This text was first published by G. G. Cameron.[159] The following is a transliteration of the passages relating to Shalmaneser's tenth,

[157]Cf. B. Mazar, "Geshur and Maacah," *JBL* 80 (1961), 16–28.

[158]The inscription is housed in the Iraq Museum and classified as IM 54669.

[159]Cameron ("Annals of Shalmaneser III," 6–26) provides a transliteration and translation of the text. Important also in Cameron's article is his discussion of the various editions of Shalmaneser's texts (see also above n. 50). Another transliteration may be found in Michel, "Die Assur-Texte," *WO* 1, 455–75.

eleventh, and fourteenth *palê* when he was again confronted by the anti-Assyrian coalition.[160]

Column II

55) AŠ 10 BAL.MEŠ-*ia* 8-*šú* ^{ÍD}A.RAT *e-bir* URU.MEŠ-*ni ša* ^{I}*sa-an-gar*

56) ^{URU}*gar-ga-miš-a-a ap-púl aq-qur* AŠ IZI *áš-ru-up*

57) TA URU.MEŠ-*ni ša* ^{URU}*gar-ga-miš-a-a at-tu-muš*

58) *a-na* URU.MEŠ-*ni ša* ^{I}*a-ra-me ša aq-tí-rib* ^{URU}*ar-ni-e* <URU.>*šar*$_4$ *ti-šú* KUR-*ud*

59) *a-di* 1 ME URU.MEŠ-*ni ša li-me-ti-šú ap-púl aq-qur* AŠ IZI *áš-ru-up*

60) GAZ.MEŠ-*šú-nu a-duk šal-la-su-nu áš-lu-la* AŠ *u*$_4$*-me-šú-ma*

61) ^{Id}IM-*id-ri ša* ^{KUR}ANŠE-*šú* ^{d}*ir-ḫu-li-na* ^{KUR}*a-mat-a-a*

62) *a-di* 12 LUGAL.MEŠ-*ni šá ši-di tam-di a-na* Á.MEŠ *a-ḫa-miš*

63) *it-tàk-lu-ma a-na e-peš* MURUB$_4$ *u* MÈ *a-na* GAB-*ia*

64) *it-bu-ú-ni it-ti-šú-nu am-daḫ-ḫi-iṣ*

65) BAD$_5$.BAD$_5$-*šú-nu áš-ku-un* ^{GIŠ}GIGIR.MEŠ *pit-ḫal-la-šú-nu*

66) *ú-nu-ut* MÈ-*šú-nu e-kim-šú-nu*

67) *a-na šu-zu-ub* ZI.MEŠ-*šú-nu e-li-ú*

68) AŠ 11 BAL.MEŠ-*ia* TA ^{URU}*ni-nu-a at-tu-muš* 9-*šú* ^{ÍD}A.RAT

69) AŠ *mi-li-ša e-bir* 97 URU.MEŠ-*ni ša* ^{I}*sa-an-gar* KUR-*ud*

70) 1 ME URU.MEŠ-*ni ša* ^{I}*a-ra-me as-šud ap-púl aq-qur*

71) AŠ IZI *áš-ru-up ši-di* ^{I}*ḫa-ma-a-ni aṣ-bat*

72) ^{KUR}*ia-ra-qu at-ta-bal-kat*

Column III

1) *a-na* URU.MEŠ-*ni ša* ^{KUR}*a-mat-a-a at-ta-rad* ^{URU}*áš-tam-ma-ku*

2) *a-di* 89 URU.MEŠ-*ni* KUR-*ud* GAZ.MEŠ-*šú-nu a-duk šal-la-su-nu*

3) *áš-lu-la* AŠ *u*$_4$*-me-šu-ma* ^{Id}IM-*id-ri ša* ^{KUR}ANŠE-*šú*

4) ^{I}*ir-ḫu-li-na* ^{KUR}*a-mat-a-a a-di* 12 LUGAL.MEŠ-*ni*

5) *ša ši-di tam-di a-na* Á.MEŠ *a-ḫa-miš it-tàk-lu-ma*

6) *a-na e-peš* MURUB$_4$ *u* MÈ *a-na* GAB-*ia it-bu-ú-ni*

7) *it-ti-šú-nu am-daḫ-ḫi-iṣ* BAD$_5$.BAD$_5$-*šú-nu áš-ku-un*

8) 10 LIM ÉRIN.MEŠ *ti-du-ki-šu-nu* AŠ ^{GIŠ}TUKUL.MEŠ *ú-šam-qit*

9) ^{GIŠ}GIGIR.MEŠ-*šú-nu pit-ḫal-la-šú-nu ú-nu-ut* MÈ-*šú-nu*

10) *e-kim-šú-nu* AŠ *ta-ia-ar-ti-ia* ^{URU}*a-pa-ra-su*

11) URU *dan-nu-ti-šú ša* ^{I}*a-ra-me* KUR-*ud* AŠ *u*$_4$*-mi-šu-ma*

12) *ma-da-tu ša* ^{I}*qàl-pa-ru-un-da* KÙ.BABBAR KÙ.GI

---

160 Cf. the transliteration in Cameron, "Annals of Shalmaneser III," 14–15; and Michel, "Die Assur-Texte," *WO* 1 (1947–52), 466, 468.

13) AN.NA.MEŠ ANŠE.KUR.<RA.MEŠ> ANŠE.MEŠ GUD.MEŠ UDU. MEŠ SÍK ZA.GÌN.MEŠ

14) ^{TÚG}*lu-búl-ti* ^{TÚG}GADA *am-ḫur a-na* KUR-*e*

15) ^{KUR}*ḫa-ma-a-ni e-li* ^{GIŠ}ÙR ^{GIŠ}*e-ri-ni a-kis*

24) AŠ 14 BAL.MEŠ-*ia ma-a-ti* DAGAL-*tu a-na la ma-né-e*

25) *ad-ki it-ti* 1 ME LIM 20 LIM ÉRIN.ḪÁ ^{ÍD}A.RAT

26) AŠ *mi-li-ša e-bir* AŠ u_4*-mi-šu-ma*

27) ^{Id}IM-*id-ri ša* ^{KUR}ANŠE-*šú* ^{I}*ir-ḫu-li-na*

28) ^{KUR}*a-mat-a-a a-di* 12 LUGAL.MEŠ-*ni ša ši-di tam-di*

29) AN.TA *ù* KI.TA ḪI(!).[161]ÉRIN.ḪI-*šú-nu* ḪÁ.MEŠ *a-na la ma-né-e*

30) *id-ku-ú-ni a-na* GAB-*ia it-bu-ú-ni it-ti-šú-nu*

31) *am-daḫ-ḫi-iṣ* BAD$_5$.BAD$_5$-*šú-nu áš-ku-un* ^{GIŠ}GIGIR.MEŠ-*šú-nu*

32) *pit-ḫal-la-šu-nu a-ṣi-iʾ ú-nu-ut* MÈ-*šú-nu*

33) *e-kim-šú-nu a-na šu-zu-ub* ZI.MEŠ-*šú-nu e-li-ú*

In my tenth *palû* I crossed the Euphrates for the eighth time. I devastated, destroyed, and burned with fire the cities of Sangara the Carchemishite. I departed from the cities of Carchemish, approached the cities of Arame, and captured Arne, his royal city. I devastated, destroyed, and burned (it) with fire along with 100 cities of its environs. (60)I slaughtered them and plundered them.

At that time Adad-idri of Aram-Damascus, Irḫuleni the Hamathite, along with twelve kings of the seacoast trusted in their own strength and marched against me to wage battle and combat. I fought with them, (65)accomplished their defeat, and took away chariots, their cavalry, and their combat weaponry. They fled to save their lives.

In my eleventh *palû* I departed from Nineveh and crossed the Euphrates for the ninth time at its flood. I captured 97 cities of Sangara. (70)I captured, devastated, destroyed, and burned with fire 100 cities of Arame. I kept to the side of Mt. Amanus and crossed Mt. Iaraqu. (III, 1)I descended to the cities of Hamath and captured Aštammaku along with 89 cities. I slaughtered them and plundered them.

At that time Adad-idri of Aram-Damascus, Irḫuleni the Hamathite, along with twelve kings (5)of the seacoast trusted in their own strength and marched against me to wage battle and combat. I fought with them and accomplished their defeat. I slew 10,000 of their warriors with the sword and took away their chariots, their cavalry, and their combat weaponry.

(10)On my return I captured Aparasu, the fortified city of Arame. At that time I received the *maddattu* of Qalparunda, silver, gold, tin, horses, donkeys, cattle, sheep, blue wool, woolen garments, and linen garments. I ascended the mountains of Amanus and cut down timbers of cedar.

(24)In my fourteenth *palû* I mobilized the countless numbers of my widespread land with 120,000 troops and crossed the Euphrates at its floods. At that time Adad-idri of Aram-Damascus, Irḫuleni the Hamathite, along with twelve kings of the upper and lower seacoast mobilized their numerous and countless troops and marched against me. (30)I fought with them and ac-

[161]Michel notes that this ḪI is a scribal error ("Die Assur-Texte," *WO* 1, 468).

complished their defeat. I disabled their chariots and their calvary and took away their combat weaponry. They fled to save their lives.

The inscription represents the earliest known account of these campaigns of Shalmaneser against the anti-Assyrian coalition, although it is obvious that the account is no more than a summary.[162] The entry for each year follows a formulistic style and uses similar vocabulary. In addition, this annalistic text and other subsequent editions are dated by *palû*, a reference to regnal years.

The campaign for the tenth *palû* (849–848 BCE) began with the suppression of Carchemish and Bit-Agusi. Grayson suggests that Shalmaneser's lack of success against the anti-Assyrian coalition in 853 BCE must have served as an encouragement to other states like Carchemish and Bit-Agusi to resist Assyrian hegemony.[163] Both Carchemish and Bit-Agusi were among the north Syrian states that had voluntarily paid *maddattu* in 853 BCE. After dealing with these two states, Shalmaneser turned southward but was again confronted by the coalition led by Adad-idri and Irḫuleni. The formulaic *ina umišuma* in line 60 introduces this encounter. Although Shalmaneser again claims to have defeated the coalition, his own record does not bear that out. Unlike the account about Carchemish and Bit-Agusi, there is no mention of the capture of any cities. Apparently, the Assyrian king's advance in Syria-Palestine was checked once again.

In his eleventh and fourteenth *palê*, Shalmaneser was again confronted by the anti-Assyrian coalition, still headed by Adad-idri and Irḫuleni. There is no evidence that the Assyrian army did any better against the coalition than on previous occasions. In fact, Shalmaneser's failure in his eleventh *palû* is indirectly supported by his own record. Following his battle with the coalition, on his return home he had to deal again with Arame of Bit-Agusi, capturing a fortified city. He also received the *maddattu* of Qalparunda (of Pattin or Gurgum?). However, neither the

---

[162]Other almost parallel accounts may be found in the Bull Inscription (see Billerbeck and Delitzsch, "Palasttore Salmanassars," 144–51; *ARAB*, 1. §§651–55; 658–59); and the Marble-Slab Inscription (see Safar, "Further Text of Shalmaneser III," 8–10, 17–18). Another fragment of a clay tablet, Assur 12343, contains a parallel account of the tenth year and the first part of the eleventh (see Michel, "Die Assur-Texte," *WO* 1, 67–71). In the Black Obelisk (see Michel, "Die Assur-Texte," *WO* 2, 150–52; *ARAB*, 1. §§567–68; 571) the notations for these years are even briefer. In fact, there is no mention of Shalmaneser's encounter with the coalition in the tenth year. Since the event was recorded in earlier editions, there is no reason to suggest that the encounter did not take place. It is understandable why in this very late edition of the annals that the "not very successful" confrontation with the coalition would be left out.

[163]Grayson, "Ashur-dan II to Ashur-nirari V," 261–62.

capturing of cities nor the receiving of *maddattu* was mentioned in relation to his battle with the coalition.

In each of these campaigns, reference is made to the "twelve kings of the seacoast." One wonders if by now this phrase had not become a standard expression for the western anti-Assyrian coalition. More likely is the fact that by now it had become a broader regional coalition, involving almost every state in Syria-Palestine. Israel and Judah, at the time perhaps ruled by a single king, Jehoram son of Jehoshaphat,[164] must have continued its strong participation in the coalition. On the other hand, the continuous involvement of Tyre and Sidon—under Ba^{c}al-^{c}azor II (c. 855–830)—in the alliance is less certain. Since there is no record of Tyre and Sidon paying *maddattu* between 856–855 and 847–845 BCE, we may assume that they participated in the coalition on some scale, at least through the eleventh *palû* (848–847 BCE). If our dating of Band XIV of the "Bronze Gates of Balâwât" to the period of 847–845 BCE is correct and Shalmaneser received *maddattu* from Tyre and Sidon, then it is possible that Tyre and Sidon broke with the coalition before the 845–844 BCE campaign of Shalmaneser and established good relations with Assyria. In fact, the entire coalition may even have begun to disintegrate at this time before completely collapsing after the 845–844 BCE campaign.

E. III R 5, 6

III R 5, 6 is an annalistic fragment discovered in the Central Palace of Shalmaneser III at Nimrud. It describes the events of the eighteenth *palû* of Shalmaneser in great detail. The text was first published by Rawlinson.[165]

1) . . . AŠ 18 BAL.MEŠ-*ia* 16-*šú* ^{ÍD}A.RAT
2) *e-bir* ^{I}*ḫa-za-ʾi*-DINGIR *šá* ^{KUR}ANŠE-*šú*
3) *a-na gi-piš* ÉRIN.ḪI.A.MEŠ-*šú*
4) *it-ta-kil-ma* ÉRIN.ḪI.A.MEŠ-*šú*

---

[164] See J. Strange, "Joram, King of Israel and Judah," *VT* 25 (1975), 191–201; Miller in *HAIJ*, 280–84; J. H. Hayes and P. K. Hooker, *A New Chronology for the Kings of Israel and Judah and Its Implications for Biblical History and Literature* (Atlanta: John Knox, 1988), 33–36.

[165] Rawlinson, *Cuneiform Inscriptions*, 3. pl. 5, no. 6. Cf. the transliteration in Michel, "Die Assur-Texte," *WO* 1, 265–67; and H. S. Sader, *Les États araméens de Syrie: Depuis leur fondation jusqu'à leur transformation en provinces assyriennes* (Beiruter Texte und Studien 36; Beirut: Franz Steiner, 1987), 231–32.

5) *a-na ma-a*ʾ*-diš id-ka-a*
6) ^{KUR}*sa-ni-ru* ŠU.SI KUR^{e}
7) *šá pu-ut* ^{KUR}*lab-na-na a-na dan-nu-ti-šú*
8) *iš-kun it-ti-šú am-daḫ-ḫi-iṣ*
9) BAD$_5$.BAD$_5$-*šú áš-kun* 16 LIM
10) ÉRIN.MEŠ *ti-du-ki-šú* AŠ ^{GIŠ}TUKUL.MEŠ
11) *ú-šam-qit* 1 LIM 1 ME 21 ^{GIŠ}GIGIR.MEŠ-*šú*
12) 4 ME 70 *pit-ḫal-lu-šú it-ti uš-ma-ni-šú*
13) *e-kim-šú a-na šu-zu-ub*
14) ZI.MEŠ-*šú e-li* EGIR-*šú ar-te-di*
15) AŠ ^{URU}*di-maš-qi* URU *šarru-ti-šú e-sir-šú*
16) ^{GIŠ}KIRI$_6$-*šú ak-kis a-di* KUR^{e}
17) ^{KUR}*ḫa-ú-ra-ni a-lik* URU.MEŠ^{ni}
18) *a-na la ma-ni a-púl a-qur*
19) AŠ IZI.MEŠ GÍBIL^{up} *šal-la-su-nu*
20) *a-na la ma-ni áš-lu-la*
21) *a-di* KUR^{e} ^{KUR}*ba-a*ʾ*-li-ra-a*ʾ*-si*
22) *šá* SAG *tam-ti*$_4$ *a-lik ṣa-lam šarru-ti-ia*
23) AŠ *lìb-bi áš-qup* AŠ *u*$_4$*-me-šú-ma*
24) *ma-da-tu šá* ^{KUR}*ṣur-ra-a-a*
25) ^{KUR}*ṣi-du-na-a-a šá* ^{I}*ia-ú-a*
26) DUMU *ḫu-um-ri-i am-ḫur*

In my eighteenth *palû*, I crossed the Euphrates for the sixteenth time. Hazael of the land of Imērišu (= Aram-Damascus) relied on the mass of his troops, $^{(5)}$mobilized his troops in multitude, and made Mount Saniru, a mountain facing the Lebanon, his stronghold. I fought with him and accomplished his defeat. 16,000 $^{(10)}$of his soldiers I slaughtered with the sword. 1,121 of his chariots, 470 of his cavalry, together with his camp, I took away from him. To save his life, he left. I followed him $^{(15)}$and besieged him in Damascus, his royal city. I cut down his orchards. I marched as far as the mountains of Hauran. I destroyed, devastated, and burned with fire countless cities, $^{(20)}$and carried away their countless spoil. I marched as far as the mountains of Baʿli-raʾsi, which faced the sea, and erected a stela of my royal self there. At that time I received the *maddattu* of the Tyrians $^{(25)}$and Sidonians, and of Jehu[166] the (Bit)-Ḫumrite.[167]

---

166 The identification of *Ia-ú-a* with Jehu has been widely accepted by scholars. P. K. McCarter ("'Yaw, Son of Omri': A Philological Note on Israelite Chronology," *BASOR* 216 [1974], 5–7), however, has suggested that *ia-ú-a* (or *ia-a-ú* in the Marble-Slab inscription) may merely represent the divine name "Yaw," and can be regarded as a hypocoristic form of either Joram or Jehu. He concludes that *ia-ú-a* is more likely Joram on the basis of the epithet *mār ḫumri* and the chronological problems of the reigns of Ahaziah and Joram. M. Weippert ("*Jau(a) mār Ḫumrî*—Joram oder Jehu von Israel?" *VT* 28 [1978], 113–18) has challenged McCarter's argument and persuasively shown that *ia-ú-a* represent **Yahhūʾa*, i.e., Jehu.

167 According to H. Tadmor ("The Historical Inscriptions of Adad-nirari III," *Iraq* 35 [1973], 149), the phrase ^{I}*ia-ú-a mâr ḫu-um-ri-i* ought not be translated as "Jehu son of

On this campaign, in his eighteenth year (841–840 BCE), Shalmaneser, who had previously confronted strong opposition and was forced to turn back at the Orontes River without penetrating further, encountered only the forces of Aram-Damascus. Several notable differences between the account for this campaign and those of Shalmaneser's earlier campaigns in Syria-Palestine (in his sixth, tenth, eleventh, and fourteenth regnal years) are conspicuous. First, the king of Aram-Damascus is no longer Adad-idri—who had so ably led the anti-Assyrian coalition against Shalmaneser's earlier incursions into the region—but rather Hazael. Second, Irḫuleni of Hamath—who was always mentioned in the earlier campaigns together with the king of Aram-Damascus as a co-leader of the coalition—does not appear in the present account. Third, missing also from the account of this campaign is the reference to the "twelve kings of the seacoast." Fourth, while the earlier accounts made no mention of kings in central and southern Syria and Palestine paying *maddattu* to Shalmaneser, the present text records the reception of *maddattu* from Tyre and Sidon and Jehu.

The differences enumerated above reveal quite unambiguously the disintegration of the anti-Assyrian coalition that had adeptly prevented Assyrian expansion in Syria-Palestine between 853–852 and 845–844 BCE. A number of events which took place in the region between 845–844 and 841–840 BCE contributed to the dissolution of regionalism, directly and indirectly. First and foremost was the dynastic change in Aram-Damascus.[168] Assyrian evidence for this event comes from a "summary inscription"[169] of Shalmaneser III, *KAH I*, 30.[170] Obverse, lines 25–27 of the text read as follows:

Omri," but as "Jehu, the king of Bit-Ḫumri." He cites parallel cases (see Parpola, *Neo-Assyrian Toponyms*, 75–92) where "the kings of Bit-(A)gusi, Bit-Adini, and Bit-Dakuri etc. are called *mār Agūsi*, *mār Adīni* and *mār Dakūri*." Tadmor's argument is weak, however, since *māru* is not used in Akkadian for "king." The phrase DUMU [URU]GN is, however, used to denote a citizen or native of a city or a country (*CAD*, 10/1. 315–16). Therefore, *mār ḫu-um-ri-i* should be seen as a synonym to the gentilics [KUR]*ṣur-ra-a-a* and [KUR]*ṣi-du-na-a-a*. Cf. J. Hughes, *Secrets of the Times: Myth and History in Biblical Chronology* (JSOTSup 66; Sheffield: JSOT, 1990), 183 n. 55. See also n. 78 above.

[168]So Briquel-Chatonnet, *Les relations*, 111–12.

[169]For a description of this form in Neo-Assyrian inscriptions, see Tadmor, "Historical Inscriptions," 141.

[170]The cuneiform text was published by L. Messerschmidt, *Keilschrifttexte aus Assur historischen Inhalts. Heft I* (Leipzig: J. C. Hinrichs, 1911), no. 30. For a transliteration of the text, see Michel, "Die Assur-Texte," *WO* 1, 57–63. An English translation may be found in *ARAB*, 1. §§679–83. A recent study of the text relating to Aram-Damascus was done by Pitard (*Ancient Damascus*, 134–38).

25) ^{Id}IM-*id-ri* KUR-*šú e-mi-id*

26) ^{I}*ḫa-za-ʾi*-DINGIR DUMU *la ma-ma-na*

27) ^{GIŠ}GU.ZA *iṣ-bat*

Adad-idri died. Hazael, the son of a nobody, seized the throne.

Hazael is identified in this text not as a descendant of Adad-idri, but as "the son of a nobody," a term used to designate a commoner.[171] This dynastic change significantly impacted the regional alliance—one that had most probably been forged through treaties. It is possible that treaties in the ancient Near East made among rulers were considered binding only during the life of the dynasty.[172] In the event of a usurpation, the treaty was no longer binding and had to be contracted anew. If this is true, then it is understandable why the entire coalition disintegrated following the death of Adad-idri (or his son, Ben-Hadad; cf. 2 Kgs 8:7–15), and no state fought alongside Hazael when Shalmaneser appeared on the scene again during this campaign. Left on his own, Hazael, nonetheless, refused to surrender. According to Shalmaneser, Hazael's forces were dealt a severe defeat. Damascus was besieged but did not fall into the hands of the Assyrians. Eventually, Shalmaneser turned his attention southward and destroyed some cities in the Hauran area.

Hamath, which is mentioned in all earlier campaigns of Shalmaneser and was probably second in importance only to Aram-Damascus in the coalition, is notably absent. The Assyrian king would have marched past Hamath on his way to Damascus. Al-

---

[171]The issue of the conflict between this text and 2 Kgs 8:7–15, where the Aramean king murdered by Hazael is identified as Ben-Hadad, has been noted by scholars. Two solutions have been proposed. The first argues that the Assyrian text indicates that Hazael overthrew Adad-idri and suggests that the name of the king of Aram in the Kings text was secondarily added when other stories of Ben-Hadad were incorporated into the narratives of the Omride dynasty (so, e.g., Miller, "Elijah Cycle," 448, n. 37; and E. Lipiński, "Le Ben-Hadad II de la Bible et l'histoire," in *Proceedings of the Fifth World Congress of Jewish Studies*, vol. 1, ed. P. Peli [Jerusalem: R. H. Hacohen, 1969], 172–73). The second entertains the possibility that the Kings account is accurate, since there is enough time for a throne change between 845–844 and 841–840 BCE. The Assyrian account is thus presumed to be a mistake (so Jepsen, "Israel und Damaskus," 158–59).

Pitard (*Ancient Damascus*, 132–38) recently argued that both proposals are equally viable and must be taken seriously. In particular, he provides new evidence in support of Jepsen's position. Basically, he argues that *KAH I*, 30 is a "summary inscription." Therefore, events relating to a geographical area have been telescoped. The inscription has collapsed Shalmaneser's encounters with Aram-Damascus over a period of time (from 853–852 to 841–840 BCE) into a brief account, giving the impression that very little time passed between events. Thus, contends Pitard, the Assyrian text cannot be used as evidence that Hazael murdered Adad-idri. In fact, the Assyrian text does not claim that Hazael killed Adad-idri. A Ben-Hadad may have succeeded Adad-idri only to be replaced by Hazael!

[172]Tadmor, "Assyria and the West," 39–40.

though it is quite certain that the Assyrian army would have taken a route along the Orontes Valley to the Beqa[c] Valley—and hence had to go through Hamathite territory—in order to reach Damascus, it is surprising that there is no mention of any encounter with Hamath, an important enemy in Assyria's earlier attempts to penetrate the region. Hamath may have withdrawn from the coalition with the usurpation of the Damascus throne by Hazael and submitted to the Assyrians,[173] thereby allowing the Assyrian army passage through its territory without any resistance.

When Shalmaneser was at Ba[c]li-Ra'ši,[174] he received *maddattu* from Jehu of Israel and the king of Tyre and Sidon, who is identified as Ba[c]li-ma-AN-zēr, the Tyrian, in the Marble-Slab Inscription (see below). Jehu's capitulation, which is well documented in Assyrian sources,[175] sharply contrasts with the resistance of Hazael. Therefore, it is obvious from Assyrian texts that Hazael of Aram-Damascus and Jehu of Israel were following contrary foreign policies in relating to Assyria. There are two main issues to be dealt with here. The first pertains to Israelite-Aramean relations. While the Assyrian texts only hint at this relation via the different courses of action each state took vis-à-vis Assyria, biblical texts reveal clearly the hostility between them. 2 Kings 8:28–29 and 9:14b–15a describe the event that led to the eventual incapacitation of king Jehoram, namely, the battle the Israelites had to wage against Hazael of Aram-Damascus at Ramoth-gilead.[176] As

---

[173]M. C. Astour, "841 B.C.: The First Assyrian Invasion of Israel," *JAOS* 91 (1971), 384.

[174]The place is most commonly identified with Rās en-Nāqūra; so E. Lipiński, "Note de topographie historique: Ba[c]li-Ra'ši et Ra'šu-Qudšu," *RB* 78 (1971), 84–92 and Pitard, *Ancient Damascus*, 148, n. 4. For other identifications, see Astour, "First Assyrian Invasion," 384–86.

[175]See also the Marble-Slab Inscription and the Black Obelisk Inscription.

[176]The relationship of the two texts is a debatable issue. Many scholars agree that 9:14b–15a once served as the original introduction to the Jehu narrative, but was subsequently adapted at 8:28–29 in connection with the reign of Ahaziah of Judah. Thereupon its function as introduction to the reign of Jehu became redundant. This was first suggested by I. Benzinger (*Die Bücher der Könige* [KHC 9; Leipzig: J. C. B. Mohr [Paul Siebeck] 1899], 148–49) and followed by many others, including M. Noth (*The Deuteronomistic History* [2d ed.; JSOTSup 15; Sheffield: JSOT, 1981], 72); J. A. Montgomery (*A Critical and Exegetical Commentary on the Books of Kings*, ed. H. S. Gehman [ICC; Edinburgh: T. & T. Clark, 1951], 396, 400); J. Gray (*I & II Kings* [OTL; 2d ed.; Philadelphia: Westminster, 1970], 543); O. H. Steck (*Überlieferung und Zeitgeschichte in den Elia-Erzählungen* [WMANT 26; Neukirchen-Vluyn: Neukirchener Verlag, 1968], 32, nn. 1–2); Timm (*Die Dynastie Omri*, 138); A. F. Campbell (*Of Prophets and Kings: A Late Ninth-Century Document [1 Samuel–2 Kings 10]* [CBQMS 17; Washington, DC: Catholic Biblical Association of America, 1986], 22); L. M. Barré, *The Rhetoric of Political Persuasion. The Narrative Artistry and Political Intentions of 2 Kings 9-11* (CBQMS 20; Washington, DC: Catholic Biblical Association of America, 1988), 11–13. McKenzie (*Trouble With Kings*,

we have noted, throughout most of its history the Omride dynasty enjoyed friendly relations with Aram-Damascus, in particular participating actively in the anti-Assyrian coalition that held off Shalmaneser III's incursion into Syria-Palestine on several occasions. It was only late in the reign of Jehoram that this relationship turned sour and the Arameans of Damascus encroached into Israelite territory. What caused this switch in political relations between the two states?

Evidence points, as we have noted, first of all, to the dynastic change in Aram-Damascus as the most likely catalyst for the break-up of the anti-Assyrian coalition as well as the reversal of Israelite-Aramean relations. Whether Hazael was shunned by his neighbors because of his usurpation of the Damascus throne and the likely annihilation of the powerful and revered dynasty of Adad-idri or whether he voluntarily went on the offensive against them cannot be determined. Hazael may have initiated the hostilities between Israel and Aram-Damascus.[177] 2 Kings 9:14b indicates that Jehoram's presence at Ramoth-gilead was a defensive move against the aggressor, Hazael: ויורם היה שמר ברמת גלעד הוא וכל־ישראל מפני חזאל מלך־ארם. It is against this broader background that the battle of Ramoth-gilead was waged,[178] in-

---

71–73), following J. C. Trebolle-Barrera (*Jehú y Joás. Texto y composición literaria de Reyes 9–11* [Institución San Jerónimo 17; Valencia: [s. n.], 1984], 110–25), suggests that the LXX^{L} and the Old Latin at 10:36 reflect the original form and placement of the notice of Jehu's conspiracy against Ahaziah and that the notice has been fragmented in the MT and dispersed in 8:28–29 and 9:14–15a. In its present context, 9:14b–15a shows signs of being an insertion as it clearly disrupts the natural sequence of vv 13 and 15b. In addition, Gray observes that it was inserted "to account for the absence of Joram when Jehu was anointed and acclaimed king at Ramoth Gilead" (*I & II Kings*, 543).

[177]Cf. Miller, "House of Ahab," 314, n. 4; and Pitard, *Ancient Damascus*, 145–46.

[178]Astour ("First Assyrian Invasion," 383–89), on the contrary, argues that the Israelites under Jehoram were fighting the Assyrians instead of the Arameans (cf. also G. W. Ahlström, "The Battle of Ramoth-Gilead in 841 BCE," *"Wünschet Jerusalem Frieden": Collected Communications to the XIIth Congress of the International Organization for the Study of the Old Testament, Jerusalem 1986*, ed. M. Augustin and K.-D. Schunck [Beiträge zur Erforschung des Alten Testaments und des Antiken Judentums 13; Frankfurt am Main: Peter Lang, 1988], 157–66). Astour contends that Jehoram had "continued his father's policy of alliance with Aram and resistance to Assyria" (387). He, however, fails to take into account the fact that with Hazael's usurpation of the throne of Damascus and his eradication of the dynasty that had been a moving force in the old coalition, a new political situation had arisen. With the end of the old dynasty, states that were once part of the anti-Assyrian coalition probably no longer saw themselves as bound by treaty agreements. Israel, under Jehoram, must have seen itself freed from a treaty agreement made between his predecessors and Adad-idri. In addition, 2 Kgs 8:28–29 and 9:14b–15a specifically mention Hazael by name as the aggressor against Israel. Astour disregards this information entirely. His only supposed evidence for Assyrian aggression against the Israelites comes from Hosea 10:13–15, where he identifies "Shalman" as Shalmaneser III. It is unlikely that the prophet Hosea would support his preaching with an allusion to a situation that took place more than a century prior to his time. Instead, it is more likely that Hosea was referring to a

augurating a new period of hostility between Samaria and Damascus that was to last until Pekah's takeover of Samaria in 734 BCE. According to 2 Kgs 10:32–33, Aram-Damascus's aggression against Israel continued during the reign of Jehu, resulting in the loss of Israelite territory in the Transjordan.

In Tyre, a shift in policy toward Assyria was taking place. If our interpretation of Band XIV of the Balâwât inscriptions is correct, then Tyre under Ba^{c}al-^{c}azor II again established friendly relations with Assyria by sending *maddattu* to Shalmaneser sometime between 847 and 844 BCE. The text indicates that the Assyrian king received it personally, that is, while on campaign. The most likely time for Shalmaneser to have received this *maddattu* was during or after the campaign against Damascus in 845–844 BCE. Tyre may have been the first of the coalition members to seek cordial relations with Assyria.

The second issue relates to Assyrian-Israelite relations. It is quite certain that Israel's anti-Assyrian stance, evident particularly at the battle of Qarqar in 853–852 BCE, continued throughout the duration of the Omride dynasty. With Jehu's usurpation of the Israelite throne, chronicled in 2 Kings 9–10,[179] a change in Israelite policy toward Assyria occurred.

In 2 Kgs 8:28–29, the historical setting of Jehu's coup is located in the context of the Israelite-Aramean war at Ramoth-gilead (cf. 2 Kgs 9:14b–15a) at which time king Jehoram was in-

---

situation close at hand, namely that he was speaking of Shalmaneser V's recent onslaught of Beth-Arbel and warning the Israelites that the same fate awaited them.

[179]In its present form, the account of Jehu's *coup d'état* is composite and heavily redacted. Although scholars generally agree that the core account upon which additions were subsequently made is "historical," and that it was written to justify the bloody coup, there is no consensus with regard to its date of origin (see, for instance, J. Wellhausen, *Die Composition des Hexateuchs und der historischen Bücher des Alten Testaments* [4th ed.; Berlin: Walter de Gruyter, 1963], 285–87; Noth, *Deuteronomistic History*, 72). Scholars have identified the following as secondary additions to these two chapters: 9:7–10a, 14–16, 25–26, 27b–29, 36–37; 10:1a, 10–17, 18–28, 29–36 (see Barré, *Rhetoric of Political Persuasion*; Y. Minokami, *Die Revolution des Jehu* [GTA 38; Göttingen: Vandenhoeck & Ruprecht, 1989]; McKenzie, *Trouble With Kings*, 70–79). It must be noted, however, that there is very little consensus regarding most of these additions. Scholars' evaluation of these additions is determined by a number of factors: (1) what they consider to be the core document, its function, and when it was written; (2) their understanding of the DtrH, and the levels of redaction that shaped the entire work; and (3) whether or not they posit any post-DtrH writer(s) in their hypotheses (for an excellent review of the scholarship on the deuteronomistic history, see McKenzie, *Trouble With Kings*, 1–19 and the bibliography listed there). McKenzie, for example, working on a revised Nothian model of a single DtrH, isolated the following as belonging to DtrH: 9:7a, 8–9, 15a, 16aα, 25–26, 36a, 37; 10:1a, 10–17, 29-36, and the rest of the additions as from post-DtrH writers: 9:7b, 10a, 14, 15a, 16aβ, 27b–29, 36b; 10:18–28 (*Trouble With Kings*, 78).

capacitated.[180] With the king having to leave the battlefield due to an injury, the Israelite army was left under the command of Jehu. The stage was set for Jehu to pull off a coup. It is not certain what the major motivation for the coup was. Although the DtrH pointed to the murder of Naboth as the reason for the coup,[181] the major motivation may well have been political. Cogan and Tadmor have rightly noted that "violent dynastic changes in Israel can frequently be traced to dissatisfaction with foreign military policies, which led army officers to take matters into their own hands."[182] Thus it can be surmised that Jehu advocated a foreign policy different from that of king Jehoram and that the policy in question related to Assyria. Jehoram, like his predecessors, held to an anti-Assyrian policy.[183] That the policy advocated by Jehu was pro-Assyrian is substantiated by his submission and payment of

---

[180]Literarily, the present form of the story links the *coup* with Jehu's designation and anointment as king over Israel by a prophet, identified here as Elisha, who instigated the revolution by designating Jehu as the next king of Israel. Hayes and Hooker (*New Chronology*, 42) suggest the possibility that Elijah was originally the prophet who instigated Jehu's coup, and that Elisha was the נער sent to anoint Jehu. This finds support in the Elijah narrative where Elijah was the prophet who was divinely commissioned to anoint Jehu (1 Kgs 19:15–18). The animosity that existed between Elijah and the Omrides makes it understandable why Elijah should have had an interest in getting rid of the Omrides. It is true that prophets are known to have played significant roles and exerted great influence in the politics of Israel and Judah. Yet the historical accuracy of the prophet's role in Jehu's coup is questionable. In Hosea's attack on the Jehu dynasty (Hos 1:4–5), there is no mention of a prophetic connection with his coup. It is possible that the prophetic participation was written into the narrative as a divine sanction for the revolt. In addition, there are enough similarities between Jehu's anointing and that of David and Saul to suggest that it was a later literary invention (so Campbell, *Of Prophets and Kings*, 17–23). According to Campbell, "it is clear that all three have been put together to express the conviction that God's guidance of his people was manifested through the action of a prophet empowered to designate Israel's kings through the rite of anointing" (23).

[181]See Barré, *Rhetoric of Political Persuasion*, 14; McKenzie, *Trouble With Kings*, 73–74.

[182]M. Cogan and H. Tadmor, *II Kings* (AB 11; Garden City, NY: Doubleday, 1988), 119.

[183]E. Lipiński ("An Assyro-Israelite Alliance in 842/841 B.C.E.?" in *Proceedings of the Sixth World Congress of Jewish Studies*, ed. A. Shinan [3 vols.; Jerusalem: Jerusalem Academic Press, 1975–77], 1. 273–78) suggests that a military alliance was established between Israel and Assyria in 842 BCE. He bases his argument on the lack of reference to Israel in what is perhaps the third edition of Shalmaneser's annals (the "Baghdad Text"), composed probably in 842 BCE. His other evidence is taken from 1 Kings 22, which he interprets as Jehoram's attack on Aram-Damascus from the south in collaboration with Assyria's attack from the north. The conclusion drawn from both pieces of evidence by LipinÅski are problematic. The lack of reference to Israel in the annals is due more probably to how later accounts of campaigns against the anti-Assyrian coalition had referred to the coalition—as "Adad-idri of Aram-Damascus, Irḫuleni of Hamath, together with twelve kings of the seacoast"—than as evidence of an alliance between Israel and Assyria in 842 BCE. 1 Kings 22, moreover, comes from the period of the Jehu dynasty rather than from the reign of Jehoram (see above, pp. 35–38).

maddattu to Shalmaneser III in 841–840 BCE.[184] Aramean aggression towards Israel, started shortly before the death of Jehoram, directly influenced Jehu's change in foreign policy. Jehu could use Assyria's help to complete the coup as well as to deal with the Aramean aggression as was done by Menahem almost a century later (see 2 Kgs 15:19–20 and the discussion of the text below).

Jehu's payment of *maddattu* to Shalmaneser was a very significant event in Assyrian-Israelite relations. It was an event that was not only recorded in inscriptions but also depicted in relief as well.[185] Bearing in mind that Israel was already contending with an Aramean offensive, Jehu's submission to Assyria was a tactical move to avoid further assault; this time by an appeal to a superpower whom Israel had earlier resisted by participating in the coalition. Moreover, since Jehu seized power during a turbulent time, his payment of *maddattu* to Shalmaneser should be seen as an attempt to buy Assyria's support for his reign.[186] On some occasions the one "who gave the *madattu* received from the great king his right to sit on the local throne."[187] A switch in Israel's foreign policy thereby took place, one which was all the more significant to the Assyrian king after having fought the anti-Assyrian coalition, in which Israel was a major participant, for more than a decade. This new policy adopted by Jehu must have been seen as a victory for Shalmaneser. Jehu could probably have restored the Israelite-Aramean relations, already severed when Hazael usurped the throne in Damascus, and with Aram-Damascus have fought against the Assyrians. Instead, Jehu chose to follow a new policy and bought the support of Shalmaneser in usurping the Israelite throne, thereby leaving Hazael to battle the Assyrians alone. As will be shown later, this new pro-Assyrian policy established by Jehu was to remain in effect for the duration of the Jehu dynasty.

---

[184]See pp. 57–59.

[185]See below, pp. 62–66, on the treatment of the Black Obelisk.

[186]See Smith, "Jehu and the Black Obelisk," 98.

[187]So Smith, "Jehu and the Black Obelisk," 96. He uses as evidence of such a gesture a text of Kilamuwa of Yʾdy-Samʾal where king Kilamuwa claims to have hired the king of Assyria to help him deal with an adversarial king (95; see *ANET*, 654–55). Barrakab, the son of Panamu of Yʾdy-Samʾal declares, "I was seated by my Lord Rakabel and my Lord Tiglath-pileser upon the throne of my father" (*ANET*, 655). See Parpola and Watanabe, *Neo-Assyrian Treaties*, XX–XXI, for further examples of Assyrian intervention in royal succession.

If Jehu's payment of *maddattu* represented Israel's submission to Assyrian sovereignty and to a policy determined by Assyria, can the same motivation be attributed to the actions of Tyre and Sidon in 845–844 BCE (?) and 841–840 BCE? While it is likely that the payment of *maddattu* did symbolize Tyre and Sidon's submission to Assyria's hegemony, the evidence is not conclusive. Tyre and Sidon had had a history of paying *maddattê* to Assyria. However, as has been noted earlier, those *maddattê* were probably to be seen as "diplomatic gifts" to purchase cordial relations with Assyria in order to secure their own commercial interests in the region rather than as tribute that was paid annually. Could the gifts in 845–844 and 841–840 BCE perhaps be yet another attempt on the part of the Phoenicians to do likewise?

There are substantial differences between the *maddattu* paid by Israel and that by Tyre and Sidon. First, Israel's payment seems to have been viewed by the Assyrian monarch as much more important than that of the Phoenicians, since the former was later depicted in relief while the latter was not. Second, while Jehu was an usurper—whose tribute was given for political as well as personal reasons—the king of Tyre and Sidon, Ba^{c}li-ma-AN-zēr (c. 855–830 BCE), was not.[188] His motive for paying *maddattu* to Shalmaneser was probably very different, namely, that it was to assure a continued commercial relationship rather than buy political security.

Another issue that needs to be addressed is the nature of Israelite-Tyrian relations during this period. Since the Assyrian text speaks of the two states paying *maddattu* on a similar occasion, is that an indication that there were cordial relations between them? Biblical evidence, albeit indirect, seems to suggest that this was not the case. A major part of Jehu's coup was the slaughter of the royal house, which involved three separate assaults. The first was an attack on Jehoram and Ahaziah, the kings of Israel and Judah respectively, at Jezreel (2 Kgs 9:17–24, 27). With the death of both monarchs, Jehu turned his attention towards Jezebel (2 Kgs 9:30–37). It is most interesting to note that in all the accounts of usurpation in Israel—and there were many—only Jezebel as the queen mother is singled out as a threat to the success of a coup who must be removed. No other queens share that distinction. This may have been due to her continual influence in the politics

[188]See Josephus, *Ag. Ap.*, 1.18 §124, where the ḳing is identified as Βαλέζωρος (Baalazor), the son of Ethbaal.

of the Omrides and her support by the Tyrians even after the death of her husband, Ahab. In the eyes of the narrator, while the Omrides were known to have close association with the Phoenicians, it was Jezebel who came to embody everything Phoenician, including culture and religion. Exterminating Jezebel was therefore seen as a necessary step to stamping out Phoenician influence. Her death would have made ongoing Phoenician intervention in Israelite affairs less likely. The murder of Jezebel was quickly followed by the massacre of the descendants of Ahab (2 Kgs 10:1–17). In exterminating the royal houses of Israel and Judah, Jehu in essence repealed the pro-Phoenician policy of the Omride dynasty. The murder of Jezebel, the daughter of Ethbaal and sister (or half-sister) of the reigning king, Ba^{c}al-^{c}azor (= Ba^{c}li-ma-AN-zēr), was probably viewed by the Tyrian royal house as an atrocious act, one that momentarily severed the good relations between Israel and Tyre.

Although no states seem to have supported Aram-Damascus, only Tyre and Sidon and Israel are said to have paid *maddattu* to Assyria. Hamath's capitulation has been dealt with earlier. While this cannot be proven conclusively, other smaller states may have similarly capitulated and submitted to the Assyrians when the coalition disintegrated.[189]

F. The Marble-Slab Inscription

The Marble-Slab inscription was discovered in the *liben* of the outer wall of the ancient royal city of Aššur in 1950. This edition of the annals of Shalmaneser III, inscribed on the first day of the month of *Tašrītu* of Shalmaneser's twentieth *palû*, like III R 5, 6, contains a detailed account of his eighteenth *palû* (col. III, lines 45b–53 to col. IV, lines 1–15a).[190] This text closely parallels III R 5, 6 except in the tribute section, beginning in col. IV, line 10b, although some interesting variations appear elsewhere.[191]

10) . . . *ma-da-tu šá* ^{I}*ba-ʾ-li-ma*-AN-*zēr*

11) ^{I}*ṣur-ra-a-a šá* ^{I}*ia-a-ú* DUMU ^{I}*ḫu-um-ri-i*

12) *am-ḫur* AŠ *ta-ia-ar-ti-ia a-na*

13) ^{KUR}*lab-na-na lu e-li ṣa-lam šárrū-ti-ia*

---

[189]On what Egypt may have done, see Redford, *Egypt, Canaan, and Israel*, 339–40.

[190]The inscription was first published by Safar, "Further Text of Shalmaneser III," 3–21.

[191]Cf. the transliteration in Michel, "Die Assur-Texte," *WO* 2, 38–39.

14) *it-ti ṣal-me ša ^{I}tukul-ti-apil-é-šár-ra*

15) *šárri rabî a-lik pa-ni-ia ú-še-ziz*

> The tribute of Ba^{c}li-ma-AN-zēr, the Tyrian, and of Jehu, the (Bit)-Ḫumrite, I received. On my return, I climbed the Lebanon. I erected a stela of my royal self beside the stela of Tiglath-pileser, the great king, my predecessor.

In addition to the differences in the tribute section the Marble-Slab inscription shows other variations from III R 5, 6. First, Shalmaneser claims to have slaughtered 16,020 soldiers (col. III, line 51) instead of the 16,000 given in III R 5, 6. Second, the place Ba^{c}li-raʾsi is further modified as "opposite Tyre" (*šá pu-ut* ^{KUR}*ṣur-ri*; col. IV, line 9). Third, instead of referring to Tyre and Sidon by their geographical names in gentilic form, ^{KUR}*ṣur-ra-a-a* and ^{KUR}*ṣi-du-na-a-a*, they are referenced by their ruler, Ba^{c}li-ma-AN-zēr, the Tyrian. This king is to be identified with Βαλέζωρος (= Ba^{c}al-^{c}azor) of the Tyrian annals copied by Menander of Ephesus which Josephus cites.[192] This is additional support that at the time only one king ruled over the two states. Fourth, instead of the form *ia-ú-a* (which occurs in III R 5, 6; the reliefs of the Black Obelisk; and the Kurbaʾil Statue, lines 29–30[193]), a variant form *ia-a-ú* occurs for the name of Jehu. Such irregularities in cuneiform representation of foreign names are common.[194] The name of Sûa of Gilzanu, for example, is represented in three different forms in Shalmaneser's inscriptions.[195] In all probability, the variations can be accounted for by the way a particular scribe heard the name being articulated or different scribal conventions.

G. The Black Obelisk Inscription

Lines 97–99 and 102–104 of the Black Obelisk describe Shalmaneser III's campaigns to the west in his eighteenth *palû* (841–840 BCE) and twenty-first *palû* (838–837 BCE) respectively. In addition, panel B of the reliefs, accompanied by a text, depicts a figure, perhaps Jehu, bowing before Shalmaneser presenting *maddattu*.

---

[192] Josephus, *Ag. Ap.*, 1.18 §124; cf. Katzenstein, *History of Tyre*, 116–18.

[193] J. V. Kinnier-Wilson, "The KurbaʾilStatue of Shalmaneser III," *Iraq* 24 (1962), 108–11.

[194] McCarter, "Yaw, Son of Omri," 5.

[195] Smith, "Jehu and the Black Obelisk," 94.

Lines 97–99, 102–104:[196]

97) . . . AŠ 18 BAL.MEŠ-*ia* 16-*šú* ^{ÍD}A.RAT *e-bir* ^{I}*ḫa-za-ʾi*-DINGIR

98) *šá* ^{KUR}ANŠE-*šú a-na* MÈ *it-ba-a* 1 LIM 1 ME 21 ^{GIŠ}GIGIR.MEŠ-*šú* 4 ME 70 *pit-ḫal-lu-šú it-ti*

99) *uš-ma-ni-šú e-kim-šú*

102) . . . AŠ 21 BAL.MEŠ-*ia* 21-[*šú*] ^{ÍD}A.RAT *e-bir a-na* URU.MEŠ^{ni}

103) *šá* ^{I}*ḫa-za-'i*-DINGIR *šá* ^{KUR}ANŠE-*šú a-lik* 4 *ma-ḫa-ze-šú* KUR^{ud} *ma-da-tu šá* ^{KUR}*ṣur-ra-a-a*

104) ^{KUR}*ṣi-du-na-a-a* ^{KUR}*gu-bal-a-a am-ḫur*

In my eighteenth *palû*, I crossed the Euphrates for the sixteenth time. Hazael of the land of Imērišu (= Aram-Damascus) came forth for battle. 1,121 of his chariots, 470 of his calvary, together with his camp, I took away from him.

In my twenty-first *palû*, I crossed the Euphrates for the twenty-first time. I marched against the cities of Hazael of the land of Imērišu (= Aram-Damascus), and captured four of his cities. The tribute of the land of the Tyrians, Sidonians, and Byblians, I received.

Panel B:[197]

ma-da-tu šá ^{I}*ia-ú-a* DUMU ^{I}*ḫu-um-ri-i* KÙ.BABBAR.MEŠ KÙ.GI.MEŠ *sap-lu* KÙ.GI *zu-qu-ut* KÙ.GI *qa-bu-a-te*^{MEŠ} KÙ.GI *da-la-ni*^{MEŠ} KÙ.GI AN.NA.MEŠ ^{GIŠ}*ḫu-ṭar-tú šá qāt šárru* ^{GIŠ}*pu-aš-ḫa-ti am-ḫur-šu*

The tribute of Jehu, the (Bit)-Ḫumrite. Silver, gold, a golden bowl, a golden vase, golden goblets, golden pitchers, tin, a *ḫutartu* for the hand of the king, and *puašḫatu*,[198] I received from him.

This text for the eighteenth *palû* of Shalmaneser is the shortest of all the texts that report on this campaign of 841–840 BCE,[199] and it adds nothing to the other texts already considered. On the other hand, the Black Obelisk is the only intact inscription that relates the events of Shalmaneser's twenty-first *palû*.[200] During this year (838–837 BCE), Shalmaneser again campaigned in Syria-Palestine and battled Hazael alone.

---

[196]Cf. Michel, "Die Assur-Texte," *WO* 2, 154.

[197]Cf. Michel, "Die Assur-Texte," *WO* 2, 141.

[198]The meaning of *pu-aš-ḫa-ti* is unknown. Michel suggests that it is a kind of weapon (*ibid.*). Luckenbill translates "javelins" (*ARAB* I, §590), but on the basis of *bu-dil-ḫa-ti* (so Michel, *ibid.*). Oppenheim transcribes as *pu-ru*$_4$*-ḫa-ti* and leaves it untranslated (*ANET*, 281, n. 2), while D. W. Thomas suggests that it is a kind of fruit (*DOTT*, 48–49).

[199]The only other text available for this campaign that is not treated here is the Bull Inscription, first published by A. H. Layard, *Inscriptions in the Cuneiform Character from Assyrian Monuments* (London: Harrison and Son, 1851), pls. 12–16, 46–47. The only variation between the Layard and Black Obelisk texts concerns the number of Hazael's chariots taken by Shalmaneser; the Layard text gives a figure of 1,131.

[200]Another inscription which refers to this *palû*, discovered at Nimrud, is unfortunately badly damaged. The text is given in J. Laessøe, "A Statue of Shalmaneser III, from Nimrud," *Iraq* 21 (1959), 154, fragment E, lines 9–19, esp. 11–16.

The eponym chronicle for the twenty-first (838–837 BCE) and twenty-second (837–836 BCE) years reads *a-na* KUR*ma-la-ḫi* and *a-na* KUR*da-na-bi* respectively.[201] Both cities are located in the Damascus area. On the basis of the eponym chronicle, Pitard suggests that the account on the Black Obelisk for the twenty-first *palû* conflates two successive campaigns to the Damascus area.[202] Given the fact that the Black Obelisk is a late edition of the annals and contains numerous errors,[203] such conflation could have taken place. Moreover, by conflating the two *palê* into one, the scribe would have tendentiously smoothed over the difficulty that Shalmaneser had in suppressing Hazael. The entries in the eponym chronicle, however, probably do not reflect two campaigns but one, which took more than a year to complete. At the end of 838–837 BCE, the Assyrian army was encamped at Malaḫu, and at the end of 837–836 BCE at Danabu.

While campaigning against Hazael (838–836 BCE), Shalmaneser personally received the tribute or diplomatic gifts from Tyre, Sidon, and Byblos. These Phoenician states were willing to pay to remain on good terms with the Assyrians rather than risk invasion. It is difficult to tell whether the Phoenicians saw these gifts as indications of their subjection to Assyrian hegemony.

While it is clear from III R 5, 6 and the Marble-Slab inscriptions that Jehu paid tribute in 841–840 BCE, it is uncertain if the text accompanying the relief on the Black Obelisk should be related to the events of 841–840 BCE. Scholars have generally assumed that the "depiction" of Jehu on the relief reflects the payment of the tribute noted in III R 5, 6 and the Marble-Slab inscription. This assumption may be correct. Beyond the fact that Jehu paid tribute in 841–840 BCE, what further information may be gleaned from this relief? The Black Obelisk, it should be remembered, is probably the final edition of Shalmaneser's annals, erected towards the end of his reign. The reliefs concern five different geographical regions and the submission of each of the kings depicted occurred at different periods during the reign of Shalmaneser. Sûa of Gilzanu, for example, is depicted in panel A;

[201] Ungnad's earlier reading of *s[u(?)-ú(?)]-ḫi* for the year 838 BCE is questionable ("Eponymen," 433). The reading of *ma-la-ḫi* is now considered almost certain. See Reade, "Assyrian Campaigns," 251–60; and Pitard, *Ancient Damascus*, 150.

[202] Pitard, *Ancient Damascus*, 149–50.

[203] For example, Dayān-Aššur served as the *limmu* during the sixth regnal year (853–852 BCE) of Shalmaneser; in the Black Obelisk, however, his *limmu* is dated to the fourth regnal year (*ARAB*, 1. §561). Cf. Reade, "Assyrian Campaigns," 254–55.

this king according to the Monolith Inscription (col. I, line 28; col. II, line 61) paid tribute to Shalmaneser in his accession year as well as his third *palû*. The relief, therefore, recalls Sûa's submission to Assyrian hegemony early in the reign of Shalmaneser. Similarly, the panel relating to Jehu is concerned with the fact that Jehu paid tribute and submitted to the Assyrians. A closer analysis of the relief and accompanying inscription reveals important information about Jehu's submission. The most significant piece of evidence comes from the phrase, ^{GIŠ}*ḫuṭartu ša qāt šarri*, which Elat suggests is an indication of the peaceful submission of Jehu. He adds that

> the *ḫuṭārtu* was not a sceptre, a symbol of royal authority, which is designated by *ḫaṭṭu*. This latter word, as distinct from *ḫuṭārtu*, is often mentioned in neo-Assyrian documents, but never included in a tribute or handed over by a vassal king to his Assyrian overlord. It thus seems to us that the *ḫuṭārtu* was rather a symbol of protection or ownership of property . . . .[204]

Similarly, the phrase is used in relation to Sûa of Gilzanu, except that the word is in the plural (^{GIŠ}*ḫu-ṭar-a-te*^{MEŠ}).[205] Elat's argument is based on the fact that the same word is used of a slave mark signifying possession by a particular owner in the late Babylonian period.[206] He argues that the same symbolic meaning must be maintained for the late Babylonian period as well as the Neo-Assyrian period and concludes that when Jehu and Sûa handed over *ḫuṭārtu* to Shalmaneser III, they were symbolically placing their states (Bit-Ḫumri and Gilzanu respectively) under the special protection of the king of Assyria.[207]

Several conclusions may be drawn from the relief of the Black Obelisk regarding Israelite-Assyrian relations during the reign of Jehu. First, the payment of tribute on the relief indicates Jehu's "purchase" of the right to rule over Israel, that is, Assyrian sanction of his rule in 841–840 BCE. Second, the use of the word *ḫuṭārtu* indicates the placement of Bit-Ḫumri (Israel) under special Assyrian protection. Third, the depiction of Jehu on the relief denotes the significance that this act had for Assyria and probably that a pro-Assyrian policy was established for the first time in Israel. Fourth, since the obelisk was erected late in the reign of

---

[204]Elat, "Campaigns of Shalmaneser III," 33–34.

[205]Smith explains that the word is used here in the plural, because Sûa was accompanied by his brothers when he presented tribute to Shalmaneser (cf. Monolith Inscription, col. II, line 61; Smith, "Jehu and the Black Obelisk," 96).

[206]Elat, "Campaigns of Shalmaneser III," 34; cf. *CAD*, 6. 264–65.

[207]*Ibid.*; cf. also Smith, "Jehu and the Black Obelisk," 96.

Shalmaneser, the relief is also indicative of Jehu's continuing submission to the Assyrians.

III. SYNOPSIS

The foregoing analysis reveals that during the period of the Omride dynasty, regional politics and cooperation among the Syro-Palestinian states was at its height. This cooperative stance in Syria-Palestine probably developed in two phases. On the four campaigns of Ashurnasirpal II (883–859 BCE) to the west (in the period 877–876 to 866–865 BCE), "virtually no opposition was encountered."[208] *Maddattu* was received only from the Phoenicians. The formation of economic and commercial cooperation among the south Syro-Palestinian states—the first phase—probably developed during this period. In Israel, this phase was presided over by Omri. With the more aggressive policy of Assyrian domination carried out by Shalmaneser, this cooperation moved, probably after Shalmaneser's action against Bit-Adini and its provincialization (856–855 BCE), to the formation of a military coalition. In Israel, Ahab presided over this move. The entire region was united to halt the encroachment of Assyrian control over regional commerce.[209] The strong coalition was able to check Shalmaneser's advance on at least four occasions. Each time the Assyrian army was turned back at the Orontes. Under the leadership of Adad-idri of Aram-Damascus and Irḫuleni of Hamath, central and southern Syria-Palestine was able to hold off Assyrian encroachment for more than a decade. Ahab of Israel was not only a major participant, but also probably a leader in the formation of the coalition. It is reasonable to speculate that Tyre was involved in the coalition for a time in the 850s and early 840s. With almost all other states closely aligned, it would not have been to the benefit of Tyre, either politically or commercially, to advocate a different stance and stay away from participation in the coalition, especially since Egypt was also supporting the western anti-Assyrianism. The absence of any reference to Phoenician troops involved in the conflict at Qarqar in 853 BCE could have been due to the fact that they participated as part of the Israelite contingent.

---

[208]Grayson, "Ashur-dan II to Ashur-nirari V," 256.

[209]The general prosperity of Israel during this time was probably the consequence of Israel's participation as a full-fledged member of the regional coalition. With states in Syria-Palestine able to control the flow of commerce themselves, instead of having an outside power siphoning off goods from the region, the states in the entire region in cooperation with one another probably enjoyed a period of prosperity.

A new situation had developed by the eighteenth year of Shalmaneser's reign (841–840 BCE). The anti-Assyrian coalition in Syria-Palestine that had been successful in fending off Shalmaneser's several attempts to penetrate further beyond the Orontes River no longer existed. Aram-Damascus, Tyre and Sidon, and Israel, onetime members—directly or indirectly—of the coalition, all responded differently to Shalmaneser on this campaign. First, Aram-Damascus, now ruled by Hazael, was in direct opposition to Assyria. Isolated from its former allies, Aram-Damascus was left to fight the Assyrians alone. Second, Tyre, interested in protecting its commercial interests and monopoly in the region opted for diplomatic cooperation with the Assyrians by giving "diplomatic gifts" to the Assyrian king. Apparently, as long as Tyre was willing to present the Assyrian king with enormous "diplomatic gifts" occasionally, Assyria was content with Tyre's symbolic acknowledgment of its sovereignty. Third, Israel under Jehu submitted politically to Assyria. As has been observed above, both the domestic and regional situations with which Jehu was confronted made that a politically astute move. On the one hand, Jehu was able to receive Assyrian support and sanction for his personal coup. On the other hand, through Israel's political subjugation to Assyria and the placement of the state under Assyrian protection, Jehu was able to receive help from its suzerain in dealing with the Arameans. Shalmaneser's attack on Hazael in 841–840 BCE may have prevented the Arameans from carrying out more immediate aggression against Israel.

With regard to the new relationship between these three western states, first, it is clear that Israel and Aram-Damascus were antagonistic to each other, illustrated by their disparate response to Assyria. In addition, it has been noted that the Hebrew Bible provides evidence that during the reign of Jehu, Hazael of Aram-Damascus conducted further aggression against Israel and annexed its Transjordanian territory (cf. 2 Kgs 10:32–33). Second, while Assyrian texts do not provide any information to determine the nature of Israelite-Tyrian relations, indirect evidence suggests that the relation between them was anything but cordial. The cooperative relations existing during the Omride dynasty were probably severed as a consequence of Jehu's coup and subsequent murder of Jezebel, the queen mother and Tyrian princess (cf. 2 Kgs 9:30–33). Finally, the Assyrian sources are also silent with regard to the relation between Aram-Damascus and Tyre. It has been suggested, however, that some ties existed between them during this period, although the ties were probably confined to commerce.[210] This suggestion is not unreasonable, given the fact that Tyrian relations with Israel had been broken and that Tyre would thus need an alternate route in order to reach the Gulf of Aqabah for its commercial interests.[211] Thus, after the collapse of this western united front, the region moved into a new phase—one in which the states functioned more independently of one another but a phase in which Aram-Damascus set out to dominate the region.

[210]So Katzenstein, *History of Tyre*, 184. He alludes to the discovery of carved ivories at Arslan Tash in Syria, with one bearing the name of Hazael, as evidence of this commercial tie (cf. I. Ephᶜal and J. Naveh, "Hazael's Booty Inscription," *IEJ* 39 (1989), 192–200; F. Thureau-Dangin et al., *Arslan Tash* [Bibliothéque Archéologique et Historique 16; Paris: Paul Geuthner, 1931], pl. XLVII, 112; *KAI*, no. 232).

[211]On the importance of the Gulf of Aqabah trade route, see Briquel-Chatonnet, *Les relations*, 268–70.

CHAPTER TWO

THE REIGN OF ADAD-NIRARI III

I. INTRODUCTION

The eponym chronicle is an important source of information for the reign of Shalmaneser's successor and Adad-nirari III's predecessor, Šamši-Adad V (823–811 BCE). The eponym chronicle becomes all the more significant given the fact that there are very few inscriptional texts available from the reign of this monarch. The following is the eponym chronicle from the reign of Šamši-Adad V:

Regnal Year	*Dates*	*Reported Event*[1]
1	823–822 BCE	*si-ḫu* revolt
2	822–821 BCE	*si-ḫus* revolt
3	821–820 BCE	*si-ḫu*[2] [. . .]-*ri-is*[3] revolt . . . -ris
4	820–819 BCE	*a-na* KUR*man-na-a-a* at Mannai
5	819–818 BCE	. . .]-*šum-me*[4] . . . shumme
6	818–817 BCE	[*a-na* KUR*til-li*]-*e* at Tille
7	817–816 BCE	[*a-na* KUR*til-li*]-*e* at Tille
8	816–815 BCE	*a-na* KUR*til-l*[*i-e*] at Tille
9	815–814 BCE	*a-na* KUR*za-ra-a-t*[*e*] at Zarate

[1]Information for this column for the years 823–822 to 816–815 BCE is derived from Eponym Canon C^{b} 4 (Ungnad, "Eponymen," 433) and STT 46 + 348 (Gurney and Finkelstein, *Sultantepe Tablets* I, #46; Gurney and Hulin, *Sultantepe Tablets* II, #348) and for the years 815–814 to 811–810 BCE from Eponym Canon C^{b} 1 (Ungnad, "Eponymen," 428).

[2]So STT 348.

[3]So Eponym Canon C^{b} 4 (Ungnad, "Eponymen," 433).

[4]STT 348 reads KUR at the end of the line

10	814–813 BCE	*a-na* ^{URU}*di-ri* DINGIR GAL *a-na* ^{URU}*di-ri it-ta-lak* at Der The great god went to Der
11	813–812 BCE	*a-na* ^{KUR}*aḫ-sa-na* at Aḫsana
12	812–811 BCE	*a-na* ^{KUR}*kal-di* at Chaldea
13	811–810 BCE	*a-na* ^{KUR}KÁ.DINGIR^{KI} at Babylon

According to the eponym chronicle, the final years of the reign of Shalmaneser III were characterized by a major rebellion that broke out in 827–826 BCE and continued into the reign of Šamši-Adad V. This revolt, according to an annalistic text of Šamši-Adad, was started by Aššur-daʾʾin-apli, another son of Shalmaneser, and was supported by twenty-seven cities.[5] Šamši-Adad claims that it was he who eventually suppressed the rebellion. Since the eponym canon for Šamši-Adad's third regnal year (821–820 BCE) still recorded a revolt at the end of the year, the rebellion must have extended into his fourth regnal year (820–819 BCE) before he finally put an end to it.

Following the suppression of the rebellion, Šamši-Adad was preoccupied throughout his reign with curtailing troubles in the northeastern frontier (820–819 to 815–814 BCE) and in Babylonia (814–813 to 811–810 BCE).[6] The eponym chronicle reveals that Šamši-Adad did not mount any campaign to the west throughout his reign. As a result, some rulers in the west rebelled, that is, withheld their tribute.[7] The absence of Assyria in the west meanwhile provided the occasion for Hazael of Aram-Damascus to expand his territory and dominate affairs in Syria-Palestine.[8] Biblical sources furnish evidence that Hazael subjugated Israel, Philistia, and Judah. First, 2 Kgs 10:32–33 reports that during the reign of Jehu, "YHWH began to cut off parts of Israel. Hazael defeated them throughout the territory of Israel: from the Jordan eastward, all the land of Gilead, the Gadites, and the Reubenites, and the Manassites, from Aroer, which is by the valley of the Arnon, that

---

[5] *ARAB*, 1. §715.

[6] See Saggs, *Assyria*, 78; Grayson, "Ashur-dan II to Ashur-nirari V," 269–71; cf. *ARAB*, 1. §§716–26.

[7] So the Sabaʾa Stela (ll. 14–15) and Sheikh Hammad Stela (ll. 1–5) of Adad-nirari III (see below, pp. 84–88).

[8] Cf. Pitard, *Ancient Damascus*, 151–58.

is, Gilead and Bashan." While it is not certain if all these areas were lost during the reign of Jehu, it is clear that Hazael was able to carry out his expansionist policy and encroach on Israelite territory. Second, 2 Kgs 12:17–18 recounts Hazael's aggression toward Philistia and Judah, capturing Gath and forcing the submission of Jehoash of Judah to Aram-Damascus's hegemony. Pitard, arguing against A. Jepsen[9] and B. Mazar,[10] asserts that there is insufficient evidence to support any claim that Hazael expanded his dominance north of Damascus.[11] Even without the northern expansion, Pitard is probably right to conclude that "the size of Hazael's empire was significant enough to make Damascus the capital of one of the most powerful states of Syria, one that Assyria would have to deal with as it began to stir once again at the end of the ninth century."[12]

With the accession of Adad-nirari III (810–783 BCE), Assyrian activities in the west resumed. A major campaign to the west, lasting three or four years, was conducted to re-subjugate the states that had rebelled against Assyrian hegemony during the reign of Adad-nirari's predecessor as well as to inaugurate a new policy of strength toward the west. Inscriptional materials from the reign of Adad-nirari that pertain to his campaigns in the west are not numerous. In fact, there is not a single annalistic text preserved from his long reign. The texts that deal with his military activities in the west are the Antakya Stela, the el-Rimah Stela, the Calah Slab, the Saba'a Stela, the Sheikh Hammad Stela, the Scheil and Millard Fragment, and the Pazarcik Stela (obverse).

II. ASSYRIAN INSCRIPTIONS

A. The Eponym Chronicle

The absence of annalistic texts from the reign of Adad-nirari III highlights the significance of the eponym chronicle in helping to establish the chronology of Assyria's involvement in the west and the nature of that involvement during this period. Texts from Adad-nirari's reign are "summary inscriptions" and provide few

---

[9]Jepsen, "Israel und Damaskus," 168.

[10]B. Mazar, "The Aramean Empire and Its Relations with Israel," *BA* 25 (1962), 108–16.

[11]Pitard, *Ancient Damascus*, 152–58.

[12]*Ibid.*, 158.

clues for dating. The following is the eponym chronicle for the period of the reign of Adad-nirari III.

Regnal Year	*Dates*	*Reported Event*[13]
1	810–809 BCE	*i-na* KUR in the land
2	809–808 BCE	*a-na mad-a-a* at Madai
3	808–807 BCE	*a-na* ^{URU}*gu-za-na* at Guzana
4	807–806 BCE	*a-na* ^{KUR}*man-na-a-a* at Mannai
5	806–805 BCE	*a-na* ^{KUR}*man-na-a-a* at Mannai
6	805–804 BCE	*a-na* ^{KUR}*ar-pad-da* at Arpad
7	804–803 BCE	*a-na* ^{URU}*ḫa-za-zi* at Ḫazazi
8	803–802 BCE	*a-na* ^{URU}*ba-ʾ-li* at Ba^{c}li
9	802–801 BCE	*a-na* UGU *tam-tim mu-ta-nu* to the sea. A plague
10	801–800 BCE	*a-na* ^{URU}*ḫu-bu-uš-ki-a* at Ḫubuškia
11	800–799 BCE	*a-na mad-a-a*[14] at Madai
12	799–798 BCE	*a-na mad-a-a* at Madai
13	798–797 BCE	*a-na* ^{URU}*lu-u-ši-a* at Lušia
14	797–796 BCE	*a-na* ^{KUR}*nam-ri* at Namri
15	796–795 BCE	*a-na man-ṣu-a-te*[15] at Manṣuate
16	795–794 BCE	*a-na* ^{URU}*di-e-ri* at Der
17	794–793 BCE	*a-na* ^{URU}*di-e-ri* at Der
18	793–792 BCE	*a-na mad-a-a* at Madai

[13]Information for this column is derived from Eponym Canon C^{b} 1 (Ungnad, "Eponymen," 428–30).

[14]The determinative KUR before *mad* (= KUR) is constantly omitted in the eponym chronicle.

[15]The determinative is omitted.

19	792–791 BCE	*a-na mad-a-a* at Madai
20	791–790 BCE	*a-na* ^{KUR}*ḫu-bu-uš-ki-a* at Ḫubuškia
21	790–789 BCE	*a-na* ^{KUR}*i-tu-ʾ-a* at Ituʾa
22	789–788 BCE	*a-na mad-a-a* at Madai
23	788–787 BCE	*a-na mad-a-a* [URU_4 *ša* É ^{d}AG *ša* ^{KUR}NIN]A^{KI} *kar-ru* at Madai. The foundation of the temple of Nabû at Nineveh was laid
24	787–786 BCE	*a-na mad-a-a* ^{d}AG *a-na* E.GAL GIBIL *e-ta-rab* at Madai. Nabû entered the new temple
25	786–785 BCE	*a-na* ^{KUR}*ki-i*[*s*]-*ki* at Kiski
26	785–784 BCE	*a-na* ^{KUR}*ḫu-bu-uš-ki-a* DINGIR GAL *a-na* ^{URU}*di-ri* [*it-ta-*]*lak* at Ḫubuškia. The great god went to Der
27	784–783 BCE	*a-na* ^{KUR}*ḫu-bu-uš-ki-a* at Ḫubuškia
28	783–782 BCE	*a-na* ^{KUR}*i-tu-ʾ-u* at Ituʾu

According to the eponym chronicle, Adad-nirari did not begin military expeditions to the west until his sixth regnal year.[16] Beginning with the sixth year, however, the Assyrian army is noted in the eponym chronicle to have operated in the west for three (or four?) successive years. At the end of 805–804 BCE, the Assyrian army was encamped at Arpad (identified with modern Tell Refād) in northern Syria. The following year (804–803 BCE), the Assyrians were at Ḫazazi, also located in northern Syria. Ḫazazi, identi-

[16]Briquel-Chatonnet (*Les relations*, 120), following E. Schrader (*Keilinschriftliche Bibliothek* [2 vols.; Berlin: H. Reuther, 1889–90], 1. 208–9), suggests that the campaign against Arpad in the eponym chronicle took place in the fifth regnal year, 806–805 BCE. How that dating was derived, however, is not stated.

On the basis of a misreading of the el-Rimah Stela (where the phrase *ina ištēt šatti* was mistranslated as "in [my] first year"; see below, esp. n. 39) and its correlation with the eponym chronicle, earlier scholars have speculated on a co-regency between Adad-nirari and his mother Semiramis. This view is, however, no longer viable following a correction of the reading of the phrase. See, e.g., S. Page, "A Stela of Adad-nirari III and Nergal-ereš from Tell al Rimah," *Iraq* 30 (1968), 139–53; cf. S. Page, "Adad-nirari III and Semiramis: The Stelae of Saba'a and Rimah," *Or* 38 [1969], 458; W. Schramm, "War Semiramis assyrische Regentin?," *Historia* 21 (1972), 513–21; Tadmor, "Historical Inscriptions," 147.

fied with modern ᶜAzāz, is situated in the vicinity of Arpad, about 25 km to the northwest.[17] The eponym chronicle listed Baᶜli as the location of the army for the year 803–802 BCE. The identification of Baᶜli is, unfortunately, uncertain. Various identifications have been proposed: (1) Baalbek in Lebanon;[18] (2) Baᶜli-raʾši (identified with Rās en-Nāqūra) of Shalmaneser III's inscriptions;[19] (3) Baᶜli-ṣapuna, located north of Ras Shamra;[20] and (4) Abila.[21] All that can be safely said is that, the name being West Semitic, Baᶜli was probably located in Syria.[22] The eponym notation "to the sea" for the year 802–801 BCE is ambiguous as it can refer either to the Mediterranean Sea, the Persian Gulf, or to any body of water, if "sea" is taken literally. Brinkman has, however, pointed out that no other eponym gives as destination a body of water. He suggests instead that "to the sea" more plausibly refers to the Sealand of southern Mesopotamia.[23] Adad-nirari may have been in the west, therefore, for three successive years rather than four. Since the eponym chronicle listed three different locations for those years, are they to be conceived as three different campaigns? Because they were all locations in Syria, it is more likely that this was a single campaign that lasted for over three years. Moreover, Ḫazazi, in the vicinity of Arpad, most probably belonged to the kingdom of Arpad; thus the Assyrian army at the time of the Akîtu festival in 803 BCE was still stationed in Arpadite territory. The single campaign can be understood as having been carried out in two phases: the first phase was conducted in northern Syria, with Arpad as the main target, in 805–804 and 804–803 BCE, while the second phase was directed against southern Syria—if Baᶜli is located there—in 803–802 BCE. The eponym chronicle thus provides indirect evidence of the difficulty Adad-nirari had in dealing with western states in his first

---

17 Cf. Millard and Tadmor, "Adad-nirari III in Syria," 59; S. Parpola, *The Correspondence of Sargon II, Part I: Letters from Assyria and the West* (SAA 1; Helsinki: Helsinki University Press, 1987), s.v. "Map of Assyria."

18 R. de Vaux, "La Chronologie de Hazael et de Benhadad III, Rois de Damas," *RB* 43 (1934), 514; Poebel, "Assyrian King List," 84; E. Honigmann, "Baᶜalbek," *RLA*, 1. 327–28.

19 See n. 174 in chapter one above.

20 H. Cazelles, "Une nouvelle stèle d'Adad-nirari d'Assyrie et Joas d'Israël," *CRAIBL* (1969), 115, n. 15.

21 See Cazelles, *ibid.*

22 A. R. Millard, "Adad-nirari III, Aram, and Arpad," *PEQ* 105 (1973), 161–62.

23 J. A. Brinkman, *A Political History of Post-Kassite Babylonia, 1158–722 B.C.* (AnOr 43; Rome: Pontifical Biblical Institute, 1968), 217, n. 1359; cf. also Pitard, *Ancient Damascus*, 163.

campaign to the region. That this campaign was conducted against a coalition of western kingdoms is indicated by the Pazarcik Stela (see below).

Another western campaign was perhaps conducted in 796–795 BCE, the year which the eponym chronicle noted that the army was encamped at Manṣuate,[24] a location that has not been precisely identified. Most scholars, however, would locate it in the Lebanese Beqa^{c} Valley.[25] Lipiński has suggested modern day Masyat some 28 miles west-southwest of Hamath as its likely location.[26]

The eponym chronicle will figure importantly in the discussion of the dating of Adad-nirari's campaigns against Arpad and Aram-Damascus and his receipt of tribute from Joash of Israel and from the Phoenician states, mentioned in the inscriptions of the Assyrian king.

B. The Antakya Stela

The Antakya Stela, an inscription from the reign of Adad-nirari III, was found about 1968 near the Orontes, between Antakya and Samandag in Turkey. The stela has two sculptured human figures at the top—perhaps one representing the Assyrian king and the other the powerful *turtānu*, Šamši-ilu, who is featured prominently in the text—and consists of nineteen lines of text. In all likelihood the stela was erected by Šamši-ilu,[27] who served as *turtānu* during the reigns of Adad-nirari III (810–783 BCE), Shalmaneser IV (782–773 BCE), Ashur-dan III (772–755 BCE), and Ashur-nirari V (754–745 BCE). According to the eponym chronicle, he served as *limmu* in 780–779, 770–769, and 752–751 BCE.[28] In one of his own inscriptions from Til-Barsip, he identi-

---

[24]The name Manṣuate lacks a determinative. This phenomenon has been explained on the assumption that the name was probably used as a geographical term rather than a place name (cf. Millard and Tadmor, "Adad-nirari III in Syria," 63, n. 21).

[25]E. Honigmann, "Historische Topographie von Nordsyrien Altertum," *ZDPV* 47 (1924), 16; *idem*, "Massyas," in Pauly-Wissowa-Kroll-Mittelhaus, eds., *Real-Encyclopedie der classischen Altertumswissenschaft*, XIV/2 (Stuttgart: J. B. Metzlersche, 1930), cols. 2165–66; C. G. Hölscher, "Marsyas," in *ibid.*, col. 1986.

[26]E. Lipiński "The Assyrian Campaign to Manṣuate, in 796 B.C., and the Zakir Stela," *AION* 31 (1971), 393–99.

[27]On Šamši-ilu, see J. D. Hawkins, "The Neo-Hittite States in Syria and Anatolia," *CAH*^{2} III/1, 404–5.

[28]See Ungnad, "Eponymen," 430.

fies himself as the "governor of the land of Ḫattî."[29] The stela is presently housed at the Antakya Museum in Turkey. Although reference had already been made to it by other scholars,[30] the inscription was first published by V. Donbaz in 1990.[31] The inscription is slightly damaged on the left side.

1) ^{Id}IŠKUR-ÉRIN.TÁḪ *šárru* GAL *šárru* KAL *šar*$_4$ ŠÚ *šar*$_4$ KUR ⸢AŠ⸣
2) A ^{I}*šam-ši*-10 *šar*$_4$ *dan-nu šar*$_4$ ŠÚ *šar*$_4$ KUR AŠ «*aš-šur*»[32]
3) A ^{Id}SILIM.MA-*nu*-MAŠ *šar*$_4$ *kib-rat* 4
4) [*ta*]-*ḫu-mu šá* AŠ *bir-ti* ^{I}*za-ku-ri* KUR *ḫa-ma-ta-a-a*
5) [*u* AŠ *bir*]-*ti* ^{I}*a-tar-šúm-ki* A ^{I}*ad-ra-mu* ^{I}10-ÉRIN.TÁḪ *šar*$_4$ KUR AŠ ^{I}*šam-ši*-DINGIR ^{LÚ}*tar-ta-nu*
6) [*iš-ku*]-*nu-ni* ^{URU}*na-aḫ-la-si a-di* A.ŠÀ.MEŠ-*šú* ^{GIŠ}KIRI$_6$.MEŠ-*šú*
7) [*u d*]*i-ma-ti-šú*[33] *gab-be šá* ^{I}*a-tar-šúm-ki šu-tú* ^{fD}*ar-am-tú* AŠ *bi-ri-šú-nu*
8) [*ú-šam*]-*ši-lu-ma i-zu-zu mi-ṣir* NAM A[34] ^{I}10-ÉRIN.TÁḪ *šar*$_4$ KUR AŠ ^{I}*šam-ši*-DINGIR ⸢^{LÚ}⸣
9) [*tar*]-*ta-nu ú-za-ki-ú-ma a-na* ^{I}*a-tar-šum-ki* A ^{I}*ad-ra-mu a-na* DUMU.MEŠ-*šú*
10) [DU]MU.DUMU.MEŠ-*šú* EGIR.MEŠ *ki ri-mu-ti i-ri-mu* URU-*šú ta-ḫu-ma-ti-šú*
11) [x x] *a-na mi-ṣir* KUR-*šú ú-kín* MU *aš-šur* ^{d}IŠKUR *u* ^{d}*be-er* ^{d}BAD *aš-šur-ú*
12) [^{d}NIN.LÍ]L *aš-šur-tú* MU ^{d}30 *a-šib* ^{URU}KASKAL-*ni* DINGIR.MEŠ GAL.MEŠ
13) [*šá* K]UR *aš-šur man-nu* EGIR-*ú šá pi* NA.RÚ.A *šú-a-tú*
14) [*ú*]-*šam-sa-ku-ma mi-ṣir an-na-a* TA *qa-at* ^{I}*a-tat-šúm-ki*
15) [DUMU].MEŠ-*šú u* DUMU.DUMU.MEŠ-*šú* AŠ *dan-na-ni e-ki-mu*
16) [(x)] ⸢*u*(?)⸣ *šu-mu šaṭ-ri i-pa-ši-ṭa* MU *šá-nam-ma i-šaṭ-ṭar*
17) [*aš-šur*] ^{d}IŠKUR *u* ^{d}*be-er* ^{d}30 *a-šib* ^{URU}KASKAL DINGIR.MEŠ GAL.MEŠ *šá* KUR AŠ
18) [*šá* AŠ] NA.RÚ.A *an-né-e* MU-*šú-nu zak-ru*
19) [*i*]*k-ri-bi-šú ul i-sá-mu-ú*

---

[29] F. Thureau-Dangin and M. Dunand, *Til-Barsib* (Bibliothéque Archéologique et Historique 23; Paris: Librairie Orientaliste Paul Geuthner, 1936), 146.

[30] See, e.g., Grayson, "Ashur-dan II to Ashur-nirari V," 272, n. 191; Hawkins, "Neo-Hittite States," 399, n. 218, 400, n. 230.

[31] V. Donbaz, "Two Neo-Assyrian Stelae in the Antakya and Kahramanmaraş Museums," *Annual Review of the Royal Inscriptions of Mesopotamia Project* 8 (1990), 9.

[32] Scribal error. The original intent was probably to write just AŠ for Aššur as in lines 1, 5, 8, and 17 (see Donbaz, "Two Neo-Assyrian Stelae," 7).

[33] As reconstructed by K. Deller (so Donbaz, "Two Neo-Assyrian Stelae," 7).

[34] NAM A is difficult. Donbaz suggests a possible metathesis for *a-nam* = *annâm*.

> **Adad-nirari, the great king, strong king, king of the universe, king of Assyria, son of Šamši-Adad, the strong king, king of the universe, king of Assyria, son of Shalmaneser, the king of the four corners.**
>
> **[The boun]dary stone between Zakkur of Hamath [and] Ataršumki, son of Adramu, Adad-nirari, the king of Assyria, and Šamši-ilu, the *turtānu*, [esta]blished. The city of Naḫlasi together with its fields, gardens, [and set]tlements belonged to Ataršumki. They divided the Orontes River between them. This is the border. Adad-nirari, the king of Assyria, and Šamši-ilu, the [*tur*]*tānu*, have given it freely and clearly to Ataršumki, son of Adramu, to his sons, and his future [grand]sons. His city and its territories [. . .] to the border of his land he made firm.**
>
> **By the name of Aššur, Adad, Ber, the Assyrian Illil, the Assyrian [Mulissu], and the name of Sin who dwells in Harran, the great gods [of A]ssyria, whoever in the future speaks evil of the terms of this stela, takes this border by force from the hand of Ataršumki, [his] sons, and his grandsons, destroys the written name and writes another name, may [Aššur], Adad, Ber, Sin who dwells in Harran, and the great gods of Assyria [whose] names are recorded on this stela, not listen to his prayers.**

The inscription begins by providing the standard epithets and genealogy of Adad-nirari (lines 1–3), the king to whom this stela was "dedicated." Šamši-ilu, the powerful *turtānu* of Ḫatti (= northern Syria and Anatolia[35]), is mentioned in association with the Assyrian king. The focus of the text is a border dispute between Zakkur of Hamath and Ataršumki of Arpad along the Orontes, one that was settled most probably by the Assyrian *turtānu* rather than Adad-nirari himself since Hamath and Arpad fell under the sphere of Šamši-ilu's influence and jurisdiction. The result was a border agreement that allowed both parties equal access to the Orontes.

The inscription reveals a situation when both Hamath and Arpad were loyal subjects of Assyria. The fact that this inscription was written on Ataršumki's behalf, identifying Arpad's border with Hamath, goes to show Arpad's alliance with Assyria at the time. The settlement of this dispute should be dated to before 805–804 BCE, that is, to a time when Arpad was still a loyal subject of Assyria.[36] The eponym chronicle notes, as we have seen, that an Assyrian campaign was conducted in the west beginning in 805–804 BCE, with Arpad, which had rebelled against Assyrian hegemony, as its main target. On the other hand, the Antakya Stela cannot be dated earlier than 808–807 BCE, since the *turtānu* at that time was someone other than Šamši-ilu.[37] The border dis-

---

[35] See Hawkins, "Neo-Hittite States," 372–441.

[36] Contra Hawkins, "Neo-Hittite States," 400.

[37] The eponym chronicle (C^a 1 and C^b 1) identifies Nergal-ilāya, the *turtānu*, as the *limmu* for 808–807 BCE (see Ungnad, "Eponymen," 420, 428).

pute between Arpad (which was in rebellion against Assyria by 805–804 BCE) and Hamath (which remained loyal) probably indicates the beginning of friction between western pro- and anti-Assyrian kingdoms.

Zakkur of Hamath (cf. the discussion of the Zakkur Stela below) will feature as an important character in the reconstruction of politics in the west during this period.

C. The el-Rimah Stela

The el-Rimah Stela is an inscription of Adad-nirari III found during the 1967 season of excavation at Tell el-Rimah, Iraq directed by D. Oates. The text contains twenty-one lines inscribed across the relief of the king, of which nine were deliberately chiseled off in antiquity.[38]

1) DIŠ ^{d}IM EN *šur-bi-e* NIR.GÁL DINGIR.MEŠ URU-*ri bu-kur* ^{d}*a-nime-diš-šú-ú ra-šub-bi*

2) MAḪ *gú-gal* AN-*e u* KI-*tim mu-šá-za-nin* ḪÉ.NUN *a-šib* ^{URU}*za-ma-ḫi* EN GAL-*e* EN-*šu*

3) ^{I}10-ÉRIN.TÁḪ *šárru dan-nu šar*$_4$ ŠÚ *šar*$_4$ KUR *aš-šur* A ^{Id}*šam-ši*-^{I}IM *šar*$_4$ ŠÚ *šar*$_4$ KUR *aš-šur* A ^{Id}SILIM.MA-*nu*-MAŠ *šar*$_4$ *kib-rat* LÍMMU

4) ^{GIŠ}GIGIR.MEŠ ÉRIN.ḪÁ.MEŠ KI.KALxBAD.MEŠ *lu ad-ki* DIŠ KUR *ḫat-te* DU-*ka lu aq-bi* AŠ 1-*et* MU.AN.NA[39]

5) KUR MAR.TU^{KI} KUR *ḫat-te a-na si-ḫir-ti-šá* AŠ GÌR.II.MEŠ-*ia lu ú -šak-niš* GÚ.UN *ma-da-tu*

6) *a-na* EGIR *u*$_4$-*me* UGU-*šú-nu lu ú-kin* 2 LIM GÚ.UN KÙ.BABBAR 1 LIM GÚ.UN URUDU 2 LIM GÚ.UN AN.BAR

7) 3 LIM *lu-bùl-ti bir-me u* ^{TÚG}GADA.MEŠ *ma-da-tu ša* ^{I}*ma-ri-ʾi ša* KUR ANŠE-*šú im-ḫur*

8) *ma-da-tu šá* ^{I}*ia-ʾa-su* KUR *sa-me-ri-na-a-a* KUR *ṣur-a-a* KUR *ṣi-du-na-a-a*

9) *im-ḫur* DIŠ *tam-tim* GAL-*te šá šùl-me* ^{d}*šam-ši lu a-lik ṣa-lam* EN-*ti-ia*

10) AŠ ^{URU}*ar-wa*$_6$[40]-*di ša* MURUB$_4$ *tam-tim lu-u az-qu-pu* DIŠ KUR *lab-na-ni*

11) *lu e-li* GIŠ.ÙR 1 ME ^{GIŠ}*e-ri-ni dan-nu-te ḫi-ši-iḫ-ti* É.GAL É.KUR. MEŠ-*ia*

---

[38]Cf. the transliteration in Page, "Stela of Adad-nirari III," 139–53.

[39]Page had originally translated the phrase *ina* 1-*et* MU.AN.NA (*ina ištēt šatti*) as "in (my) first year" ("Stela of Adad-nirari III," 143). In a later article, she corrected the translation to read "in a single year" ("Adad-nirari III and Semiramis," 458). Cf. H. Donner, "Adadnirari III. und die Vasallen des Westens," in *Archäologie und Altes Testament*, Festschrift K. Galling, ed. A. Kuschke and E. Kutsch (Tübingen: J. C. B. Mohr, 1970), 55.

[40]Page transcribed this sign as *ma* but it should probably be read as *wa*$_6$.

12) *lu ak-kis ma-da-te šá šárru*^{MEŠ}*-ni* KUR *na-ʾi-ri* DÙ.MEŠ-*šú-nu lu-u im-ḫur*

13) AŠ u_4*-me-šú-ma a-na* ^{Id}IGI.DU.KAM ^{LÚ}*šá-kin* KUR *ra-ṣa-pi* KUR *la-ki-e*

14) KUR *ṣir-qu*(?) [^{URU}]*an-at* KUR *su-ḫi* x x x (x) *iṣ*(?)-*bat*(?) *man-za-zu ši*(?) x x x (x)

15) *lu aq-bi* ^{URU}BÀD-^{d}MÙŠ 12 ^{URU}*kap-ra-ni-šú* ^{URU}KAR-^{d}30 10 ^{URU}*kap-ra-ni-šú*

16) ^{URU}BÀD-EN-x 33 ^{URU}*kap-ra-ni-šú* ^{URU}BÀD-*aš-šur* 20 ^{URU}*kap-ra-ni -šú* ^{URU}BÀD-[^{Id}IGI.]DU.KAM

17) 33 ^{URU}*kap-ra-ni-šú* ^{URU}BÀD-^{d}AMAR.UTU 40 ^{URU}*kap-ra-ni-šú* ^{URU} *til*(?) ^{I}10-ÉRIN.TÁḪ

18) 1 ME 26 *kap-ra-ni-šú* BÀD-EN(?).KUR-*sa*(?)-*an*(?)-*ga-ri* 28 ^{URU}*kap-ra-ni-šú* AŠ KUR *a-za-al*(?)-*li*(?)

19) ^{URU}BÀD-^{I}10-ÉRIN.TÁḪ 15 ^{URU}*kap-ra-ni-šú* AŠ KUR *la-ki-e* $^{\mathrm{URU.d}}$IM 14 *kap-ra-ni-šú* AŠ KUR *qat-ni*

20) PAP 3 ME 31 URU.MEŠ-*ni* ERÍ.MEŠ *ša* ^{I}IGI.DU.KAM AŠ *zi-kir* EN-*šú iṣ-ba-tu-ma e-pu-šú*

21) *šá* AŠ MU.MEŠ *an-nu-ti* 1-*en* MU *i-pa-ši-ṭu-ma* DINGIR.MEŠ GAL.MEŠ *iz-zi-iš li-kil-mu-šú*

To Adad, the greatest lord, hero of the gods, mighty one (?), first-born son of Anu, who alone is fiery, the lofty irrigator of heaven and earth, who provides the rain that brings abundance, who dwells in Zamaḫu, the great lord, his lord:

I, Adad-nirari, the strong king, king of the universe, king of Assyria, son of Šamši-Adad, the king of the universe, king of Assyria, son of Shalmaneser, the king of the four corners, mobilized chariots, troops, and camps, and ordered a campaign against Ḫatti. In a single year $^{(5)}$I made Amurru and Ḫatti in its entirety kneel at my feet; I imposed tribute (and) regular tax for future days upon them. He received two thousand talents of silver, one thousand talents of copper, two thousand talents of iron, three thousand multi-colored garments and (plain) linen garments as tribute from Mariʾ of the land of Imērišu (= Aram-Damascus). He received the tribute of Joash of the land of the Samarians, of the land of the Tyrians, and of the land of the Sidonians. I marched to the great sea where the sun sets, and erected a stela of my royal self $^{(10)}$in the city of Arwad which is in the middle of the sea. I went up the Lebanon mountains and cut down timbers: one hundred mature cedars, material needed for my palace and temples. He received tribute from all the kings of Naʾiri.

At that time, I ordered Nergal-ereš, the governor of Raṣappa, Lakê, Sirqu (?), An[at], Suḫi and X to . . . $^{(15)}$Dūr-Inanna with its twelve villages, Kār-Sin with its ten villages, Dūr-EN-X with its thirty-three villages, Dūr-Aššur with its twenty villages, Dūr-[Ner]gal-ereš with its thirty-three villages, Dūr-Marduk with its forty villages, Tell(?)-Adad-nirari with its one hundred and twenty six villages, Dūr-EN-KUR-Sa(?)-an-ga-ri with its twenty-eight villages in the district of Azalli (?), DĒr-Adad-nirari with its fifteen villages in the district of Lakê, the city of Adad with its fourteen villages in the district of Qatni, $^{(20)}$a total of three hundred and thirty-one small (?) towns which Nergal-ereš founded and built in the name of his lord.

> Whoever shall blot out a single name (*or*: line) from among these names (*or*: lines), may the great gods fiercely destroy him.

Formally, the el-Rimah Stela can be classified as a "summary inscription."[41] The inscription is a brief presentation of the achievements of Adad-nirari organized according to geographical regions, beginning with Ḫatti and Amurru, regions to the west of Assyria, and ending with Naʾiri in the east. In addition, it relates the founding of new settlements in the province of which Nergal-ereš was the governor.

One unusual literary feature of this inscription is the interchange between the first and third person singular pronouns (between ll. 6a and 6b, 9a and 9b, and 12a and 12b). Page concluded that this phenomenon is characteristic of many Assyrian royal inscriptions, dating back to as early as the time of Tukulti-ninurta II (890–884 BCE).[42] Tadmor has shown, however, that this interchange in the el-Rimah Stela is probably more than a stylistic variation. Rather, the narration of the achievements of the king is a compilation made from two different sources: one relating the conquest of Ḫatti and Amurru (lines 3–6a, 9–12a), and the other a tribute list (lines 6b–8, 12b). The tribute list was inserted into the narration of the conquest at the point where *ma-da-tu* is mentioned.[43]

Lines 3–6a begins with the epithets of Adad-nirari and is followed by a general statement about a campaign against Ḫatti, a term used in Neo-Assyrian texts for the Neo-Hittite states in northern Syria and Anatolia.[44] The Assyrian king further claims to have suppressed the entire region of Amurru and Ḫatti "in a single year" and imposed tribute on the whole region. In all likelihood, Amurru refers to the region south of Ḫatti and north of Aram-Damascus, namely, central Syria.[45] The claim that the entire Anatolian and northern and central Syrian region submitted to him "in a single year" is typical of the braggadocio of Assyrian royal inscriptions.

The tribute list of lines 6b–9a names four states that paid tribute to the Assyrian king. These states—Aram-Damascus, Samaria, Tyre and Sidon—are located in southern Syria-Palestine.

---

[41]Tadmor, "Historical Inscriptions," 141.

[42]Page, "Stela of Adad-nirari III," 145.

[43]Tadmor, "Historical Inscriptions," 141–42.

[44]See Hawkins, "Neo-Hittite States," 372–441.

[45]Cf. D. J. Wiseman, "Historical Records of Assyria and Babylonia," in *DOTT*, 52.

Three issues immediately arise in dealing with this inscription. (1) When did Adad-nirari's western campaign take place? (2) Was more than one western campaign related in this inscription? (3) Were the subjugation of the Syro-Hittite states and the tribute of the Syro-Palestinian kings the results of the same campaign? These issues will be dealt with later in light of all the inscriptions of Adad-nirari III.

For our present purpose, it is important to note that Mariʾ[46] of Aram-Damascus, Joash of Samaria, and Tyre and Sidon paid tribute to Adad-nirari during this particular campaign. Unfortunately, there is no indication when the tribute was received; nor is there evidence in the inscription to suggest that Aram-Damascus, Israel, and Tyre and Sidon were part of an alliance which Adad-nirari campaigned to suppress.

D. The Calah (or Nimrud) Slab

The Calah Slab (I R 35, 1) is an inscription of Adad-nirari that was discovered in 1854 by Loftus at Nimrûd. The text was first published by E. Norris, from a paper squeeze, in the first volume of Rawlinson's folios.[47] What survives was probably the upper part of a longer inscription. The extant text has 24 lines.[48]

1) É.GAL ^{I}10-ÉRIN.TÁḪ *šárru* GAL *šárru dan-nu šar*$_4$ ŠÚ *šar*$_4$ KUR *šárru šá ina* DUMU-*šú aš-šur šar*$_4$ ^{d}*ì-gì-gì ut-tu-šú-ma mal-kut*
2) *la šá-na-an ú-mal-lu-ú qa-tuš-šú* SIPA-*su* GIM Ú.TI UGU UKÙ.MEŠ KUR *aš-šur ú-ṭí-bu-ma*
3) *ú-šar-ši-du* ^{GIŠ}GU.ZA-*šú* SANGA KÙ *za-nin* É.ŠÁR.RA *la mu- par-ku-ú mu-kil* GARZA É.KUR
4) *šá ina* ^{GIŠ}TUKUL-*ti aš-šur* EN-*šú* DU.DU-*ma mal-ki šá kib-rat* LIMMÚ-*ti*
5) *ú-šék-ni-šú a-na* GÌR.II.MEŠ-*šú ka-šid* TA KUR *si-lu-na*[49]
6) *šá na-paḫ* ^{d}UTU-*ši* KUR ZALÁG KUR *el-li-pi* KUR *ḫar-ḫar* KUR *a-ra-zi-aš*
7) KUR *me-su* KUR *ma-da-a-a* KUR *gi-zil-bu-un-da* DIŠ *si-ḫir-ti-šú*
8) KUR *mu-un-na* KUR *par-su-a* KUR *al-lab-ri-a* KUR *ab-da-da-na*

---

[46]Mariʾ, king of Aram-Damascus, is probably to be identified with Ben-Hadad III, son of Hazael, rather than with Hazael, who was well known to the Assyrians and would have been named by them. The name was either "a term of address" (equivalent to the Hebrew אדני) or an alternative name of Ben-Hadad (see, e.g., Pitard, *Ancient Damascus*, 165–66; Millard and Tadmor, "Adad-nirari III in Syria," 63, n. 22).

[47]Rawlinson, *Cuneiform Inscriptions*, 1. pl. 35, no. 1.

[48]Cf. the transliteration in Tadmor, "Historical Inscriptions," 148–50.

[49]The determinative was erroneously written as MU instead of KUR (= *šadû*).

9) KUR *na-ʾi-ri* DIŠ *paṭ gim-ri-šá* KUR *an-di-ú šá a-šar-šú ru-qu*

10) <KUR> BAD-*ḫu*[50] KUR-*ú a-na paṭ gi-rim-šú a-di* UGU *tam-tim* GAL-*ti*

11) *šá na-paḫ* ^{d}UTU-*ši* TA UGU ^{ÍD}A.RAT KUR *ḫat-ti* KUR *a-mur-ri* DIŠ *si-ḫir-ti-šá*

12) KUR *ṣur-ru*[51] KUR *ṣi-du-nu* KUR <É>-*ḫu-um-ri-i*[52] KUR *u-du-mu* KUR *pa-la-as-tú*

13) *a-di* UGU *tam-tim* GAL-*ti šá* SILIM-*mu* ^{d}UTU-*ši ana* GÌR.II-*ia*

14) *ú-šék-niš* GÚ.UN *ma-da-tú* UGU-*šú-nu ú-kin a-na*

15) KUR *šá*-ANŠE-*šú lu-ú a-lik* ^{I}*ma-ri-ʾi šárru šá* KUR ANŠE-*šú*

16) AŠ ^{URU}*di-ma-áš-qi* URU *šárru-ti-šú lu-ú e-sir-šú*

17) *pu-ul-ḫi me-lam-me šá aš-šur* EN-*šú*[53] *is-ḫup-šú-ma* GÌR.II-*ia iṣ-bat*

18) *ar-du-ti* DÙ-*uš* 2 LIM 3 ME GÚ.UN KÙ.BABBAR 20 GÚ.UN KÙ.GI

19) 3 LIM GÚ.UN ZABAR 5 LIM GÚ.UN AN.BAR *lu-búl-ti bir-me* GADA

20) ^{GIŠ}NÁ ZÚ ^{GIŠ}*ni-mat-ti* ZÚ *iḫ-zi tam-li-e* NÍG.GA-*šú* NÍG.ŠU-*šú*

21) DIŠ *la ma-ni* AŠ ^{URU}*di-ma-áš-qi* URU *šárru-ti-šú* AŠ *qí-rib* É.GAL-*šú am-ḫur*

22) *šárru*^{MEŠ}-*ni šá* KUR *kal-di* DÙ-*šú-nu ar-du-ti e-pu-šú* GÚ.UN *ma-da-tú a-na* UD-

23) *um* <*ṣa*>-*a-ti*[54] UGU-*šú-nu ú-kin* KÁ.DINGIR^{KI} BÁRA.SIPA^{KI} GÚ.DU$_8$.A

24) ^{KI} *ri-ḫat* ^{d}EN ^{d}NÀ ^{d}U.GUR *lu-ú iš-šú-ni* ^{UDU}SISKUR.MEŠ KÙ [. . .

Palace of Adad-nirari, the great king, strong king, king of the universe, king of the land (of Assyria), the king whom Aššur, king of the Igigi, had chosen in his youth and gave him a kingdom without rival; whose rule (*lit.*, shepherding) he (Aššur) made good as the plant of life for the people of Assyria, and whose throne he established securely; the holy priest, who provides magnificently for Ešarra, who is unwearied, who upholds the cult of Ekur (*or*, the temple); who went forth under the protection of Aššur, his lord, and the rulers of the four corners (5)he brought to submit at his feet; who conquered from Mount Siluna of the rising sun, the lands of Namri, Ellipi, Ḫarḫar, Araziaš, Mesu, Madai, Gizilbunda in its totality, Munna, Parsua, Allabria, Abdadana, Naʾiri to its farthest border, Andiu which lies afar off, (10)Mount BAD-*hu* to its farthest border, as far as the great sea of the rising sun; from the banks of the Euphrates—Ḫatti, Amurru in its totality, Tyre, Sidon, [Bit]-Ḫumri, Edom, Philistia, as far as the great sea of the set-

---

[50]The determinative KUR (= *šadû*) was omitted due to scribal mistake.

[51]The determinative KUR was written inverted.

[52]Tadmor argues that a scribal omission occurs here as there are no instances of a toponym with the pattern of "*māt Bit*-^{m}PN, where the element *Bit* would be omitted" ("Historical Inscriptions," 149). Thus, it should be translated "(the land of) Bit-Ḫumri" rather than "Omriland."

[53]The cuneiform text reads EN-*ia* for EN-*šú* (cf. l. 4).

[54]*ṣa* is erroneously omitted in the text.

ting sun—I brought to submit at my feet. I imposed on them talents of tribute.

Against (15)Ša-imērišu (= Aram-Damascus) I marched and Mariʾ, king of the land of Imērišu (= Aram-Damascus), I shut up in Damascus, his royal city. The fearful splendor of Aššur, his lord, overwhelmed him and he seized my feet, and he became my vassal. 2,300 talents of silver, 20 talents of gold, 3,000 talents of copper, 5,000 talents of iron, colored woolen and linen garments, (20)an ivory bed, an couch inlaid and embossed with ivory, immeasurable amount of his property and goods I received in Damascus, his royal city, in his palace.

The kings of Kaldu, all of them, became my vassals; I imposed on them talents of tribute for all time to come. Babylon, Barsip, Kutha, brought the "remnant" of Bêl, Nabû, and Nergal, pure sacrifices . . . .

This inscription is, formally, a "summary inscription." It begins with a series of royal epithets (lines 1–5) and then summarizes Adad-nirari's achievements in two geographical regions, the east and the west (lines 5–14). Among the lands in the west over which Adad-nirari displayed his authority are Ḫatti and Amurru—geographical terms used to refer to the Neo-Hittite states in Anatolia and northern Syria as well as central Syria—along with Tyre, Sidon, [Bit]-Ḫumri, Edom, and Philistia. The text proceeds to describe in detail Adad-nirari's campaign against Aram-Damascus, during which he shut up its king, Mariʾ, in Damascus, forcing him to surrender, and collected a large tribute from him in his palace in Damascus. The inscription then focuses on the area of Babylonia before the break.

As in the el-Rimah and Sabaʾa Stelae, Aram-Damascus is the main focus of the inscription; it is the only place described in detail and its king is the only one named. There is no chronological data given in this inscription for the campaign against Aram-Damascus.

The Calah Slab inscription divides the western states into two camps. On the one side is Aram-Damascus, which offered strong resistance to Adad-nirari's attempt to reassert Assyrian influence and domination in the west. On the other side are the states that offered homage to the Assyrian king, apparently voluntarily. These include the north Syrian and Anatolian states in general together with several specific Palestinian states, namely, Tyre, Sidon, [Bit]-Ḫumri, Edom, and Philistia. These states may have offered *maddattu* and homage to the Assyrians as an anti-Damascus move to break free from Damascus's control. Since the text is a summary inscription and not organized chronologically, it is not possible to ascertain the sequence of events, that is, whether the capitulation of the other states took place before or after or during the attack on Damascus. It is also impossible to determine whether the rulers of the "entire" western region offered homage during a single campaign. An attempt to reconstruct the sequence of events will be made later in correlation with other inscriptional material.

*E. The Saba*ʾ*a Stela*

The Sabaʾa Stela was discovered in 1905 in the desert south of the Sinjar hills. The text consists of thirty-three lines, inscribed below a depiction of the king, of which some are badly worn and only partially legible.[55]

1) [DIŠ] ⸢^{d}⸣IŠKUR *gú-gal* AN *u* ⸢KI-*tim* DUMU⸣ ^{d}*a*-⸢*nim*⸣ *qar*-⸢*du*⸣ *šar*-⸢*ḫu*⸣
2) ⸢*gít*⸣-*ma*-⸢*lu*⸣ *pu-un*-⸢*gu*⸣-*lu ku-bu-uk-kuš a-šá*-⸢*rid*⸣
3) ^{d}*í-gì-gì qar-rad* ^{d}GÍŠ.U *šá ḫi-it-lu-pu nam-ri-ri ra-kib*
4) [U$_4$].⸢MEŠ⸣ GAL.MEŠ *ḫa-líp me-lam-me ez*-⸢*zu*⸣-*te mu-šam-qit* ḪUL.MEŠ
5) [*na-a*]-⸢*ši*⸣ *qi-na*-⸢*an*⸣-*zi* KÙ-*te mu-šab-riq* NIM.GÍR EN GAL-*e* EN-*šú*
6) [^{I}10-ÉRN].⸢TÁḪ⸣ *šárru* GAL-*u šárru dan-nu šar$_4$* ŠÚ *šar$_4$* KUR *aš-šur šárru la šá-na*-⸢*an*⸣ SIPA *tab-ra-te*
7) [PA.TE].SI MAḪ *šá ni-iš qa-ti-šú* ⸢*na*⸣-*dan zi-bi-šú iḫ-šu-ḫu*
8) [DINGIR].⸢MEŠ⸣ GAL.⸢MEŠ⸣ SIPA-*su* GIM *šam-me* TI.LA UGU UKÙ.MEŠ
9) [KUR *aš*]-⸢*šur*⸣ *ú*-⸢*ṭi*⸣-*bu-ma ú-ra-pi-šú* KUR-*su* A ^{I}*šam-ši*-10 *šárru dan-nu*
10) [*šar$_4$* ŠÚ] ⸢*šar$_4$*⸣ KUR *aš-šur* A.⸢A⸣ ^{I}SILIM.MA-*nu*-MAŠ *šá-pir mal-ki* PAP-*eš mu-šá-pi*-(erasure)-*iḫ*
11) [KUR.KUR][56].MEŠ KÚR.MEŠ AŠ MU.5.KÁM <*šá*> AŠ ^{GIŠ}GU.ZA *šárru-ti* GAL-*iš*
12) [*ú*]-⸢*ši*⸣-*bu-ma* KUR *ad-ki* ⸢ÉRIN⸣.ḪI-*at* KUR *aš-šur* ⸢DAGAL⸣.MEŠ DIŠ KUR *ḫat-te*-⸢*e*⸣[57]

---

[55] Cf. the transliteration in Tadmor, "Historical Inscriptions," 144–45. The text was originally published by E. Unger, *Reliefstele Adadniraris III. aus Sabaʾa und Semiramis* (Publicationen der Kaiserlich Osmanischen Museen 2; Constantinople: A. Ihsan and Co., 1916), 8–13, pl. II.

[56] Following M. J. Seux, *Épithètes Royales Akkadiennes et Sumériennes* (Paris: Letouzey et Anê, 1967), 185, n. 69. Unger had reconstructed the signs to read *šárru* (*Reliefstele Adadniraris III*, 8 and pl. II).

[57] The early reading of the destination of the campaign was *ana* KUR *pa*-(erasure)-*la-áš*-[*tú*], translated by Luckenbill as "against Palashtu (Palestine)" (*ARAB*, 1. §734). Tadmor challenged this reading and initially suggested instead to read *ana* KUR *ḫat*-(erasure)-*te* ⸢GAL-*te*⸣ and translated as "against the ⸢great⸣ land of Ḫatti" ("A Note on the Saba'a Stele of Adad-nirari III," *IEJ* 19 [1969], 46–48).

13) [*a-na*] ⸢DU⸣ *lu aq-bi* ^{ÍD}*pu-raṭ-te* AŠ *me-li-šá e-bir šárru*^{MEŠ}*-ni*

14) [KUR *ḫat-te*][58] ⸢DAGAL⸣*-te šá* AŠ *tar-ṣi* ^{I}*šam-ši*-10 AD*-ia id-nin-ú-ma*

15) ⸢*ik-lu*⸣-[*ú* IGI.DU$_8$]*-šú-un* AŠ *qí-bit aš-šur* ^{d}⸢X⸣.UTU[59] ^{d}IŠKUR ^{d}*iš-tar* DINGIR.[MEŠ]

16) ⸢*tik*⸣*-li-*⸢*ia*⸣ [*pul*]-⸢*ḫu me-lam*$^!$*-mu*$^!$⸣ *is-ḫu-pu-šú-nu-te-ma* GÍR.[II. MEŠ-*ia*]

17) *iṣ-ba-tú* GÚ.UN *ma*⸢*da*⸣-[*tú* . . .] ⸢x x x⸣ [. . .]

18) DIŠ KUR *aš-šur ú-ru-ni am-*[*ḫur* DIŠ KUR *šá*-ANŠE*-šú* DU]

19) *lu aq-bi* ^{I}*ma-ri-iʾ* ^{URU}*di-maš-qi* ⸢*lu*⸣ [*e-sir-šú* . . .]

20) ME GÚ.UN KÙ.GI 1 LIM GÚ.UN KÙ.BABBAR <x> GÚ.UN [. . . *am-ḫur*]

21) ⸢AŠ⸣ *u*$_4$*-me-šú-ma ú-še-piš-ma ṣa-lam be-lu-te-ia li-ta-*[*at qur*]*-di-ia*

22) ⸢*ip*⸣*-šit qa-ti-ia* AŠ *qir-bi-šú al-ṭur* AŠ AN *za-ban-ni* ⸢*ul*⸣*-ziz*$^?$*-šú* ⸢NA$_4$$^?$⸣

23) ⸢x⸣*-ri* ^{d}IGI.DU.KAM ^{LÚ}GAR.KUR ^{URU}*ni-mit-*^{d}15 ^{URU}*ap-ku* ⸢^{URU}*ma*$^?$⸣*-ri-e*

24) KUR *ra-ṣa-pi* KUR *qat-ni* ^{URU}BÀD*-duk*-1-LIM ^{URU}*kar-*^{I}AŠ-PAP-A ^{URU}*sir*⸣*-qu*

25) KUR *la-qi-e* KUR *ḫi-in-da-*⸢*nu*⸣ ^{URU}*an-at* KUR *su-ḫi* $^{\text{URU.d}}$[*aš-šur*]-LU*-bat*

26) NUN*-ú* EGIR*-ú šá ṣa-lam šu-a-tú ul-tú* KI*-šú i-x-*⸢x . . . x . . . ⸣*-ni-ma*

27) ⸢*man*⸣*-nu lu* AŠ SAḪAR.ḪI.A *i-kát-ta-mu lu* AŠ É Á.⸢SÁG⸣ [xx] *u-še-ra-be*

28) MU *šárru* EN*-ia u* MU *šaṭ-ri i-pa-ši-ṭu-ma* MU*-šú i-šaṭ-ṭar aš-šur* AD ⸢DINGIR.MEŠ⸣

29) *li-ru-ur-šu-ma* NUMUN*-šú* MU*-šú* AŠ KUR *li-ḫal-li-qu* ^{d}[AMAR⸣.UTU[. . .]

30) ⸢*šárru*⸣*-su lis-kip* ŠU.II IGI.MEŠ*-šú ka-mu-su lim-nu-šú* ^{d}UTU DI.KU$_5$ ⸢AN *u* KI⸣

31) *ik-le-tú ina* KUR-⸣*šú li-šab-ši-ma a+a*$^!$ *i-ṭu-lu a-ḫa-*⸢*meš* ^{d}IŠKUR⸣

32) *gú-gal* AN*-e* KI-⸢*tim*⸣ MU *lis-su-uḫ* GIM *tib e-ri-bu-u* ⸢*lit*⸣*-bi-ma*

33) *li-šam-qit* KUR*-su*

[To] Adad, the canal inspector of heaven and earth, the son of Anu, the magnificent hero, the perfect one, the mighty one in strength, foremost among the Igigi, valiant among the Anunnaki, who is enveloped in awe-inspiring light, who rides the great [days], who is covered with terrible splendor, who brings low the wicked (5)with his shining whip, who hurls the

---

[58] So Tadmor, "Note on Saba'a Stele," 47, n. 13. Unger reconstructed the signs to read KÚR.MEŠ and translates the phrase *šárru*^{MEŠ}*-ni* [KÚR.MEŠ] ⸢DAGAL⸣*-te* as "die Könige [die feindlichen, zahl]reichen" (*Reliefstele Adadniraris III*, 10–11); cf. *ARAB*, 1. §734.

[59] Unger reads ^{d}⸢Sin⸣ $^{\text{[d]}}$Šamaš (*Reliefstele Adadniraris III*, 10), while H. Genge reads ^{d}⸢AMAR⸣.UTU (*Stelen neuassyrischen Könige, Teil I, Die Keilinschriften* [Diss., Freiburg im Breisgau, 1965], 14, 117–18).

thunderbolt, the great lord, his lord; [Adad-nirari], the great king, strong king, king of the universe, king of Assyria, king without a rival, the wonderful shepherd, the exalted viceroy, whose thoughts are the raising of his hands and the giving of his offering, whose rule the great gods made beneficial as the food of life for the people of Assyria, and whose land they enlarged; son of Šamši-Adad, the strong king, king of the universe, king of Assyria, grandson of Shalmaneser, ruler of princes, destroyer of hostile lands.

In the fifth year since I magnificently sat on the royal throne, I mobilized the country, and ordered the numerous army of Assyria to campaign against Ḫatti. I crossed the Euphrates at its flood. The kings of the ⌜wide⌝ [land of Ḫatti], who in the time of Šamši-Adad, my father, had rebelled, and ⌜withheld their tribute⌝, at the command of Aššur . . . Adad, Ishtar, the gods in whom I trust, [terror] overwhelmed them and they kissed my feet. I received the heavy tribute . . . which they brought to Assyria.

I ordered a campaign against Ša-imērišu (= Aram-Damascus). [I shut up] Mariʾ in Damascus. 100 talents of gold, 1000 talents of silver . . . talents of . . . [I received].

At that time I had a stela of my royal self made. The power of my might, the deeds of my hands, I inscribed thereon. I set it up in Zabanni . . . .

The inscription (?) of Nergal-ereš , governor of Nimit . . . , Apku, Marê (?), Raṣappa, Qatni, Dūr-karpati (?), opposite Kar-Aššur-naṣir-apli, Sirqu, the lands of Lakê and Ḫindanu, the city of Anat, the land of Suḫi, and the city of [Aššur]-iṣbat.

The future prince who shall remove this stela from its place, whoever shall cover it with dust or shall bring it into a house of "disease of the face (?)," who shall blot out the name of the king, my lord, or my written name, and write his own name (in their stead), may Aššur, the father of the gods, curse him, may he destroy his seed, his name, in the land. May Marduk . . . overthrow his kingdom, counting out for him hands and eyes that are "bound." May Šamaš, judge of heaven and earth, bring darkness into his land, . . . together. May Adad, the canal inspector of heaven and earth, destroy his name, may he come on like a locust swarm and bring low his land.

The Sabaʾa Stela is a composite text and, like the el-Rimah Stela, can be categorized as a "summary inscription." After an extended prologue which extols the deity Adad and the king Adad-nirari III by naming their epithets (lines 1–11a), the inscription describes a campaign that Adad-nirari undertook in Ḫattî (lines 11b–18a) and a second campaign or a second phase of the same campaign against Aram-Damascus (lines 18b–20). To commemorate those achievements, Nergal-ereš, a governor of one of the provinces of Assyria, set up the stela.

The chronological statement *ina ḫamušti šatti <šá> ina kussê šarrūti rabiš ūšibūma* in lines 11b–12a has evoked a great deal of scholarly discussion. Should this statement be taken literally and thus lines 11b–20 read as an excerpt from the royal annals? Does it relate only to the campaign against Ḫattî, or include the campaign against Aram-Damascus as well? How does it relate to the eponym chronicle? How one interprets this chronological reference depends upon how one understands Adad-nirari's western campaigns mentioned in his other inscriptions and the eponym list and the relative chronology of the reign of king Joash of Israel (see below).

At this point, it is important to note only that the inscription relates that Adad-nirari mobilized the Assyrian army for a campaign in the west (Ḫatti) in his fifth year. It goes on to describe Adad-nirari's reassertion of authority over some states which had rebelled against his father, Šamši-Adad, and withheld their tribute. The text, in particular, refers to Adad-nirari's campaign to Aram-Damascus, where he suppressed its king, Mariʾ, in Damascus and collected a large tribute from him. As with the two preceding stelae already dealt with, the question remains whether the campaign against Aram-Damascus was a second campaign or the second phase of the same western campaign.

F. The Sheikh Hammad Stela

The Sheikh Hammad Stela (BM 131124) is a fragment of a summary inscription found in 1879 near the mound of Sheikh Hammad by H. Rassam. The text was not published until 1973 by A. R. Millard and H. Tadmor.[60] Rassam had initially thought that the stela belonged to Shalmaneser III (II in Rassam's designation),[61] but Millard and Tadmor noticed its similarities with the el-Rimah Stela and identified it as belonging to Adad-nirari III. The nine lines of text preserved have been restored and read by Millard and Tadmor as follows:[62]

1) [^{I}10-ÉRIN.TÁḪ *šárru* GAL-*u šárru*] *dan-nu šar*$_4$ ŠÚ *šar*$_4$ KUR *aš-šur* A ^{I}*šam-ši*-10
2) [*šar*$_4$ ŠÚ *šar*$_4$ KUR *aš-šur* A ^{I}SIL]IM.MA-*nu* MAŠ *šar*$_4$ *kib-rat* 4-*ti*
3) [AŠ *qí-bit* ^{d}*aš-šur* ^{GIŠ}GIGIR.MEŠ ÉRIN.MEŠ K]I.KALxBAD *lu-u ad-ki a-na* KUR *ḫat-t*[*i*]
4) [DIŠ DU *lu aq-bi* ^{Í}]^{D}A.RAT AŠ *mi-li-šá e-bir*
5) [. . . DIŠ ^{URU}*pa-qi-ra-ḫu*]-*bu-na*[63] *a-ta-rad* ^{I}*a-tar-šum-k*[*i*]

---

[60]Millard and Tadmor, "Adad-nirari III in Syria," 57–64.

[61]H. Rassam, *Asshur and the Land of Nimrod* (Cincinnati: Curts and Jennings/New York: Eaton and Mains, 1897), 311–12.

[62]Millard and Tadmor, "Adad-nirari III in Syria," 58.

[63]So Pazarcik Stela, line 12 (Donbaz, "Two Neo-Assyrian Stelae," 9).

6) [^{URU}*ar-pa-da-a-a u šárru*^{MEŠ}]*-ni šá* KUR [*ḫat*]*-ti šá i-si-ḫu-*[*m*]*a*
7) [DIŠ Á*-šu-nu it-tak-lu-ma p*]*u-ul-ḫi me-lam-me šá aš-šur* E[N-ia]
8) [*is-ḫu-pu-šu-nu-ma* . . . AŠ *iš-t*]*e-et* MU.AN.NA KUR *ḫat-t*[*i*]
9) [DIŠ *si-ḫir-ti-ša* . . .] *ak*[*-šu-ud*]

[Adad-nirari, the great king,] strong [king], king of the universe, king of Assyria, son of Šamši-Adad, [the king of the universe, king of Assyria, son of Sh]almaneser, the king of the four corners: [at the command of Aššur] I mobilized [chariots, troops, and c]amps [and ordered them to campaign] against Ḫatti. I crossed the Euphrates at its flood . . . and went down [to Paqiraḫu]buna. Ataršumki [the Arpadite and the kings] of [Ḫat]ti who had rebelled and [trusted in their own strength,] the fearful splendor of Aššur my [l]ord [overwhelmed them . . . . In a sin[gle year, Ḫatti in [its totality . . .] I con[quered . . .].

Although the left side of the inscription is broken, enough of the royal names have been preserved to make the restoration and its ascription to Adad-nirari III tenable. In fact, the Pazarcik Stela from the reign of Adad-nirari (see below) makes it certain that the Sheikh Hammad Stela is an inscription of Adad-nirari. In the Sheikh Hammad inscription, in addition to describing the resubmission of the kings of Ḫatti who had revolted against his father, Šamši-Adad V, Adad-nirari identifies a certain Ataršumki among the rebel kings, who was probably the leader of the rebellion. The Pazarcik Stela also names Ataršumki of Arpad as the leader of a coalition against which Adad-nirari fought at the city of Paqiraḫubuna.[64]

G. The Scheil and Millard Fragment

This is a fragmentary stone slab, the details of whose discovery are unknown. Only ten lines of the entire inscription remain. First published by V. Scheil,[65] the inscription was edited and republished by Millard and Tadmor.[66] The following is a transliteration of the text with Millard's restoration in brackets:

1) *i-šu-ṭu ni-ir* [*bēlūti* . . .]
2) *šá* AŠ *tar-ṣi* ^{I}*šam-ši-*[*adad abīya isiḫu-ma idninu-ma*]
3) EN.MEŠ *šá* ^{ÍD}A.[RAT *ittišu ušbalkitu alāk girrīya*]
4) *iš-me-ma* ^{I}*a-tar-š*[*úm-ki ana emūq ramanišu*]
5) *it-ta-kil-ma* DIŠ *e-*[*piš qabli illik abiktašu aškun-ma*]

---

[64]Cf. Pazarcik Stela, lines 11–15 (Donbaz, "Two Neo-Assyrian Stelae," 9).

[65]V. Scheil, "Notules, XXXV. Fragment d'une inscription de Salmanasar, fils d'Aššurnaṣirapal," *RA* 14 (1917), 159–60.

[66]Millard and Tadmor, "Adad-nirari III in Syria," 60–61.

6) *uš-ma-nu-šú* TE[67]*-kim* [. . .]

7) *ni-ṣir-ti* É.[GAL-*šu alqâ* . . . [I]*ataršúmki*]

8) DUMU [I]*a-ra-me u*[*l-tu kussî šarrūtišu ušetbišu šallassu*]

9) DIŠ *la ma-ni am-ḫ*[*ur* . . .]

10) *li*-[. . .]

. . . [who] bore the yoke of lordship . . . who [had rebelled and revolted] in the time of Šamši-[Adad my father, and caused] the rulers of Eup[hrates to rebel with him,] he heard [of my approaching.] Ataršumki trusted [in his own strength and came forward to battle. I defeated him and] took away his encampment [. . . I took] the treasure of his pa[lace . . . Ataršumki,] son of Arame, [I deposed] fr[om his royal throne. His booty] beyond account [I received . . . .

This inscription is fragmentary and omits the name of the king to whom it belongs. Its ascription to Adad-nirari III is based on its similarity to the Sheikh Hammad Stela, where Ataršumki is named as a rebellious king. If Millard's restoration is accepted, then the inscription is another account of Adad-nirari's campaign against Ataršumki of Arpad, the leader of a wider regional rebellion.[68]

In his campaign, Adad-nirari suppressed the rebellion, defeated Ataršumki, looted his palace, removed him from the throne, and carried away a huge booty. Unfortunately, the fragment does not provide any chronological data to help date this campaign and much of its content has been reconstructed.

H. The Pazarcik (Kahramanmaraş) Stela

The Pazarcik Stela was discovered at the village of Kizkapanli in the Pazarcik area (modern day Kahramanmaraş) in Turkey. This stela, which functioned as a boundary stone, contains two inscriptions. The obverse is an inscription of Adad-nirari III, while the reverse is an inscription from the reign of Shalmaneser IV.

---

[67]Scheil suggests that the sign TE stands for KAR ("Fragment d'une inscription de Salmanasar," 159–60), and should be read as *ekēmu*. Scheil is probably correct as it can be easily seen how the mistake could have arisen from a scribal error. Cf. the similar phrase BÀD *uš-ma-ni-šu e-kim-šú* in an inscription of Shalmaneser III, *KAH* 30, line 31.

[68]If Millard's reconstruction is correct, Arpad's relation with Assyria would have been one that changed rapidly, from rebellion in the reign of Šamši-Adad V to submission in the pre-805 BCE years of Adad-nirari III to rebellion against Adad-nirari in 805–804 BCE. It is to be noted, however, that Millard's reconstruction is purely conjectural and may not be accurate. For instance, while Millard's reconstruction suggests that the rebellion of western rulers during the reign of Šamši-Adad was led by Ataršumki, the king of Arpad, no such evidence may be derived from the Saba᾿a Stela. Millard's reconstruction must, therefore, be viewed with caution.

The stela must have originally been set up by Adad-nirari (or his *turtānu*, Šamši-ilu) as a "boundary stone" to mark the border between Kummuḫ and Gurgum. The stela was reinscribed on the reverse during the reign of Shalmaneser IV (782–773 BCE) and given to Ušpilulume, king of Kummuḫ, by Šamši-ilu, the *turtānu*, as a sign of Assyrian commitment to helping Kummuḫ protect its boundary. The stela is presently housed at the Kahramanmaraş Museum in Turkey. For the present, it is the inscription on the obverse that demands our attention. The inscription, consisting of twenty-three lines, is well-preserved.[69]

1) *ta-ḫu-ma šá* ^{I}10-ÉRIN.TÁḪ *šar*$_4$ KUR *aš-šur*
2) A ^{I}*šam-ši*-10 *šar*$_4$ KUR *aš-šur*
3) ^{SAL}*sa-am-mu-ra-mat* MUNUS.É.GAL
4) *šá* ^{I}*šam-ši*-10 *šar*$_4$ KUR *aš-šur*
5) AMA ^{I}10-ÉRIN.TÁḪ *šárru* KAL *šar*$_4$ KUR *aš-šur*
6) *kal-lat* ^{Id}SILIM.MA-*nu*-MAŠ
7) *šar*$_4$ *kib-*<*rat*> 4-*ti* AŠ *u*$_4$*-me* ^{I}*uš-pi-lu-lu-me*
8) *šar*$_4$ ^{URU}*ku-mu-ḫa-a-a a-na* ^{I}10-ÉRIN.TÁḪ *šar*$_4$ KUR *aš-šur*
9) ^{SAL}*sa-am-mu-ra-mat* MUNUS.É.GAL
10) ^{ÍD}*pu-rat-tú ú-še-bi-ru-u-ni*
11) ^{I}*a-tar-šum-ki* A ^{I}*ad-ra-a-me* ^{URU}*ár-pa-da-a-a*
12) *a-di* 8 *šárru*^{MEŠ}*-ni šá* KI-*šú* AŠ ^{URU}*pa-qira-ḫu-bu-na*
13) *si-dir-ta-šú-nu* KI-*šú-nu am-taḫ-iṣ uš-ma-na-šú-nu*
14) *e-kim*[70]*-šú-nu-ti a-na šu-zu-ub* ZI.MEŠ-*šú-nu*
15) *e-li-ú* AŠ MU.AN.NA *šá-a-te*
16) *ta-ḫu-mu šú-a-tú* AŠ *bir-ti* ^{I}*uš-pi-lu-lu-me*
17) *šar*$_4$ ^{URU}*ku-mu-ḫa-a-a* AŠ *bir-ti* ^{I}*qa-al-pa-ru-da*[71]
18) A ^{I}*pa-la-lam šar*$_4$ ^{URU}*gúr-gu-ma-a-a ú-še-lu-ni*
19) *man-nu šá* <TA> ŠU-*at* ^{I}*uš-pi-lu-lu-me*
20) DUMU.MEŠ-*šú* DUMU.DUMU.MEŠ-*šú e-ki-mu*
21) *aš-šur* ^{d}AMAR.UTU ^{d}IŠKUR ^{d}30 ^{d}UTU
22) *a-na di-ni-šú lu la i-za-zu*
23) *ik-kib aš-šur* DINGIR-*ia* ^{d}30 *a-šib* ^{URU}KASKAL

The boundary stone of Adad-nirari, king of Assyria, son of Šamši-Adad, king of Assyria, (and of) Sammu-rāmat, the palace-woman of Šamši-

[69]See Donbaz, "Two Neo-Assyrian Stelae," 8–9.

[70]The *Winkelhaken* is missing from this sign.

[71]Donbaz has noted that this last sign is an anomaly ("Two Neo-Assyrian Stelae," 10).

Adad, king of Assyria, mother of Adad-nirari, the strong king, king of Assyria, daughter-in-law of Shalmaneser, the king of the four corners.

At that time, Ušpilulume caused me—Adad-nirari, king of Assyria, and Sammu-rāmat, the palace-woman—to cross the Euphrates. Ataršumki, son of Adramu, of the city of Arpad, together with eight kings who were with him at the city of Paqiraḫubuna, I fought a pitched battle with them. I took away from them their camp. To save their lives they dispersed.

In this year, this boundary stone was set up between Ušpilulume, king of the Kummuḫites, and Qalparuda, son of Palalam, king of the Gurgumites.

Whoever takes it away from the hand of Ušpilulume, his sons, or his grandsons, may Aššur, Marduk, Adad, Sin, and Šamaš not defend (him) at his court case. Abomination of Aššur, my god, and Sin who dwells in Ḫarran.

The inscription begins by identifying the king who authorized this "boundary stone," including a brief genealogy as well as the identity of his mother, Sammu-rāmat (= Semiramis), who must have been an important queen-mother. Besides noting that the boundary stone was set up to settle a border dispute between Ušpilulume, king of Kummuḫ, and Qalparuda, king of Gurgum, the inscription recalls a battle that Adad-nirari fought with Ataršumki, king of Arpad, and eight allies. According to the text, this campaign was carried out in response to the bidding of Ušpilulume, who must have been an ally of Adad-nirari. Since importance is placed on the inscription as a boundary stone, the background of the campaign was probably that an anti-Assyrian coalition, headed by Arpad, was brewing in the west, especially in northern Syria and Anatolia. An attempt was made by the coalition to force Ušpilulume of Kummuḫ, who had chosen to remain loyal to Assyria, to join the coalition. To put down the anti-Assyrian alliance, Adad-nirari conducted a campaign in the west, thereby preventing Kummuḫ from suffering any loss of territory.

That a western coalition, most probably anti-Assyrian, was in existence during this period is supported by the Zakkur Stela.[72] Specifically, the inscription describes a military expedition led by Bar-Hadad of Aram-Damascus against Zakkur, king of Hamath and Luᶜaš. The alliance consisted of sixteen states[73] which included Damascus, Arpad, Que, Umq, Gurgum, Samᵓal, Melid,

---

[72]For the text see *KAI*, no. 202 and for text and translation, see *TSSI*, 2. 8–13. Much has been written on this inscription. For bibliography, see Fitzmyer and Kaufman, *Aramaic Bibliography*, 13–14.

[73]So the reconstruction of J. C. L. Gibson in *TSSI*, 2. 8. The number is actually uncertain. The Aramaic text reads עשר . . . ש. E. G. H. Kraeling reconstructed the number as "seventeen" (*Aram and Israel* [New York: Columbia University Press, 1918], 99–100).

two kings who could no longer be identified because the stela is broken, and seven others who were not named. The king of Arpad is given as ברגש (Bar-guš = Bit-Agusi), which is the dynastic name rather than the name of the reigning monarch, Ataršumki, who appears in previously discussed Assyrian sources. The coalition laid siege to Hadrach by building a wall and a moat around it. Zakkur claims in the inscription that upon praying to Baalšamayn, Hadrach was spared from falling into the hands of the coalition. How the siege was broken, however, is not described and cannot be determined from the text.

The Zakkur text offers important clues to western politics of the time. First, the inscription reveals a strong regionalism in the west, particularly in Syria and western Anatolia. This coalition was almost certainly anti-Assyrian as had been the coalition in the mid-ninth century BCE. The seven states that were not named were most probably states subservient to Aram-Damascus. Arpad, listed immediately after Aram-Damascus, was probably a major participant in the coalition and a leader of the northern Syrian and Anatolian states.[74] This thesis is supported by the Pazarcik Stela (lines 11–15) which mentions Ataršumki (= ברגש in the Zakkur Stela) at the head of an alliance of nine kingdoms. It is noteworthy that Kummuḫ does not appear to be a member of the coalition (although it could have been one of the two states missing from the lacunae). If the Zakkur Stela dates from the same period as the Pazarcik Stela, then it is understandable why Kummuḫ was not involved in the coalition.[75] Gurgum, the other party involved in the border dispute with Kummuḫ on the Pazarcik Stela, is mentioned in the Zakkur Stela as a participant in the coalition. It makes sense, therefore, that the border dispute was adjudicated by the Assyrians on Kummuḫ's behalf over against Gurgum.

Second, the military campaign launched against Zakkur by the anti-Assyrian coalition suggests that Hamath was subject to Assyria during this time. It was noted in the previous chapter that with the usurpation of Hazael in Aram-Damascus, the anti-Assyrian coalition which was successful in preventing Shalmaneser's advance into Syria-Palestine in the mid-ninth century BCE collapsed. Hamath, a co-leader in this coalition, reversed its policy

---

[74]So already Hawkins, "Neo-Hittite States," 403. Arpad probably participated as co-leader of the coalition with Aram-Damascus in the same way Hamath did in the mid-ninth century (cf. Pitard, *Ancient Damascus*, 172–73).

[75]Cf. Hawkins, "Neo-Hittite States," 400; also *idem*, "Von Kummuh nach Kommagene," *Antike Welt* 6 (1975), 8–9.

and submitted to Assyria. In all likelihood, Hamath had remained loyal to Assyria since the time of Hazael's usurpation of the throne in Damascus. This siege of Hadrach was therefore carried out by the new coalition in an attempt to force Zakkur to join the alliance against Assyria. With Lu^{c}aš and Hamath remaining pro-Assyrian, a major geographical gap between Arpad and Damascus would have weakened the coalition front against the Assyrians. With the strengthening of the Assyrians under Adad-nirari, the western coalition of north Syrian and Anatolian states was attempting to involve the entire region in a strong anti-Assyrian stance. Before this reassertion of Assyrian influence in the west, the pro-Assyrian policy of Hamath had not been a cause for contention.

Third, while the Zakkur Stela reveals Aram-Damascus's influence in the region during this period, it also indicates the weakening of its power after its zenith under Hazael, vis-à-vis its inability to force, let alone coerce, Hamath and Lu^{c}aš into joining the anti-Assyrian coalition, as Hamath had done in the mid-ninth century BCE.

Finally, the coalition's siege of Hadrach was most probably lifted in association with Adad-nirari's campaign in the west, noted not only in the Pazarcik Stela but also in other inscriptions as well. The date for this campaign will be dealt with in the following section.

III. SYNOPSIS

A. History of Interpretation

Scholars generally agree, on the basis of the eponym list's reference to Arpad, that the suppression of the north Syrian coalition led by Ataršumki of Arpad occurred in 805 BCE. But there is wide disagreement regarding the course of Adad-nirari's early military activity in the west, and especially the date of his campaign against Damascus and his personal receipt of tribute from Joash of Israel and the Phoenician states. Several dates have been proposed based on the interpretation of two factors: (1) how the chronological datum "in the fifth year" of the Saba$^{\supset}$a Stela is interpreted; and (2) the particular chronological scheme adopted for the reign of Joash.

Some scholars have tended to discount the chronological datum of the Saba᾿a Stela, the latest being Pitard, who writes:

> Once it is accepted that the reference to the fifth year has little or no chronological value, there is nothing *a priori* to prevent assigning the campaign to any year in which a western campaign occurred.[76]

Such has indeed been done. Dates of 803, 802, 798, and 796 BCE have been proposed by different scholars.

Lipiński[77] opts for a date of 803 BCE. He discounts 805 BCE because that was the year Adad-nirari campaigned in northern Syria, and in particular against Arpad (according to the eponym list). Agreeing with Brinkman,[78] he argues that the campaign of 802 BCE "to the sea" refers to the coastal region in southern Babylonia. He further contends that the campaign of 796 BCE "to Manṣuate" should be associated with the Zakkur inscription and not the el-Rimah Stela.[79] Therefore, the only viable date is 803 BCE. Lipiński supports his dating by noting that the *limmu* for 803 BCE was Nergal-ereš, governor of Raṣappa, who dedicated the el-Rimah Stela to Adad-nirari. Moreover, Baᶜli, which he identifies with Baᶜli-ra᾿ši, is listed as the destination for that same year. Lipiński suggests that Joash became a coregent with his father, Jehoahaz, in 805 BCE. When Jehoahaz died in 803 BCE, Joash paid tribute to Adad-nirari, the "savior" who delivered Israel from the yoke of Damascus (2 Kgs 13:5).

Jepsen,[80] Soggin,[81] and Donner[82] all argue that the campaign during which Adad-nirari subjugated Damascus and received tribute from Joash of Israel should be associated with that of 802 BCE, "to the sea" of the eponym list, assuming that it refers to the Mediterranean Sea.[83] Furthermore, they all follow Begrich's chronological scheme[84] in which Joash's reign is calculated from

---

[76]Pitard, *Ancient Damascus*, 164–65.

[77]Lipiński "Ben-Hadad II," 157–73.

[78]See n. 23 above.

[79]Lipiński "Assyrian Campaign to Manṣuate," 393-99.

[80]A. Jepsen, "Ein neuer Fixpunkt für the Chronologie der israelitischen Könige?" *VT* 20 (1970), 359–61.

[81]J. A. Soggin, "Ein ausserbiblisches Zeugnis für die Chronologie des Jĕhô᾿āš/Jô᾿āš, König von Israel," *VT* 20 (1970), 366–68.

[82]H. Donner, "Adadnirari III," 57.

[83]The association of the campaign against Damascus with the eponym notation "to the sea" has been followed by Bright, *History*, 256; Sader, *Les États araméens*, 267; and Briquel-Chatonnet, *Les relations*, 124–25, who dates the campaign to 803 rather than 802 BCE.

[84]J. Begrich, *Die Chronologie der Könige von Israel und Juda* (Tübingen: J. C. B. Mohr, 1929).

802–801 BCE to 787–786 BCE. Thus, Joash would have been king and could have paid tribute in 802 BCE. Jepsen suggests that Joash paid the tribute in order to ensure Assyria's support in his rebellion against Damascus at the death of Hazael.[85] Soggin, on the other hand, suggests that Joash paid the tribute in an attempt to secure the support of Assyria and to benefit from Adad-nirari's presence in Syria, since Joash was already troubled on two fronts: by Judah in the south (2 Kgs 13:12; 14:8–14), and Damascus in the north (2 Kgs 13:22–25).[86]

Page[87] dates the campaign to Damascus, during which Adad-nirari also received the tribute of Joash of Israel, to 798 BCE or later. She contends that three different Assyrian campaigns were conducted in Syria-Palestine during the reign of Adad-nirari, in 806, 802, and 798 BCE or later. She reads the Sabaʾa and el-Rimah Stelae as providing evidence for the 806 BCE campaign. Support for the 802 BCE campaign is derived from the eponym list's destination "to the sea," which she understands as the Mediterranean coast. Adopting Thiele's chronology for Joash, the beginning of whose reign is assigned to 798 BCE, Page argues that "a third expedition to Syria-Palestine must be added to those of 806 and 802, and it took place during or after 798 B.C."[88]

Tadmor,[89] Millard,[90] Miller,[91] and Pitard[92] are among the proponents of the 796 BCE date. Several arguments have been used to support this dating: (1) The reference to the "fifth year" in the Sabaʾa inscription as the date of the western campaign conflicts with that of the eponym list, which cites *man-na-a-a* (Mannai), located in the east, as the destination of the campaign. (2) If Damascus was subjugated in the same campaign that resulted in the defeat of Arpad and its coalition partners, as recorded in the Sheikh Hammad and the Scheil and Millard Fragments, one would expect that the significant double victory would have been recorded as an element in a single campaign in Adad-nirari's in-

[85]Jepsen, "Chronologie der israelitischen Könige," 360.

[86]Soggin, "Chronologie des Jĕhôʾāš," 368.

[87]Page, "Stela of Adad-nirari III," 147–49, 152–53.

[88]*Ibid.*, 149. Page's interpretation is primarily based on Thiele's chronology which she adopts, and not on any Assyrian evidence. She even failed to correlate her argument with the reference to Manṣuate in the Eponym list.

[89]In Millard and Tadmor, "Adad-nirari III in Syria," 61–64; see also Tadmor, "Historical Inscriptions," 146–48.

[90]Millard, "Adad-nirari III, Aram, and Arpad," 161–64.

[91]Miller in *HAIJ*, 292–93.

[92]Pitard, *Ancient Damascus*, 164–65.

scriptions. (3) If Damascus had been defeated in an earlier campaign, there is no reason why Adad-nirari should conduct a campaign "against Manṣuate" in 796 BCE. (4) According to the eponym list, 796 BCE was the only year that Adad-nirari reached southern Syria-Palestine, assuming Manṣuate to be located there; as such, this is the most likely occasion for Adad-nirari to have subjugated Damascus and collected tribute from Joash of Israel. (5) Regardless of the chronological scheme one adopts, the year 796 BCE as the campaign date would not create any chronological problem for the mention of Joash in the el-Rimah text.

Shea and Cody are among the few scholars who have attempted to associate the events of the various inscriptions with the reference to the fifth year in the Saba᾽a inscription. Shea[93] contends that all the inscriptions (the el-Rimah Stela, the Sheikh Hammad Stela, the Scheil and Millard Fragment, the Saba᾽a Stela, and the Calah [Nimrud] Slab) and the *limmu* reference "to Arpad" refer to the same campaign and should be dated to 805 BCE. He argues this by first linking the Sheikh Hammad Stela, the Scheil and Millard Fragment, and the eponym list on the basis of the references to Arpad. Then he connects the campaign of the Saba᾽a Stela with the campaign against Arpad. Although, according to his understanding of the eponym list, the campaign against Arpad should be placed in Adad-nirari's sixth regnal year, he nonetheless correlates it with "the fifth year" of the Saba᾽a Stela. Since the el-Rimah Stela shares with the Saba᾽a Stela a similar stylistic form and structure, the campaign noted in the el-Rimah Stela should also be dated to 805 BCE. Finally, the Calah slab "shares enough features in common" with the Saba᾽ă and el-Rimah Stelae that the western campaign mentioned in it should also be correlated. Shea then describes this campaign as a "circle tour" of Syria in which Adad-nirari suppressed the entire northern and southern Syria "in one year."[94]

Since this campaign occurred in 805 BCE, at which time Joash of Israel also paid tribute to Adad-nirari, then Joash must have been on the throne by 805 BCE. To accommodate this theory, Shea constructs a chronology for the period based on the argument that the reigns of Jehu and Jehoahaz of Israel together have been inflated by seven years. By discounting the seven years of Athaliah's reign, contending that she was acting as queen regent

---

V. H. Shea, "Adad-nirari III and Jehoash of Israel," *JCS* 30 (1978), 102–9.
bid., 110.

for Joash of Judah, and reducing the reigns of Jehu and Jehoahaz together by seven years, Shea is able to place Joash of Israel on the throne in 805 BCE.[95]

Cody,[96] also accepting "the fifth year" of the Saba'a Stela and correlating it with the reference to "in my first year"[97] of the el-Rimah Stela, dates the campaign against Damascus and the year Joash paid tribute to 805 BCE. Since the *limmu* reference to Arpad dates to Adad-nirari's sixth year, he argues, following Poebel, that the campaign of the Saba'a text was ordered in 806 BCE, but carried out only in 805 BCE.[98] To fit Joash into his proposed chronological scheme, Cody posits a coregency between Joash and his father Jehoahaz (from ca. 806 to ca. 801 or 798–797 BCE).[99]

B. Critique

There are weaknesses in the preceding proposals. (1) It is a mistake to discount totally the chronological datum, "the fifth year" in the Saba'a Stela, for whatever reason. Tadmor has contended that the Saba'a Stela inscription is not an excerpt from the royal annals, arguing that regnal formulas were written with *palû* instead of *šattu*. Nevertheless, there are at least two occurrences where *šattu* is used; compare the phrase *i-na* 4-*te ša-at-te š*[*a*] in Aššur-bêl-kala's annals[100] and the reference to Sargon II's third year of reign as his third *šattu*.[101] (2) The eponym chronicle for the fifth year of Adad-nirari refers to *man-na-a-a* (Mannai), a country located in the east, as the location of the Assyrian army at the conclusion of the new year festival of Nisan 805 BCE. It is the eponym for Adad-nirari's sixth regnal year, however, that records Arpad as the army's location at the end of the year. The data in

---

[95] *Ibid.*, 111–13.

[96] A. Cody, "A New Inscription from Tell āl-Rimaḥ and King Jehoash of Israel," *CBQ* 32 (1970), 325–40.

[97] Cody was working on Page's original translation; her revised translation reads, "in a single year" (see above, n. 39). To explain this supposed chronological discrepancy between the Saba'a and el-Rimah stelae, Cody postulates a coregency of Adad-nirari and his mother Semiramis (330), first articulated by Unger (*Reliefstele Adadniraris III*, 16–20) but already challenged by Poebel ("Assyrian King List," 81–84).

[98] Cody, "New Inscription," 329; cf. Poebel, "Assyrian King List," 84.

[99] *Ibid.*, 333–37.

[100] E. F. Weidner, "Die Annalen des Königs Aššurbêlkala von Assyrien," *AfO* 6 (1930–31), 84, part III, line 22. It is clear that *šattu* and *palû* (if the restoration of part I, line 25 is right) are used interchangably. See also Grayson, *ARI*, 2. 48–49.

[101] H. Winckler, *Die Keilinschrifttexte Sargons* I (Leipzig: E. Pfeiffer, 1889), 122.

the eponym chronicle thus makes it highly unlikely that Adad-nirari mobilized his army and conducted a western campaign across the Euphrates in his fifth year. It is, however, not unreasonable to assume that a slight scribal error has occurred in the Sabaʾa Stela, since the cuneiform signs for five (𒐊) and six (𒐋) are very close in form.[102] Allowing a probable scribal error of "the fifth year" for "the sixth year," there would be no discrepancy between the dating of the campaign against Arpad in the Sabaʾa Stela and the eponym chronicle. Thus, Pitard's contention that "the reference to the fifth year has little or no chronological value" and that "there is nothing . . . to prevent assigning the campaign to any year in which a western campaign occurred" is without much basis. (3) The Sheikh Hammad and Pazarcik Stelae and the Scheil and Millard Fragment that note the defeat of Arpad and its coalition partners were probably inscribed prior to the defeat of Damascus and the inscribing of the Sabaʾa Stela. However, Damascus's capitulation soon became the most significant victory in the entire region. Although the defeat of Arpad is hinted at in the Sabaʾa Stela, it is now overshadowed by the defeat of Damascus, and the two episodes are presented in the summary inscriptions as parts of a general rebellion. (4) To use the eponym reference to Manṣuate as an argument about the proximity of the Assyrian army to Damascus and a 796 BCE date is unconvincing. The Assyrian army could easily have moved into southern Syria in any of the years it was on campaign in the west. Moreover, the location of Manṣuate, which is written in the eponym chronicle without a determinative, in south-central Syria is not a certainty. It may not have been located in Syria-Palestine at all. (5) Arguing for a date of 802 as the year Adad-nirari suppressed Damascus and collected tribute from Joash of Israel can only be sustained if the "sea" really refers to the Mediterranean Sea. This, as Brinkman has convincingly argued, is probably not the case.

There are several specific weaknesses in the arguments of Shea and Cody. (1) Given the literary form of the inscriptions (as summary inscriptions) and their composite nature, it is difficult to sustain an argument that they all refer to a single campaign in a single year. (2) That the north Syrian rebellion was longstanding and regional in character is alluded to in the inscriptions. It is, therefore, highly unlikely for an Assyrian king to have been able

---

[102]So already noted by Hughes, *Secrets of the Times*, 196, n. 68.

to suppress northern Syria and conduct a campaign against Damascus in a single year, particularly in his first campaign to the region. Moreover, the eponym chronicle listed Ḫazazi, in the vicinity of Arpad (see above), as the location of the army in the following year (804–803 BCE). (3) Shea's attempt to reconstruct biblical chronology on the basis of Adad-nirari's inscriptions to bring it in line with Assyrian chronology is highly problematic. There is no legitimate reason to discount Athaliah's reign from the chronology of Judean rulers. (4) Admittedly, Cody was working with an earlier and mistaken translation of the el-Rimah Stela whereby he had to postulate a coregency between Adad-nirari and Semiramis. Nevertheless, to posit a coregency between Joash and his father Jehoahaz in order to date Joash's payment of tribute in 805 BCE is a serious weakness. In addition to the lack of biblical data to support such a theory, as Cody himself admits, there are no coregencies in either Israel and Judah that can be convincingly proposed and sustained,[103] contrary to what Thiele has argued.[104]

C. Reconstruction

To begin with, the eponym list provides important and perhaps the most reliable chronological information pertaining to Adad-nirari's activities in the west and should constitute the basis for any reconstruction. Throughout the period between Nisan 805 and Nisan 802 BCE, the Assyrians were in the west. The location of the Assyrian army at Arpad, Ḫazazi, and Baᶜli makes it logical to see the three years as part of a long but single campaign to put down a longstanding rebellion in the region.[105] The place references in the eponym chronicle, as has been earlier demonstrated, do not report the full activity of the year but only the location of the main Assyrian army during the new year festival at the end of the year. Although the chronicle says the Assyrian army is at Arpad, Ḫazazi, and Baᶜli, this only indicates the army's location at the time of the three Akîtu festivals. Throughout the remainder of the time, the army could have campaigned widely in the region.

---

[103]See Hayes and Hooker, *New Chronology*, esp. 12.

[104]E. R. Thiele, *The Mysterious Numbers of the Hebrew Kings: A Reconstruction of the Chronology of the Kingdoms of Israel and Judah* (3d ed.; Grand Rapids: Zondervan, 1984).

[105]Cf. Hughes, *Secrets of the Times*, 196–97, who suggests that both the Sabaʾa and Rimah stelae condense the three-year conquest of northern Syria into a single campaign.

The Antakya Stela records a border agreement between Arpad and Hamath, negotiated through the *turtānu*, Šamši-ilu. This event should be dated to before the Assyrian campaign in the west in 805–802 BCE, rather than 796 BCE, as suggested by Hawkins.[106] There is no necessity to correlate this event with the eponym chronicle since the arbitration did not involve the main Assyrian army. This event, therefore, is not mentioned in the eponym chronicle. Moreover, a date of 796 BCE is too late, as Ataršumki, son of Adramu, was replaced by his son Bar-Hadad following the 805–802 BCE campaign in the west.[107] The Antakya Stela thus provides evidence of a loyal Ataršumki—not too long before he rebelled and coöperated with Aram-Damascus in leading a coalition against Assyria—on whose behalf Šamši-ilu arbitrated the border dispute with Hamath.

It has been noted in the previous chapter that during the reign of Hazael, Aram-Damascus underwent a period of expansion, particularly in the area south of Damascus. Aram-Damascus's expansion was to a certain extent assisted by a period of decline and weakness in Assyria. Although Aram-Damascus probably did not extend its territorial holdings north of Damascus,[108] its influence in the north was significant nonetheless. Evidence of this, as we have seen, comes from the Zakkur Stela, which notes that Bar-Hadad, son of Hazael, joined with Arpad to lead a coalition of north Syrian and Anatolian states against Zakkur of Hamath and Lu^{c}aš, who had remained loyal to Assyria. It is likely that the king of Arpad was none other than Ataršumki,[109] who had rebelled and joined forces with Bar-Hadad of Damascus in an attempt to force Zakkur into joining the anti-Assyrian coalition. The siege of Hadrach, therefore, most probably took place in 806–805 BCE. Adad-nirari's anticipated attack against the western regionalism precipitated the attack against Zakkur.[110]

---

[106]Hawkins, "Neo-Hittite States," 400, 403.

[107]This is the Bar-Hadad of the Melqart Stela. In the most recent study of the Melqart Stela, Puech has argued quite convincingly that the name of the father of Bar-Hadad should be reconstructed to read עתרסמן and identified with Ataršumki, king of Arpad ("Stèle de Bar-Hadad," 311–34; cf. Pitard, "Bir-Hadad of the Melqart Stela," 3–21). If the restoration of the Scheil and Millard Fragment is correct (see above, pp. 88–89), then Ataršumki was probably removed from the throne by Adad-nirari.

[108]Pitard, *Ancient Damascus*, 152–58.

[109]Contra Puech ("Stèle de Bar-Hadad," 333–34) who suggests that the king of Arpad of the Zakkur stela was Bar-Hadad of the Melqart stela. He dates the siege of Hadrach to 796 in association with the Assyrian campaign to Manṣuate.

[110]A similar situation existed in 734–733 BCE, when Ahaz of Jerusalem was attacked by an anti-Assyrian coalition during the days of Tiglath-pileser III.

The first major battle was fought against Arpad and its coalition partners. This expedition began after Nisan 805 BCE, Adad-nirari's sixth regnal year, erroneously written as the "fifth" in the Sabaʾa Stela, and the army crossed the Euphrates early in the spring when the river was at flood stage. The Sheikh Hammad and Pazarcik Stelae and the Scheil and Millard Fragment report this campaign as well. The Sheikh Hammad and Pazarcik Stelae allude to the fact that this campaign was conducted to suppress a regional rebellion under the leadership of Ataršumki, king of Arpad. The Sabaʾa Stela additionally suggests that some of the revolting kings of Ḫattî had begun rebelling and withholding their annual tribute during the reign of Šamši-Adad V, a period when Assyria was notably absent from the west. It is not possible to determine whether Arpad was among the rebellious states during the reign of Šamši-Adad V. Even if Arpad had taken advantage of Assyria's weakness to withhold tribute during the reign of Šamši-Adad, it must have renewed its allegiance to Assyria early in the reign of Adad-nirari, resulting in Assyria's help in settling its border dispute with Hamath (so the Antakya Stela). With the arrival of Adad-nirari in the district of Arpad, the siege of Hadrach was broken, as Ataršumki and his coalition had to redirect their attention to battling the Assyrians. If our understanding of the eponym list and the Sabaʾa Stela is correct, then Assyrian military activity against Arpad and its allies must have taken about two years, as the eponym list records the location of the army in that area for two consecutive years (Arpad and Ḫazazi).

According to the Calah Slab, Israel, Tyre, Sidon, Edom, and Philistia paid tribute to Adad-nirari. It is possible that the whole of central and southern Syria-Palestine had been under the domination of Aram-Damascus prior to the death of Hazael (probably in 806 BCE).[111] In the estimation of Pitard, Israel, Judah, and Philistia—and probably also Ammon, Moab, and Edom—were all subjugated by Hazael.[112] Evidence for the subjugation of Israel comes from 2 Kgs 10:32–33. The loss of Israelite territory that began during the reign of Jehu continued into the reign of Jehoahaz (cf. 2 Kgs 13:25). Pitard surmizes that Hazael encroached into

[111] Millard and Tadmor, "Adad-nirari III in Syria," 64.

[112] Pitard, *Ancient Damascus*, 151–52. See his map on p. 157 that shows the extent of Hazael's control. See also Miller in J. A. Dearman and J. M. Miller, "The Melqart Stele and the Ben-Hadads of Damascus: Two Studies," *PEQ* 115 (1983), 101; Ephʿal and Naveh, "Hazael's Booty Inscription," 192–200; Ahlström, *History of Ancient Palestine*, 607–10.

Israelite territory "to such an extent that Israel must have been virtually, if not in actuality, a vassal to Aram."[113] Philistia's suppression by Hazael is attested by 2 Kgs 12:17a, which reads: "At that time, Hazael, king of Aram, went up and fought against Gath and captured it." It is likely that other Philistine cities met the same fate. Judah, at the time ruled by Jehoash, was not spared either. 2 Kings 12:17b–18 notes that when Hazael pushed against Jerusalem, Jehoash had to empty the treasures of the temple and the palace and to offer them as tribute to Hazael, thereby submitting to Aram-Damascus's hegemony. Hazael's domination of Syria-Palestine probably extended as far south as the port-city of Elath.[114] Evidence for this is derived from 2 Kgs 16:6:

בעת ההיא השיב רצין מלך־ארם את־אילת לארם וינשל את־
היהודים מאילות וארמים באו אילת וישבו שם עד היום הזה

At that time, Rezin, king of Aram, restored Elath to Aram and drove out the Judeans from Elath. Then the Arameans came to Elath and have dwelt there to this day.

There is little consensus on how the verse should be read and interpreted. Most would eliminate רצין from v. 6a and emend ארם to ארום throughout the rest of the verse. The verse would then read: "At that time the king of Edom recovered Elath for Edom, and drove the Judeans from Elath; and the Edomites came to Elath, where they live to this day."[115] On the other hand, there are translations that read "Aram/Arameans" throughout the verse,[116] "Aram" in v. 6a, and "Edomites" in v. 6b.[117] Most recently, Irvine suggests translating v. 6 as "At that time Rezin the king of Syria restored Elath to Edom and drove out the Judeans from Elath. And the Edomites entered Elath and have lived there unto this day."[118] Irvine's translation is, however, based on historical conclusions rather than textual evidence. The only support for any emendation is in v. 6b. While the *ketib* reads וארמים, the *qere* reads ואדמים.

[113]Pitard, *Ancient Damascus*, 151.

[114]On Elath, see J. F. Zorn, "Elath," *ABD*, 2. 429–30; see also the related article by M. Lubetski, "Ezion-geber," *ABD*, 2. 723–26.

[115]So NRSV. Cf. NEB, JB, TEV; also Montgomery, *Kings*, 458; Cogan and Tadmor, *II Kings*, 184; Gray, *I & II Kings*, 632; Jones, *1 and 2 Kings*, 2. 535–36; E. Würthwein, *Die Bücher der Könige* (2 vols.; ATD 11; Göttingen: Vanderhoeck and Ruprecht, 1984), 2. 386.

[116]See particularly KJV and NASB. So also T. R. Hobbs, *2 Kings* (WBC 13; Waco: Word Books, 1985), 207.

[117]So NIV and NJPSV.

[118]S. A. Irvine, *Isaiah, Ahaz, and the Syro-Ephraimitic Crisis* (SBLDS 123; Atlanta: Scholars Press, 1990), 85.

Other than that, there is no textual support either for the elimination of רצין or for the change from ארם to ארום. Thus, it is best to stay with the MT and emend only the *ketib* to the *qere*, and read:

בעת ההיא השיב רצין מלך־ארם את־אילת לארם וינשל את־
היהודים מאילות ואדומים באו אילת וישבו שם עד היום הזה

At that time, Rezin, king of Aram, restored Elath to Aram and drove out the Judeans from Elath. Then the Edomites came to Elath and have dwelt there to this day.

Although the context of the verse is a much later period, namely, the reign of Rezin (mid-eighth century BCE), the verse provides evidence that Elath was in the hands of Aram-Damascus at an earlier period before it was restored to Israelite and Judean control in the time of Jeroboam II and then returned to Aramean control. The reign of Hazael seems to be the most logical period for Aram-Damascus to have had control of Elath, that is, at a time when Aram-Damascus was at its height of expansion in the south. Moreover, with the control of Elath, Hazael would have had direct control and domination of the Red Sea trade originating from Elath. There is no evidence that Hazael subjugated Tyre and Sidon. It is likely that with the breakdown of relations with Israel following Jehu's coup, the Phoenicians established relations with Hazael. With Aram-Damascus directly controlling Transjordan and the port of Elath, Tyre and Sidon would thus have continued to have access to the trade route via the Red Sea to the Arabian and African coasts.

Judah, although not mentioned in the Calah Slab, was probably regarded as vassal or a subordinate part of Israel as in the earlier period.[119] The payment of tribute to Adad-nirari from states under Aram-Damascus's domination—Israel, Edom, and Philistia—would have constituted an act of rebellion against Damascus and an acknowledgement of homage to Assyria. The "tribute" of Tyre and Sidon, while it may not have been an act of rebellion against Aram-Damascus, was also a recognition of Assyria's strength and influence in the affairs of Syria-Palestine. This "tribute" may again have been, as it was on previous occasions, more diplomatic gift than submission to Assyria's suzerainty. The tribute or diplomatic gift from these states could have been paid at

---

[119]Moab was probably a subordinate to Aram-Damascus and without a king. Amos 2:3 (from the mid-eighth century BCE) speaks of a שפט rather than a מלך ruling over Moab. Cf. Amos 1:15 and 2:1 where both Ammon and Edom were ruled by a מלך.

anytime when the Assyrian army was in the west, but in all probabilty, before Damascus was subdued by Adad-nirari. Although Israel and Tyre and Sidon were noted to have paid tribute or presented diplomatic gifts at the same time, there is insufficient evidence to suggest that they were allies. On the contrary, strained relations between the Israelites and the Phoenicians that began during the reign of Jehu probably continued into the reigns of Jehoahaz and Joash.

The battle against Damascus probably began after Nisan 803 BCE when the army moved from Ḫazazi. The subjugation of Damascus could have taken place between Nisan 803 and Nisan 802 BCE, because by the end of the year, the main army was reported to have been located at Baᶜli. Joash of Israel could have delivered his tribute personally to Adad-nirari after Nisan 803 BCE when the Assyrian army was in southern Syria, that is, during Joash's first regnal year on the Israelite throne (804–803 BCE).[120] Tyre, Sidon, Edom, and Philistia could have done the same. The payment of tribute by a vassal or the contribution of a diplomatic gift by a cooperative state was an annual affair and was only noted in the royal inscriptions when the king was present in the region to collect the tribute personally. Tribute sent directly to the Assyrian royal court by a vassal would not have been reported, as a rule, in the king's annals or other inscriptions.

Since the states dominated by Damascus had rebelled and submitted to the Assyrians, Damascus was probably left to fight the Assyrians on its own. The defeat of Damascus was an important victory not only because it weakened Aram-Damascus but also because it reaffirmed Assyria's influence in Syria-Palestine after a period of absence. No wonder it eventually overshadowed the defeat of Arpad as the most significant victory in the west.

In the aftermath of a weakened Aram-Damascus—which had suffered not only from the failure of the Bar-Hadad-led coalition against Zakkur of Hamath and Luᶜaš (so Zakkur Stela) but also in the defeat of Damascus (so especially the Calah Slab and the Sabaʾa Stela)—Joash of Israel soon moved to reclaim Israelite territories lost to Aram-Damascus (cf. 2 Kgs 13:25). It is in this context that the accounts of the three battles between Aram-Damascus and Israel in 1 Kings 20 and 22 should be located.[121] These

---

[120]See Hayes and Hooker, *New Chronology*, 47–48, for the reign of Joash of Israel.

[121]While most scholars who associate 1 Kings 20 and 22 with the period of the Jehu dynasty identify the king of Israel in those accounts as Joash, in concurrence with 2 Kgs

battles with Israel hastened the decline of Aram-Damascus and eventually led to the temporary demise of its domination in southern Syria and Palestine.

If Aram-Damascus was dealt with in 803–802 BCE, what then does one do with the Manṣuate campaign in 796–795 BCE, which most scholars associate with the defeat of Damascus? Two solutions may be offered. First, as has been noted, the location of Manṣuate remains a problem. The possibility that Manṣuate was not located in Syria cannot be ruled out. If that be the case, then there is little evidence that Adad-nirari mounted another campaign in the west after 805–802 BCE. Second, even if Manṣuate can be conclusively located in the Beqa^{c} Valley of Lebanon, the army's presence could have been merely a show of Assyrian force in the west without any major battle being fought. Or, it could have been an expedition to collect timber from the forests of Lebanon for building purposes. Adad-nirari had done the same at the conclusion of his 805–802 BCE campaign (cf. the el-Rimah Stela, lines 10–11).

After a period of domination by Aram-Damascus during the reign of Hazael, when states in Syria-Palestine functioned and related to Assyria independently, if at all, a new phase of political relations in Syria-Palestine is discernible. This period witnesses the resurgence of a north Syrian-Anatolian coalition led by Aram-Damascus, sparked by the succession of Ben-Hadad to the throne of Damascus. According to the Zakkur Stela, sixteen states were involved in the coalition; none of the states named, however, was from south of Damascus. Arpad, under Ataršumki, was a coleader of the coalition (as evident also from the Pazarcik Stela, obverse). An unsuccessful attempt was made by the coalition to force Zakkur, the king of Hamath and Lu^{c}aš, to join the coalition in order to create a strong united front against Assyria throughout Anatolia and all of Syria.

This phase of political cooperation did not last long. Adad-nirari mounted a major campaign in 805–802 BCE to crush the rebellion. In the process, Arpad was captured and Aram-Damascus considerably weakened.

During this phase of political and commercial relations, Israel, under Jehoahaz, remained antagonistic to Aram-Damascus. In

13:25 (so, e.g., Jepsen, "Israel und Damaskus," 157; Whitley, "House of Omri," 144–45; Pitard, *Ancient Damascus*, 122–24), Miller argues that it was Jehoahaz ("Omride Wars," 442–43; *HAIJ*, 300).

fact, Aram-Damascus's aggression toward Israel had continued during the reign of Ben-Hadad (2 Kgs 13:3). However, during Adad-nirari's 805–802 BCE campaign, Israel must have received a reprieve from the aggression of Aram-Damascus. 2 Kings 13:5 noted that "YHWH gave Israel a savior," who is most probably to be identified with Adad-nirari.[122] On the other hand, with Aram-Damascus continuing to control the trade routes, and in particular the seaport of Elath, Tyre probably had good relations with Aram-Damascus, at least commercially. There is no evidence—direct or indirect—to suggest that the relations between the Israelites and the Phoenicians were anything but strained.

[122]Contra J. Briend, "Jeroboam II sauveur d'Israël," *Mélanges bibliques et orientaux en l'honneur de M. Henri Cazelles*, ed. A. Caquot and M. Delcor (AOAT 212; Neukirchen-Vluyn: Neukirchener Verlag, 1981), 41–49.

CHAPTER THREE

THE REIGNS OF SHALMANESER IV, ASHUR-DAN III, AND ASHUR-NIRARI V

I. INTRODUCTION

The sources for the reigns of Shalmaneser IV (782–773 BCE), Ashur-dan III (772–755 BCE), and Ashur-nirari V (754–745 BCE)—and thus for any portrayal of the political relations of states in southern Syria-Palestine—are scanty, with very few inscriptional materials being available. The eponym chronicle—itself sketchy—is the main source for tracing the activities of these kings.

A weakening of the central Assyrian administration characterizes this period. This weakening of the central government is illustrated by the lack of source material and royal inscriptions.[1] The decline of the authority and influence of the central administration during the first half of the eighth century BCE was caused by two major factors. First, there was the diffusion of authority and power into the hands of strong provincial governors, begun already in the reign of Adad-nirari III. These governors included such figures as Nergal-ereš, the governor of Raṣappa and Ḫindanu—provinces along the middle Euphrates—who was responsible for setting up the el-Rimah and Sabaʾa Stelae of Adad-nirari.[2] These stelae enumerate the regions under his jurisdiction and the settlements founded by him.[3] Two other officials of significance were Bēl-tarṣi-iluma, the governor of Calah, who set up

[1]So already Grayson, "Ashur-dan II to Ashur-nirari III," 276–79; cf. Saggs, *Assyria*, 82–84. For inscriptional material from this period, see W. Schramm, *Einleitung in die assyrischen Königsinschriften. Zweiter Teil: 934–722 v. Chr.* (Handbuch der Orientalistik I/5; Leiden/Köln: E. J. Brill, 1973), 120–24.

[2]See chapter two above.

[3]On Nergal-ereš, see e.g., D. Oates, "The Excavations at Tell al Rimah, 1967," *Iraq* 30 (1968), 128–32; J. N. Postgate, *Neo-Assyrian Grants and Decrees* (Studia Pohl, ser. maior 1; Rome: Pontifical Biblical Institute, 1969), 115–17; Tadmor, "Historical Inscriptions," 148; Grayson, "Ashur-dan II to Ashur-nirari V," 273–74; cf. Schramm, *Einleitung*, 113.

two inscribed statues in honor of Adad-nirari and Semiramis,[4] and Bēl-ḫarrān-bēlu-uṣur, the *nāgir ekalli*, who built a city, named it after himself, and subsequently set up a stela to commemorate its founding.[5] Perhaps the most important official was Šamši-ilu, the *turtānu* and governor of Ḫatti, who not only had a long career but also "the virtual authority of a king,"[6] and who is known to have arbitrated border disputes between rival kingdoms and to have led major campaigns conducted with the main Assyrian military force.[7]

A second factor that led to the weakening of the central Assyrian government was Urartian expansion from their territory around Lake Van to the southeast toward Media and to the southwest toward Anatolia and Syria-Palestine. Urartu[8] had long been a major Assyrian opponent, struggling with Assyria for control of trade routes.[9] Urartu was at its height of expansion during the reign of Argishti I (about 786–764 BCE).[10] Early in his rule, Argishti conducted numerous campaigns to expand his control and influence. This brought Urartu into direct confrontation with Assyria, putting the latter on the defensive. The eponym chronicle noted that several campaigns were carried out against the Urartians between 781–780 and 774–773 BCE. One of Šamši-ilu's inscriptions suggests that it was he, rather than the Assyrian king, who led these campaigns against the Urartians.[11] During the reign of Argishti, Urartu

> commanded not only the important trade routes leading from Mesopotamia and Iran to the rich metal-working areas of Kulkhai (Colchis) and the Aras

---

[4]*ARAB*, 1. §§744–45.

[5]*ARAB*, 1. §§823–27.

[6]Grayson, "Ashur-dan II to Ashur-nirari V," 278.

[7]See Antakya and Pazarcik stelea (Donbaz, "Two Neo-Assyrian Stelae"); cf. also Hawkins, "Neo-Hittite States," 404–5.

[8]For studies on Urartu, see, e.g., B. B. Piotrovsky, *The Ancient Civilization of Urartu* (New York/London: Cowles/Cresset, 1969); H.-J. Kellner, *Urartu. Ein wiederentdeckter Rivale Assyriens* (Prähistorische Staatssammlung München, Museum für Vor- und Frühgeschichte, Ausstellungskataloge 2; Munich: Buchdruckwerkstätte Pichlmayr, 1976); P. E. Zimansky, *Ecology and Empire: The Structure of the Urartian State* (SAOC 41; Chicago: Oriental Institute, 1985).

[9]See R. D. Barnett, "Urartu," *CAH*^{2} III/1, 314–71, esp. 333–56; H. W. F. Saggs, *The Greatness that was Babylon: A Survey of the Ancient Civilization of the Tigris-Euphrates Valley* (rev. ed.; London: Sidgwick & Jackson, 1988), 98–100; L. D. Levine, "East-West Trade in the Late Iron Age: A View from the Zagros," in *Le plateau iranien et l'Asie centrale des origines à la conquête islamique* (Colloques internationaux du Centre national de la recherche scientifique 567; Paris: Editions du Centre national de la recherche scientifique, 1977), 171–86.

[10]On the reign of Argishti I, see Barnett, "Urartu," 344–48.

[11]See Thureau-Dangin and Dunand, *Til-Barsib*, 146–48, lines 11–18.

> valley, but also those arteries running westwards into Anatolia and south and south-westwards into the plains and foothills of north Syria.[12]

Argishti's expansionistic policy was continued by his son, Sardurri II (about 764–735 BCE). There is evidence that during his reign, Sardurri helped organize a strong anti-Assyrian coalition of north Syrian and Anatolian states that included Arpad, Melid, Gurgum, and Kummuḫ.[13]

In spite of the weakness of the central government, Assyria continued its involvement in the west during the reigns of Shalmaneser IV, Ashur-dan III, and Ashur-nirari V. Assyrian strength in the region was exercised through the dominating presence of the *turtānu*, Šamši-ilu, who claimed the title of "governor of Ḫatti" (*sāpir māt Ḫatti*) for himself.[14] The entire region of Anatolia and Syria-Palestine must have come under his sphere of domination.[15] With a weak central government, he was the *de facto* Assyrian king of the West. Both the discovery of his inscriptions at Til-Barsip (in Bit-Adini[16]) and his claim of Kar-Shalmaneser as the city of his lordship[17] point to Til-Barsip as the center of his administration. Šamši-ilu was appointed as the *turtānu* early in the reign of Adad-nirari III, probably before 806–805 BCE, the year he settled the border dispute between Arpad and Hamath.[18] He remained the *turtānu* during the reigns of Shalmaneser IV, Ashur-dan III, and Ashur-nirari V, appearing as the *limmu* in 780–779, 770–769, and 752–751 BCE. He was no longer the *turtānu* in the reign of Tiglath-pileser III (see the *limmu* for the year 742–741 BCE); it is not known, however, when he died or was replaced as *turtānu*. In an inscription attributed to Shalmaneser IV, Šamši-ilu is noted to have led a campaign against Ḫadiānu of Aram-Damascus,[19] a campaign which can be correlated with the one noted in the eponym chronicle for the year 773–772 BCE.

---

[12]Barnett, "Urartu," 347.

[13]Layard 71a + 71b + 72a; see *ARAB* 1. §769.

[14]Thureau-Dangin and Dunand, *Til-Barsib*, 146, line 9.

[15]In the Til-Barsip inscriptions, Šamši-ilu claimed to have dominated territories as far as Muški in the west and Namri in the east (Thureau-Dangin and Dunand, *Til-Barsib*, 146, lines 9–10).

[16]Bit-Adini was already provincialized early in the reign of Shalmaneser III, who changed the name of Til-Barsip to Kar-Shalmaneser (*ARAB*, 1. §§602–3; cf. Grayson, "Ashur-dan II to Ashur-nirari V," 260).

[17]Thureau-Dangin and Dunand, *Til-Barsib*, 148, lines 19–20.

[18]See chapter two above, pp. 75–78; contra Hawkins, "Neo-Hittite States," 400.

[19]So Pazarcik Stela, reverse (Donbaz, "Two Neo-Assyrian Stelae," 9–10); see below, pp. 108–109.

Scholars have attempted to identify Šamši-ilu in non-Assyrian texts. First, in the Sefire inscriptions mention is made of a certain Bar-gaʾyah of KTK, with whom Matiʾ-ilu of Arpad made a treaty. These texts clearly identify Bar-gaʾyah as the superior party in the treaty. Although the identity of Bar-gaʾyah and the kingdom of KTK has been an issue of great dispute, Lemaire and Durand have surmised that Bar-gaʾyah is to be identified with Šamši-ilu.[20] They argue that Bar-gaʾyah was a dynastic name, equivalent to Bar-guš of the Zakkur Stela and Bit-Agusi in Assyrian inscriptions. Moreover, גאיה is assumed to be an Aramaic variant of the Assyrian *gaʾuni* in the Monolith Inscription.[21] They further suggest that KTK should be identified with a royal city in Bit-Adini that appears in the Monolith Inscription of Shalmaneser III.[22] Although in the Monolith Inscription only two signs of the place name are legible, namely, *ki . . . ka*, they note that Malamat had reconstructed the name to read *ki*-[*it*]-*ka*$_4$.[23] In addition, they note that Durand and Charpin have proposed restoring the name to read *ki*-[*tá*]-*ka*$_4$ upon examination of photographs of the inscription. This city, Kit(t)a/i/uka, is in turn to be associated with Til-Barsip.

Lemaire and Durand's proposal is fraught with problems. (1) There is no evidence that Šamši-ilu was descended from a royal family of Syrian stock. Moreover, it is unlikely that a Syrian would have been appointed to the very powerful position of *turtānu* in the Assyrian administration. (2) The association of גאיה with *gaʾuni* is uncertain. Even if the identification is correct, Gaʾuni is clearly distinguished from Bit-Adini in the Monolith Inscription. Lemaire and Durand do not explain how Gaʾuni became Bit-Adini. (3) The identification of KTK with *ki . . . ka* of the Monolith Inscription is based on the reconstruction of a place name and is certainly questionable. Even if the name is correctly reconstructed, there is no evidence that the place later became known as Til-Barsip. In sum, the identification of Bar-gaʾyah with Šamši-ilu cannot be sustained.

Second, reference is made in Amos 1:5 to תומך שבט מבית עדן "the one who holds the scepter from Beth-Eden" (= Bit-Adini).

---

[20]A. Lemaire and J.-M. Durand, *Les Inscriptions Araméennes de Sfiré et l'Assyrie de Shamshi-ilu* (Hautes Études Orientales 20; Genève/Paris: Droz, 1984), esp. 37–58.

[21]Cf. *ARAB*, 1. §599.

[22]Lemaire and Durand, *Les Inscriptions Araméennes de Sfiré*, 47–51.

[23]See A. Malamat, "A New Proposal for the Identification of KTK in the Sefire Inscriptions," in *M. Razin Volume, Census Lists and Genealogies and Their Historical Implications*, ed. S. Bendor (Haifa: University of Haifa, 1976), 7–11 [Hebrew].

Malamat, in his analysis of the biblical text in light of the Til-Barsip inscriptions of Šamši-ilu, suggested identifying the Assyrian *turtānu* with "the one who holds the scepter in Beth-Eden."[24] Malamat has been followed by Hawkins[25] and Hayes.[26] Hayes, in particular, goes on to suggest that Amos 1:5 reveals the existence of a coalition made up of Rezin of Aram-Damascus—the primary target of the oracle—Pekah, יושב מבקעת־און, a rival king of Israel, and Šamši-ilu. In this context the verb ישב means "to sit enthroned."[27] The same verb is used in the phrase ישב על כהסאי in the Sefire inscriptions;[28] its parallel, *wašābu* in Akkadian, is used, for example, in the eponym chronicle in association with the enthronement of kings.[29] Thus, יושב מבקעת־און refers to a ruler in the Valley of Aven rather than the inhabitants[30] and is used in parallel to תומך שבט מבית עדן. Moreover, Hayes correctly suggests a coalition between the three parties, because the only reason the two rulers would have been mentioned in an oracle on Aram-Damascus was because they were in league with Aram-Damascus. Yet, it is precisely because the text speaks of an alliance that the identification of "the one who holds the scepter from Beth-Eden" with Šamši-ilu is suspect. Contrary to Hayes, there is no reason why an Assyrian governor of Šamši-ilu's stature and power—and who was virtually the Assyrian king of the west—would enter into an alliance with Aram-Damascus, a state frequently diametrically opposed to Assyrian presence and domination in Syria-Palestine. Moreover, coalitions in the west were often formed in order to oppose Assyria's domination of the region and control of trade routes. Thus, Šamši-ilu's participation in the coalition would have meant rebellion against the Assyrian central administration, which seems unlikely. Therefore, while it

---

[24]A. Malamat, "Amos 1:5 in the Light of the Til-Barsip Inscriptions," *BASOR* 129 (1953), 25–26.

[25]Hawkins, "Neo-Hittite States," 404.

[26]J. H. Hayes, *Amos, the Eighth-Century Prophet: His Times and Preaching* (Nashville: Abingdon, 1988), 74–79.

[27]For similar usages in the Hebrew Bible, see W. G. E. Watson, "David Ousts the City Rulers of Jebus," *VT* 20 (1970), 501–2; F. I. Andersen and D. N. Freedman, *Amos* (AB 24A; New York: Doubleday, 1989), 253–54.

[28]Sefire iii. 17 (*KAI*, no. 224; *TSSI*, 2. 48).

[29]See, e.g., the eponym chronicle for 745–744 BCE, where the phrase *ina* GIŠ*kussê ittušib* is used for the accession of Tiglath-pileser III to the Assyrian throne.

[30]So, e.g., NRSV.

is true that Beth-Eden in Amos 1:5 refers to Bit-Adini, the identification of the ruler with Šamši-ilu cannot be sustained.[31]

While Šamši-ilu appears in several Assyrian inscriptions and was a powerful force in Syro-Palestinian politics for over half a century, it is doubtful if the non-Assyrian texts such as the Sefire inscriptions and Amos 1:5 contain references or allusions to him.

II. ASSYRIAN INSCRIPTIONS

A. The Eponym Chronicle

The nature and extent of Assyrian activity in the west, no doubt under the primary leadership of Šamši-ilu, can be seen in the eponym chronicle for the three kings under whom Šamši-ilu served as *turtānu*.

Regnal Year	*Dates*	*Reported Event*[32]
Shalmaneser IV		
1	782–781 BCE	*a-na* ^{KUR}*i-tu-ʾu* at Ituʾu
2	781–780 BCE	*a-na* ^{KUR}*ur-ar-ṭi* at Urartu
3	780–779 BCE	*a-na* ^{KUR}*ur-ar-ṭi* at Urartu
4	779–778 BCE	*a-na* ^{KUR}*ur-ar-ṭi* at Urartu
5	778–777 BCE	*a-na* ^{KUR}*ur-ar-ṭi* at Urartu
6	777–776 BCE	*a-na* ^{KUR}*i-tu-ʾu* at Ituʾu
7	776–775 BCE	*a-na* ^{KUR}*ur-ar-ṭi* at Urartu
8	775–774 BCE	*a-na* ^{KUR}*e-ri-ni* at the Cedar Mountain
9	774–773 BCE	*a-na* ^{KUR}*ur-ar-ṭi* ^{KUR}*nam-ri*[33]

---

[31]See below (p. 130) for a proposal of the identity of "the one who holds the scepter from Beth-Eden."

[32]Information for this column is derived from Eponym Canon C^b 1 (Ungnad, "Eponymen," 430).

[33]This notation is unusual; no other notations involving the location of the main army has two place names. Naturally, the main army could not be located at two separate places at one time. Bearing in mind that this was the period in which Urartu was at the zenith of its expansion, it is likely that Namri was under Urartian control. Saggs has suggested that when Tiglath-pileser mounted a counter-pressure on Urartu, the Assyrian king began with a

		at Urartu and Namri
10	773–772 BCE	*a-na* ^{URU}*di-maš-qa* at Damascus
Ashur-dan III		
1	772–771 BCE	*a-na* ^{URU}*ḫa-ta-ri-ka* at Ḫatarikka
2	771–770 BCE	*a-na* ^{URU}*ga-na-na-a-ti* at Gannanati
3	770–769 BCE	*a-na* ^{URU}*ma-ra-ad* at Marad
4	769–768 BCE	*a-na* ^{KUR}*i-tu-ʾu* at Ituʾu
5	768–767 BCE	*i-na* KUR in the land
6	767–766 BCE	*a-na* ^{KUR}*gán-na-na-ti* at Gannanati
7	766–765 BCE	*a-na mad-a-a* at Madai
8	765–764 BCE	*a-na* ^{KUR}*ḫa-ta-ri-ka mu-ta-nu* at Ḫatarikka. A plague
9	764–763 BCE	*i-na* KUR in the land
10	763–762 BCE	*i-na* ^{ITI}SIG$_4$ ^{d}UTU AN.MI GAR^{an} in the month of Simanu an eclipse of the sun occurred
11	762–761 BCE	*si-ḫu* AŠ ^{URU}ŠÀ.URU revolt in the city of Aššur
12	761–760 BCE	*si-ḫu* AŠ ^{URU}4-*ḫa* revolt in Arrapḫa
13	760–759 BCE	*si-ḫu* AŠ ^{URU}4-*ḫa* revolt in Arrapḫa
14	759–758 BCE	*si-ḫu* AŠ ^{URU}*gu-za-na mu-ta-nu* revolt in Guzana. A plague
15	758–757 BCE	*a-na* ^{URU}*gu-za-na* SILIM^{mu} AŠ KUR at Guzana. Peace in the land
16	757–756 BCE	AŠ KUR in the land
17	756–755 BCE	AŠ KUR in the land
18	755–754 BCE	*a-na* ^{KUR}*ḫa-ta-ri-ka*

---

campaign in Namri (*The Greatness that was Babylon: A Sketch of the Ancient Civilization of the Tigris-Euphrates Valley* [New York: Hawthorn, 1962], 107; cf. the eponym chronicle of 744–743 BCE). The double reference thus probably indicates that the campaign was against the Urartians in the region of Namri.

		at Ḫatarikka
Ashur-nirari V		
1	754–753 BCE	*a-na* ^{KUR}*ar-pad-da* TA ^{URU}*aš-šur ta-a-a-ar-tú* at Arpad Return from the city of Aššur
2	753–752 BCE	*i-na* KUR in the land
3	752–751 BCE	*i-na* KUR in the land
4	751–750 BCE	*i-na* KUR in the land
5	750–749 BCE	*i-na* KUR in the land
6	749–748 BCE	*a-na* ^{KUR}*nam-ri* at Namri
7	748–747 BCE	*a-na* ^{KUR}*nam-ri* at Namri
8	747–746 BCE	*i-na* KUR in the land
9	746–745 BCE	*si-ḫu* AŠ ^{URU}*kal-ḫi* revolt in Calah
10	745–744 BCE	AŠ ^{ITI}GU$_4$ UD 13 KÁM [$^{\text{I.GIŠ}}$TUKUL]-*ti*-DUMU.UŠ.É- *šár-ra* AŠ ^{GIŠ}GU.ZA *it-tu-šib* [AŠ ^{ITI}]DU$_6$ *a-na bi-rit* ÍD *it-ta-* *lak* On the 13th of Aiaru, Tiglath- pileser ascended the throne. In the month of Tašrītu, he marched to the region between the rivers

In the years between 780–779 and 752–751 BCE, when it is known that Šamši-ilu served as *turtānu*, there were no major anti-Assyrian coalitions or rebellions in the west. While the main Assyrian army was in the west for at least six years and on four different campaigns (in 775–774, 773–772, 772–771, 765–764, 755–754, and 754–753 BCE), these were most likely conducted against attempts by individual states or minor coalitions to revolt against Assyrian hegemony. The results were inconsequential as these rebellions were quickly suppressed by Šamši-ilu. Two of these expeditions to the west occurred in the reign of Shalmaneser IV. In 775–774 BCE, the Assyrian army was noted to have been located "at the Cedar Mountain" (= Lebanon), a notation that could refer to only an expedition to secure timber for building projects in Assyria rather than to a military campaign. A western campaign was undertaken by the Assyrians in 773–772 BCE, when the location of the army at the turn of the year was Damascus. This campaign is most certainly to be correlated with the one mentioned in the Pazarcik Stela (reverse).

B. The Pazarcik Stela

This text begins by identifying the monarch to whom this inscription was attributed, namely, Shalmaneser (IV), son of Adad-nirari and grandson of Šamši-Adad. Lines 4–13, following the introduction, reads as follows:[34]

4) ^{I}*šam-ši*-DINGIR ^{LÚ}*tar-ta-nu*
5) *ki-i a-na* KUR ANŠE-*šú i-lik-ú-ni*
6) *ma-da-tú šá* ^{I}*ḫa-di-a-ni* KUR ANŠE-*šú-a-a*
7) KÙ.BABBAR KÙ.GI URUDU ^{GIŠ}NÁ *šárru-ti-šú*
8) ^{GIŠ}*né-mat-tú šárru-ti-šú* DUMU.MUNUS-*su*
9) KI *nu-du-ni-šá ma-a*ʾ*-di*
10) NÍG.GA É.GAL-*lim la ma-ni am-ḫur-šú*
11) AŠ *ta-a-a-ár-ti-ya ta-ḫu-mu šú-a-tu*
12) a-*na* ^{I}*uš-pi-lu-lu-me šar*$_4$ ^{URU}*ku-mu-ḫa-a-a*
13) *a-din* . . .

When Šamši-ilu, the *turtānu*, (5)marched to Aram-Damascus, the *maddattu* of Ḫadiānu of the Arameans of Damascus—silver, gold, copper, his royal bed, his royal couch, his daughter with her enormous dowry, (10)the countless property of his palace—I received from him.

On my return, this boundary stone to Ušpilulume, king of the Kummuḫites I gave . . . .

That this was a campaign directed at Aram-Damascus is evident from the text. In addition, it is quite certain that the campaign was led by the *turtānu*, Šamši-ilu, rather than Shalmaneser himself. This is supported by the usage of the third person singular in the verbal form *illikūni* in line 5. Although the referent of the first person singular in the term *amḫur* (line 10) is the king, without doubt it was Šamši-ilu who encountered Aram-Damascus and received the *maddattu* on the king's behalf. Likewise, it must have been Šamši-ilu who reconfirmed the boundary of Kummuḫ (with Gurgum; cf. lines 11–13)—already established during the reign of Adad-nirari III (cf. Pazarcik Stela, obv. ll. 16–18)—even though the action was attributed to Shalmaneser. This text also reveals

[34]See Donbaz, "Two Neo-Assyrian Stelae," 9.

that it was Ḫadiānu, the king of Aram-Damascus against whom the campaign was undertaken. Ḫadiānu must have begun to rebel against Assyrian hegemony and policies to warrant this attack from Šamši-ilu.

There is perhaps indirect evidence from the Hebrew Bible that this campaign was undertaken to check the expansion of Aram-Damascus into northern Galilee.[35] The evidence comes from Isa 8:23—a verse that belongs to the larger literary unit of 8:21–9:6[36]—which may be translated as follows:

> Like the time (כָּעֵת) the former one (הָרִאשׁוֹן) treated contemptibly (הֵקַל) the land of Zebulun and the land of Naphtali, so also the latter one (וְהָאַחֲרוֹן) has treated harshly (הִכְבִּיד) the Way of the Sea, Beyond the Jordan, and Galilee of the Nations.

The verse is a comparative sentence with כְּ in כעת introducing the protasis and וְ in והאחרון introducing the apodosis.[37] The verse compares two parallel situations.[38] Although most scholars take הראשון and האחרון as adjectives qualifying עת,[39] they should

---

[35]On the Galilee as a disputed territory between Israel and Aram-Damascus, see below (pp. 122–23).

[36]Several issues have arisen in the history of interpretation of this text, vis-à-vis its translation, verb tenses, compositional unity, and date and authorship (see Irvine, *Syro-Ephraimitic Crisis*, 1990], 215–16 and nn. 1–5 for a discussion and bibliography concerning these issues).

According to Irvine, this text is best understood as a single speech of the eighth-century prophet and "as an address to a Jerusalemite audience shortly after Pekah's coup in Samaria and Ahaz's move toward independence from the northern kingdom" (216). It is in this larger literary, rhetorical, and historical context that 8:23 is located.

Scholars generally regard 8:23aα as a gloss on v. 22b (see, e.g., H. Wildberger, *Isaiah 1–12: A Commentary* [Continental Commentaries; Minneapolis: Fortress, 1990], 377, 381–82; and O. Kaiser, *Isaiah 1–12* [OTL; 2d ed.; Philadelphia: Westminster, 1983], 200–201) or an editor's bridge between the gloomy picture of vv. 21–22 and the pronouncement of hope in 8:23aβ–9:6 (see R. E. Clements, *Isaiah 1–39* [NCBC; Grand Rapids: Eerdmans, 1980], 104). Irvine, however, disagrees with the view that it is from a later hand and argues instead that it serves as a transition to the following subunit (Irvine, *Syro-Ephraimitic Crisis*, 220).

[37]On comparative clauses, see B. K. Waltke and M. O'Connor, *An Introduction to Biblical Hebrew Syntax* (Winona Lake, IN: Eisenbrauns, 1990), 641–42. While it is true that in most instances, the apodosis would be introduced by כן, there are at least three instances where ו is used for that function, namely, Exod 16:34; Num 1:19; and Hos 9:13. On the translation of Hos 9:13, see J. K. Kuan, "Hosea 9:13 and Josephus's *Antiquities* IX, 277–287," *PEQ* 123 (1991), 103–8.

[38]Contra, e.g., H. L. Ginsberg, "An Unrecognized Allusion to Kings Pekah and Hoshea of Israel," *Benjamin Mazar Volume*, ed. M. Avi-Yonah *et al.* (ErIsr 5; Jerusalem: Israel Exploration Society, 1958), 61*–65*, who interprets them as contrasting situations; G. R. Driver, "Isaianic Problems," in *Festschrift für Wilhelm Eilers*, ed. G. Wiessner (Wiesbaden: Otto Harrasowitz, 1967), 46–47, 49; and NRSV.

[39]So, e.g., H. Barth, *Die Jesaja-Worte in der Josiazeit. Israel und Assur als Thema einer productiven Neuinterpretation der Jesajaüberlieferung* (WMANT 48; Neukirchen-Vluyn: Neukirchener Verlag, 1977), 141–45; and O. Kaiser, *Isaiah 1–12*, 203.

more correctly be construed as personal subjects of הקל and הכביד.[40]

One of the problems in the interpretation of the verse lies in determining how the two verbs ought to be translated. First, there is the issue of tense. Although both verbs are conjugated as perfective, there is a tendency among English versions to translate הקל in the past and הכביד in the future.[41] There is, nonetheless, no justification for such a rendering. Both verbs refer to past events, as numerous scholars have argued.[42] הקל, the hiphil of קלל, literally means "to make light." When construed in this manner, it always takes the compound preposition מעל.[43] There are four occurrences in which the verb takes a direct accusative without a preposition.[44] In these cases, it is best to construe a metaphorical meaning different from the literal and "to treat with contempt" is appropriate in these contexts. While the contextual meaning of הקל is easy to determine, the same cannot be said of its counterpart הכביד. The literal meaning of הכביד, the hiphil of כבד, is "to make heavy." The term with this meaning is used rather frequently in the Hebrew Scriptures.[45] Although the NRSV translates הכביד as "to make glorious"[46] in this verse, the only other place where this meaning is attested is Jer 30:19. This would give the verb an opposite meaning to הקל. Yet, as has been noted earlier, the syntax of the verse requires a parallel meaning. In 2 Chron 25:19, the meaning "to boast" fits the context best. By comparing the meanings of the verb in Mishnaic Hebrew, Aramaic, and Akkadian, Emerton proposes translating הכביד as "to

---

[40]So Ginsberg, "An Unrecognized Allusion," 61*–65*; G. R. Driver, "Isaianic Problems," 47; J. A. Emerton, "Some Linguistic and Historical Problems in Isaiah VIII. 23," *JSS* 14 (1969), 158–60; and Irvine, *Syro-Ephraimitic Crisis*, 222. Driver and Emerton have rightly observed that while הראשון and האחרון are masculine, עת is feminine; as such they should not be considered as modifiers of עת because of gender disagreement.

[41]The NRSV, e.g., translates the two verbs as: ". . . he brought into contempt . . . he will make glorious . . . "; so also the NIV, TEV, and JB. Cf. also A. Alt, "Jesaja 8, 23–9, 6. Befreiungsnacht und Krönungstag," in *Festschrift Alfred Bertholet zum 80. Geburtstag gewidmet*, ed. W. Baumgartner *et al.* (Tübingen: J. C. B. Mohr [Paul Siebeck], 1950), 32–35; Wildberger, *Isaiah 1–12*, 384.

[42]So, e.g, Emerton, "Problems in Isaiah VIII. 23," 158; Driver, "Isaianic Problems," 46–47, 49; and Irvine, *Syro-Ephraimitic Crisis*, 222. Cf. also the Geneva Bible and KJV.

[43]Exod 18:22; 1 Sam 6:5; 1 Kgs 12:10 (= 2 Chron 10:10); Jonah 1:5. In 1 Kgs 12:4, 9 (2 Chron 10:4, 9), however, the two prepositions מן and על are separate.

[44]2 Sam 19:44; Isa 8:23; 23:9; Ezek 22:7.

[45]1 Kgs 12:10, 14 (= 2 Chron 10:10, 14); Isa 47:6; Lam 3:7; Hab 2:6. In Exod 8:11, 28; 9:34, 10:1; Isa 6:10; Zech 7:11 אזן and לב are the objects of the verb.

[46]Cf., e.g., Ginsberg, "An Unrecognized Allusion," 61*; Barth, *Jesaja-Worte*, 141–45; and Kaiser, *Isaiah 1–12*, 203.

treat harshly."[47] This meaning can be construed perhaps also in Neh 5:15 (although the verb is used with the preposition על), where the context makes it unambiguous that the people were subjected to harsh treatment by the former governors.

While there is scholarly agreement that Isa 8:23 reflects Israel's loss of territories, there is no consensus regarding who was/were responsible for the losses. Most scholars identify Tiglath-pileser III as the antagonist, who carried out these onslaughts in connection with the Syro-Ephraimitic crisis.[48] Driver contends that הראשון and האחרון refer to Tiglath-pileser III and Shalmaneser V respectively.[49] On the other side of the spectrum are scholars who argue that the two substantives refer to two Israelite kings instead. Ginsberg identifies them as Pekah and Hoshea respectively, while Irvine identifies them as Jeroboam II and Menahem. According to Ginsberg, the verse bemoans Hoshea's failure to recover the Israelite territories that Pekah had lost.[50] Ginsberg's translation is problematic and hence his interpretation must remain questionable. According to Irvine, although הראשון and האחרון refer to Jeroboam II and Menahem, it was the Syrians who had actually encroached on and annexed Israelite territories.[51] In other words, the two Israelite kings were only *passively* responsible for the losses. The text of Isa 8:23, however, suggests, on the contrary, that the people mentioned were *actively* responsible, that is, they "treated contemptibly and harshly" those territories. Irvine's interpretation is therefore untenable on this point.

---

[47] Emerton, "Problems in Isaiah VIII. 23," 164–65.

[48] C. F. Whitley ("The Language and Exegesis of Isaiah 8:16–23," *ZAW* 90 [1978], 41–42) argues that it alludes to two separate campaigns against Israel, the first in 734 BCE and the second in 733/732 BCE. Emerton, however, argues that the two lines are parallel reflections of Tiglath-pileser's annexation of the northern regions of Israel ca. 732 BCE ("Problems in Isaiah VIII. 23," 156, 170). On the contrary, Alt ("Jesaja 8, 23–9, 6," 32–38, 45–49) and Barth (*Jesaja-Worte*, 141–66), suggest that the first line describes Tiglath-pileser's invasion of Israel during the Syro-Ephraimitic crisis, while the second anticipates the future liberation of Israelite territories. While it is true that 2 Kgs 15:29 describes the capture of territories in Gilead and Galilee by Tiglath-pileser during the reign of Pekah, less certain is the fact that they were taken from the Israelites and as such the Assyrians were responsible for reducing Israel to a rump state in 734–732 BCE (so Irvine, *Syro-Ephraimitic Crisis*, 224; see also his chaps. 2 and 3). Moreover, the likelihood that two different individuals are meant is stronger. On the issue of the southern border of Aram-Damascus, see most recently, S. A. Irvine, "The Southern Border of Syria Reconstructed," *CBQ* 56 (1994) 21–41.

[49] Driver, "Isaianic Problems," 48.

[50] Ginsberg, "An Unrecognized Allusion," 61*–65*.

[51] Irvine, *Syro-Ephraimitic Crisis*, 225.

The following proposal rests on three decisions. First, the terms, הראשון and האחרון, refer to two separate persons. Second, the verse refers to territories that Israel lost. Third, as Irvine rightly notes, it was the Arameans of Damascus who were responsible for those losses. Since the verse is located in the context of the Syro-Ephraimitic crisis, Rezin must be its immediate referent, האחרון. Conversely, הראשון should be taken as a reference to Ḫadiānu, Rezin's predecessor, mentioned in the Pazarcik Stela. If this interpretation is correct, the biblical text provides evidence that Ḫadiānu harassed Israel during his reign in the second quarter of the eighth century BCE. The regions that were lost to Ḫadiānu included "the land of Zebulun and the land of Naphtali," that is, Upper Galilee. Ḫadiānu's expansion of Aram-Damascus's territory most likely invited Šamši-ilu's campaign in 773–772 BCE. The successful campaign of the main Assyrian army led by Šamši-ilu was an effort to curtail Aram-Damascus's expansion in Syria-Palestine.

The western campaign that began in 773–772 BCE, the last regnal year of Shalmaneser IV, during which Šamši-ilu took direct action against Ḫadiānu of Aram-Damascus, continued into the following year, the first regnal year of Ashur-dan III (772–771 BCE). The eponym chronicle recorded the location of the main Assyrian army as Ḫatarikka (= Hadrach, the capital of Lu^{c}aš) for that year. The Zakkur Stela, as has been noted, reveals that the state of Lu^{c}aš, with its capital at Hadrach, was under the control of Hamath towards the end of the ninth century BCE.[52] It has also been surmised that Hamath had submitted to Shalmaneser III by 841–840 BCE and began following a pro-Assyrian policy.[53] How long Hamath maintained its pro-Assyrian policy, however, is not certain. It is plausible that the attack on Hadrach is an indication that Hamath had rebelled by 773–772 BCE and was in league with Aram-Damascus. That, however, is not the only possible interpretation of the eponym notation. It is equally plausible that Lu^{c}aš had broken away from Hamath and become an independent state again. Choosing to follow a policy different from Hamath—one that was anti-Assyrian—it entered into an alliance with Damascus. If this interpretation is correct, then there is no evidence that Hamath had strayed from its pro-Assyrian policy

[52] See chapter two above, pp. 92–93.

[53] See chapter one above, pp. 54–55.

during this time. It probably remained loyal to Assyria until the reign of Tiglath-pileser III.[54]

III. ŠAMŠI-ILU AND SYRO-PALESTINIAN POLITICS

During the reign of Ashur-dan III, two other western campaigns were recorded, in 765–764 and 755–754 BCE. Both campaigns were again undertaken in northern Syria as the eponym chronicle for each of those years recorded Ḫatarikka as the location of the main army. These campaigns were most probably led by Šamši-ilu as well. Both these campaigns were precipitated by attempts by Ḫatarikka—most likely with the cooperation of neighboring states—to shake off Assyrian hegemony.

The campaign against Arpad in 754–753 BCE, the first regnal year of Ashur-nirari V, was probably an extension of the campaign against Ḫatarikka in 755–754 BCE. With Šamši-ilu and the main Assyrian army occupied with putting down the rebellion at Ḫatarikka, Arpad seized the opportunity to revolt as well. After dealing with Ḫatarikka the army moved north to Arpad. It is likely that the new monarch, Ashur-nirari V, returned from Assyria to join his forces at Arpad. The eponym chronicle, besides mentioning the location of the main army at Arpad at the turn of the year, added *ištu* ^{URU}*aššur taʾʾarṭu* ("return from the city of Aššur"). This notation could have referred to the king going back to the capital city at the end of the year 754–753 BCE to officiate in the Akîtu festival. As soon as his official function was completed, he returned to Arpad. The fragmentary treaty text between Ashur-nirari and Matiʾ-ilu of Arpad probably resulted from this campaign.[55] The surviving portions of the text are primarily curses against Matiʾ-ilu if he breaks the treaty. It has been suggested that the circumstance that led to the making of this treaty was not a military defeat of Arpad but rather "a political surrender in the face of the advancing Assyrian troops."[56] The eponym notations for the year make this suggestion doubtful. More likely a siege was laid or a battle waged against Arpad, which was able to hold out for a time. With no conclusion of the campaign in sight, Ashur-nirari had to return to the city of Aššur for the Akîtu festival while the campaign continued under the leadership of Šamši-

---

[54]See chapter four below, pp. 149–50.

[55]See Parpola and Watanabe, *Neo-Assyrian Treaties*, 8–13; *ARAB*, 1. §§749–60.

[56]Parpola and Watanabe, *Neo-Assyrian Treaties*, XXVII.

ilu. When the king returned from Assyria, Arpad surrendered or was defeated, leading to the treaty between Ashur-nirari and Matiʾ-ilu.

The Sefire inscriptions reporting a treaty between Matiʾ-ilu and Bar-gaʾyah of KTK have been mentioned above in connection with Šamši-ilu. Similarities between these Aramaic inscriptions and the Assyrian treaty text with Matiʾ-ilu have been noted by scholars.[57] Attempts to identify Bar-gaʾyah and his kingdom KTK have not been convincing.[58] Recently, Parpola and Watanabe suggested a plausible identification of Bar-gaʾyah (literally, "son of majesty") with Ashur-nirari V, and KTK—either as an epithet or pseudonym—with Assyria.[59] Thus, they hold that these Aramaic texts are counterparts of the Assyrian text. They surmise that pseudonyms were used for the Assyrian king and country because Assyria was a hated sovereign and that this would protect Matiʾ-ilu from being dethroned by the anti-Assyrian faction in Arpad.[60]

While attractive this proposal is not without problems. It is not clear why an Aramaic version of the treaty would have been needed. Moreover, it is farfetched to suggest that pseudonyms would have helped save Matiʾ-ilu's throne, as if anti-Assyrian Arpadites would not have been able to decipher the pseudonyms.

During this period of strong Assyrian presence in the west in the person of Šamši-ilu, anti-Assyrian activities of Syro-Palestinian states were effectively curtailed. Israel, now under the reign of Jeroboam II (788–748 BCE), continued its expansion,[61] begun already during the reign of Joash. Of the long reign of Jeroboam II, the narrator of the book of Kings has very little to say except that "he restored the border of Israel from the entrance of Hamath as far as the Sea of Arabah" (2 Kgs 14:25) and that he "returned Damascus and Hamath to Judah in Israel" (2 Kgs 14:28). There are two issues that need to be addressed. First, what is the extent

---

[57]*Ibid.*; on the Sefire inscriptions, see *KAI*, no. 222–24; *TSSI*, 2. 18–56.

[58]See Lemaire and Durand, *Inscriptions Araméennes de Sfiré*, 20–21, for a summary of proposed identifications.

[59]This proposal had earlier been made by J. Cantineau, "Remarques sur la stèle araméenne de Sefiré-Soudjin," *RA* 28 (1931), 167–78 (cf. also G. Dossin, "*BR G'YH* roi de *KTK*," *Muséon* 57 [1944], 147–55; and G. Contenau, "La cryptographie chez les Mésopotamiens," in *Mélanges bibliques rediges en l'honneur Andre Robert* [Travaux de l'Institut Catholique de Paris 4; Paris: Bloud & Gay, 1957], 17–21).

[60]Parpola and Watanabe, *Neo-Assyrian Treaties*, XXVII–XXVIII.

[61]See E. Lipiński, "Jéroboam II et la Syrie," *Storia e Tradizioni di Israele: Scritti in onore di J. Alberto Soggin*, ed. D. Garrone and F. Israel (Brescia: Paideia, 1991), 171–76.

of the kingdom of Israel during Jeroboam II's reign? Hayes suggests that the statement in 2 Kgs 14:25 "denotes the territory from southern Lebanon to the area west of the Jordan at the northern end of the Dead Sea."[62] Jeroboam's territory thus would have included all Galilee in the north and southward to the northern border of Judah. The reference to "as far as the Sea of Arabah" probably implies that Jeroboam's territory included also the region of Gilead in Transjordan, territory already won back from Damascus by Joash (cf. 1 Chron 5:17). The reclaiming of these territories would have come about at the expense of Hamath and Damascus, a factor possibly indicated by the enigmatic reference in 2 Kgs 14:28: ואשר השיב את־דמשק ואת־חמת ליהודה בישראל.[63]

Jeroboam's control of Galilee is a disputed issue. The Galilean region was contested for by Israel, Damascus, Tyre, and perhaps Hamath. Aramean and Israelite control of the region seems to have varied from time to time. Both states had vested interests in the area, for important trade routes passed through it to the coastal cities of Acco, Achzib, Tyre, and Sidon. Thus, whoever controlled the region also enjoyed expanded trade relations with the Phoenicians. 1 Kings 15:20 indicates that Upper Galilee was taken by Ben-Hadad I of Aram-Damascus during the reign of Baasha, king of Israel. The text reads, "Then Ben-Hadad listened to King Asa and sent commanders of his armies against the cities of Israel. He conquered Ijon, Dan, Abel-beth-maacah, all Chinneroth, and all the land of Naphtali." Lower Galilee at that time seems to have remained in the hands of Israel. That Israel continued to control part of the Jezreel Valley and thus perhaps at least portions of Lower Galilee during the Omride dynasty is supported by evidence from 1 Kings 21 and 2 Kgs 9:14–26, both of which mention that the Omrides had a winter palace at Jezreel. No other biblical nor non-biblical inscriptional materials, however, relate to the region at this time, much less indicate that the Omrides controlled territory north of Jezreel. Thus it is uncertain whether the Omrides reclaimed any of Upper Galilee. Ahlström suggests that Upper Galilee may have been returned to Israel by Aram-Damascus as a reward for Ahab's participation in the anti-Assyrian coalition.[64] It has also been argued that archaeological evidence from Hazor and Dan from this period shows architectural styles

---

[62] Hayes, *Amos*, 22.

[63] On this text, see further below, p. 123–24.

[64] Ahlström, *History of Ancient Palestine*, 592.

and construction techniques similar to those of the Ahab level at Samaria and Megiddo, suggesting that Upper Galilee—and Hazor in particular—had reverted to Israelite control.[65] Even if Israel had controlled the whole Galilee during the Omride dynasty, it was probably lost to Aram-Damascus again during the reign of Hazael, along with other Israelite territories. While Joash had begun recovering territories for Israel, particularly in the Transjordan, it was Jeroboam II who retook Israelite territories in the Galilee.[66] This probably happened early in his reign since in the 770s BCE, Aram-Damascus had again encroached upon Upper Galilee (cf. the earlier discussion of Isa 8:23). Šamši-ilu's dominating presence in Syria-Palestine in no small part kept Damascus and other states under control and contributed to Israelite territorial expansion under Jeroboam. With Šamši-ilu keeping check on the activities of anti-Assyrian states in the region, particularly Aram-Damascus, a situation was created that enabled Israel to reclaim territories that had earlier been held under David and Solomon. Moreover, as a pro-Assyrian state, Israel may even have received direct help from the Assyrians. Already in the reign of Jehoahaz, Assyrian presence in the region is probably alluded to in the "savior" Yahweh gave Israel to deliver it from the hands of Aram-Damascus (2 Kgs 13:5).

A second issue relates to 2 Kgs 14:28, which suggests that Israel dominated Hamath and Damascus during the reign of Jeroboam II. The MT ואשר השיב את־דמשק ואת־חמת ליהודה בישראל, literally translated "and how he returned Damascus and Hamath to Judah in Israel," is difficult. Emendations have been suggested, based not only on the difficulty of the text but also on historical considerations. Burney, for example, emends the text to read ואשר נלחם את־דמשק ואשר השיב את־חמת יהוה מישראל, "and how he fought Damascus and how he turned back the wrath of Yahweh from Israel."[67] Haran suggests emending ליהודה בישראל to ליהודה וישראל, construing an alliance between Judah and Israel, who were able to exert direct control over Damascus and

[65] See recently Pitard, *Ancient Damascus*, 109 and 120.

[66] See Unger, *Israel and the Arameans*, 90.

[67] C. F. Burney, *Notes on the Hebrew Text of the Book of Kings* (Oxford: Oxford University Press, 1903), 320–21. Burney's emendation has been followed by W. E. Barnes, *The Second Book of Kings* (CBSC; Cambridge: Cambridge University Press, 1908), 72 and Gray, *I & II Kings*, 616.

Hamath.[68] Hobbs translates, "and how he restored to Israel Damascus and Hamath," leaving "Judah" out.[69] Most scholars see this verse as indicating that Israel and Judah were strong enough to subject Damascus (and possibly also Hamath) to vassalage.[70] While it is not impossible that Israel was strong enough to dominate Hamath and Damascus, with the assistance of the Assyrian Šamši-ilu, it is doubtful that it did. A kingdom (or empire) that was too strong would have posed a threat to Assyrian presence and interest in the region; thus it seems unlikely that Šamši-ilu would have permitted Israel's enormous expansion in southern and central Syria.

When Jeroboam was king in Israel, Uzziah (Azariah) was reigning in Judah. The only item from the reign of Uzziah that is important for assessing the political and commercial relations between Israel/Judah, Aram-Damascus, and the Phoenicians is the restoration of Elath to Judah (2 Kgs 14:22). It has been noted in the previous chapter that Elath came under the control of Aram-Damascus during the days of Hazael's empire with Aramean encroachment on Israelite and Judean territories. Thus, when Elath was restored to Judean control, it was taken from Aram-Damascus. It has been surmised that Uzziah ruled under the shadow of Jeroboam II,[71] possibly as a vassal of Israel.[72] Thus, it is possible that the restoration of Elath to Judah was carried out under Jeroboam's leadership.[73]

Relations between Israel/Judah and Aram-Damascus were obviously antagonistic during this period. Israel and Judah, as a con-

---

[68]M. Haran, "The Empire of Jeroboam ben Joash," *VT* 17 (1967), 267–324, esp. 296; cf. K. D. Fricke, *Das Zweite Buch von den Königen* (BAT 12/11; Stuttgart: Calwer, 1972), 190.

[69]Hobbs, *2 Kings*, 175.

[70]See, e.g., Pitard, *Ancient Damascus*, 177.

[71]So *HAIJ*, 310; but cf. J. Bright, *A History of Israel* (3d ed.; Philadelphia: Westminster, 1981), 258.

[72]For a long period of its history, Judah was a subordinate state to Israel, beginning with the reign of Omri. This situation again existed after Amaziah of Judah challenged Israel's sovereignty and was soundly defeated by the forces of Joash of Israel (2 Kgs 14:8–14), reducing Judah to vassal status. Judah's vassaldom most probably continued during the reign of Uzziah. Cf. Hayes, *Amos*, 23–24.

[73]The referents in 2 Kgs 14:22 are not entirely clear. A straightforward reading would imply that Uzziah was being referred to as the one who rebuilt Elath and returned it to Judah. In addition, המלך would refer to Amaziah (so NRSV). However, Amaziah met a violent death (cf. 2 Kgs 14:19–20) and thus the phrase "slept with his fathers"—one that is often used to denote a king's peaceful death—is not applicable to him. The verse perhaps originally referred to Jeroboam II, whose father Joash "slept with his fathers" (2 Kgs 14:16). It was he who recaptured Elath from Aram-Damascus but handed it over to the control of Judah.

sequence of the restraining presence of Šamši-ilu, were strong enough to continue regaining territories lost during a lengthy period of subjugation by Aram-Damascus. Losing Elath to Israel and Judah meant not only Aramean loss of control of the Red Sea port but also it allowed Israel to recover a major commercial alliance with the Phoenicians. The Phoenicians needed Elath for access to the Red Sea trading route to carry on commerce with the Arabian and African coasts. With much of the Transjordan also under Jeroboam's control, the Phoenicians could only gain access to Elath through Israelite and Judean territories. Thus, it was only to Phoenician advantage to have cordial relations with Israel and Judah once Elath was restored to Uzziah's control. Such a commercial relation would undoubtedly benefit both Israel and Judah economically as well.

The prosperous states of Israel and Judah and their cooperative commercial relations with Phoenicia were threatened by new political conditions which developed in Syria-Palestine in the 750s BCE, changing the region's international relations. A new king by the name of Rezin (Raᶜyān or Raqyān in Assyrian inscriptions) had ascended the throne of Damascus. While it cannot be proven conclusively, in all likelihood Rezin's accession took place in the 750s,[74] during the final decades of Jeroboam's reign. In addition, in Israel, a rival claimant to the kingship appeared on the scene, namely, Pekah son of Remaliah. One piece of evidence for Pekah's counter monarchy is found in the twenty-year reign assigned him in 2 Kgs 15:27.

Scholars have noted that external evidence has fixed the number of years from Menahem's payment of tribute to Tiglath-pileser in 738–737 BCE to the fall of Samaria in 722–721 BCE at sixteen. Biblical chronology assigns two years to Pekahiah, twenty to Pekah, and nine to Hoshea, a total of thirty-one years.[75] Confronted with this dilemma, most scholars dealing with biblical chronology have tended to reduce the length of Pekah's reign. Albright, for example, reduced his reign to six years.[76] Recently, Hughes has argued that the twenty years assigned to Pekah is a

---

[74]See Pitard, *Ancient Damascus*, 189, and Sader, *Les États Araméens de Syrie*, 288. Hayes suggests the 760s (*Amos*, 26). The last king of Aram-Damascus mentioned in Assyrian sources before Rezin is Ḫadianu. See the discussion on Šamši-ilu and Ḫadianu above, pp. 115–20.

[75]Even if one accepts Thiele's dating of 743 BCE for Menahem's payment of tribute (*Mysterious Numbers*, 154), the number of years until the fall of Samaria is twenty-one.

[76]W. F. Albright, "The Chronology of the Divided Monarchy of Israel," *BASOR* 100 (1945), 22, n. 26.

"schematic round number."[77] Attempts such as these to reduce the length of Pekah's reign have not been entirely convincing. Moreover, Judean synchronisms with the reigns of Pekah in 2 Kgs 15:27, 32 and 16:1 imply a lengthy reign for him.

Other scholars have argued that the number belonged to an original source and must be taken seriously. That Pekah ruled as a rival king for several years before his usurpation of the throne in Samaria has been proposed. This suggestion was first put forward by C. Lederer in 1888.[78] The best and most comprehensive argument for a rival kingship of Pekah, however, was made by H. J. Cook in 1964.[79] His main arguments may be summarized as follows:

(1) The term שליש, used to describe Pekah in relation to Pekahiah in 2 Kgs 15:25, is used in the Hebrew Scriptures both of a class of warriors connected with chariots and of officers whose rank is not specified. Therefore, this official title could have been given to Pekah at an earlier time (during the reign of Menahem) and does not necessarily involve his personal attendance upon Pekahiah.[80]

(2) Assyrian inscriptions employed different terms for the states of Menahem and Pekah. Menahem is referred to as "Menahem of Samaria," while the domain of Pekah at the time of his overthrow is designated as "Bit-Ḫumri,"[81] the normal Assyrian designation for Israel. Thus Menahem ruled over only the district of Samaria, while Pekah after gaining control over Samaria ruled over other sections of the country as well.

(3) The names Ephraim and Israel, as they are used in Hosea (who prophesied during this particular period), are not interchangeable designations for the northern kingdom. In fact, there is no evidence in the Hebrew Scriptures that they were used as equivalent terms. Moreover, the term "Ephraim" was used to de-

---

[77]Hughes, *Secrets of the Times*, 201.

[78]C. Lederer, *Die biblische Zeitrechnung vom Auszuge aus Ägypten bis zum Beginne der babylonischen Gefangenschaft* (Speier: F. Kleeberger, 1888), 135–38.

[79]H. J. Cook, "Pekah," *VT* 14 (1964), 121–35. Cf. also M. Vogelstein, *Fertile Soil: A Political History Under the Divided Monarchy* (New York: American Press, 1957), 30–31.

[80]The term שלישו may well be an apposition defining Remaliah rather than Pekah. Remaliah could have remained loyal to the royal house even though his son, Pekah, had taken a different course of action. If the term is in apposition to Remaliah, then there is no necessity to speculate when Pekah would have served as a שליש in the royal army of the Menahem dynasty. On the term שליש, see the recent works by D. Schley, "The *šālišîm*: Officers or Special Three-man Squads?," *VT* 40 (1990), 321–26; and O. Margalith, "A Note on *šālîšîm*," *VT* 42 (1992), 266.

[81]*ARAB*, 1. §816.

note the northern kingdom after it was reduced to a rump-state during and after the Syro-Ephraimitic crisis. Thus, there is evidence that in Hosea (chaps. 4, 5, 8, and 10), Ephraim and Israel refer to two separate rival kingdoms: Ephraim, centered in Samaria and under Menahem's control, and the rest of Israel, under Pekah's domination.[82]

(4) Pekah seized control of parts of Israel east of the Jordan and in Galilee in 752 BCE at the same time that Menahem seized the throne in Samaria and ruled as a rival king until 740 BCE, when he became king also in Samaria after assassinating Pekahiah.

Since Cook's work, scholars have increasingly accepted the hypothesis that Pekah ruled as a rival king in Transjordan,[83] or at least are open to the idea.[84] While Cook's main thesis is essentially correct, his suggestion that Pekah became a rival king at the time when Menahem usurped the throne in Samaria is suspect. In order to accommodate that, he accepted Thiele's argument that Menahem paid tribute in 743 BCE instead of 738 BCE (on the basis of Layard 50a + 50b + 67a),[85] a date more generally accepted by Assyriologists and biblical historians. If, indeed, Menahem paid tribute to the Assyrians as late as 738 BCE, and his final year on the throne was 737–736 BCE,[86] then his ten-year reign would have begun in 747–746 BCE (his first regnal year being 746–745 BCE). Pekah, who was removed from the throne following Tiglath-pileser's campaign to the west in 734–732 BCE, then, must have begun his rule as a rival king during the twilight years of Jeroboam II. What were the conditions during the last years of Jeroboam's reign that could have made this possible?

During the reign of Jeroboam II, Israel, as we have noted above, was able to expand its territorial boundaries, recapturing areas in Transjordan (so Amos 6:13–14) and the Galilean region.

---

[82]Hos 5:5, e.g., reads: וענה גאון־ישראל בפניו וישראל ואפרים יכשלו בעונם כשל גם־יהודה עמם ("The pride of Israel will answer in his face, and Israel and Ephraim shall stumble because of their wrongdoing, even Judah has stumbled with them"). This text makes it quite unambiguous that three kingdoms co-existed during that time.

[83]So, e.g., Thiele, *Mysterious Numbers*, 129; *idem*, "Coregencies and Overlapping Reigns Among the Hebrew Kings," *JBL* 93 (1974), 194–98; Hayes and Hooker, *New Chronology*, 60–62. Thiele, in the first edition of his chronology, had considered this possibility but eventually ruled it out (*The Mysterious Numbers of the Hebrew Kings: A Reconstruction of the Chronology of the Kingdoms of Israel and Judah* [Chicago: University of Chicago Press, 1951], 113–14).

[84]So, e.g., Bright, *History*, 273, n. 8; Cogan and Tadmor, *II Kings*, 174, 179.

[85]Cook, "Pekah," 122; cf. Thiele, *Mysterious Numbers*, 154–59.

[86]So Hayes and Hooker, *New Chronology*, 56, 62.

This must have happened during the early and middle part of Jeroboam's reign, for his control had begun to disintegrate in the last years of his reign.[87]

Although the exact date that Rezin ascended the throne of Damascus cannot be known, the 750s seem to be a likely period. Presumably, at this time when Israel was on the decline, Rezin seized the opportunity to wrench away Israelite holdings in the Transjordan and Galilee.[88] The oracle against Damascus in Amos 1:3–5 probably describes Rezin's reestablishment of Aramean control in Gilead.[89]

Against this background, a plausible scenario that led to Pekah's establishment of a rival kingship in Transjordan may be reconstructed. When Rezin usurped the throne in Damascus,[90] he, in imitation of Hazael, began to expand Damascus's influence. Pekah, probably a Transjordanian himself, and his supporters collaborated with Rezin when the latter made his advance southward. For his support and collaboration, Pekah was made a puppet ruler, subject to Rezin, over the Transjordanian and Galilean territories that he helped win from the control of Jeroboam. That Pekah had cooperated with Rezin long before he was on the throne in Samaria is evidenced also from 2 Kgs 15:37,[91] where together they threatened Judah during the reign of Jotham (759–744 BCE). It is interesting to note that in the text, while Rezin is identified as רצין מלך ארם, Pekah is referred to only as פקח בן־רמליהו.

Another event that affected the politics in Syria-Palestine was the death of Šamši-ilu. The eponym chronicle notes that he was

---

87As rightly noted by Cogan and Tadmor, *II Kings*, 164. Contra M. Haran ("The Rise and Decline of the Empire of Jeroboam ben Joash," *VT* 17 [1967], 266–97), who argues that Israelite expansion occurred late in the reign of Jeroboam II.

88See *HAIJ*, 323–25; Hayes, *Amos*, 26–27; Irvine, *Syro-Ephraimitic Crisis*, 105.

89See Hayes, *Amos*, 72, and below.

90That Rezin was an usurper may be gathered from a fragment of the annals of Tiglath-pileser III which identifies Ḫādara as the ancestral house of Rezin (Layard 72b + 73a; cf. P. Rost, *Die Keilschrifttexte Tiglat-Pilesers III* [Leipzig: E. Pfeiffer, 1893], lines 205–6; *ARAB*, 1. §777; see Pitard, *Ancient Damascus*, 182–83).

91This verse is often regarded as archival (so, e.g., Gray, *I & II Kings*, 630), but recently E. Ben-Zvi has called into question this assumption and suggests instead that it is derived from a prophetic source ("Tracing Prophetic Literature in the Book of Kings: The Case of II Kings 15,37," *ZAW* 102 [1990], 100–105). Regardless of its source, Cogan and Tadmor are probably correct to note that, like 2 Kgs 10:32, it "derives from sound historical tradition and shows that the pressure of Aram and Israel upon Judah had started prior to the attack on Ahaz" in the so-called Syro-Ephraimitic crisis (Cogan and Tadmor, *II Kings*, 182). Cf. B. Oded, "The Historical Background of the Syro-Ephraimitic War Reconsidered," *CBQ* 34 (1972), 153–54. Contra J. Begrich, "Der syrisch-ephraimitische Krieg und seine weltpolitischen Zusammenhänge," *ZDMG* 83 (1927), 214–15, who doubts the historical accuracy of this verse.

the *limmu* for the last time in the year 752–751 BCE. Although there is no conclusive evidence, it is plausible that Šamši-ilu died not long after 752–751 BCE. If he had begun his tenure as *turtānu* early in the reign of Adad-nirari III—prior to 806–805 BCE, as we have suggested[92]—by 752–751 BCE he would have already been in office for more than half a century.

With the death of Šamši-ilu, the strong Assyrian presence in the west no longer existed. Rezin of Aram-Damascus seized the opportunity to begin organizing an anti-Assyrian alliance. This alliance is reflected in part in Amos 1:5, in the context of an oracle against Aram-Damascus.[93] According to Amos, the ruler of the Valley of Aven (יושב מבקעת־און) and the ruler of Beth-Eden (תומך שבט מבית עדן) were members of the coalition. As has been suggested above, the ruler of the Valley of Aven is to be identified with Pekah.[94] Although the location of the Valley of Aven remains uncertain since it appears in only this text, Kallai-Kleinmann has identified Beth-aven (mentioned in 1 Sam 13:5; 14:23; Hos 5:8) with Tell Maryam in the Wadi es-Suweinit 1 km west of Mukhmas.[95] The Valley of Aven was thus probably the Suweinit Valley and its continuation as the Wadi Qelt to the Jordan River. Pekah, with the backing of Rezin, appears to have begun encroaching on territories west of the Jordan after securing his hold in Transjordan.

---

[92]See chapter two above, pp. 77–78.

[93]The superscription in Amos 1:1 provides two pieces of information for the dating of Amos's prophetic ministry, namely, the reigns of king Uzziah of Judah and king Jeroboam II of Israel and "two years before the earthquake." According to the chronology of Hayes and Hooker (*New Chronology*, 50–55), Uzziah was king over Judah from 785 to 760 BCE, but since he abdicated and died only in 734 BCE, he was assigned a reign of fifty-two years (cf. 2 Kgs 15:2). Jeroboam II reigned over Israel from 788 to 748 BCE. Because of the long reigns of these two kings, the chronological data are too general to be helpful. The other datum, "two years before the earthquake," is perhaps more helpful. Since earthquakes are not uncommon in Syria-Palestine (see D. H. Kallner-Amiran, "A Revised Earthquake Catalogue of Palestine," *IEJ* 1 [1950–51], 223–46; *IEJ* 2 [1952], 48–65), this particular earthquake must have been significantly powerful and unforgettable (cf. Zech 14:4–5); evidence of it is attested in the remains of Stratum VI of Hazor dated to the mid-eighth century BCE (see Y. Yadin, *Hazor II: An Account of the Second Season of Excavations, 1956* [Jerusalem: Magnes: 1960], 24–26, 36–37; cf. P. J. King, *Amos, Hosea, Micah—An Archaeological Commentary* [Philadelphia: Westminster, 1988], 21, 38). The mid-eighth century BCE, thus, appears to be the most probable date of Amos's ministry. However, if our interpretation of Amos 1:5 in relation to the death of Šamši-ilu is correct, then Amos's ministry could be dated more precisely to after 751 BCE.

[94]So Hayes, *Amos*, 76

[95]Z. Kallai-Kleinmann, "Notes on the Topography of Benjamin," *IEJ* 6 (1956), 180–87; cf. P. M. Arnold, "Beth-aven," *ABD*, 1. 682. See also N. Na'aman, "Beth-aven, Bethel and Early Israelite Sanctuaries," *ZDPV* 103 (1987), 13–21.

That Beth-Eden in Amos 1:5 is to be identified with Bit-Adini is quite certain. But who was the ruler being referred to? Our earlier discussion has called into question the identification of the ruler with Šamši-ilu. Andersen and Freedman, dating this text to the reign of Ben-Hadad son of Hazael, suggest that the king of Damascus was the one referred to as the ruler of the Valley of Aven (identified as the Beqa^{c} Valley) and the ruler of Beth-Eden.[96] Their interpretation assumes that Amos was talking about events already decades removed from his time, which seems unlikely. Moreover, there is no evidence that Aram-Damascus was able to extend its control as far north as Bit-Adini, especially during the reign of Ben-Hadad when the power of Aram-Damascus was declining, due in large part to the presence of Šamši-ilu in Syria-Palestine.

The following proposal is based on the suggestion that Šamši-ilu died not long after or during the year that he last served as *limmu* (752–751 BCE). With the death of Šamši-ilu, a rebellion broke out, leading to the defacement of his monuments at Til-Barsip and Arslan Tash.[97] A native of Bit-Adini, who was able to take over the throne, then joined the anti-Assyrian coalition headed by Rezin.

Another member of the coalition was Tyre. This may be surmised from Amos's oracle against Tyre,[98] one that is best understood in the context of Israelite-Phoenician relations.[99] One of the two wrongdoings that Amos accuses Tyre of committing was forgetting the ברית אחים, "a covenant of brothers."[100] E. Gerstenberger and J. Priest have pointed out the prominence of the concept of "brotherhood" in treaty relationships in the ancient

---

[96]Andersen and Freedman, *Amos*, 256.

[97]The defacement of the monuments is noted by Thureau-Dangin and Dunand, *Til-Barsib*, 142; J. E. Reade, "The Neo-Assyrian Court and Army: Evidence from the Sculptures," *Iraq* 34 (1972), 89, 93–94. It makes better sense to argue that the defacement was done deliberately by anti-Assyrian natives of Bit-Adini rather than by an Assyrian king. Although Šamši-ilu often assumed an independence from the Assyrian king in his inscriptions, there is no evidence that he ever opposed the Assyrian monarch.

[98]The question of the authenticity of this oracle as belonging to the prophet Amos has long been debated. For a discussion of the issues, see J. Barton, *Amos's Oracles Against the Nations: A Study of Amos 1.3–2.5* (SOTSMS 6; Cambridge: Cambridge University Press, 1980), 24, 32. See also K. N. Schoville, "A Note on the Oracles of Amos against Gaza, Tyre and Edom," *Studies on Prophecy*, ed. D. Lys *et al.* (VTSup 26; Leiden: E. J. Brill, 1974), 55–63; M. Haran, "Observations on the Historical Background of Am. I.2–II.6," *IEJ* 18 (1968), 202–12.

[99]Cf. Briquel-Chatonnet, *Les relations*, 132–37.

[100]See M. Fishbane, "The Treaty Background of Amos I.11 and Related Matters," *JBL* 89 (1970), 313–18.

Near East.[101] In addition, the same concept is used elsewhere in the Hebrew Bible to describe the relationship between Hiram of Tyre and Solomon (1 Kgs 9:13) and between the king of Israel and Ben-Hadad of Aram-Damascus (1 Kgs 20:32–33). That ברית אחים is used here in Amos as a reference to the relationship between Israel and Tyre has been proposed by earlier scholars.[102] Most of these scholars, however, see it as a reference to the treaty established at an earlier time, either during the Solomonic or the Omride period. But it is more probable that Amos was referring to a situation close at hand rather than one a century or more removed. As noted above, the Israelite-Phoenician relation, broken at the time of Jehu's extermination of the Omride dynasty, was restored sometime during the reign of Jeroboam II.[103] What Amos was condemning Tyre for, then, was the breaking of this "covenant of brothers" during the final years of Jeroboam's reign.[104] This probably came about as the result of a new alignment between Tyre, Aram-Damascus, and Pekah's rival kingdom following the accession of Rezin to the Aramean throne. In addition, the expansion of Damascene control into Galilee, Transjordan, and Elath made Damascus a more promising commercial partner. That Tyre was an ally of Rezin of Aram-Damascus is supported by an Assyrian inscription from the time of Tiglath-pileser III (ND 4301 + 4305; see next chapter). This cooperation, certainly in existence during the reign of Tiglath-pileser, probably began back in the 750s.[105]

The reason for Tyre's break with Israel and alliance with Rezin and his anti-Assyrian coalition was commercial.[106] Elath was retaken by Rezin according to 2 Kgs 16:6. The annalistic note relating to Elath (reading with the MT),[107] although placed in Ahaz's reign, most probably comes from the 750s, that is during

---

[101]E. Gerstenberger, " Covenant and Commandment," *JBL* 84 (1965), 38–51; J. Priest, "The Covenant of Brothers," *JBL* 84 (1965), 400–406.

[102]See, e.g., A. S. Kapelrud, *Central Ideas in Amos* (Oslo: Aschehoug, 1956), 24; T. H. Robinson and F. Horst, *Die Zwölf Kleinen Propheten* (HAT 1/14; Tübingen: J. C. B. Mohr [Paul Siebeck], 1938), 70; Priest, "Covenant of Brothers," 403–6.

[103]So already Hayes, *Amos*, 88–89.

[104]So also S. Cohen, "The Political Background of the Words of Amos," *HUCA* 36 (1965), 153–60. Cohen further suggests that Israel was on the defensive at this time.

[105]Contra W. T. Pitard, "Rezin," *ABD*, 4. 708–9, who argues that the coalition was probably formed between 737 and 735 BCE. During Tiglath-pileser's campaigns in Syria-Palestine (743–740 and 738–737 BCE), the members of the coalition would have curtailed their anti-Assyrianism and, as we know, even offered *maddattu* to Tiglath-pileser.

[106]See Briquel-Chatonnet, *Les relations*, 136–37.

[107]See chapter two above, pp. 102–103.

the reign of Jotham. The importance of Elath for access to the Gulf of Aqabah for commerce with the Arabian and African coasts has been already noted. As such, it was a vital port for the commercial interests of the Arameans and Phoenicians. Thus, it is not surprising that Rezin would have retaken it early in his reign. Tyre, needing access to the trade route would not have hesitated to break off relations with Israel and to cooperate with Rezin in the anti-Assyrian coalition.

We have argued that Isa 8:23 is best interpreted against the background of Israel's loss of territory to Aram-Damascus. הראשון refers to Ḫadiānu, who took "the land of Zebulun and the land of Naphtali," that is, Upper Galilee, from the Israelites. Conversely, האחרון must refer to Rezin, under whose reign an attempt to create a "Greater Aram" paralleling that of Hazael was launched. It was he who "treated harshly the way of the sea, the land beyond the Jordan, and Galilee of the nations." It has been noted that since his usurpation of the throne in Damascus sometime during the middle of the eighth century BCE, he began to encroach upon Israelite territories and supported Pekah as a rival king. In all likelihood, he wrenched away the coastal regions, Transjordan, and all Galilee from Jeroboam II and subsequently made Pekah his puppet over these territories. Amos 1 and 6:13 attest to Jeroboam's troubles in the coastal regions and Gilead, while Hos 1:5 may reflect his difficulties in Galilee.[108] Isaiah 9:10–11a probably indicates a similar situation of Israelite loss of territorial holdings. The text reads:

> So YHWH exalted the adversaries of Rezin over it,
> and spurred on its enemies;
> Arameans from the east and Philistines from the west,
> and they devoured Israel by the mouthful.

The phrase "the adversaries of Rezin," have created problems for scholars. Most would emend צרי to צריו or צרריו and delete רצין.[109] There is, however, no textual support for such an emendation. The phrase is a possessive genitive construction, not to be understood as the adversaries "against" Rezin but in the sense that Rezin "owns" the adversaries or, as Irvine rightly construes, that they are "in the charge" of Rezin.[110] The enemies are further

---

[108]So Irvine, *Syro-Ephraimitic Crisis*, 225.

[109]See, e.g., O. Procksch, *Jesaia I* (KAT 9; Leipzig: A. Deichert, 1930), 100–101; Wildberger, *Isaiah 1–12*, 220; and Kaiser, *Isaiah 1–12*, 219; also the NEB, JB, TEV, and NRSV.

[110]Irvine, *Syro-Ephraimitic Crisis*, 239–40 and n 12.

identified as Arameans and Philistines. The historical allusion is quite clear: it refers to the time when Rezin and his anti-Assyrian allies "devoured" Israelite territories "by the mouthful" during the last years of Jeroboam's reign and reduced Israel to a rump state (cf. Amos 1:3–8).[111]

IV. SYNOPSIS

Following Adad-nirari's 805–802 BCE campaign and the establishment of Šamši-ilu as the dominant Assyrian presence in the west, a new phase in the politics in the west was introduced, lasting from the late 800s to the 750s BCE. This was a period of independent national actions, with only limited cooperation between states. Šamši-ilu's presence in the west curtailed anti-Assyrian activities. Rebellions were quickly put down. With Šamši-ilu's dominating presence, pro-Assyrian states like Israel and Judah were able to regain territorial holdings lost to Aram-Damascus at the height of its expansion. Joash of Israel was able to take back some territories from Ben-Hadad (2 Kgs 13:25; cf. 1 Kings 20 and 22:1–38). It was, however, during the reign of Jeroboam II that Israel regained most, if not all, of its traditional territories, including all Galilee and much of Transjordan (cf. 2 Kgs 14:25, 28; see discussion above). The important seaport of Elath was restored to Judean control (2 Kgs 14:22). With Elath back in Israelite/Judean control, close relations with Tyre were renewed. This was the "covenant of brothers" in Amos 1:9, a covenant that Tyre would eventually break.

With the usurpation of the throne of Damascus by Rezin, another phase of political and commercial relations in Syria-Palestine ensued. This phase coincided with the death of Šamši-ilu in the late 750s BCE, which greatly reduced the Assyrian presence in the west. This was the phase in which a major anti-Assyrian coalition of Syro-Palestinian rulers headed by Rezin was first formed. This situation is reflected in Amos 1 (see discussion above); the coalition included Pekah, a puppet of Rezin and a rival king of Israel; Bit-Adini, now under a local ruler; Tyre, which had broken its relations with Israel under Jeroboam II; and possibly

[111]Cf. *ibid.*, 240. Kaiser's suggestion that this passage reflects the Philistine wars in the time of Saul and the Philistine and Aramean collaboration against Israel in the second half of the ninth century is without justification (*Isaiah 1–12*, 222, 224) and assumes that the Israelite audience listened to the speech with a long history of Israel at the back of their minds!

also the Philistine cities of Gaza, Ashdod, Ashkelon, and Ekron. Aggressive actions were taken by the coalition against Israel which resulted in the loss of territory which Israel had regained early in the reign of Jeroboam II (cf. Isa 8:23; 9:10–11a). Rezin likewise moved to retake the port of Elath and place it under Aramean control (2 Kgs 16:6). With Elath no longer in Israelite hands, it is understandable why Tyre would choose to break off relations with Israel and join the coalition headed by Rezin.

CHAPTER FOUR

THE REIGN OF TIGLATH-PILESER III

I. INTRODUCTION

During the *limmu* year of Nergal-naṣir (746–745 BCE) a revolt was noted to have occurred in the city of Calah. The eponym entry for that year reads:

[AŠ *li-me* | ^{Id}*nergal-naṣir*^{ir} | *ša* ^{URU}*na-ṣi-bi-na* | *si-ḫu* AŠ ^{URU}*kal-ḫi*

In the *limmu* of Nergal-naṣir, (governor) of Naṣibina, revolt in the city of Calah

This revolt probably began several months before Nisan 745 BCE. In conjunction with that revolt Pul, who may have been the governor of Calah,[1] seized the throne of Assyria on 13 Iyyar and assumed the throne name of Tiglath-pileser (III).[2] His reign (744–727 BCE) was marked by renewed incursions into the west. The Assyrian empire under Tiglath-pileser III was at the zenith of its expansion. Tiglath-pileser conducted a series of expeditions in the west, beginning with a major campaign in northern Syria (and Anatolia) in 743–739 BCE, in 738–737 BCE in Kullani, and another in Syria-Palestine in 734–731 BCE. There, among other matters, he dealt with the anti-Assyrian coalition of the so-called Syro-Ephraimitic alliance, of which Aram-Damascus, Israel, and Tyre were the leaders. The Assyrian king annexed many territories, turning them into Assyrian provinces and relocating conquered populations. By the time of his death in 727 BCE, the entire Eastern Mediterranean Seaboard had become part of the Assyrian empire, either as provinces or as vassal states.[3]

---

[1]So F. X. Kugler, *Sternkunde und Sterndienst in Babylon* 11/2 (Münster in Westfalen: Aschendorff, 1912), 125, n. 3; Olmstead, *History of Assyria*, 174; Saggs, *Assyria*, 83.

[2]On Tiglath-pileser, see most recently, A. K. Grayson, "Assyria: Tiglath-pileser III to Sargon II (744–705 B.C.)," *CAH*^{2} III/2. 71–85.

[3]On the expansion of the Assyrian empire under Tiglath-pileser III, see Saggs, *Assyria*, 85–92; Grayson, "Tiglath-pileser III to Sargon II," 74–83.

Several inscriptions from his reign contribute to our understanding of the regional politics in Syria-Palestine in general and the relations between the Israelites, the Phoenicians, and the Arameans of Damascus during this period. Before these texts are analyzed, however, it is significant to look at the eponym chronicle for the reign of Tiglath-pileser III, because it provides a broad background as well as important information on the activities of the Assyrian king for the entire period.

II. ASSYRIAN INSCRIPTIONS

A. Eponym Chronicle

The value of the eponym chronicle to the historian for the reconstruction of Assyrian history has been noted in Chapter One. The following is the eponym list from the reign of Tiglath-pileser III, beginning with his accession year, the tenth regnal year of Ashur-nirari V.

Regnal Year	*Dates*	*Reported Event*[4]
10	745–744 BCE	AŠ ^{ITI}GU$_4$ UD 13 KÁM [$^{\text{I.GIŠ}}$TUKUL]-*ti*-DUMU.UŠ.É-*šár-ra* AŠ ^{GIŠ}GU.ZA *it-tu-šib* [AŠ ^{ITI}]DU$_6$ *a-na bi-rit* ÍD *it-ta-lak* On the 13th of Aiaru, Tiglath-pileser ascended the throne. In the month of Tašrītu, he marched to the region between the rivers
1	744–743 BCE	*a-na* ^{KUR}*nam-ri* at Namri
2	743–742 BCE	*i-na* ^{URU}*ar-pad-da* *d*]*i-ik-tú ša* ^{KUR}*ur-ar-ṭi di-kàt* in Arpad a defeat of Urartu was inflicted[5]
3	742–741 BCE	*a-na* ^{URU}*ar-pad-da*

---

[4]Eponym Canon C^b 1; A. Ungnad, "Eponymen," 430–31.

[5]See H. Tadmor, "Azriyau of Yaudi," *Studies in the Bible*, ed. C. Rabin (ScrHier 8; Jerusalem: Magnes, 1961), 253–54, for the history of the translation of this notation. Tadmor's translation, "A defeat on Urartu was inflicted in Arpad," is questionable, since according to the Nimrûd Slab Inscription (*ARAB*, 1. §785) and II R 67 (= K 3751; see *ARAB*, 1. §797), the defeat of Sardurri took place in Kummuḫ. The notation then should be treated as two separate phrases, the first locating the main Assyrian army in Arpad and the second reporting the defeat of Urartu as an important event, although it did not take place in Arpad.

		at Arpad
4	741–740 BCE	*a-na* ^{URU}(ditto) *a-na* 3 MU.MEŠ *ka-šid* at (the same city); after three years it was captured
5	740–739 BCE	*a-na* ^{URU}*ar-pad-da* at Arpad
6	739–738 BCE	*a-na* ^{KUR}*ul-lu-ba* ^{URU}*bir-tu ṣab-ta-at* at Ulluba a fortress was taken
7	738–737 BCE	^{URU}*kul-la-ni-i ka-šid* Kullani was captured
8	737–736 BCE	*a-na mad-a-a* at Madai
9	736–735 BCE	*a-na* GÌR.II ^{KUR}*na-al* at the foot of Mt. Nâl
10	735–734 BCE	*a-na* ^{KUR}*ur-ar-ṭi* at Urartu
11	734–733 BCE	*a-na* ^{KUR}*pi-liš-ta* at Philistia
12	733–732 BCE	*a-na* ^{KUR}*di-maš-qa* at Damascus
13	732–731 BCE	*a-na* ^{KUR}*di-maš-qa* at Damascus
14	731–730 BCE	*a-na* ^{URU}*šá-pi-ia* at Šapiya
15	730–729 BCE	*i-na* KUR in the land
16	729–728 BCE	LUGAL ŠU.II ^{d}EN BAD^{bat} the king took the hand of Bêl
17	728–727 BCE	LUGAL ŠU ^{d}EN BAD^{bat} ^{URU}*di*-[. . .] the king took the hand of Bêl. The city of Di[. . .][6]
18	727–726 BCE	*a-na* ^{URU}[. . .] [^{Id}SILIM.MA-*n*]*u*-MAŠ AŠ ^{GIŠ}[GU.ZA *it-tu-šib*]

[6]Following G. Smith, "New Fragment," 322, 325, 331. Delitzsch's cuneiform text of the Eponym Canon C^{b} reads a *Winkelhaken* as the beginning part of a sign (*Assyrische Lesestücke*, 94), presumably *di*, which was omitted in Ungnad ("Eponymen," 432). Smith suggests that a revolt occurred during this year. He is followed most recently by Irvine (*Syro-Ephraimitic Crisis*, 25, n. 6), who suggests that the place referred to is Damascus. While Irvine is probably right that the city of Damascus is being referred to, his (so also Smith's) conjecture that the line originally recorded a revolt cannot be substantiated. This is not the formula of how a revolt is recorded in the eponym chronicle. The usual formula is *si-ḫu ina* GN. It is more likely that the reference is to the capture of the city and a revolt can only be indirectly inferred.

at [. . .]
[Shalma]neser [ascended] the
[throne].

The eponym list establishes that Tiglath-pileser III was an extremely active king, mounting military campaigns every single year from his accession year (745–744 BCE) to his fourteenth regnal year (731–730 BCE). In his second regnal year (743–742 BCE), Tiglath-pileser was already campaigning in the west, where he dealt principally with Arpad for three years (743–742, 742–741, 741–740 BCE) before conquering it. The following year (740–739 BCE), the army was still stationed at Arpad, most probably to carry out mop-up operations in the vicinity. During all these years when the main army was stationed at Arpad, smaller excursions may have been carried out against other states. That Arpad was involved in a wider coalition that rebelled against Assyrian hegemony is borne out by a fragmentary annalistic text (Layard 71a + 71b + 72a).[7] The states involved in the coalition included Urartu, Melid, Gurgum, and Kummuḫ. The Assyrian king was back in the west in his seventh regnal year (738–737 BCE), this time capturing Kullani (= Calneh) in northern Syria.

At the end of the year 734–733 BCE, that is, in the spring of 733 BCE, the army was reported to be at Philistia. The notations for the following two years (733–732 and 732–731 BCE) noted the presence of the military in the land of Damascus. If the entry URU*di*-[. . .] for the year 728–727 BCE refers to the city of Damascus, then the Assyrians must have returned to Syria-Palestine after an absence of three years. If Damascus had fallen in 732–731 BCE, it must have rebelled again and had to be recaptured.

B. Layard 45b + III R 9, 1

Layard 45b[8] and III R 9, 1[9] are fragments belonging to Tadmor's Series C_1 of the annals.[10] Layard 45b consists of 16 lines of

[7]See H. Tadmor, "Introductory Remarks to a New Edition of the Annals of Tiglath-Pileser III," *Proceedings of the Israel Academy of Sciences and Humanities* II/9 (1967), 180. Cf. *ARAB*, 1. §769.

[8]Texts named after Layard were originally published in cuneiform in his *Inscriptions in the Cuneiform Character*; the name and numbering of the texts refer to the page numbers in this volume. Layard had no knowledge of the cuneiform signs he was lithographing (see E. A. W. Budge, *The Rise and Progress of Assyriology* [London: M. Hopkinson, 1925], 90).

[9]Texts named with the letter "R" refer to those published by Rawlinson, *Cuneiform Inscriptions*. The Roman numeral refers to the volume, the first Arabic numeral to the

text, divided into two columns, A and B. In Rost's edition of the annals,[11] column A is numbered as lines 74–81, followed by column B as lines 82–89. According to Tadmor's analysis, however, the order of the two columns is not only reversed but also is interrupted by III R 9, 1. The sequence, thus, is as follows: column B (of Layard 45b) + III R 9, 1 + Column A (of Layard 45b). For the purpose of this study, only lines 82–89 (of Layard 45b) and 90–91 (of III R 9, 1), which is a tributary list, demand our attention. The following is a transliteration of the text:[12]

82) *ša* ^{I}*ma* [. . .]
83) *ina muḫ-ḫi* [. . .][13] ^{I}*ra-ḫi-a-ni* [KUR *ša*-ANŠE.NITÁ-*šú-a-a* . . .]
84) 3 GUN KÙ.GI [. . .] GUN KÙ.BABBAR [. . .]
85) 20 GUN ŠIM *la-du-nu* [. . .] .MEŠ [. . .]
86) ^{I}*ku-uš-ta-áš-pi* KUR *ku-um-muḫ-*[*a-a* . . .]
87) KUR *ṣur-ra-a-a* ^{I}*ú-ri-ia-ik* KUR [*qu-ú-a-a* . . .]
88) ^{I}*pi-si-ri-is* URU *gar-ga-miš-a-a* ^{I}*tar-ḫu-la-ra* [*gur-gu-ma-a-a* . . .]
89) AN.BAR KUŠ.AM.SI ZÚ.AM.SI SÍK.ZA.GÌN.SA5 [. . .]
90) [. . .]-*šú-nu ma-ʾa-at-tu*
91) [. . . *ar*]-*pad-da* [. . .]

. . . of Ma . . . . Thereupon . . . Ra^{c}yān[14] [the Ša-imērišu-ite], . . . 3 talents of gold, . . . x talents of silver, . . . $^{(85)}$20 talents of *ladunu* . . . . Kuštašpi the Kummuḫ[ite], . . . the Tyrian, Uriak [the Queite], Pisiris the Carchemishite, Tarḫulara [the Gurgumite], . . . iron, elephant hide, ivory, red purple garments . . . $^{(90)}$their . . . , in large (quantity) . . . Arpad . . . .

From what is preserved of the text, it can be surmised that the states involved in this tributary list were basically from northern

---

plate, and the second Arabic numeral to the text number in the plate. Thus, III R 9, 1 is from volume 3 of Rawlinson's *Cuneiform Inscriptions*, pl. 9, no. 1.

[10]Tadmor, "Introductory Remarks," 180. Tadmor has been involved in a major study of the annals of Tiglath-pileser III since the 1960s. Employing artistic, typological, and palaeographic criteria, Tadmor distinguishes six parallel recensions of the annals (Series A, B, C_1, C_2, D, and E) which once decorated the walls of Tiglath-pileser's palace ("Introductory Remarks," 177–78).

[11]Rost, *Keilschrifttexte*.

[12]The numbering of the lines of Tiglath-pileser's annals follows that of Rost's edition since it is the most readily available and widely used edition. Moreover, the text is not numbered in Layard's transcription.

[13]Rost's reconstruction of *ina íli-*[*su-nu*] [*aš-kun*] is purely conjectural (*Keilschrifttexte*, 14). The two signs after *ina* clearly read *muḫ-ḫi*. *ina muḫḫi* is an adverbial phrase that probably begins this tributary list.

[14]The Akkadian form of *ra-ḫi-a-ni* is an attempt to reproduce the Aramaic *ra^{c}yān*; so B. Landsberger, *Samʾal: Studien zur Entdeckung der Ruinenstaette Karatepe* (Ankara: Türkischen Historischen Gesellschaft, 1948), 1. 66–67, n. 169. In the Iran Stela, the name is written as *ra-qi-a-nu*, representing the Aramaic form רקין. This name has come into Hebrew as רצין (= Rezin). For the etymology and comparative Semitics of this name, see Pitard, *Ancient Damascus*, 181–82.

Syria.[15] Aram-Damascus and Tyre appear to be the southernmost states from whom tribute was received.[16] Because of the fragmentary nature of the text, it is possible that there were more states named than is now preserved. For one thing, Samaria was probably listed at the end of line 86. An Analogy with the Iran Stela and Layard 50a + 50b + 67a (for these texts, see below), the reference to Samaria would have come before Tyre. The order of the states in the three lists can be seen in the following chart:

Layard 45b +	*Iran Stela*	*Layard 50a +*
Ša-imērišu	Kummuḫ	Kummuḫ
Kummuḫ	Ša-imērišu	Ša-imērišu
....	Samaria	Samaria
Tyre	Tyre	Tyre
Que	Byblos	Byblos
Carchemish	Que	Que
Gurgum	Melid	Carchemish
	Tabalu	Hamath
	Atuna	Sama'l
	Tuḫana	Gurgum
	Ištunda	Melid
	Ḫušemna	Kaska
	Kaska	Tabalu
	Carchemish	(A)Tuna
	Sama'l	Tuḫana
	Gurgum	Ištunda
	Arabia	Ḫušemna
		Arabia

Together with the gentilic ending for Kummuḫ before it and the name of the king of Tyre after it, this would have required between eighteen and twenty-one signs. Although the text is broken, on the basis of the length of other annalistic texts of Tiglath-pileser, there is certainly room for this number of signs in a single line to include the name of Menahem and Samaria. The historical implications for this will be dealt with later. Whether any other Palestinian states paid tribute at this time is uncertain.

[15]Hawkins ("Neo-Hittite States," 372–441) designates these states including Damascus as Syro-Hittite. Even with the collapse of the Hittite Empire, the Assyrians continued to refer to the area as the "land of Ḫatti" or as "Ḫatti and Amurru."

[16]It is likely that some of these states had already been paying tribute in previous years. This receipt of tribute by Tiglath-pileser gets noted in the text because the Assyrian king received it personally while on campaign in the region. Tribute sent to the capital under normal conditions was generally not so noted.

Since Arpad is mentioned at the end of the tabulation of tribute received, it is likely that Tiglath-pileser received the tribute of these leaders in Arpad.[17] It is also plausible that ^{I}*ma* in line 82 is the first sign of the name Matiʾ-ilu[18] and that the broken text related Tiglath-pileser's campaign against him or the defeat of Arpad.

Most recently Pitard has again argued that the account of this tribute list is parallel to that of Layard 50a + 50b + 67a and that the event should be dated to Tiglath-pileser's eighth year (737–736 BCE).[19] In advocating this dating, he cites Tadmor's earlier treatment of the text, where Tadmor argues a position he has since abandoned.[20] In his 1967 article, Tadmor dated Layard 45b to Tiglath-pileser's sixth and seventh *palê*[21] (740–739 and 739–738 BCE respectively) with lines 82–89 probably relating to the sixth.[22] Unfortunately, because of the nature of the article Tadmor does not offer any reasons for the dating. Rost in his edition of the annals dated these lines to Tiglath-pileser's third *palû* (743–742 BCE).

The only certainty about the dating of this fragment is that there is no consensus among scholars. The alleged parallel between this fragment and Layard 50a + 50b + 67a cannot be sustained.[23] Although it is true that in most cases the rulers appear in the same order as Layard 50a + 50b + 67a, the greatest discrepancy is the order of the first two rulers (see chart above). In Layard 50a + 50b + 67a, like all other subsequent tribute lists of Tiglath-pileser III, Kuštašpi of Kummuḫ is listed first. In Layard 45b, however, Rezin of Ša-imērišu is listed prior to Kuštašpi of Kummuḫ. Moreover, it is also evident that he occupies a promi-

---

[17]Rost read line 91 as *ina qabal* URU *ar-pad-da am-ḫur*, purportedly on the basis of a squeeze of the text.

[18]Cf. M. Weippert, "Menahem von Israel und seine Zeitgenossen in einer Stelenin-schrift des assyrischen Königs Tiglathpileser III. aus dem Iran," *ZDPV* 89 (1973), 36.

[19]Pitard, *Ancient Damascus*, 183.

[20]Cf. Tadmor, "Azriyau of Yaudi," 255–56.

[21]In correlating the eponym chronicle with the annals of Tiglath-pileser III, it is apparent that the king's *palû* dating begins with his accession year, that is, the year that the new king first mounted a campaign. The same is true for the reign of Sargon II (see Tadmor, "Campaigns of Sargon," 30–31). The word is best translated as "campaign year." Since it is presumed that the Assyrian army would be on military campaign every year subsequently, years are dated consecutively from the first *palû* regardless of whether the king was leading the campaign or a campaign actually took place.

[22]Tadmor, "Introductory Remarks," 180, 186. So also W. H. Shea, "Menahem and Tiglath-pileser III," *JNES* 37 (1978), 48; Oded, "Phoenician Cities," 42.

[23]Contra also M. Cogan, "Tyre and Tiglath-pileser III: Chronological Notes," *JCS* 25 (1973), 96–97.

nent place in the list and is cited individually as having paid a specific amount of tribute. His submission must therefore have been regarded by Tiglath-pileser as of particular import. Thus, Rezin must have been at that time the most powerful ruler in Syria-Palestine and the strongest potential threat to Assyrian domination of the region. Because of the prominence given to Rezin, it is probable that his suppression or submission took place early in the reign of Tiglath-pileser. Rezin's suppression or submission could have been used to demonstrate the Assyrian king's success in the west and to help consolidate his power in Assyria itself.

The eponym chronicle lists Arpad as the location of the Assyrian troops on Tiglath-pileser's second to sixth regnal years (743–742 BCE to 739–738 BCE). This western campaign started in the king's second regnal year, perhaps as early as the spring of the year. According to the annals text Layard 71a + 71b + 72a, Sardurri of Urartu, Matiʾ-ilu of Arpad, Sulumal of Melid, Tarḫulara of Gurgum, and Kuštašpi of Kummuḫ opposed the Assyrians during Tiglath-pileser's third *palû* (that is, his second regnal year, 743–742 BCE).[24] This anti-Assyrian movement was encouraged and supported by Urartu in the same way that Egypt probably had supported the Syro-Palestinian coalition of the 850s BCE. Tiglath-pileser's campaign in his second regnal year was an attempt to crush a rebellion. Further evidence for Urartian support of the coalition is derived from the eponym chronicle for the year 743–742 BCE, *ina* ^{URU}*arpadda dîktu ša* ^{KUR}*urarṭi dikat* ("in Arpad; a defeat of Urartu was inflicted"), where the Assyrian army defeated the Urartians in Kummuḫ.[25] Although Tiglath-pileser was able to defeat Urartian forces rather quickly in Kummuḫ, he was less successful in dealing with Arpad (and perhaps also the rest of the members of the coalition). It was three years before he finally captured Arpad.[26] The fact that Tiglath-pileser fought Urartu in Kummuḫ during this "Arpad" campaign indicates that he campaigned widely in the eastern Mediterranean Seaboard and that the notation about military engagement in the eponym chronicle should not be taken as inclusive or exhaustive.[27]

[24] This text is fragmentary and it is true that the numeral before *palû* is broken. Tadmor assigns it to the third *palû* ("Introductory Remarks," 180). This dating is quite certain since the eponym chronicle for the second regnal year notes that the Urartians were defeated in conjunction with the campaign against Arpad.

[25] See n. 5 above.

[26] So the notation in the eponym chronicle for 741–740 BCE: *ana* ^{URU}(*arpadda*) *ana* 3 *šanâti*^{meš} *kašid* = "at (Arpad), after three years it was captured."

[27] So Hayes and Hooker, *New Chronolgy*, 60.

In one of these excursions during the period 743–740 BCE, Tiglath-pileser III probably went down to help Menahem of Israel. Evidence for this event comes from 2 Kgs 15:19–20. In this text, Tiglath-pileser is identified as Pul. The text reads:

> In his days,[28] Pul, king of Assyria, came into the land, and Menahem gave Pul a thousand talents of silver to help him confirm his hold on the royal power. Menahem paid out the silver on behalf of Israel because of all the warriors to give to the king of Assyria, fifty shekels of silver per man. The king of Assyria then returned and did not remain there in the land.

The phrase בא פול מלך־אשור על־הארץ is not to be interpreted as Assyria's invasion of Israel, as rightly noted by Hobbs.[29] The usual phrase used to express an invasion is עלה or עלה על. This usage occurs on eleven occasions in the books of Kings, namely, 1 Kgs 14:25; 15:17; 20:1, 22; 2 Kgs 6:24; 12:18; 17:3; 18:9, 13, 25; 23:29. In each of these instances, the meaning of an invasion or attack is clear: the place invaded is affixed to the preposition על. In three cases, the attack is made even more explicit with the addition of other verbs of warfare, לחם in 2 Kgs 12:18 and צור in 1 Kgs 20:1 and 2 Kgs 6:24. Conversely, בוא על, which *may* connote an attack occurs only twice in the books of Kings, once here in the text under discussion and the other in 2 Kgs 25:1. From both cases, however, the meaning of an invasion is neither implicit nor explicit in the usage. From 2 Kgs 25:1, one only knows that Jerusalem was invaded by Nebuchadnezzar because of the further qualification, ויחן עליה ויבנו עליה דיק סביב.[30] Without such additional qualification in 2 Kgs 15:19, then, it is unlikely that any invasion occurred or was meant.

If Tiglath-pileser did not come to Israel as an invader, why then was he there? Hobbs's suggestion that Tiglath-pileser had come to Israel to provide Menahem with military assistance against threats and at Menahem's request (see Hos 5:13) is most attractive and intelligible. This is supported in part by 2 Kgs 15:19, which points out Tiglath-pileser's presence in Israel and notes that "Menahem gave Pul a thousand talents of silver to help

---

[28]Reading בימיו with LXX, which places it at the beginning of v. 19, for MT's כל־ימיו at the end of v. 18. Verse 19aα finds its parallel in 2 Kgs 23:29: "In his days, Pharaoh Neco, king of Egypt, went up against . . . ."

[29]Hobbs, *2 Kings*, 199. Hobbs's translation of the text, however, does not agree with his discussion (cf. p. 188).

[30]In three other instances, בוא alone was used (2 Kgs 15:29; 25:8, 25), and any indication of attack is made explicit and further qualified by other activities of warfare, as in the "taking" (לקח) of places in 2 Kgs 15:29 or the "burning" (שרף) of buildings in 2 Kgs 25:8 or the "striking down" (נכה) of persons in 2 Kgs 25:25.

him confirm his hold on the royal power." The context of the verse makes it certain that what Menahem paid Tiglath-pileser was not a tribute but a payment for military assistance rendered. The amount of money (a thousand talents of silver) that Menahem paid Tiglath-pileser was unusually high but not without parallels. A. Šanda[31] has compared this amount with the 2,300 talents of silver which Adad-nirari III exacted from Mariʾ, king of Aram-Damascus, in 804–803 BCE,[32] and the 30 talents of gold and 800 talents of silver which Sennacherib received from King Hezekiah in 701 BCE.[33] Cogan and Tadmor[34] note that Menahem's payment is comparable to the tribute of 10 talents of gold and 1,000 talents of silver exacted by Tiglath-pileser from Hulli king of Tabalu[35] and of 50 or 150 talents of gold and [2,000 talents of silver] from Mêtenna king of Tyre.[36] They further state that both Hulli and Mêtenna were usurpers and their payments in fact bought Assyrian support and legitimization of their rule. That Menahem's payment was also an attempt to buy Assyrian support for his rule is illuminated by the phrase להיות ידיו אתו להחזיק הממלכה בידו. Menahem had usurped the Israelite throne at a politically tumultuous time and had to suppress resistance before his claim to the throne was complete. It is likely that in early times his hold on the royal power was constantly challenged. In addition, there was Pekah, a rival king, who must have posed a continuous threat to his kingship.[37] It is likely that Menahem continued the pro-Assyrian stance established by Jehu and continued throughout his dynasty; there is no indication to the contrary. As a loyal Assyrian vassal it is only logical that Menahem would seek the suzerain's help in strengthening his hold on the kingdom when the latter was in the vicinity. It is known from Assyrian sources that Tiglath-pileser was in Syria-Palestine from 743–742 to 740–739 BCE, during which time the main Assyrian army was stationed at Arpad for four consecutive years. In any of these years, the Assyrian king and a contingent of his army could have come south to Israel

---

[31] A. Šanda, *Die Bücher der Könige* (2 vols; EHAT 9; Münster: Aschendorff, 1911–12), 2. 186.

[32] See the Calah Slab, line 18; cf. Tadmor, "Historical Inscriptions," 148–50; *ANET*, 281–82.

[33] *ANET*, 288.

[34] Cogan and Tadmor, *II Kings*, 172.

[35] *ARAB*, 1. §802.

[36] *ARAB*, 1. §803.

[37] The possibility of Pekah and his rival kingship over the Transjordan has been dealt in the previous chapter. See also Hobbs, *2 Kings*, 199.

to assist Menahem with his internal problems. In exchange for Tiglath-pileser's help, Menahem contributed to Tiglath-pileser a sizable payment. Assyrian texts also indicate that Tiglath-pileser personally collected tribute from Menahem during his first western campaign from 743–742 to 740–739 BCE (if our reconstruction of Layard 45b is correct), and subsequently in 739–738 BCE (so the Iran Stela) and 738–737 BCE (so Layard 50a + 50b + 67a). A likely scenario is that when the Assyrian king first campaigned in Syria-Palestine in 743–742 BCE, Menahem—a loyal Assyrian subject—paid tribute and subsequently seized the opportunity to enlist Tiglath-pileser's help to deal with the political harassment of both internal and external enemies.

Verse 20a of 2 Kgs 15 sheds further light on the kind of help Menahem received. The verse reads:

ויצא מנחם את־הכסף על־ישראל על כל־גבורי החיל לתת למלך
אשור חמשים שקלים כסף לאיש אחד

"To exact" or "to levy" a tax is the common translation of ויצא.[38] Hobbs notes, however, that such a translation of the hiphil of יצא is incorrect and impossible, since it usually means "to send out" or "to bring out."[39] Thus, what Menahem did was not to exact or levy the silver from Israel, but rather to pay out the silver *on behalf of*[40] Israel. The phrase על כל־גבורי החיל has been variously translated and interpreted. The NRSV, for instance, translates it as "from all the wealthy." Cogan and Tadmor translate it as "every man of means" and interpret it as designating the wealthy Israelites from whom Menahem exacted the silver to pay the king of Assyria.[41] Two things need to be noted. First, while it is true that גבורי החיל took on the connotation of the privileged economic class,[42] the three other occasions where the phrase occurs in the books of Kings (1 Kgs 11:28; 2 Kgs 5:1; 24:14) always refer to "warriors." The expression should be translated no differently here. Second, על כל־גבורי החיל is not in apposition to על־ישראל. The use of על here is different from the preceding one,

[38]So, e.g., Cogan and Tadmor, *II Kings*, 170; Jones, *1 and 2 Kings*, 2. 526; NRSV.

[39]Hobbs, *2 Kings*, 199.

[40]For this usage of על, see Waltke and O'Connor, *Hebrew Syntax*, 217.

[41]Cogan and Tadmor, *II Kings*, 172; so also Hayes in *HAIJ*, 328; Jones, *1 and 2 Kings*, 2. 526.

[42]Cf., e.g., 1 Sam 9:1 and Ruth 2:1; see also R. de Vaux, *Ancient Israel: Its Life and Institutions* (New York: McGraw-Hill, 1961), 70, 72.

in that it is employed here to explain why the silver was paid,[43] that is, "*because of* all the warriors," those mercenaries whom Tiglath-pileser supplied to help strengthen Menahem's power in Israel.[44] The amount for each mercenary was fifty shekels of silver. In all likelihood, it was through this event that Menahem was able to hold on to power till his natural death,[45] in 736 BCE, after a reign of ten years, always remaining a loyal Assyrian vassal.

The relationship of the tribute list in the Iran Stela and that of Layard 45b remains uncertain. If the tribute list in Layard 45b is to be dated no later than Tiglath-pileser's sixth *palû* (740–739 BCE), then this list predates that in the Iran Stela. Thus the Tyrian king cannot be Hiram as Rost suggested.[46] According to Cogan's suggestion, it is more likely that the Tyrian king was the same king mentioned in the Iran Stela, namely, Tubail,[47] who preceded Hiram on the throne of Tyre.

C. The Iran Stela

Other than the fact that this stela was found in western Iran, no details of its discovery are known. Although fragmentary, the inscription clearly falls under the genre of "summary inscription." Like other royal inscriptions of the genre, it begins with a catalog of divine epithets (col. I, lines 1–20), followed by a series of royal epithets (col. I, lines 21–33). The inscription then summarizes the achievements of the monarch according to geographical regions. The section of our focus, col. II, lines 1–23, is a list of the Anatolian and Syro-Palestinian kings upon whom Tiglath-pileser III imposed tribute. The text was published by L. D. Levine;[48] col. II, lines 1–23 is transliterated by him as follows:

1) MAN.MEŠ *šá* KUR *ḫat-ti* KUR *a-ri-me šá* UŠ *tam-ti*[*m*][49]

---

[43]For this usage of על, see Waltke and O'Connor, *Hebrew Syntax*, 218.

[44]So already noted by Hobbs, *2 Kings*, 200.

[45]The narrator states that he "slept with his ancestors" (2 Kgs 15:22), a phrase used of kings who died of natural causes.

[46]Rost, *Keilschrifttexte*, 14, l. 86.

[47]Cogan, "Tyre and Tiglath-Pileser III," 98, n. 13. So also Katzenstein, *History of Tyre*, 204.

[48]L. D. Levine, *Two Neo-Assyrian Stelae from Iran* (Toronto: Royal Ontario Museum, 1972), 11–24. See also his article "Menahem and Tiglath-Pileser: A New Synchronism," *BASOR* 206 (1972), 40–42.

[49]Following M. Weippert ("Menahem von Israel," 31), who notes that Levine's reading of *uš-pe-lu* is syntactically questionable, and that it is impossible to read the last sign as LU. Instead he suggests reading UŠ as a logogram for *šiddu* and restoring *tam-tim*

2) *šá* SILIM ^{d}*šam-ši* KUR *qid-ri* KUR *a-ri-b*[*i*]
3) ^{I}*kuš-taš-pi* URU *ku-muḫ-a-*[*a*]
4) ^{I}*ra-qi-a-nu* KUR *ša*-ANŠE.NITÁ-*šú-a-*[*a*]
5) ^{I}*mi-ni-ḫi-im-m*[*e*] KUR *sa-m*[*e-*]*ri-i-na-a-*[*a*]
6) ^{I}*tu-ba-ìl* URU *ṣur-a-*[*a*]
7) ^{I}*si-pàṭ-ba-ìl* KUR *gub-la-a-*[*a*]
8) ^{I}*ú-ri-ik* KUR *qu-ú-a-*[*a*]
9) ^{I}*su-lu-mal* KUR *mi-lid-a-*[*a*]
10) ^{I}*ú-as-sur-me* KUR ⸢*ta*⸣*-bal-a-*[*a*]
11) ^{I}*uš-ḫi-ti* KUR *a-tú-na-a-*[*a*]
12) ^{I}*ur-bal-la-a* KUR *tú-ḫa-na-a-*[*a*]
13) $^{[I]}$*tu-ḫa-me* KUR *iš-tu-un-di-a-*[*a*]
14) ^{I}*u-i-ri-mi* KUR *ḫu-šem-na-a-*[*a*]
15) ^{I}*da-di-ìl* KUR *ka*$^{()}$*š -ka-a-*[*a*]
16) ^{I}*pi*!*-si-ri-is* URU *gar-*[*g*]*a-miš-a-*[*a*]
17) ^{I}*pa-na-am-mu* [KUR *sa-m*]*a-al-la-a-*[*a*]
18) ^{I}*tar-ḫu-la-ru* KUR [*gur*]*-gu-ma-a-*[*a*]
19) SAL *za-bi-bi-e šar-ra*[*t*] KUR *a-ri-b*[*i*]
20) *bíl-tú ma-da-tú* ⸢KÙ⸣.BABBAR GUŠKIN AN.NA AN.BAR
21) KUŠ.AM.SI ZÚ.AM.SI *ta-kil-tú ar-ga-man-nu*
22) *lu-bul-ti bir-me* GADA ANŠE.A.AB.BA.MEŠ
23) ANŠE *na-qa-a-ti* UGU-*šú-nu ú-*⸢*kin*⸣

The kings of Ḫatti, Aram on the banks of the sea of the setting sun, Qedar, and Arabia.[50] Kuštašpi the Kummuḫite, Raqyān[51] the Ša-imerišu-ite, (5)Menahem the Samarian, Tubail the Tyrian, Sipatbail the Byblian, Urik the Queite, Sulumal the Melidite, (10)Uassurme the Tabalite, Ušḫiti the Atunaite, Urballa the Tuḫanaite, Tuḫame the Ištundite, Uirimi the Ḫušemnaite, (15)Dadi-il the Kaskaite, Pisiris the Carchemishite, Panammu the Samaʾlian, Tarḫulara the Gurgumite, Zabibe the queen of Arabia, (20)tribute and gifts, silver, gold, tin, iron, elephant hide, ivory, blue purple

---

and translates the phrase as "vom Ufer the Meeres." He is followed by R. Borger in *TUAT* (378).

[50]Weippert suggests treating KUR *a-ri-bi* as an appositive of KUR *qid-ri* ("Menahem von Israel," 31). While this is possible and solves the problem of the duplication of Arabia in line 19, it is more likely that they are two separate entities, and together with Ḫatti and Aram, they refer to the entire region from which Tiglath-pileser extracted tribute. "Ḫatti" refers to Anatolia and north Syria, while "Aram" refers to central Syria and southward (as does the phrase "all Aram" including upper and lower Aram in the Sefire inscriptions). Qedar and Arabia probably refer to the region along the fringes of the Arabian and Syrian deserts. For an extensive work on the Arabs, see I. Ephʿal, *The Ancient Arabs: Nomads on the Borders of the Fertile Cresent 9th–5th Centuries B.C.* (Jerusalem/Leiden: Magnes/E. J. Brill, 1982), esp. 221–27 on the Qedarites.

[51]Raqyān, written as *ra-qi-a-nu* in Akkadian, apparently reflects an Old Aramaic form of the name of the king (see n. 14 above).

and red purple garments, trimmed linen garments, dromedaries, she-camels, I imposed upon them.

This list begins with a general description of the geographical region involved, namely, Ḫatti, Aram, Qedar, and Arabia (lines 1–2)—the western part of the Fertile Crescent. It then names the rulers of the region upon whom Tiglath-pileser had imposed tribute. Most of the states are from northern Syria and Anatolia, with the exception of Aram-Damascus, Israel, Tyre, Byblos (located in southern Syria and northern Palestine), and Arabia. Israel is the southernmost state listed.

The similarity between this tribute list and other lists has been noted by Levine.[52] In comparing the present list with the annals list, Levine notes that "the only differences . . . are the inclusion of Hamath in the annals and the substitution of the name of Tubail in the stele for that of Hiram."[53] In both the annals texts (Layard 50a + 50b + 67a and Layard $69a_1$ + $69b_2$), however, the place where the name of the Tyrian king was inscribed is broken.

Layard 50a + 50b + 67a:	[ ] *ṣur-a-a*
Layard $69a_1$ + $69b_2$:	[ ]

Nevertheless, in III R 9, 3,[54] an annals text republished by G. Smith, the name of the king of Tyre was restored as ^I^*ḫi-ru-um-mu*. M. Cogan alleges that he has Tadmor's confirmation that Smith's restoration is reliable, since it was based on a squeeze of the text copied by Rawlinson.[55] It should be noted, additionally, that the Iran Stela provides a list of states on whom Tiglath-pileser imposed tribute (UGU-*šu-nu ú-kin*, col. II, lines 23 and 29) to be sent yearly to the capital (*šat-ti-šam-ma am-da-na-ḫa-ra* AŠ ⸢*qé*⸣-*reb* KUR *aš-š*[*ur*], col. II, line 30).[56] It is not itself a list of tributaries and their payment of tribute.

---

[52]Levine, *Two Neo-Assyrian Stelae*, 22–23.

[53]*Ibid*., 22. Although not as important, there is also a difference is the order of the listing of the states after Que.

[54]See Rawlinson, *Cuneiform Inscriptions*, 3. plate 9, no. 3. Tadmor suggests that this is "an ecclectic text, pieced together from several partly parallel documents" ("Introductory Remark," 177).

[55]Cogan, "Tyre and Tiglath-Pileser III," 97 and n. 9.

[56]The statement, "I received yearly in Aššur," follows a list of tribute imposed on the rulers of Mannai, Ellipi, Namri, and Singibutu. Contrary to Levine's suggestion that this latter tribute list belongs to the events of the campaign of 737–736 BCE (*Two Neo-Assyrian Stelae*, 24), it is better to treat this list in relation to the campaign and provincialization of Ulluba in 739–738 BCE. A show of force by Tiglath-pileser must have brought about the submission of these rulers in the Zagros. For the location of Mannai, Ellipi, and Namri see L. D. Levine, *Contributions to the Historical Geography of the Zagros in the Neo-Assyrian Period* (diss., University of Pennsylvania, 1969).

According to the annals (Layard 50a + 50b + 67a and Layard 69a_1 + 69b_2), Enilu of Hamath was one of the states that paid tribute to Tiglath-pileser in the latter's eighth *palû* (738–737 BCE). That was the same year in which Tiglath-pileser suppressed a rebellion, led by a certain *az-ri-a-*[*ú*]/*az-ri-ia-a-ú*,[57] that involved

---

[57]The identity of *az-ri-a-*[*ú*]/*az-ri-ia-a-ú* has been vigorously debated. Earlier scholars, such as E. Schrader (*Die Keilinschriften und das Alte Testament* [Giessen: J. Ricker, 1872], 116), identified him with Azariah/Uzziah of Judah without much hesitation. This was done by linking this text to another, K 6205 (III R 9, 2), where lines 104 and 105 read as follows:

[. . .] *a-a-u* KUR *ia-u-da-a-a* GIM [. . .]
[. . .] *ṣ*/*z-ri-ia u* KUR *ia-u-di* [. . .]

In earlier scholarship, the lines were reconstructed to read:

[*áz-ri-i*]*a-a-u* KUR *ia-u-da-a-a* GIM [. . .]
[*á*]*z-ri-ia-u* KUR *ia-u-di* [. . .]

With such a reconstruction of K 6205, it is easy to see how the identification with Ahaziah/Uzziah of Judah was made. H. Winckler ("Das syrische Land Yaudi und der angebliche Azarja von Juda," *Altorientalische Forschungen* 1 [1893], 1–23) challenged this identification and argued that *az-ri-a-*[*ú*] was the ruler of Yaʾudi-Samʾal, equating *ia-u-di* with יאדי. Winckler's identification was not without problems and was subsequently challenged by W. H. Haydn ("Azariah of Judah and Tiglath-Pileser III," *JBL* 26 [1909], 182–88), D. D. Luckenbill ("Azariah of Judah," *AJSL* 41 [1925], 217–32), E. Thiele ("The Chronology of the Kings of Judah and Israel," *JNES* 3 [1944], 155–62), Albright ("Chronology of the Divided Monarchy of Israel," 18, n. 8), and Tadmor ("Azriyau of Yaudi," 232–71), who reverted to the earlier identification with Azariah/Uzziah. Although the coalition of states which *az-ri-a-*[*ú*]/*az-ri-ia-a-ú* purportedly headed was in north and central Syria, these scholars apparently did not find such an identification problematic. Tadmor, for example, argued that Judah under Azariah was "the strongest of the South-Syrian states at that time" (266), strong enough to head a coalition of north Syrian states into battle against Tiglath-pileser III.

In 1974, Na'aman ("Sennacherib's 'Letter to God,'" 25–38) brought the debate to a conclusion when he showed that K 6205 belongs together with another fragmentary text (BM 82-3-23, 131), which had been ascribed by Tadmor ("Campaigns of Sargon," 80–84) to Sargon II. Na'aman argues instead that the two fragments belong to the time of Sennacherib, and the king of Judah referred to in K 6205 was Hezekiah. In another article, Na'aman ("Looking for KTK," *WO* 9 [1977–78], 229–39) proposes that *az-ri-a-*[*ú*]/*az-ri-ia-a-ú* of III R 9, 3 was the king of the north Syrian city of Hadrach. Recently, Cogan and Tadmor (*II Kings*, 166) have argued that the name *az-ri-a-*[*ú*]/*az-ri-ia-a-ú* is not Aramean, but Israelite, and suggests that he could have been an Israelite/Judean who gained prominence in the region of Hamath. Azriyau is generally assumed to be the leader of the anti-Assyrian coalition suppressed by Tiglath-pileser. Hughes has, however, argued that there is no evidence to support such an assumption and pointed out that the translation of *ekēmu ana* in the phrase *ša i-na ḫi-iṭ-ṭi u gul-lul-ti a-na* ^{I}*az-ri-ia-a-ú e-ki-i-mu* as "had gone over to" (so *ARAB*, 1. §770) is unprecedented. He proposed instead to translate the phrase as "which they (the rebels) had unlawfully taken away from Azriyau" and inferred from this translation that Azriyau could have been the ruler of Hamath who remained a loyal Assyrian subject during that rebellion (*Secrets of the Times*, 198, n. 73). While it is correct that *ekēmu* should be translated as "to take away from, annex, conquer, capture" (*CAD* 3. 65–67), *ana* (i.e., "to, for," etc.) is not usually used with *ekēmu* (as already noted by Tadmor, "Azriyau of Yaudi," 267). Hence Hughes's suggestion goes beyond what the evidence can bear. Rather, one should translate the phrase with A. L. Oppenheim as "which they had (unlawfully) taken away for Azriau" (*ANET*, 283). Hughes's suggestion that Azriyau was the ruler of Hamath is further weakened by the fact that Enilu was the king of Hamath who paid tribute to Tiglath-pileser in that same year. Therefore, without other convincing evidence, it is best to stick to earlier suggestions that *az-ri-a-*[*ú*]/*az-ri-ia-a-ú* was the leader of

Ḫatarikka and some coastal cities as well as the nineteen districts of Hamath (Layard 65; Tadmor's Series C_2). Whether the city of Hamath itself was involved in the rebellion is uncertain as neither the city nor its king are mentioned in the text. Although Tadmor has suggested that Hamath remained loyal to Assyria and as such it was not provincialized after Azriyau's rebellion was suppressed, it is more probable to posit that Hamath was involved.[58] This explains why it was not listed in the Iran Stela as one of the states upon which Tiglath-pileser imposed tribute. Moreover, the city of Hamath must have capitulated when Tiglath-pileser returned to the west to deal with the rebellion, while districts that had belonged to Hamath chose to remain loyal to Azriyau and persisted with the rebellion. This is probably why Hamath did not suffer the same fate as the rest of its districts.

Although it is clear that the tribute list on this stela predates the list in the annals, less clear is its precise date. Levine argues for a date in 737 BCE and that the stele was written and erected at the conclusion of Tiglath-pileser's campaign to Media.[59] That campaign most probably did not conclude until the ninth regnal year of Tiglath-pileser (736–735 BCE). Cogan, however, has called into question Levine's dating, noting in particular that a Tyrian king by the name of Hiram paid tribute to Tiglath-pileser in 738–737 BCE (Tiglath-pileser's eighth *palû*; Layard 50a + 50b + 67a) and again sometime between 734 and 731 BCE (ND 4301 + 4305).[60] Levine's dating, then, would necessitate seeing a quick succession of Tyrian kings during this period—a Hiram followed by Tubail, followed by a second Hiram. This was quite unlikely. Rather, as Cogan rightly deduces, the tribute list on the Iran Stela predates that of Layard 50a + 50b + 67a.[61] Cogan proceeds to suggest that it "could well be a summary list, reflecting this 740 B.C. tribute,"[62] namely, that of Layard 45b. Although this date

---

an anti-Assyrian coalition and to acknowledge that the nation of his reign cannot now be determined.

[58]Tadmor, "Azriyau of Yaudi," 266–68.

[59]The eponym list for the year 737–736 reads: *a-na mad-a-a*.

[60]Cogan, "Tyre and Tiglath-Pileser III," 97–98.

[61]*Ibid.*

[62]*Ibid.*, 98, n. 13. This dating of the tribute list in the "Iran stela" is adopted by, among others, N. Na'aman ("Historical and Chronological Notes on the Kingdoms of Israel and Judah in the Eighth Century B.C.," *VT* 36 [1986], 81–82) and Hughes (*Secrets of the Times*, 200–201). Na'aman associates its erection with the Assyrian campaign against Media in 737–736 BCE, which he suggests is described in detail in the inscription. In reality, nowhere is Media mentioned in the inscription. Its association with Media was first suggested by Levine on other grounds. Even if the erection of the stela can be dated to

would solve the problem of the succession of the Tyrian kings, the fact that the stela was found in western Iran makes Cogan's dating questionable as the Assyrian army was still in Arpad at the end of the year 740–739 BCE. This tribute list should instead be dated between Tiglath-pileser's sixth and eighth *palû* (740–739 and 738–737 BCE). The fact that the stela was discovered in western Iran requires one to associate its erection with an Assyrian campaign in that vicinity. Levine's suggestion of the Median campaign as the occasion of the erection of the stela has been shown to be no longer viable. The stela should instead be associated with Tiglath-pileser's campaign to Ulluba. The eponym list for the king's sixth regnal year (739–738 BCE) reads *a-na* ^{KUR}*ul-lu-ba* ^{URU}*bir-tu ṣab-ta-at* (= "at Ulluba, a fortress was taken"). Ulluba was located in the vicinity of the modern day Iranian-Iraqi border, between the Tigris and one of its tributaries, the Greater Zab, and south of the Hakkāri Mountains, about 100 km north of Nineveh.[63] After the capture of Arpad in 741–740 BCE, the Assyrian army remained in the vicinity of Arpad for another year to mop up rebellious elements in Syria-Palestine. This was the year (740–739 BCE) when Tiglath-pileser probably received tribute from Rezin of Aram-Damascus, Kuštašpi of Kummuḫ, Tubail of Tyre, and others (Layard 45b). It was during this same period (sixth or seventh *palû*) that Tutammû of Unqi was defeated and his territory provincialized (III R 9, 1, line 92). In 739–738 BCE, when the Assyrian army was on its way back to Assyria, Ulluba was taken and provincialized (see eponym chronicle and Layard 65, line 133 [*ARAB*, 1. §770], where in his eighth *palû* [738–737 BCE], Tiglath-pileser settled the deportees from the districts of Hamath following a rebellion, "in the province of the land of Ulluba"). Thus, the Iran Stela was most probably erected at the conclusion of the long western campaign (743–739 BCE) and

737–736 BCE, would it not make better sense to include the tribute list of 738–737 BCE instead? Thiele (*Mysterious Numbers*, 126–28), on the other hand, wants to date Menahem's tribute payment in the stela to 743 or 742 BCE. His argument is that the inscription follows a counterclockwise movement, beginning with Tiglath-pileser's first *palû*, which he dates to 745 BCE, and followed by events of consecutive years. This argument goes beyond the evidence in the text. This is a summary inscription and not an annalistic text and thus not a yearly account of the achievements of the king. Although it begins with the king's first *palû*, that is, his first campaign year, it summarizes events according to geographical regions and mentions the main event that led to the erection of the stela.

[63]See Barnett, "Urartu," 324–325, map 13; Grayson, "Tiglath-pileser III to Sargon II," 75.

following the provincialization of Ulluba. This tribute list, then, is one that dates to Tiglath-pileser's seventh *palû* (739–738 BCE).[64]

The name "Menahem the Samarian" occurs twice in the inscriptions of Tiglath-pileser III, once here in the Iran Stela and again in the annals (Layard 50a). The only thing we can safely conclude from the tribute list in the Iran Stela is that Menahem was one of the many Anatolian and Syro-Palestinian rulers upon whom Tiglath-pileser imposed *biltu* and *maddattu*.

The question of the identity of Tubail of Tyre remains a puzzle. Katzenstein had argued that Tubail of Tyre was Ethbaal II,[65] although there is no other evidence of this Ethbaal either from Phoenician or other sources. The question arises whether the Akkadian *tu-ba-il* represented the Phoenician אתבעל, *ʾittōbaᶜl*. Katzenstein seems to think so, equating Tubail with Ethbaal. Recently, Pitard has supported this identification, stating that "the Akkadian form *tu-ba-il* is certainly meant to render Phoenician אתבעל, Ittobaᶜl, a common royal name at Tyre and Sidon."[66] He argues that Tubail is equivalent to the name ^{I}*tu-ba-ʾa-lum* found in Sennacherib's annals.[67] Although there is no contemporary evidence to support this equation, the identification is most probable. Pitard's identification is based on the argument that a prosthetic א was often omitted. Perhaps the best evidence for this comes from the Ahiram sarcophagus, where the name of the king who made the sarcophagus is given as תבעל or [א]תבעל, if the reconstruction is correct.[68] It has been recognized that in the Phoenician language "omission of first syllable beginning originally with /ʾ/ is attested."[69] Compare, for example, the name אחרם in the Ahiram sarcophagus inscription and חרם in the Baal Lebanon inscription.[70]

---

[64]Shea suggests that this tribute list is a version of Layard 45b ("Menahem and Tiglath-pileser," 49). He is followed recently by Briquel-Chatonnet, *Les relations*, 143–45. This, however, cannot be, since Layard 45b is a statement of tribute received while the Iran Stela is a statement of tribute imposed.

[65]Katzenstein, *History of Tyre*, 129, 194, 204–5.

[66]Pitard, *Ancient Damascus*, 185, n. 104. See also Briquel-Chatonnet, *Les relations*, 141–43.

[67]D. D. Luckenbill, *The Annals of Sennacherib* (Chicago: University of Chicago Press, 1924), 30, 169.

[68]See, e.g., L. H. Vincent, "Les Fouilles de Byblos," *RB* 34 (1925), 184 and pl. VIII. Yet one wonders if the reconstruction is necessary or if the name had originally been written just תבעל (*tōbaᶜl*).

[69]S. Segert, *A Grammar of Phoenician and Punic* (München: C. H. Beck, 1976), 77.

[70]*KAI*, nos. 1 and 30; *TSSI*, 3. 12–16; 66–68. See also W. F. Albright, "Notes on Early Hebrew and Aramaic Epigraphy," *JPOS* 6 (1926), 78–79; Z. S. Harris, *A Grammar*

If ^{I}*tu-ba-ʾa-lum* goes back to an original אתבעל in Phoenician, it is possible that ^{I}*tu-ba-ìl* does as well. Nevertheless, the case of ^{I}*tu-ba-ìl* is more complex and less certain.[71] First, the "ba^{c}l" element is almost always rendered *ba-ʾa-lu/i* in Assyrian inscriptions.[72] The Iran Stela would be the only place where *ba-ìl* stands for the "ba^{c}l" element,[73] although it may not necessarily be the case. Second, the name transcribed as ^{I}*tu-ba-ìl* by Levine can equally be transcribed as ^{I}*ṭú-ba-ìl*. In this case, the name can certainly represent the Canaanite טבאל, read as *ṭōbʾēl* or *ṭābĕēl*, in which case the DINGIR sign (*ìl*) is an accurate representation of the Canaanite אֵל. Contrary to Pitard, this is certainly *not* impossible. In this case, Tubail may be identified with *Ṭābĕʾal*/*Ṭābĕʾēl* of Isa 7:6, as has already been proposed by A. Vanel.[74]

D. Layard 50a + 50b + 67a

Layard 50a + 50b + 67a belongs to Tadmor's Series B of Tiglath-pileser's annals. The cuneiform text was republished by G. Smith in III R 9, 3,[75] which Tadmor, however, suggests is "an eclectic text, pieced together from several partly parallel documents." Layard 50a + 50b + 67a is fragmentary and consists of twenty-four lines of text, recording the military and political achievements of Tiglath-pileser III in his eighth and ninth *palê* (738–737 and 737–736 BCE). These accomplishments include the war against Aramean tribes in Syria under the leadership of the governor of Naʾiri (Layard 50a, lines 1–3),[76] the repopulating of

---

of the Phoenician Language (AOS 8; New Haven: American Oriental Society, 1936), 31; Segert, *Grammar*, 77.

71 Contra Pitard, *Ancient Damascus*, 185.

72 See, e.g.,, ^{I}*si-pi-iṭ-[ṭí]-bi-ʾi-li* in Layard 50a, line 10; ^{I}*si-bi-it-[ti]-bi-ʾi-li* and ^{I}*ma-ta-an-bi-ʾi-li* in K 3751 (II R 67), lines 7 and 10; *a-na* ^{URU}*ba-ʾ-li* in the eponym chronicle of 802–801 BCE (Ungnad, *RLA*, 2. 429); ^{KUR}*ba-ʾ-li-ṣa-pu-na* (Rost, *Keilschrifttexte*, 20); ^{I}*tu-ba-ʾa-lum* in Sennacherib's annals (Luckenbill, *Annals of Sennacherib*, 30); ^{I}*ba-ʾa-lu* in Esarhaddon's treaty with Baal of Tyre (R. Borger, *Die Inschriften Asarhaddons Königs von Assyrien* [AfO 9; Osnabrück: Biblio-Verlag, 1967], 107–9, §69).

73 Cf. the name ^{I}*si-pàṭ-ba-ìl* on line 7, where *ba-ìl* occurs probably through "corruption."

74 A. Vanel, "Tâbe'él en Is. VII 6 et le roi Tubail de Tyr," *Studies on Prophecy: A Collection of Twelve Papers*, ed. G. W. Anderson *et al.* (VTSup 26; Leiden: E. J. Brill, 1974), 17–24.

75 See Rawlinson, *Cuneiform Inscriptions*, 3. plate 9, no. 3. Rost furnishes a transliteration of the text with a German translation in his edition of the annals (*Keilschrifttexte*, 24–28, ll. 141–64).

76 Layard 65, a parallel text, alludes to other governors who were involved in this campaign (cf. Rost, *Keilschrifttexte*, ll. 133–40).

the land of Unqi (Layard 50a, lines 3–9), and the receipt of tribute from western states, from Anatolia in the north to Palestine in the south (Layard 50a, lines 10–12; Layard 50b + 67a, lines 1–5). This last item is the focus of our attention, and the following is a transliteration of the text:[77]

Layard 50a

150) . . . *ma-da-at-tu ša* ^{I}[78]*ku-uš-ta-áš-pi* URU *ku-um-mu-ḫa-a-a* ^{I}*ra-ḫi-a-nu* KUR *šá* ANŠE.NÍTA-*šu-a-a* ^{I}*me-ni-ḫi-im-me* URU *sa-me-ri-na-a-a*

151) [^{I}*ḫi-ru-um-mu* URU][79] *ṣur-a-a* ^{I}*si-pi-iṭ-*[*ṭì*]*-bi-ʾi-li* URU *gu-ub-la-a-a* ^{I}*ú-ri-ik-ki* KUR *qu-ú-a-a* ^{I}*pi-si-ri-is* URU *gar-ga-*[*miš*][80]*-a-a* ^{I}*e-ni-*DINGIR

152) [URU *ḫa-am-ma*][81]*-ta-a-a* ^{I}*pa-*[*na-am-mu*][82]*-u* URU *sa-am-ʾa-la-a-a* ^{I}*tar-ḫu-la-ra* KUR *gúr-gu-ma-a-a* ^{I}*su-lu-ma-al* [KUR][83] *me-lid-da-a-a* ^{I}*da-di-i-lu*

Layard 50b + 67a

153) URU *kas-ka-a-a* ^{I}*ú-as-sur-me* KUR *ta-bal-a-a* ^{I}*uš-ḫi-it-ti* KUR *tu-na-a-a* ^{I}*ur-bal-la-a* KUR *tu-ḫa*[84]*-*[*na-*[85]]*a-a* ^{I}*tu-*[*ḫa-am-me* URU *ís-tu-un-da-a-a*][86]

154) ^{I}*ú-ri-im-mì-i* URU *ḫu-šem*[87]*-na-a-a* ^{SAL}*za-*[*bi-bi-*[88]]*e šar-rat* KUR *a-ri-bi* KÙ.GI KÙ.BABBAR AN.NA AN.BAR KUŠ.AM.SI [ZÚ.AM.SI][89]

---

[77]The enumeration of the lines of the text follows that of Rost. A parallel list can be found in Layard $69a_1$ + $69b_2$ (Tadmor's Series A).

[78]Layard copied the sign as  , and indicated its uncertainty with a question mark. Smith rightly corrected the sign to read the determinative for a personal name.

[79]As already noted above (pp. 148–49), Hiram's name does not show up in Layard 50a but in III R 9, 3. Cogan's reconstruction is almost certain ("Tyre and Tiglath-Pileser III," 97, n. 9).

[80]Restored following Smith. This sign is missing in Layard's text. We can only guess whether the sign was mistakenly left out by the original scribe or by Layard in his copying.

[81]Restored following Smith.

[82]Restored following Smith.

[83]Restored following Smith.

[84]Following Smith; cf. Iran stela, rev. 12. Layard copied as  , and indicated its uncertainty with a question mark.

[85]Uncertain in Layard's copy; restored following Smith.

[86]Restored following Smith.

[87]Following Smith; cf. "Iran stela," rev. 14. Layard's copy reads as two signs, *bi-ta*, obviously an error.

[88]Restored following Smith.

[89]Restored following Smith.

155) *lu-bul-ti bir-me* ^{TÚG}GADA SÍK[90] *ta-[kil-*[91]*]tu* [SÍK *ar*[92]]*-ga man-nu* ^{GIŠ}ESIG ^{GIŠ}TÚG *mim-ma aq-ru ni-ṣir-ti šarru-ú-ti* ^{UDU}ARAD.MEŠ *pal-[ku-ti ša* SÍK.MEŠ*-šú-nu]*[93]

156) *ar-ga-man-nu ṣar-pat iṣ-ṣur* AN*-e mut-tap-ri-šú-ti šá a-gap-pi-šú-nu a-na ta-kil-te ṣar-pu* ANŠE.KUR.RA.MEŠ ANŠE.GÌR.NUN.NA. MEŠ GU4.NÍTA.MEŠ *ù ṣe-[e-ni* ANŠE.A.AB.BA. MEŠ]*[94]

157) $^{\text{SAL.ANŠE}}$*[a-*[95]*]na-qa-a-te a-di* ^{ANŠE}*ba-ak-ka-ri-ši-na am-ḫur . . .*

(150). . . . The tribute of Kuštašpi the Kummuḫite, Raᶜyān the Ša-imērišu-ite, Menahem the Samarian, [Hiram the] Tyrian, Sipittibiᵓli the Byblian, Urikki the Queite, Pisiris the Carchemishite, Enilu [the Hama]thian, Pa[namm]u the Samaᵓlian, Tarḫulara the Gurgumite, Sulumal the Melidite, Dadi-il the Kaskaite, Uassurme the Tabalite, Ušḫitti the Tunaite, Urballa the Tuḫanaite, Tu[ḫamme the Ištundaite], Urimmi the Ḫušemnaite, Zabibe the queen of Arabia—gold, silver, lead, iron, elephant hide, [ivory], (155)multicolored trimmed garments, linen garments, blue purple wool, red purple wool, ebony, boxwood, whatever precious things from the royal treasury; fatted sheep [whose wool is dyed] red purple, flying birds whose wings are dyed blue purple, horses, mules, cattle and sh[eep, dromedaries], female camels together with their colts—I received.

Aside from some differences alluded to earlier, this tribute list is almost identical with that of the Iran Stela. Their similarities and differences are immediately obvious when they are set side-by-side:

Iran Stela	*Layard 50a + 50b + 67a*
Kuštašpi the Kummuḫite	Kuštašpi the Kummuḫite
Raqyān the Ša-imērišu-ite	Raᶜyān the Ša-imērišu-ite
Menahem the Samarian	Menahem the Samarian
Tubail the Tyrian	[*Hiram* the] Tyrian
Sipatbail the Byblian	Sipittibiᵓli the Byblian
Urik the Queite	Urikki the Queite
Sulumal the Melidite	Pisiris the Carchemishite
Uassurme the Tabalite	*Enilu [the Hama]thian*
Ušḫiti the Atunaite	Pa[namm]u the Samaᵓlian
Urballa the Tuḫanaite	Tarḫulara the Gurgumite
Tuḫame the Ištundite	Sulumal the Melidite
Uirimi the Ḫušemnaite	Dadi-il the Kaskaite
Dadi-il the Kaskaite	Uassurme the Tabalite
Pisiris the Carchemishite	Ušḫitti the Tunaite
Panammu the Samaᵓlian	Urballa the Tuḫanaite

[90]Wrongly read as two separate signs by Layard.

[91]According to Layard, the sign is uncertain.

[92]Illegible in Layard's copy.

[93]Restored following Smith.

[94]Restored following Smith.

[95]Lacking in Layard's copy; restored following Smith.

Tarḫulara the Gurgumite	Tu[ḫamme the Ištundaite]
Zabibe the queen of Arabia	Urimmi the Ḫušemnaite
	Zabibe the queen of Arabia

While the Iran Stela lists seventeen rulers, Layard 50a + 50b + 67a has eighteen, the one additional ruler being Enilu of Hamath. Moreover, this annalistic list has Hiram of Tyre instead of Tubail. That the two lists are almost identical requires one to date them very close to one another. That in fact is the case, if the dating of the tribute list in the Iran Stela to 739–738 BCE, proposed above, is correct.

Although the dated part of the text is broken, the dating of the tribute list in this inscription to Tiglath-pileser's eighth ***palû***, that is, 738–737 BCE, is secure and almost unanimously accepted by scholars.[96] This date is supported by the fact that line 5 of Layard 50b + 67a, which states "female camels together with their colts—I received," is followed without any break by the dated heading ***i-na*** IX ***palî-ia***. It is clear from both the annals (Layard 50a, line 3)[97] and the Eponym chronicle that Tiglath-pileser conducted a western campaign in his eighth ***palû***, during which time he received the tribute of these Anatolian and Syro-Palestinian rulers. According to the annals, the booty that was taken by his governors was "brought before me in Ḫatti."[98] The eponym chronicle for 738–737 BCE, moreover, recorded the capture of Kullani (biblical Calneh/Calno) in northern Syria.

It has been noted that Hamath does not appear in the tribute list in the Iran Stela. This has led Cogan to raise the possibility that the Azriyau affair was still not settled at the time of the compilation of the list in the Iran Stela.[99] It is, however, more probable that Hamath was involved in the rebellion, as was suggested above. If Hamath had remained loyal to the Assyrian king, tribute would have been imposed on it along with the other Ana-

---

[96]Because Thiele puts Menahem's final year as 742 BCE, he seeks to argue that this tribute list must be dated to 743 BCE (*Mysterious Numbers*, 139–62). Tadmor has convincingly refuted Thiele's arguments ("Azriyau of Yaudi," 258–59). Thiele, likewise, dates the list in the Iran stela to 743 or 742 BCE (128), and although he recognizes the differences between the two lists, he seems to ignore them.

[97]According to Layard 65, this was the campaign in which the Assyrian king dealt with the anti-Assyrian revolt led by Azriyau. On line 4, Rost suggested reading the first three signs as ***ma*** (***âlu***) ***Kul***- and restored [***la-ni***] to produce the city of Kullani, although Layard had copied the third sign as KUR. If Rost's restoration is correct, the annals provide further confirmation of the capture of Kullani, which appears in the eponym chronicle.

[98]See *ARAB*, 1. §771.

[99]Cogan, "Tyre and Tiglath-pileser III," 98, n. 13.

tolian and Syro-Palestinian states. Hamath's subsequent capitulation probably saved it from provincialization by the Assyrians.

Hiram (II) of Tyre must have succeeded Tubail on the Tyrian throne between the time of the erection of the Iran Stela and the end of the eighth *palû* (i.e., sometime in 738–737 BCE), when the official records of the annals listed the kings from whom Tiglath-pileser had personally received tribute.

E. Layard $69a_1$ + $69b_2$

Layard $69a_1$ + $69b_2$ belongs to Tadmor's Series A of Tiglath-pileser's annals. It is a parallel text to Layard 50a + 50b + 67a. The following is a transliteration of the two fragments:[100]

150) [. . .] ^{I}*ku-uš-ta-áš-pi* URU *ku-um-mu-ḫa-a-a* ^{I}*ra-ḫi-a-nu* KUR *šá* ANŠE.NÍTA-*šu*-[. . .]

151) [. . .]-*bi-*ʾ*i-li* URU *gu-ub-la-a-a* ^{I}*ú-ri-ii-ik-ki* KUR *qu-ú*-[. . .]

152) [. . .]-*na-am-mu-u* URU *sa-am-*ʾ*a-la-a-a* ^{I}*tar-ḫu-la-ra* KUR *gúr-gu*-[. . .]

153) [. . .]-*sur-me* KUR *ta-bal-a-a* ^{I}*uš-ḫi-it-te* KUR *tu-na-a-a* ^{I}*ur-bal-la*-[. . .]

154) [. . .]-*a* ^{SAL}*za-bi-bi-e šar-rat* KUR *a-ri-bi* KÙ.G[I . . .]

155) [. . .] *ár-ga-man-nu* ^{GIŠ}ESIG ^{GIŠ}TÚG [. . .]

[. . .] Kuštašpi the Kummuḫite, Raᶜyān the Ša-imērišu-[. . .]
[. . .]biʾli the Byblian, Urikki the Que [. . .]
[. . .]nammu the Samaʾlian, Tarḫulara the Gurgum [. . .]
[. . .]surme the Tabalite, Ušḫitti the Tunaite, Urballa [. . .]
[. . .]ite, Zabibe the queen of Arabia—gold, [. . .]
[. . .]red purple wool, ebony, boxwood [. . .]

This text does not add anything new to what is already known from Layard 50a + 50b + 67a.

Rezin of Aram-Damascus is presented in the texts of Tiglath-pileser as a prominent power in Syria-Palestine, one upon whom tribute was imposed (so the Iran Stela) and one who paid tribute to the Assyrian king (so Layard 45b, Layard 50a + 50b + 67a, and Layard $69a_1$ + $69b_2$). Nonetheless, non-Assyrian texts indicate that Rezin was a troublemaker in the area and whose actions were contrary to Assyrian policies and interests, even before Assyrian texts indicate that he was the ringleader in a western anti-Assyrian coalition. Our earlier treatment of Amos 1; 2 Kgs 15:37; and

[100]The enumeration of the lines of this text follows that of Rost.

16:6[101] provides evidence that as early as the 750s BCE, Rezin was already assembling a coalition in an attempt to dominate regional politics and commerce. In so doing, political and commercial pressure was exerted on pro-Assyrian states such as Israel and Judah, which suffered territorial losses.

That Rezin and the anti-Assyrian coalition was stirring up trouble again not long after 738–737 BCE is evident from the so-called Syro-Ephraimitic crisis, alluded to in Isa 7:1–9.[102] The text begins in v. 1 with a summary statement about the Syro-Ephraimitic crisis.

> In the days of Ahaz son of Jotham son of Uzziah, king of Judah, Rezin king of Aram went up with Pekah son of Remaliah, king of Israel, to Jerusalem for battle against it, but he was unable to mount an attack against it.

It is evident that the wording of Isa 7:1 is very close to that of 2 Kgs 16:5, although not identical. This has led scholars to propose different explanations for their dependence. Earlier scholars suggested that 2 Kgs 16:5 is dependent on Isa 7:1.[103] The reverse is, however, assumed by more recent scholars, who posit that Isa 7:1 is derived from the Kings text.[104] A third hypothesis, perhaps more likely, is that both these texts are independent formulations, deriving from the same archival source.[105]

That Rezin is mentioned first both in this text and in the Kings text may be historically significant. Our foregoing analysis of the Assyrian texts have shown the prominence of Rezin in Syria-Palestine. In addition, it is significant to note that according to Isaiah the action against Jerusalem was principally that of Rezin. Both verbs עלה and יכל are construed in the singular. It was Rezin who "went up" against Jerusalem, and it was Rezin who "was unable" to launch an attack against Jerusalem. Literarily (and perhaps also historically), Pekah only had a secondary role.

---

[101]See chapter three above.

[102]For a comprehensive study of the text, see Irvine, *Syro-Ephraimitic Crisis*, 133–59. Cf. also J. H. Hayes and S. A. Irvine, *Isaiah, the Eighth Century Prophet: His Times and Preaching* (Nashville: Abingdon, 1987), 113–29.

[103]See, e.g., F. Delitzsch, *Biblical Commentary on the Prophecies of Isaiah* (2 vols.; 3d ed.; New York: Funk & Wagnalls, 1889), 1. 162; A. Dillman, *Der Buch Jesaja* (5th ed.; Leipzig: S. Hirzel, 1890), 64–65.

[104]See, e.g., H. Donner, *Israel unter den Völkern. Die Stellung der klassischen Propheten des 8. Jahrhunderts v. Chr. zur Aussenpolitik der Könige von Israel und Juda* (VTSup 11; Leiden: E. J. Brill, 1964), 8; Wildberger, *Isaiah 1–12*, 283, 287, 291–93; Kaiser, *Isaiah 1–12*, 116, 170–71; Clements, *Isaiah 1–39*, 79, 82.

[105]So Cogan and Tadmor, *II Kings*, 186; Irvine, *Syro-Ephraimitic Crisis*, 137.

The summary in 7:1 chronologically follows the words and actions of Isaiah in vv. 2–9 (and 10–17). Verse 2 begins by describing the demeanor of the Davidic house as well as that of its supporters upon hearing that נחה ארם על־אפרים. While the verb נחה appears to have been derived from the root נוח, with the meaning of "to rest, settle down, remain,"[106] scholars have resorted to emendation and to cognate languages in order to derive different meanings.[107] The NRSV translates the phrase as "Aram had allied itself with Ephraim," probably following G. R. Driver's suggestion of translating נחה as "become allied with" on the basis of the Arabic *naḥa* ("to lean on").[108] Irvine, however, may be right to argue that there is no reason to resort to emendations and cognate languages in an attempt to interpret the text. Thus, he suggests translating the phrase as "Syria has descended on Ephraim." He further suggests that "Syria's 'descent' on Ephraim may vividly describe Pekah's coup in Samaria in Tishri 734, and with it, the effective takeover of the whole of the northern kingdom by Syria."[109]

Of particular importance for our discussion are vv. 5–6. The text reads:

> Because Aram has plotted evil against you, with Ephraim and the son of Remaliah, saying, "Let us go up against Judah and terrify it and split it open for ourselves and let us enthrone as king in its midst the son of Tabeʾal."[110]

According to Isaiah, the "evil" action that Aram-Damascus and Ephraim are plotting against Judah is described by the three verbal forms נקיצנה, נבקענה, and נמליך. The first verb appears to be derived from the root קוץ "to feel dread, be afraid."[111] The hiphil of the verb, therefore, may be construed in the causative as "to strike fear, terrify." The second verb נבקענה derives from the root בקע "to cleave, break open or through," a term used often in association with the capture of cities.[112] The hiphil of the verb

---

[106]So *BDB*, 628, which translates the phrase as "Aram hath settled down upon Ephraim."

[107]See Irvine, *Syro-Ephraimitic Crisis*, 138–39, for emendations and meanings proposed.

[108]G. R. Driver, "Lingusitic and Textual Problems: Isaiah I–XXXIX," *JTS* 38 (1937), 37.

[109]Irvine, *Syro-Ephraimitic Crisis*, 139.

[110]LXX renders the name as Ταβεήλ.

[111]*BDB*, 880–81 gives the meaning as "feel a loathing, abhorrence, sickening dread." Cf. Wildberger, *Isaiah 1–12*, 282, 284. For proposals of emendation, see Irvine, *Syro-Ephraimitic Crisis*, 152, n. 69.

[112]See, e.g., 2 Kgs 25:4; Jer 39:2; Ezek 26:10; 30:16; 2 Chr 32:1.

literally means "to cause (it) to break open." In all likelihood, Rezin's intention was to strike fear in the midst of Judah and create dissension for his own advantage. With a show of force in Judah, Rezin and his anti-Assyrian coalition would naturally stir up the disaffection of some of the populace against the pro-Assyrian policy of the Davidic house. Moreover, according to Isaiah, Rezin had the intention of replacing the Davidic king with the son of Tabeʾal/Tabeʾel. (Again, the text uses a hiphil form of מלך meaning "to cause to rule, enthrone.") It is clear that the Hebrew spelling of טָבְאַל (literally, "good-for-nothing") is pejorative. A correct spelling of the name טָבְאֵל is found in Ezra 4:7. The Septuagint most probably preserved the original spelling of the name, Ταβεήλ. The identity of the son of Tabeʾel has baffled scholars. Several proposals have been offered. Kraeling conjectured that the son of Tabeʾel was Rezin.[113] Rignell took this further by positing that Tabeʾal was a derogatory word-play on Rezin's name. He explained that Rezin's name in Aramaic, רצון, means "well-being," while טָבְאַל expresses the opposite meaning of "not-good."[114] Albright proposed taking Tabeʾel as the name of a state in Transjordan. His proposal is based on Nimrud Letter XIV (ND 2773), dated to the reign of Tiglath-pileser, which mentions a Ayanur the Tabelite.[115] Albright suggests that the son of Tabeʾel was a Judean prince whose mother originated from Tabel. Finally, Mazar makes a connection between the names טָבְאַל and טוֹבִיָּה(וּ), suggesting that the son of Tabeʾel was an ancestor of the influential Tobiad family of the Second Temple Period.[116] Pitard rightly notes that all these suggestions are speculative.[117] We have argued earlier that it is best to follow Vanel and identify Tabeʾel with Tubail of Tyre mentioned in the Iran stela.[118] Therefore, the son of Tabeʾel was most probably a prince of the royal house of Tyre (perhaps the brother of King Hiram), a state known from the Assyrian sources to have been in league with Rezin (ND 4301 +

---

[113]Kraeling, *Aram and Israel*, 115.

[114]L. G. Rignell, "Das Immanuelszeichen. Einige Gesichtspunkte zu Jes 7," *ST* 11 (1957), 104.

[115]W. F. Albright, "The Son of Tabeel (Isaiah 7:6)," *BASOR* 140 (1955), 34–35. The reading of the gentilic KUR *ṭa-ab-i-la-a-a* is, unfortunately, uncertain. See Saggs, "Nimrud Letters, 1952—Part II," 131–33; H. Donner, "Neue Quellen zur Geschichte des Staates Moab in der zweiten Haefte der 8. Jahrhundert v. Chr.," *MIO* 5 (1957), 170–71.

[116]B. Mazar, "The Tobiads," *IEJ* 7 (1957), 236–37. See also Oded, "Syro-Ephraimitic War Reconsidered," 161–62, who follows Mazar and in addition suggests that the son of Tabeʾel was probably related to the royal family of Judah.

[117]Pitard, *Ancient Damascus*, 185, n. 104.

[118]See pp. 152–53 above.

4305, rev. line 5). It was the intention of Rezin, the leader of the anti-Assyrian coalition, to force Judah into changing its foreign policy, even if that meant removing the pro-Assyrian Ahaz and replacing him with an anti-Assyrian appointee.

The Isaianic text reveals the close alliance between Aram-Damascus, Pekah, and the Tyrians in the mid-730s BCE, an alliance which was probably forged in the 750s BCE. The mention of the "son of Tabeʾal (= Tubail)" indicates that Tubail had supported the coalition during his reign as king of Tyre.

F. II R 67

II R 67 (K 3751)[119] is a surviving fragment of a long summary inscription of Tiglath-pileser III, found in 1873 by G. Smith. It is inscribed on both sides and summarizes the achievements of Tiglath-pileser in his first seventeen *palê*, ending with a long report on the construction of his palace at Nimrud. The inscription was most probably written in 728 BCE, at the end of Tiglath-pileser's seventeenth *palû*, or his sixteenth regnal year. The focus of our attention is on the tributary list in lines 7–13, reverse.[120]

7) [*ma-da-at-tu*] *ša* ^{I}*ku-uš-ta-áš-pi* ^{KUR}*ku-muḫ-a-a* ^{I}*ú-ri-ik* ^{KUR}*qu-u-a-a* ^{I}*si-bi-it-ti-bi-ʾi-il* [^{URU}*gu-ub-la-a-a* . . .]

8) [^{I}*e-ni*]-DINGIR ^{KUR}*ḫa-am-ma-ta-a-a* ^{I}*pa-na-am-mu-u* ^{URU}*sa-am-ʾa-la-a-a* ^{I}*tar-ḫu-la-ra* ^{KUR}*gúr-gu-ma-a-a* ^{I}*su-*[*lu-ma-al* ^{KUR}*me-lid-da-a-u* . . .]

9) [^{I}*ú*]*-as-sur-me* ^{KUR}*ta-bal-a-a* ^{I}*uš-ḫi-it-ti* ^{URU}*tu-na-a-a* ^{I}*ur-bal-la-a* ^{URU}*tu-ḫa-na-a-a* ^{I}*tu-ḫa-am-*[*me* ^{URU}*ís-tu-un-da-a-a* . . .]

10) [^{I}*m*]*a-ta-an-bi-ʾi-il* ^{URU}*ar-wa*$_{6}$*-da-a-a* ^{I}*sa-ni-pu* ^{URU}*É-am-ma-na-a-a* ^{I}*sa-la-ma-nu* ^{KUR}*ma-ʾa-ba-a-a* [^{I} . . .]

11) [^{I}*mi*]*-ti-in-ti* ^{KUR}*as-qa-lu-na-a-a* ^{I}*ia-ú-ḫa-zi* ^{KUR}*ia-ú-da-a-a* ^{I}*ka*$_{4}$*-uš-ma-la-ka* ^{KUR}*ú-du-mu-a-a* ^{I}*mu-uṣ-*[. . .]

12) [^{I}*ḫa*]*-a-nu-u-nu* ^{URU}*ḫa-za-at-a-a* KÙ.GI KÙ.BABBAR AN.NA AN.BAR A.BÁRA *lu-bul-ti bir-me* ^{TÚG}GADA *lu-bul-ti* KUR-*šú-nu* ^{SÍK}ZA.GÌN.SA$_{5}$ [. . .]

13) [*mim-ma a*]*q-ru bi-nu-ut tam-tim na-ba-li ṣi-bu-ta-at* KUR-*šú-nu ni-ṣir-ti šarru-ti* ANŠE.KUR.RA.MEŠ ANŠE.GÌR.NUN.NA.MEŠ LAL-*at* ^{GIŠ}*ni-*[*i-ri* . . . *am-ḫur*]

---

[119]A copy of the cuneiform text can be found in Rawlinson, *Cuneiform Inscriptions*, 2. pl. 67, and a transliteration in Rost, *Keilschrifttexte*, 54–77. English translations may be found in Luckenbill, *ARAB*, 1. §801; Irvine, *Syro-Ephraimitic Crisis*, 40–41.

[120]This tributary list is preceded in lines 3–6 by a description of the submission of various Arab tribes and the appointment of the Idibiʾilu as *qepu*-officers "over Egypt" (cf. Irvine, *Syro-Ephraimitic Crisis*, 40, n. 61).

> [The tribute] of Kuštašpi the Kummuḫite, Urik the Queite, Sibittibiʾil [the Byblian, . . .] [E]nil the Hamathian, Panammu the Samaʾlian, Tarḫulara the Gurgumite, Su[lumal the Melidite, . . .] [U]assurme the Tabalite, Ušḫitti the Tunaite, Urballa the Tuḫanaite, Tuḫam[me the Ištundaite, . . .] (10)[Ma]tanbiʾil the Arwadite, Sanipu the Bit-Ammonite, Salamanu the Moabite, [. . .] [Mi]tinti the Ashkelonite, Jehoahaz the Judean, Kaušmalaka the Edomite, Mus[. . .] [Ha]nun the Gazaite—gold, silver, lead, iron, tin, multicolored trimmed garments, linen garments, purple garments of their lands, [. . .] [whatever pre]cious things, products of the sea and the land, commodities of their lands, the royal treasury; horses and mules stretched to the yo[ke . . . —I received].

This tribute list[121] closely resembles other tribute lists from the reign of Tiglath-pileser. The Anatolian and northern Syrian states listed in lines 7–9 had appeared in Layard 50a + 50b + 67a, dated to 738–737 BCE, and with the exception of Hamath, also in the Iran Stela, dated to 739–738 BCE. Noticeably missing from this list are any references to Aram-Damascus, Samaria/Israel, Tyre, and Arabia, states from whom Tiglath-pileser had collected *maddattu* on earlier occasions. The other states in lines 10–12 had not appeared in earlier lists of Tiglath-pileser. These states, with the exception of Arwad, were located in southern Palestine, and included Judah.

The dating of this tribute list is a matter of dispute. J. M. Asurmendi dates the list together with the inscription to 728 BCE and suggests that the list alludes to the political situation a few years after the Syro-Ephraimitic crisis.[122] Irvine has rightly repudiated this dating, noting in particular Asurmendi's failure to account for the fact that Mitinti of Ashkelon was already removed from power sometime in 733–732 BCE, according to another inscription of Tiglath-pileser (Layard 29b).[123] Therefore this list must predate Mitinti's deposal in 733–732 BCE.

I. Ephᶜal and M. Weippert, however, believe that the list comes from two different historical periods: lines 7–9 were copied from the tribute list of 738 BCE, while lines 10–12 were associated with the so-called Syro-Ephraimitic crisis.[124] Weippert, in particular, argues for the restoration of the rulers of Aram-Damascus, Samaria, and Tyre at the end of line 7, of Kaska and Carchemish at the end of line 8, and of Ḫubišna (or Ḫušemna) and

---

[121] For a recent study of this tribute list, see Irvine, *Syro-Ephraimitic Crisis*, 40–44. The following analysis follows closely the work of Irvine.

[122] J. M. Asurmendi, *La Guerra Siro-Efraimita: Historia y Profetas* (Valencia: Institutión San Jerónimo, 1982), 34–35.

[123] Irvine, *Syro-Ephraimitic Crisis*, 41–42.

[124] Ephᶜal, *Ancient Arabs*, 29, n. 76; Weippert, "Menahem von Israel," 53.

Arabia at the end of line 9[125] in an attempt to bring this list into closer conformity to the list of 738 BCE. Irvine has cast serious doubts on Weippert's suggested restoration, particularly for line 7. Weippert's restoration would have yielded the sequence of Kummuḫ, Que, Byblos, Aram-Damascus, Samaria/Israel, and Tyre. However, Irvine correctly notes that in the earlier lists the sequence is always Kummuḫ, Aram-Damascus, Samaria/Israel, Tyre, Byblos, and Que.[126] Therefore, it is unlikely that references to Aram-Damascus, Israel, and Tyre once appeared in this tribute list. In all probability, Pisiris the Carchemishite once appeared at the end of line 7, Dadi-il the Kaskaite at the end of line 8, and Urimmi the Ḫušemnaite at the end of line 9.[127]

Irvine dates the list to 734–733 BCE and suggests that it reflects the situation in Anatolia, Syria, and Palestine following Tiglath-pileser's campaign in Philistia (noted in the eponym chronicle).[128] Most of the states that had paid tribute in 738 BCE remained loyal, while Arwad and other Palestinian states were either forcibly suppressed by or voluntarily submitted to the Assyrian king. Ahaz of Judah probably submitted voluntarily.

The absence of Rezin of Aram-Damascus, Pekah of Israel, and Hiram of Tyre from this text reflects their anti-Assyrian stance, their determination to resist Assyrian hegemony, and their military opposition to Tiglath-pileser. The situation probably reflects conditions late in 734 BCE or early in 733 BCE. By Nisan 733 BCE, the Assyrian army was "at Philistia," although Tiglath pileser himself was probably in the capital for the Akîtu festival. The list implies that Tiglath-pileser received the *maddattu* personally, so the conditions reflected may not have occurred until after Tiglath-pileser's arrival in the west.[129] II R 67 suggests, albeit *ex silentio*, the continuation of a close military alliance between Pekah, Aram-Damascus, and the Tyrians that commenced when Pekah became a rival king after a period of Damascene expansion towards the end of the reign of Jeroboam II. Prior to Tiglath-pileser's arrival in Syria-Palestine, the anti-Assyrian coalition was

---

[125]Weippert, "Menahem von Israel," 53.

[126]Irvine, *Syro-Ephraimitic Crisis*, 43. So also Hughes, *Secrets of the Times*, 202–3 and nn. 83–84.

[127]Cf. the same sequence in Layard 50a + 50b + 67a.

[128]Irvine, *Syro-Ephraimitic Crisis*, 43.

[129]Samsi, queen of the Arabs, was most probably a member of this anti-Assyrian coalition, and thus was also not named in the tribute list (contra Irvine, *Syro-Ephraimitic Crisis*, 43). On Arabia's close alliance with Damascus and Tyre, especially for the sake of Arabian trade, see Ephᶜal, *Ancient Arabs*, 83.

mounting strong opposition against the Assyrian monarch. Part of the coalition's strategy was to force Ahaz of Judah to join the alliance (Isa 7:1–9). It is likely that the coalition had expanded to include most states in Syria-Palestine. In response to the strong regionalism of the time, the Assyrian campaign of 734–731 BCE was undertaken. II R 67 also suggests the different foreign policies which were advocated by Israel and Judah—anti-Assyrian and pro-coalition, and pro-Assyrian and anti-coalition, respectively.

G. ND 400

ND 400 is a fragmentary inscription discovered in 1950 at Nimrud. According to D. J. Wiseman, who first published the text, this fragment is a version of the annalistic texts of Tiglath-pileser III. The fragment consists of twenty-seven lines, of which lines 1–19 detail his Phoenicia-Philistia campaign in 734–733 BCE.[130] Lines 1–9 describe Tiglath-pileser's offensive against the Phoenician coast, lines 10–13 the defeat of a state whose name is not preserved, and lines 14–19 the suppression of Hanun of Gaza and the erection of Tiglath-pileser's royal image at the Brook of Egypt.[131] The following is a transliteration of the text.

1) [. . .]
2) [. . .] *ma-šu* AŠ *na-ba-li* [. . .]
3) [. . .] *ú-šat-bi-ik* URU *šu-a-tu a-*[. . .]
4) [. . .] MURUB$_4$ *tam-tim ar-ḫi-su-nu-ti-ma a-di* [. . .]
5) [. . . *im-qut*]*-ma it-ru-ku* ŠÀ.MEŠ*-šú* ^{TÚG}*sa-qù il-la-bi* [. . .]
6) [. . .]*-ka* ^{GIŠ}ESI *tam-lit* ZÁ.MEŠ KÙ.GI [lacuna] *a-di* [. . .]
7) [. . .] ZÚ.AM.SI Ì DÙG.GA ŠIM^{ḪÁ} *kàl-a-ma* ANŠE.KUR.RA.MEŠ KUR [. . .]
8) [. . .]*-aḫ* TA ^{URU}*ka-áš-pu-na ša* DÙ ŠÁR *tam-tim* [. . .]
9) [. . .] AŠ ŠU.II ^{LÚ}*šu-ut-*SAG*-ia* ^{LÚ}GAR.KUR ^{URU}*ṣi-*[*mir-ra* . . .]
10) [. . . GIM *ur*]*-ki-ti* LÚ.BAD.MEŠ ^{LÚ}*mun-*[*taḫ*]*-ṣi-e-šu-nu ú-mal-la-a* [*ṣeri* . . .]
11) [. . . *ma*]*r-ši-ti-šú-nu* GU$_4$.MEŠ*-šú-nu ṣi-e-ni-šú-nu* ANŠE.NÍTA*-šu-nu* [. . .]

---

130 D. J. Wiseman, "Two Historical Inscriptions From Nimrud," *Iraq* 13 (1951), 21–24, pl. XI.

131 For a detailed analysis of the entire text, see Irvine, *Syro-Ephraimitic Crisis*, 44–56. That this was a campaign in Philistia is made evident by lines 14–19, which note that Gaza was suppressed.

12) [. . .] AŠ *qí-rib* É.GAL-*šú* [. . .]

13) [. . .]-*ḫi-di-šú-nu am-ḫur-šú-nu-ti-ma* KUR-*su-nu ú*-[. . .]

14) [. . . *ḫa-nu-*]*ú-nu* ^{URU}*ḫa-az-za-ta-a-a la-pa-an* ^{GIŠ}TUKUL.MEŠ KAL. MEŠ *ip-laḫ-ma a*-[. . .]

15) [. . .] KÙ.GI 8 ME GUN KÙ.BABBAR UN.MEŠ *a-di mar-ši-ti-šú-nu* DAM-*su* DUMU.ME[Š-*šú* . . .]

16) [. . .] *ṣa-lam* DINGIR.MEŠ GAL.MEŠ EN.MEŠ-*ia ṣa-lam* LUGAL-*ti-ia ša* KÙ.GI [. . .]

17) [. . .]-*nu ú-kin ù šu-ú ul-tu* KUR *mu-uṣ-ri* GIM *iṣ-ṣu-*[*ri* . . .]

18) [. . .] *aš-šur am-nu ṣa-lam* LUGAL-*ti-ia* AŠ ^{URU}*na-ḫal mu-ṣur a-ni-* [. . .]

19) [. . .] KÙ.BABBAR *as-su-ḫa-am-ma a-na* KUR *aš-šur*^{KI} [. . .]

[. . .] on the mainland [. . .] I poured out. That city I [. . .] in the midst of the sea I trod them down together with [. . . $^{(5)}$fear of my battle] fell on him and his courage failed. He dressed himself in sackcloth [. . .] of willow set with precious stones and gold together with [. . .] ivory, fine oil, spices of all kinds, horses from (the land of) [. . .] from Kašpuna which is built entirely[132] on the sea [. . .] into the charge of my official, the governor of Ṣi[mirra . . . $^{(10)}$like gra]ss with the corpses of their warriors I filled [the plain. . .] their [pos]sessions, their cattle, their sheep, their asses [. . .] in the midst of his palace [. . .] their gifts (?) I received from them and their land I [. . . Han]un, the Gazaite, before my powerful weapons was terrified and [. . .] $^{(15)}$gold, 800 talents of silver, peoples with their possessions, his wife, [his] sons [. . .] an image of the great gods my lords, my royal image of gold [. . .] I set up and that one from Egypt like a bird [. . .] of Aššur I counted. My royal image at the Brook of Egypt [. . .] silver I seized and to Assyria [. . .]

The main issue of contention in this section of the inscription is purportedly the identity of "that city . . . in the midst of the sea." Earlier scholars like Wiseman and Alt identified the city with Arwad.[133] Others like Vogt and Ephᶜal identified it with Tyre.[134]

Recently, Irvine[135] has argued for Arwad and against Tyre. His main arguments are: (1) The tribute list of II R 67 does not mention Tyre, indicating that it, along with Aram-Damascus and Israel, was conquered later. (2) While the Philistine campaign appeared to be a kind of Assyrian *Blitzkrieg*, the account in ND 4301 + 4305 gives the impression of an extensive military action against Tyre. (3) The location of Kašpuna cannot be used in

---

[132]Contra Wiseman ("Two Historical Inscriptions," 23), who reads the two signs together as *aḫu*. The two signs should probably be read as DÙ (= *banû*) and ŠÁR (= *kiššatu*), literally meaning "built in its entirety."

[133]Wiseman, "Two Historical Inscriptions," 24; A. Alt, "Tiglathpilesers III. erster Feldzug nach Palästina," in his *Kleine Schriften* II (Munich: C. H. Beck, 1953), 157–58.

[134]E. Vogt, "Die Texte Tiglat-Pilesers III. über die Eroberung Palästina," *Bib* 45 (1964), 349–51; Ephᶜal, *Ancient Arabs*, 30.

[135]Irvine, *Syro-Ephraimitic Crisis*, 47–48.

identifying the city "in the midst of the sea." The data relating to the location of Kašpuna is at best ambiguous. Moreover, in all probability there were several Kašpunas in antiquity.

The identification of "that city" in line 3 must remain tentative. Although the general vicinity of the site was Phoenicia, it is likely that it refers to neither Arwad nor Tyre. There is not enough evidence from the text itself to indicate that "that city" is connected to or modified by "in the midst of the sea." In all probability, what line 3 is saying is that action was taken against some particular city. Line 4 goes on to elaborate on the atrocity done in the midst of the sea to the captives of the city. Thus, to reiterate, this text is too fragmentary to make any identification secure.

Lines 10–13, as has been noted, deal with the defeat of a state whose name can no longer be known. The Assyrian king boasts about the annihilation of the enemy forces in the open field and the taking of spoil. On the basis of a seemingly parallel text, III R 10, 2, Alt suggests that this text refers to the defeat of Pekah's forces.[136] As Irvine has rightly argued,[137] this suggestion cannot be sustained, as III R 10, 2 is not really a parallel text to ND 400. Moreover, the section that Alt links with the defeat of Israel (III R 10, 2, lines 5–8; see below) in fact relates to the defeat of Aram-Damascus. There is no indication that the text, as we have it, deals with Tiglath-pileser's campaign beyond the coastal regions. Therefore, the kingdom dealt with in ND 400, lines 10–13, must be located along the Mediterranean coast, between Kašpuna and Gaza.

The action against Gaza is dealt with in lines 14–19. The dating of Tiglath-pileser's campaign in Philistine territory in general and Gaza in particular to 734–733 BCE is secure. The eponym chronicle locates the main Assyrian army in Philistia at the time of the Akîtu festival in 733 BCE. The action against Hanun of Gaza may have taken place after Tiglath-pileser returned from Assyria following the conclusion of the new year festival. On the basis of other parallel accounts (III R 10, 2, lines 8–15 and ND 4301 + 4305, rev. lines 13–16), Tiglath-pileser's action against Gaza may be summarized as follows. As the Assyrian army advanced against Gaza, Hanun fled and escaped to Egypt. As such, Tiglath-pileser was able to capture the city with much resistance. Spoil, including Philistine deities, was confiscated, and

---

[136] Alt, "Tiglathpilesers III," 155–57.

[137] Irvine, *Syro-Ephraimitic Crisis*, 50.

the royal family together with a portion of the population were taken into exile. Sometime later, however, Hanun capitulated and returned and was restored to his throne.

These states along the coast were all part of the anti-Assyrian movement led by Rezin. Gaza's involvement in the coalition probably dated back to the 750s when the coalition was formed. Evidence for this comes from Amos 1:6–8, where Gaza—along with Ashdod, Ashkelon, and Ekron—was indicted by the prophet Amos for its action against Israel, probably in cooperation with Aram-Damascus, Pekah's rival state, Bit-Adini, and Tyre (see the discussion of Amos 1:3–5, 9–10 in the previous chapter; cf. Isa 9:12).

H. Layard 29b

Layard 29b belongs to Tadmor's Series C_1 of Tiglath-pileser's annals.[138] The text is fragmentary and only twelve lines have survived. The fragment apparently reports on the campaign of Tiglath-pileser in Palestine in his thirteenth *palû* (733–732 BCE). The following is a transliteration of the text.[139]

229) [. . . GIM] *im-ba-ri* [. . .]-*šú*

230) [. . . *šal-lat* ^{URU} . . .] *na-gi-e šá* ^{KUR}É-[. . . *al*]-*qa*

231) [. . . *šal-lat* ^{URU} . . .]-*bara-a* 6 ME 25 *šal-lat* ^{URU}*a*-[. . .]

232) [. . . *šal-lat* ^{URU}]*ḫi-na-tú-na* 6 ME 50 *šal-lat* ^{URU}*ku*[140]-[. . .]

233) [. . . *šal-lat* ^{URU}*ia*]-*at-bi-te*[141] 6 ME 56 *šal-lat* ^{URU}*sa*[142]- [. . .]

234) [. . .] UN.MEŠ *a-di mar-ti-šú-nu*[143] [*áš-lu-la* . . .] ^{URU}*a-ru-ma-a* ^{URU}*ma-ru-um* [. . .]

235) [. . . ^{I}*mi-ti-in-ti* ^{KUR}]*as-qa-lu-na-a-a* AŠ *a-di-*[*ia iḫ-ṭi-ma it-ti-ia*]

236) [*it-ta-bal-kit taḫ-du ša* ^{I}*ra*]-*ṣun-ni e-mur-ma* AŠ *mi-qit* [*ṭe-mi im-qut*]

---

[138]Tadmor, "Introductory Remarks," 180.

[139]The enumeration follows Rost's edition of Tiglath-pileser's annals (*Keilinschrift-texte*, 38–41). Restoration basically follows Rost unless otherwise indicated. An English translation may be found in *ARAB*, 1. §778.

[140]So H. Tadmor, *The Inscriptions of Tiglath-Pileser III* (Jerusalem: Israel Academy of Sciences and Humanities, forthcoming), cited in Cogan and Tadmor, *II Kings*, 175, 335. Rost read it as ^{URU}*qa-na* (*Keilinschrifttexte*, 38). He is followed by, among others, Y. Aharoni, who hypothesized the reading Qana (biblical Kanah) = Khirbet Qana (*The Land of the Bible: A Historical Geography* [2d ed.; Philadelphia: Westminster, 1979], 372).

[141]For the restoration of the place name ^{URU}*ia-at-bi-te*, see Aharoni, *Land of the Bible*, 372.

[142]So Tadmor, *Inscriptions of Tiglath-Pileser*, cited in Cogan and Tadmor, *II Kings*, 175, 335. Rost reads the sign as *ir* and Aharoni restores it as ^{URU}*ir-ru-na* (biblical Yiron) and identifies it with modern Yarun (*Land of the Bible*, 372).

[143]So Rost's edition; this sentence does not show up in Layard's copy.

237) [^{I}*ru-u-kip-tu* DUMU ^{I}*mi-ti-in-ti*] AŠ ^{GIŠ}GU.ZA-*šú ú-šib a-na*[. . .]

238) [. . .] *i-dul-ma ú-ṣa-la-ni* 5 ME [. . .]

239) [. . .]-*ma a-na* URU-*šu* KU_4-*ub* 15 URU.[MEŠ . . .]

240) [. . . ^{I}*i*]-*di-bi-ʾi-i-lu* ^{KUR}*a-ru-bu* [. . .]

[. . . like] a hurricane [. . . $^{(230)}$prisoners of . . .] districts of Bit-[. . . I] took away [. . . prisoners of . . .]bara, 625 prisoners of A[. . . , prisoners of] Ḫinatuna, 650 prisoners of Ku[. . . prisoners of Ia]tbiti, 656 prisoners of Sa[. . .] people together with their possessions [I took as booty . . .] Aruma, Marum $^{(235)}$[. . . Mitinti] the Ashkelonite [violated] the oath sworn [to me and revolted against me. When the defeat of Re]zin he saw, [he perished] in misfortune. [Rukibtu, son of Mitinti], sat on his throne. For [. . .] he barred and implored me. 500 [. . .] and I entered his city. Fifteen cities [. . .] Idibiʾilu of Arabia [. . .].

Although the text is fragmentary and only Bit- . . . can be read in line 230, lines 229–230 almost certainly refer to actions against Bit-Ḫazael.[144] What was noted in these and the preceding lines was the prisoners taken from Bit-Ḫazael. The text here specially speaks of those taken from "the districts of Bit-[Ḫazael]" (*na-gi-e šá* KUR É-[*ḫa-za-ʾa-i-li*]), that is, from the traditional territory under the control and governance of Aram-Damascus (see Layard 72b + 73a, line 209 [discussed below], where the number of the districts of the land of Ša-imērišu is given as sixteen).

There is general agreement among scholars that the cities listed in lines 231–234 were located in the Galilee.[145] There is, however, no agreement among scholars regarding the connection between lines 229–230 and lines 231–234. Ephʿal seems to prefer treating lines 229–230 as separate from lines 231–234, namely, that one deals with Aram-Damascus while the other deals with Israel.[146] Irvine, on the other hand, argues that lines 229–234 are all part of the same section. He notes in particular that if lines 231–234 had originally formed a separate section, a brief introduction mentioning Bit-Ḫumri or Pekah would have been included. Thus, Irvine suggests that lines 229–234 possibly recounted "Assyria's actions against the territorial holdings of Rezin in Galilee."[147]

---

[144]See, e.g., Ephʿal, *Ancient Arabs*, 24, 26; Irvine, *Syro-Ephraimitic Crisis*, 33, 35; *TUAT*, 1. 372. Aharoni, on the other hand, restores "Bit-Ḫumri" in line 230 and suggests that the Galilean region belonged to Israel and was annexed by the Assyrians from it (*Land of the Bible*, 372–74).

[145]See, e.g., Aharoni, *Land of the Bible*, 372–74; Ephʿal, *Ancient Arabs*, 24; Irvine, *Syro-Ephraimitic Crisis*, 32–35.

[146]Ephʿal, *Ancient Arabs*, 24, 26. Ephʿal leaves open the option for restoring "Bit-Ḫumri" in line 230.

[147]Irvine, *Syro-Ephraimitic Crisis*, 35.

Of the views presented, Eph^c^al's appears to be most convincing, namely, that lines 229–230 and 231–234 are two distinct units. Line 230 would refer to "Bit-Ḫazael" and is partly parallel to Layard 72b + 73a, line 209. While Irvine's observation is important, his conclusion has problems. If he is right that Galilee belonged to Rezin, would the prisoners and the cities not be mentioned before the concluding summary which lists the districts of Aram-Damascus taken by the Assyrians (reflected in line 230)? Such is indeed the case in Layard 72b + 73a, lines 206–209, which describes the cities and number of prisoners taken and then concludes with a summarizing statement about the numbers of cities and districts taken from Aram-Damascus.

Lines 231–234 thus deal with the Galilean region[148] but do so in terms indicating their distinction from the more specific districts of Aram-Damascus. It is possible that cities in the region were mentioned without any link to either Bit-Ḫumri or Bit-Ḫazael. The historical implication of this will be dealt with later (see the discussion of ND 4301 + 4305 below).

Second Kings 15:29,[149] from the account devoted to the reign of Pekah (2 Kgs 15:27–31),[150] provides further evidence of Tiglath-pileser's annexation of the Galilean region into the Assyrian empire. The verse reads as follows:

> In the days of Pekah king of Israel, Tiglath-pileser king of Assyria came and captured Ijon, Abel-beth-maacah, Janoah, Kedesh, Hazor, Gilead, the Galilee, and all the land of Naphtali, and exiled them to Assyria.

The cities named in this list have been variously identified. Ijon is identified with Tell ed-Dibbîn. The name Ijon survives in the

[148]Aharoni (*Land of the Bible*, 372) has identified the cities in this list as follows: Ḫinatuna (biblical Hannathon) = Tell el-Bedeiwijeh; Iatbiti (biblical Jotbah) = Khirbet Jefat; and Marum (biblical Merom) = Tell el-Khirbeh. In addition, E. Forrer (*Die Provinzeinteilung des assyrischen Reiches* [Leipzig: J. C. Hinrichs], 60–61) identified Aruma with biblical Rumah (= Khirbet Rume).

[149]That the verse is archivistic is accepted by most scholars (see, e.g., Gray, *I & II Kings*, 626–28; Cogan and Tadmor, *II Kings*, 179).

[150]It begins with a synchronism of Pekah's reign with the fifty-second year of Azariah king of Judah and a statement about Pekah's length of reign. It has been noted in the previous chapter that the notation of the length of Pekah's reign of twenty years is probably correct and that external evidence requires that if Pekah ruled twenty years he must have begun his reign as a rival king in Israel during the final years of Jeroboam II. The synchronism provided by the DtrH corresponds to the beginning of Pekah's reign in Samaria in 734 BCE and not the beginning of his twenty-year reign (see Hayes and Hooker, *New Chronology*, 54, 56; cf. Thiele, *Mysterious Numbers*, 129, who dates Pekah's sole reign in Samaria from 740 BCE). This introduction is followed by the DtrH's standard negative evaluation of Israelite kings (v. 28).

modern town of Marj ᶜAyun.[151] Abel-beth-maacah is identified as Abil el-Qamḥ/Tel Abil. The site is situated north of modern Qiryat Shemona.[152] The identification of Janoah is disputed. There are at least three sites that preserved the name: (1) Khirbet Yanum near Nablus, (2) Janua, located ten kilometers southeast of Megiddo, and (3) Yanuḥ, located sixteen kilometers northeast of Acco. Aharoni favors the third site.[153] J. Kaplan has suggested the site of Khirbet Niha, located in the upper Huleh valley, as the more likely site of Janoah.[154] There are several places named Kedesh: (1) Kadesh, identified as Tell Nebī Mind, (2) Kadesh-barnea, identified as ᶜAin el-Qudeirât, (3) Kedesh, identified as Tell Qadis/Tel Qedesh, located ten kilometers northwest of Hazor in the upper Galilee, and (4) Kedesh, identified as Khirbet Qedîsh/Ḥorvat Qedesh, in the ancient tribal territory of Naphtali. Scholars generally agree that Kedesh in 2 Kgs 15:29 is to be identified with Tell Qadis/Tel Qedesh in the Galilee.[155] Finally, the identification of Hazor with Tell el-Qedaḥ is almost certain.[156] These five cities listed were thus all located in the Galilee region and were possibly the locations where battles had taken place. The verse goes on to note that besides these cities, the entire region of the Galilee, Gilead, and the land of Naphtali were lost to the Assyrians.

Scholars often interpret this verse as a parallel account of the Assyrian text Layard 29b, lines 231–234,[157] namely, that they refer to Tiglath-pileser's campaign against Israelite territorial holdings. While Cogan and Tadmor caution that "one cannot be sure that the biblical and Assyrian lists refer to the same campaign," they nevertheless hold that these were territories taken from Israel.[158] Irvine, on the other hand, argues that the political status of the Kings text is actually ambiguous, in that it is not ex-

---

[151]See Cogan and Tadmor, *II Kings*, 174; Gray, *I & II Kings*, 627–28; Aharoni, *Land of the Bible*, 429; Hobbs, *2 Kings*, 202.

[152]See Cogan and Tadmor, *II Kings*, 174; Gray, *I & II Kings*, 627; Aharoni, *Land of the Bible*, 436.

[153]Aharoni, *Land of the Bible*, 373, 437. Cf. also Gray, *I & II Kings*, 628.

[154]J. Kaplan, "The Identification of Abel Beth Maacah and Janoah," *IEJ* 28 (1978), 159–60. Cf. Cogan and Tadmor, *II Kings*, 174; Hobbs, *2 Kings*, 202.

[155]So Aharoni, *Land of the Bible*, 373–74; Cogan and Tadmor, *II Kings*, 174; Gray, *I & II Kings*, 628; Hobbs, *2 Kings*, 202.

[156]See Yadin, *Hazor* (1972), 13–15; also W. G. Dever, "Qedah, Tell el-," *ABD*, 5. 578.

[157]See, e.g., Hobbs, *2 Kings*, 201–2; Aharoni, *Land of the Bible*, 371–74; Donner, *Israel unter der Völkern*, 6, especially n. 5.

[158]Cogan and Tadmor, *II Kings*, 175, 179.

plicitly stated whether the cities and regions listed belonged to Israel or Aram-Damascus. He proceeds to suggest that, together with Layard 29b, 2 Kgs 15:29 refers to the holdings of Aram-Damascus in the Galilee and elsewhere that were captured by Tiglath-pileser.[159] Irvine may be right concerning the ambiguity of 2 Kgs 15:29. His suggestion that these regions belonged to Aram-Damascus, while not indicated in Layard 29b, is probably correct (see the discussion below on ND 4301 + 4305). As was suggested above, Tiglath-pileser's campaign in the Galilee most probably took place in 733–732 BCE.

The next section of Layard 29b (lines 235–239) proceeds to deal with events in Ashkelon. Mitinti had paid tribute earlier in 734–733 BCE, but must have quickly changed his mind and thrown in his lot with Rezin and the anti-Assyrian coalition the following year. With the defeat of Rezin, Mitinti fell from power. Ephᶜal and Irvine suggest that his fall was the result of a *coup d'état*.[160] He was succeeded by Rukiptu his son, who most probably gained the recognition of the Assyrian king after he paid a substantial amount of tribute.

I. Layard 72b +73a

Layard 72b + 73a belongs to Tadmor's Series C_2 of Tiglath-pileser's annals.[161] This inscription, which contains sixteen lines of text, is fragmentary and relates to Tiglath-pileser's campaign in Syria-Palestine in 734–732 BCE. The following is a transliteration of the text.[162]

195) [. . .][163]

196) [. . .] *pa-ni-šu* [. . .]

197) [. . .] ^{LÚ}EN ^{GIŠ}GIGIR.MEŠ *ù* [. . . ^{GIŠ}]TUKUL.MEŠ-*šú-nu ú-šab-bir-ma* [. . .]

198) [. . .] ANŠE.KUR.RA.MEŠ-*šú-nu a*[*ṣ-bat* . . . ^{LÚ}*mun*]-*daḫ-ṣi-šu na-ši* ^{GIŠ}PAN [. . .]

---

[159]Irvine, *Syro-Ephraimitic Crisis*, 32–34.

[160]Ephᶜal, *Ancient Arabs*, 24; Irvine, *Syro-Ephraimitic Crisis*, 36.

[161]Tadmor, "Introductory Remarks," 179–80.

[162]The enumeration follows Rost's edition of Tiglath-pileser's annals (*Keilinschrift-texte*, 34–39).

[163]Line 195 (line 1 of Layard 72b) is so fragmented that it is difficult to make any sense from it. Rost's reading of (*amílu*) *ḳu*-[*ra-di*]-*šu ak*-[*šud*] . . . *u-šam-ḳit ina* (*iṣu*) *kakki-ia* does not find textual support in Layard's copy.

199) [. . .] *ka-ba-bi as-ma-ri-e* AŠ ŠU.II *ú-šá*[*m-qit*]*-su-nu-ti-ma* MÈ-*šu-nu* [. . .]

200) [. . . *u-paṭ*]*-ṭir šu-u a-na šu-zu-ub* ZI.MEŠ-*šú e*-[*di*]*-nu-uš-šu ip-par-ši-id-ma* [. . .]

201) [. . .] ^{d}NIN.KILIM ^{LÚ}GAL URU-*šú* KU$_4$-*ub* ^{LÚ}SAG.KAL. MEŠ-*šú bal-ṭu-us-su-nu* [. . .]

202) [. . .] *za-qi-pa-a-ni ú-še-li-ma ú-šad-gi-la* KUR-*su* 40-*àm* 5 ÉRIN. MEŠ *uš-ma-ni* [. . .]

203) [. . . *i-na pi-ḫa*]*-at* URU-*šu aq-ṣur-ma* GIM *iṣ-ṣur qu-up-pi e-ṣir-šú* ^{GIŠ}KIRI$_6$.MEŠ-*šú* [. . .]

204) [. . .] *ṣip-pa-a-te ša ni-i-ba la i-šu-u ak-kis-ma* 1-*en ul e-zib* [. . .]

205) [. . . ^{URU}]*ḫa-a-da-ra* É AD-*šú ša* ^{I}*ra-ḫi-a-ni* KUR *šá*-ANŠE.NÍTA-*šú-a-a* [. . .]

206) [. . .] *i-ʾa-al-du al-me ak-šud* 8 ME UN.MEŠ *a-di mar-ši-ti-šú-nu* [. . .]

207) [. . .] GU$_4$.NÍTA.MEŠ-*šú-nu ṣi-e-ni-šú-nu aš-lu-la* 7 ME 50 *šal-la-at* ^{URU}*ku-ru-uṣ-ṣa-a* [. . .]

208) [. . .] ^{URU}*ir-ma-a-a* 5 ME 50 *šal-la-at* ^{URU}*me-tu-na aš-lu-la* 5 ME 91 URU.MEŠ [. . .]

209) [. . .] *ša* 16 *na-gi-e ša* KUR *šá*-ANŠE.NÍTA-*šú ki-ma* DU$_6$ *a-bu-bi u-ab-bit*[164] [. . .]

210) [. . . ^{SAL}]*sa-am-si šar-rat* KUR *a-ri-bi ša ma-mit* ^{d}*šá-maš te-ti-qu-ma* [. . .]

[. . .] before him [. . .]. The chariot-commanders and [. . .] their weapons I broke [. . .] their horses I [seized . . .] his fighters who carried bows [. . .] shields and spears, I over[threw] with my own hands and their battle formation [. . .] (200)I [broke up]. He fled alone in order to save his life and [. . . like] a big weasel he entered his city. His officers alive [. . .], had them impaled, and showed (them) to his land. 45(?) soldiers I assembled [in the vicin]ity of his city and like a bird in a cage I shut him in. His gardens [. . .] trees without number I cut down and left not one (standing). (205)[. . . the city] of Ḫadara, the ancestral home of Rezin the Ša-imērišu-ite, [. . . where] he was born, I besieged and captured. 800 people together with their possessions [. . .] their cattle, their sheep I took as spoil. 750 prisoners from the city of Kuruṣṣa, [. . .] from the city of Irmaia, 550 prisoners from the city of Metuna, I took as spoil. 591 cities [. . .] of the sixteen districts of the land of Ša-imērišu I destroyed, like mounds after a flood.

(210)[. . .] Samsi, the queen of Arabia, who broke the oath of Šamaš and [. . .].

It is clear that lines 205–209 refer to the defeat of Rezin and the capture of Aramean cities. It is less certain whether lines 195–204 refer to the attack on Aram-Damascus as well since the referent of the third person singular pronouns is not preserved. However, since lines 205-206, immediately following the description of the battle, go on to deal with the capture of Rezin's ancestral

---

[164]Following Rost.

home, Ḫadara, it is likely that lines 195–204 described the attack on Aram-Damascus. The preserved text begins by narrating the defeat of Rezin's army, followed by Rezin's escape to the capital city, against which a siege was subsequently laid. The text continues to describe the capture of other cities, including Ḫadara, the ancestral city of Rezin. The attack on the outlying regions of Aram-Damascus must have taken place in 733–732 BCE,[165] before the siege was put on the capital city of Damascus.[166] Apparently, Damascus held out since the eponym chronicle for the following year (732–731 BCE) again listed Damascus as the location of the main army.

This text (line 209) mentions specifically the "sixteen districts of Ša-imērišu" (16 *na-gi-e ša* KUR *ša* ANŠE-*šu*) that were taken by Tiglath-pileser. The phrase is parallel to *na-gi-e ša* KUR É-[*ḫa-za-ʾa-i-li*] of Layard 29b, line 230, and refers to the traditional territory under the control of Aram-Damascus.

Line 210 begins a new section relating to how Tiglath-pileser dealt with Samsi, the queen of Arabia. Unfortunately, after the statement on Samsi breaking the oath of Šamaš, the text is broken.

J. Layard 66

Layard 66 is the only text which Tadmor has classified as Series E of Tiglath-pileser's annals.[167] Tadmor, however, has noted that the events in the text may not be entirely chronological and has expressed some reservations with this classification. Ephᶜal, on the other hand, remarks that the unusual geographical order of the Arabs before Israel precludes the text from being classified as a summary inscription.[168] The text is very fragmentary and contains only eighteen lines. The following is a transliteration of the text.[169]

211) [. . .] ^{URU}[. . .]

212) [. . . *a*]-*na* ^{URU}*e*-[. . .]

213) [. . . ^{KUR}]*a-ri-bi i-na* ^{KUR}*sa*-[. . .]

---

165 Tadmor dates this text to Tiglath-pileser's thirteenth *palû* ("Introductory Remarks," 180). Cf. also Ephᶜal, *Ancient Arabs*, 26, and Irvine, *Syro-Ephraimitic Crisis*, 29.

166 Irvine is right to note that although the text presents the siege on Damascus as having taken place before other Aramean cities were captured, the reverse is probably the more correct chronological order of events (*Syro-Ephraimitic Crisis*, 30–31).

167 Tadmor, "Introductory Remarks," 180.

168 Ephᶜal, *Ancient Arabs*, 33.

169 Cf. Rost's edition of the annals, lines 211–228 (*Keilschrifttexte*, 36–39).

214) [. . . *i*]-*na* KARAŠ-*šá* [. . .]
215) [. . .] *taš-ḫu*[170]-[*tú-ma* . . .]
216) [. . . ^{KUR}*aš*]-*šur a*-[*di* . . .]
217) [. . . *áš*]-*kun-ma* ^{LÚ}[. . .]
218) [. . .].II-*ia ú-šak*-[*niš* . . .]
219) [. . .]-*a-a* ^{URU}*ḫa*-[*a*-]*a*-[. . .]
220) [. . .]-*ti-a-a* ^{LÚ}[. . .]
221) [. . . *mi*]-*ṣir* KUR.KUR *šá* SILIM *ša*[*m-ši* . . .]
222) [. . .]-*ti be-lu-ti-ia al*-[. . .]
223) [. . .] KÙ.GI KÙ.BABBAR ANŠE.[. . .]
224) [. . . Š]IM^{ḪÁ} DÙ.A-*ma ma-da-ta-šú-nu ki*-[*i* . . .]-*a*
225) [. . .]-*ši-qu* GÌR.II[. . .]-*di-šu*(?)-*ni-šú-nu* [. . .]-*a* É.GAL *si*-[. . .]-*ad*[171]
226) [. . .] ^{I}*i-di-bi*-[ʾ*i*]-*i-lu a-na* [. . .]-*ti* UGU [. . .] *ap-qid*
227) [. . . *i*]-*na gir-re-te-ia maḫ-ra-a-te gi*-[*m*]*ir* URU.MEŠ [. . .] *am-nu-ú*
228) [. . .]-*li-šú áš-lu-lu-ma* ^{URU}*sa-me-ri-na e-di-nu-uš ú-maš*-[*šir* . . .] LUGAL-*šú-nu*

[. . .] to E[. . .] Arabia, at Mt. Sa[. . .][172] within her camp [. . .] (215)she was terrified [. . .] Assyria to [. . .] I appointed, and [. . .] I made bow at my [. . .]. [. . .]a, Ḫaia[. . .], (220)[. . .]te, [. . . the bor]der of the countries of the setting sun [. . .] of my lordship [. . .] gold, silver, [. . .], all kinds of spices, their tribute as (225)[. . .] feet [. . .] a palace [. . .]. Idibiʾilu for [. . .] over [. . .] I appointed. [. . . o]n my earlier campaigns all of the cities [. . .] I counted [. . .] his [. . .] I led away and Samaria alone I le[ft . . .] their king [. . .].

This fragmentary inscription recorded Assyrian action in Syria-Palestine in 733–731 BCE.[173] Lines 213–218 deal with the subjugation of Samsi queen of Arabia (cf. the parallel accounts in III R 10, 2, lines 19–26; ND 400, lines 24–27; ND 4301 + 4305, rev. lines 17–22). This is followed by the report of the submission of various nomadic groups and their presentation of tribute (lines 218–225) and the appointment of Idibiʾilu as the *atûtu*-officer[174] at the Egyptian border (line 226). Given the content of this text with its discussion of Samsi followed by the notations on various Arab tribes and Idibiʾilu, this fragmentary text is probably only the end

[170]Following Ephʿal, *Ancient Arabs*, 34.

[171]The end of the line is difficult to transliterate and it is impossible to know to what it refers.

[172]The probability that this refers to Mt. Saqurri rather than Sabaʾ, as restored by Rost, is supported by ND 400:24 (see Wiseman, "Two Historical Inscriptions," 23–24) and III R 10, 2:19 (see Ephʿal, *Ancient Arabs*, 33).

[173]Tadmor dates the account to 732 BCE ("Introductory Remarks," 186).

[174]For a description of this official, see Ephʿal, *Ancient Arabs*, 93, n. 297.

of a much longer text that described Tiglath-pileser's 734–731 BCE campaign and the disposition of Syro-Palestinian states which resulted. Other texts describing these western actions generally contain references to Samsi as the last major figure opposed to Tiglath-pileser. References to the Arab tribes and/or Idibiʾilu appear also in Layard 29b, line 240 and II R 67, lines 3–6 (the latter text not given in the earlier discussion of II R 67).

Most scholars argue that since line 228 mentions Samaria, the section has to do with Assyrian action against Israel, vis-à-vis the reduction of the Israelite state.[175] Ephᶜal, however, recognizes the problem of seeing these "earlier campaigns" as being conducted against Israel.[176] Irvine on the basis of his understanding and interpretation of other texts, argues that this section cannot refer to Assyrian military action against Israel.[177] He contends that the cities mentioned in line 227 can only be inferred as Israelite on the basis of the mention of Samaria. He suggests instead that line 227 refers to cities confiscated from Rezin.

Irvine's suggestion that line 227 refers to Assyrian action against Aram-Damascus is difficult to sustain. It is unlikely that only one line was ascribed to Aram-Damascus, with no detail about the actions against Rezin. It is more likely that line 227 is a general summary statement about various cities mentioned throughout the earlier portion of the inscription. The specific reference to Samaria in line 228, at the end of the text, is unusual. It breaks with the normal pattern in which Bīt-Ḫumri is discussed following notations about Aram-Damascus. This unusual placement of the reference to Samaria was no doubt the result of the special treatment accorded Samaria. Unlike all the other opponents of Tiglath-pileser, Pekah and Samaria were not directly attacked by Tiglath-pileser. The task of handling the renegade Samarian was left to Hoshea and his pro-Assyrian supporters.[178]

---

[175]See, e.g., Forrer, *Provinzeinteilung*, 59; Begrich, "Syrisch-ephraimitische Krieg," 27.

[176]Ephᶜal, *Ancient Arabs*, 33.

[177]Irvine, *Syro-Ephraimitic Crisis*, 39–40.

[178]This situation is reflected in III R 10, 2, lines 15–18, and 2 Kgs 15:30. Hosea 2:1–3 (English 1:10–2:1) is perhaps an allusion to the action of the Israelites and the Judeans in dealing with Pekah. The Israelites and the Judeans (who were subordinates to the Israelites) would "appoint" a new head, namely, Hoshea, who would lead an uprising against Pekah.

K. III R 10, 2

III R 10, 2 is a summary inscription discovered by A. H. Layard in 1849 at Nimrud.[179] Ephᶜal notes that this inscription, written on a stone slab, is probably part of a larger inscription covering several slabs.[180] The campaigns covered in this inscription were directed against Syro-Palestinian states. The following is a transliteration of lines 1–26:

1) [. . .] ^{URU}*ḫa-ta-rik-ka a-di* ^{KUR}*sa-ú-a*
2) [. . . ^{URU}]*gu-u*[*b-la* ^{URU}]*ṣi-mir-ra* ^{URU}*ar-qa-a* ^{URU}*zi-mar-ra*
3) [. . . ^{URU}]*us-nu-ú* [^{URU}*si-an-nu* ^{URU}]*ri-iʾ-ra-ba-a* ^{URU}*ri-iʾ-si-ṣu-u*
4) [. . .] URU.MEŠ *re-*[. . . *ša tam-tim*] *e-li-te a-bil* 6 ^{LÚ}*šu-ut-*SAG. MEŠ-*ia*
5) [. . . ^{LÚ}EN.NAM.MEŠ UGU]*šú-nu áš-kun* [. . . ^{URU}*r*]*a-áš-pu-(ú)-na*[181] *šá a-aḫ tam-tim e-li-ti*
6) [. . .]*ni-te* ^{URU}*ga-al-*[*ʾa-za* . . . ^{URU}]*a-bi-il-*[. . .] *šá* ZAG^{KUR}É-*ḫu-um-ri-a*
7) [. . . ^{KUR}É-*ḫa-za-ʾa-i-*]*li*[182] *rap-šú a-na si-*[*ḫir-šú*] *a-na mi-ṣir* ^{KUR}*aš-šur ú-tir-ra*
8) [. . . ^{LÚ}*šu-ut-*SAG.]MEŠ-*ia* ^{LÚ}EN.NAM.MEŠ [UGU-*šú-nu áš-*]*kun* [*ḫa-a-nu-ú-nu* ^{URU}*ḫa-az-za-at-a-a*
9) [. . . *šá la pa-an* ^{GIŠ}]TUKUL.MEŠ-*ia ip-par-ši-*[*du-ma a-na* ^{KUR}]*mu-uṣ-ri in-nab-tú* ^{URU}*ḫa-az-zu-tu*
10) [. . . *ak-šud* NÍG.GA-*šú*] NÍG.ŠU-*šú* DINGIR.MEŠ-*ni*[-*šú aš-lu-la* . . .]-*ia ù* NÁ LUGAL-*ti-ia*
11) [. . . *i*]-*na qí-rib* É.[GAL-*šú ul-ziz* . . .] DINGIR.MEŠ KUR-*šu-nu am-nu-ma*
12) [. . . *bi-lat ma-da-at-tu*] *ú-kín-šu-nu-ti* [. . . *aš*]-*ḫup-šu-ma ki iṣ-ṣu-ri*
13) [. . . *i*]*p-par-šid-ma* [. . .] *a-na* KI-*šu ú-tir-šu-ma*
14) [. . .] KÙ.GI KÙ.BABBAR *lu-bul-ti bir-me* GADA
15) [. . .] GAL.MEŠ ^{GIŠ}[. . . *am*]-*ḫur* ^{KUR}É-*ḫu-um-ri-a*
16) [. . .] *il-lut* LÚ [. . . *pu*]-*ḫur* UN.MEŠ-*šu*

---

[179]There are two versions of the same text. G. Smith's version was published in 1870 and may be found in Rawlinson, *Cuneiform Inscriptions*, 3. pl. 10, no. 2. P. Rost published a new edition in 1893, in his *Keilschrifttexte*, 78–83, which contains a number of differences. See Irvine, *Syro-Ephraimitic Crisis*, 62–69, for the most recent study of the text.

[180]Ephᶜal, *Ancient Arabs*, 28, n. 71.

[181]Following Rost, *Keilschrifttexte*, 78. On the basis of ND 400, line 8, Wiseman ("Two Historical Inscriptions," 24) has suggested reading [^{URU}*k*]*a-áš-pu-ú-na* instead.

[182]When Wiseman published ND 4301 + 4305 ("A Fragmentary Inscription," 120–21) he noted that the restoration of [*nap-ta-*]*li* proposed by F. Hommel, *Geschichte Babyloniens und Assyriens* (Berlin: G. Grote, 1885), 664–65, is without support. ND 4301 + 4305 rev. 3 confirms the restoration of [^{KUR}É-*ḫa-za-ʾa-i-*]*li*.

17) [. . . NÍG.ŠU-*šú-nu a-na*] ^{KUR}*aš-šur ú-ra-a* $^{[I]}$*pa-qa-ḫa* LUGAL-*šú-nu is-ki-pu-ma* ^{I}*a-ú-si-i*ʾ

18) [. . . *a-na* LUGAL-*ti*]-*na* UGU-*šú-nu áš-kun* 10 GUN KÙ.[GI . . .] GUN KÙ.BABB[AR . . .]-*ti-šú-nu am-ḫur-šú-nu-ma*

19) [. . . *a-na* ^{KUR}*aš-šur ú-ra*]-*áš-šú-nu*[183] *ša* ^{SAL}*sa-am-si šar-rat* ^{KUR}*a-ri-bu* [AŠ ^{KUR}*sa*][184]-*qu-ur-ri*

20) [. . . *a*]-*duk* 1 [LIM x] ME UN.MEŠ 30 LIM ANŠE.A.AB.BA.MEŠ 20 LIM GU_4.NÍTA.MEŠ

21) [. . .] 5 LIM ŠIM^{ḪÁ} DÙ.A-*ma* 11 *tu*-[*u*][185] *né-mat-ti* DINGIR. MEŠ-*ni-šá*

22) [. . . NÍG.]GA-*šá e-kim-ši ù ši-i a-na šu-zu-ub* ZI.MEŠ-*šá*

23) [. . . *ana ma-a*]*d-ba-ar a-šar ṣu-ma-me* GIM ^{SAL}ANŠE.EDIN.NA

24) [. . .]*ri-šá ḫu-ra-da-at* UN.MEŠ-*šá i-na* $MURUB_4$ KARAŠ-*šá*

25) [. . . *la pa-an* ^{GIŠ}TUKUL.]MEŠ-*ia* KALA.MEŠ *taš-ḫu-tú-ma* ANŠE. A.AB.BA.MEŠ ^{ANŠE}*a-na-qa-a-te*

26) [. . . *a-di maḫ*]-*ri-ia taš-šá-a* ^{LÚ}*qe-e-pu* AŠ *muḫ-ḫi-šá áš-kun-ma*

[. . .] Ḫatarikka as far as Mt. Saue, [. . .] Byblos, Ṣimirra, Arqa, Zimarra, [. . .] Usnu, [Siannu], Riʾraba, Riʾsiṣu, [. . .] cities [. . .] of the Upper Sea I subjugated. Six of my officers [. . . (5)as governors over] them I appointed. [. . . R]ašpuna, which is on the coast of the Upper Sea [. . .], Galʾaz[a], Abil-[. . .], which are on the border of Bit-Ḫumri [. . .] the widespread [land of Bit-Ḫaza]el in its en[tirety] I brought back within the border of Assyria. [. . . officers of] mine as governors [over them I ap]pointed. Hanun of Gaza [. . . who before] my weapons fled [and to] Egypt escaped. Gaza (10)[. . . I conquered. His goods], his possessions, his gods [I carried away. . . .] of mine and my royal couch [. . .] within [his] palace [I set up . . .] gods of his land I counted and [. . . tribute and tax] I imposed on them [. . . over]threw him and like a bird [. . .] he fled and [. . .] to his place I restored him. [. . . gold], silver, colored garments, linen garments (15)[. . .] great [. . . I re]ceived. Bit-Ḫumri [. . .] the entirety of its people [. . . together with their possessions to] Assyria I led away. Pekah their king they deposed and Hoshea [. . . for king]ship over them I appointed. Ten talents of g[old . . .] talents of silv[er . . .] I received them and [. . . to Assyria I le]d them. As for Samsi queen of Arabia, at Mt. Saqurri (20)[. . . I] killed. 1,000 + x-hundred people, 30,000 dromedaries, 20,000 cattle, [. . .], 5,000 (bags) of all kinds of spices, 11 pedestals, resting places of her gods, [. . .] her property I seized. And she, to save her life, [. . . to the de]sert, an arid place, like a wild ass [. . .] her [. . .], the might of her people, within her camp (25)[. . . before] my powerful [wea]pons she became terrified, and dromedaries, she-camels [. . . be]fore me she brought. I appointed a *qepu*-officer over her and [. . .].

This text is a close parallel of ND 4301 + 4305 (discussed below) in that the content is arranged geographically rather than

[183]Following Rost, *Keilschrifttexte*, 80; *TUAT*, 374, restores the line to read "[Tribute and tax] I imposed on them."

[184]Following Ephᶜal, *Ancient Arabs*, 33.

[185]Following Ephᶜal, *Ancient Arabs*, 34.

chronologically. Like ND 4301 + 4305, the text first records Tiglath-pileser's campaign in northern Syria (743–739 BCE), resulting in the provincialization of that region (lines 1–5).[186] The text moves on to deal with the campaign of 734–731 BCE in southern Syria and Palestine, beginning with line 5. The action against Aram-Damascus is treated first (lines 5–8).[187] The section purportedly describes the territory under Rezin's control at the time Tiglath-pileser annexed and turned Aram-Damascus into an Assyrian province. One of the issues in relation to this section and its parallels in ND 4301 + 4305 and K 2649[188] is the delineation of the southern border of Aram-Damascus at the time of Assyrian annexation in 732–731 BCE.

In comparing III R 10, 2 with ND 4301 + 4305 and K 2649, Taḍmor reconstructed a fuller text describing the borders of Aram-Damascus.[189]

> [*māt* Bīt] ^{m}*Ḫaza'ili rapšu ana siḫiršu ultu š*[*ad Labna*]*na adi libbi* ^{URU}*Gal'aza u* ^{URU}*Abil*[*akka*] *ša pāṭi māt* ^{m}*Ḫumria ana miṣir māt Aššur utirra šutrešeja*
>
> The widespread [land of Beth] Hazael in its entirety from M[ount Leba]non as far as the town of Gilead and the town of Abel-Beth-Maacah which are on the borderland of the land of Beth Omri I restored to the territory of Assyria. Officials of mine as governors I appointed over them.

On the basis of his reconstructed text, Tadmor suggested that the boundary of Aram-Damascus on the eve of its conquest by the Assyrians in 733–732 BCE extended from the Lebanon in the northwest to Abel-Beth-Maacah on the eastern border of the Galilee and to Ramoth-gilead in the Transjordan. Therefore, the lands of Bashan and Golan were included in its boundaries. Thus, according to Tadmor, the Galilean hill country and the region of Gilead south of Ramoth-gilead belonged to Pekah at the time of the Assyrian invasion.[190] From Aramean territory, the Assyrian provinces of *Dimašqa* (= Damascus), *Haurīna* (= Hauran), and *Qarnini* (= Qarnaim) were established, while from Israelite terri-

---

[186]On the provincialization of Ḫatarikka and Ṣimirra, see K. Kessler, "Die Anzahl der assyrischen Provinzen des Jahres 738 v. Chr. in Nordsyrien," *WO* 8 (1975), 56–63.

[187]Earlier scholarship proposing that these lines deal with Israel is no longer viable, following the discovery of ND 4301 + 4305. Hommel had restored line 7 to read, "the widespread [land of the House of Naphta]li" (*Geschichte Babyloniens und Assyriens*, 664–65), but with the parallel text of ND 4301 + 4305, reverse lines 3–4, it is almost certain that line 7 should be restored to read, "the widespread [land of Bit-Ḫaza]el." See especially H. Tadmor, "The Southern Border of Aram," *IEJ* 12 (1962), 115.

[188]For this text, see Rost, *Keilschrifttexte*, 86.

[189]Tadmor, "Southern Border of Aram," 118.

[190]*Ibid.*, 118–21.

tory, the provinces of *Magiddu* (= Megiddo) and *Gal'aza* (= Gilead) were set up.

Most recently, Irvine has argued against Tadmor's conception of the southern border of Aram-Damascus.[191] He begins by questioning Tadmor's reconstructed Assyrian text, noting the borders of Aram-Damascus, in particular the three place names, Mount Lebanon, Gilead, and Abel-Beth-Maacah. First, Irvine points out that the restoration of ^{KUR}*La-ba-na-na* is purely conjectural as the cuneiform text published by Wiseman shows only very minimal traces to support Tadmor's reconstruction. Irvine goes on to argue that the restoration of *Kašpuna* in line 5 of III R 10, 2, a specific reference to the more general "Mount Lebanon," is likewise uncertain. He argues for the restoration of *Kašpuna* in the lacuna of line 4 together with all the other cities of the Upper Sea and proposes to retain Rost's older reading of *Rašpuna*,[192] identified as Rishpon (ʾArsuf), north of Tel Aviv,[193] for line 5.

Second, Irvine argues that the reading ^{URU}*Galʾaza* is probably the correct reading in both III R 10, 2 and K 2649 and that it is equivalent to the Hebrew גלעד. He, however, questions Tadmor's identification of the town as biblical Ramoth-gilead. He notes that in the Hebrew Bible, Ramoth-gilead is referred to as such (1 Kgs 4:13; 22:3; 2 Kgs 8:28; 9:1, 14) or as "Ramoth in Gilead" (Deut 4:43; Josh 20:8; 21:38; 1 Chr 6:65) or Ramah (2 Kgs 8:29; 2 Chr 22:6), but not as Gilead. On the other hand, there is evidence of a city by the name of Gilead in biblical and non-biblical texts.[194] Irvine prefers to identify this city with Khirbet Jelᶜad, located six miles south of the Jabbok River.

Third, Irvine seriously challenges the restoration ^{URU}*A-bil*[*akka*] in line 6 and its identification with Abel-Beth-

---

[191]Irvine, "Southern Border of Syria," 31–38. See also his *Syro-Ephraimitic Crisis*, 65–67.

[192]H. Tadmor argues that Rost's reading of *Rašpuna* is an error ("'Rashpuna'—A Case of Epigraphic Error," *Nahman Avigad Volume* (ErIsr 18; Jerusalem: Israel Exploration Society, 1985), 180–82. [Hebrew]

[193]See Forrer, *Provinzeinteilung*, 60; F. M. Abel, *Géographie de la Palestine* (2 vols.; Paris: J. Gabalda, 1933, 1938), 2. 103.

[194]The only non-biblical text is *UT* 170:2 (C. Gordon, *Ugaritic Textbook* [AnOr 38; Rome: Pontifical Biblical Institute, 1965]). Biblical evidence cited includes Hos 6:8; 12:12; Judg 10:17; 12:7. See J. Begrich, "Syrisch-ephraimitische Krieg," 228; M. Noth, "Beiträge zur Geschichte des Ostjordanlandes, 1. Das Land Gilead as Siedlungsgebiet israelitischer Sippen," *PJ* 37 (1941), 69–71; *idem*, "Gilead und Gad," *ZDPV* 75 (1959), 35–40; R. G. Boling, *Judges* (AB 6A; Garden City, NY: Doubleday, 1975), 194.

Maacah.[195] He points out that in Smith's copy of the cuneiform text, only *Abil*-[. . .] is preserved clearly. Therefore, it is uncertain if *Abilakka* (= Abel-Beth-Maacah) is the correct restoration. Because there are numerous place-names in the Hebrew Bible that begins with אָבֵל[196] (the Hebrew equivalent of *abil*), there is no certainty about which city was referred to. Having argued for the preference of Rašpuna over against Kašpuna and the identification of Gilead with Khirbet Jel^{c}ad, Irvine proceeds to suggest אבל מחולה as a likely candidate (restoring *Abil-maḫul* in line 6), to be identified with either Tell Abu Sifre[197] or Tell Abu Ṣuṣ.[198] Both sites are located about ten miles south of Beth-shean.

Irvine concludes that the southern border of Aram-Damascus at the time of Tiglath-pileser's annexation reached deep into territory traditionally claimed by Israel. In Transjordan, the boundary included not only the areas of Bashan and Golan, but also the region of Gilead from the Yarmuk to the Jabbok and beyond. West of the Jordan, Aram-Damascus's territory included the Galilee, the Jezreel Valley, the northern edge of the Ephraimite hill country, and the Plain of Sharon.

Irvine is certainly right in challenging Tadmor's reconstruction of the Assyrian text and in pointing out the weaknesses of Tadmor's conclusions concerning the southern border of Aram-Damascus. His identification of ^{URU}*Galʾaza* with Khirbet Jel^{c}ad and his argument for retaining Rost's restoration of Rašpuna are quite convincing. While his general conclusion that the southern border of Aram-Damascus at the time of Tiglath-pileser's annexation extended into territory once claimed by Israel is probably correct, his proposal for restoring *Abil-maḫul* (אבל מחולה) for ^{URU}-*abil*-[. . .] must, however, be viewed with caution. In Rawlinson's copy of the text, the two signs after *a-bi-il* are discernible as *ak-maš*. Moreover, if the space that Rawlinson has provided for

[195] Cogan and Tadmor, *II Kings*, 174, have recently pointed out the uncertainty of this identification, first made by Schrader, *Keilinschriften*, 144. Alt proposed to regard the place as "Abel of Acco" ("Tiglathpilesers III," 156, n. 2).

[196] אבל השטים (Num 33:49); אבל כרמים (Judg 11:33); אבל מחולה (Judg 7:22; 1 Kgs 4:12); אבל מצרים (Gen 50:11); אבל מים (2 Chr 16:4); אבל בית־מעכה (1 Kgs 15:20; 2 Kgs 15:29; cf. 2 Sam 20:14, 15).

[197] So W. F. Albright, "Bronze Age Mounds of Northern Palestine and the Hauran," *BASOR* 19 (1925), 18; Gray, *I and II Kings*, 133.

[198] So H. Rösel, "Studien zur Topographie der Kriege in den Büchern Josua und Richter," *ZDPV* 92 (1976), 23; Aharoni, *Land of the Bible*, 313; see also D. V. Edelman, "Abel-meholah," *ABD*, 1. 11–12.

the damaged signs is accurate, then there is no way to fit *ma-ḫul* into the space.

A larger question lies behind the discussion of the southern border of Aram-Damascus, namely, who had control of the territories in the Galilee and Gilead that were lost to the Assyrians in 734–732 BCE, the Arameans of Damascus or the Israelites. According to Tadmor, Israel held those territories, while Irvine suggests Aram-Damascus. A proposal regarding this issue will be offered below when all other evidence is assessed.

From Aram-Damascus, III R 10, 2 moves on to describe the subjugation of Gaza in 734–733 BCE (lines 8–15). This account is similar to the reports in ND 400, lines 14–18 and ND 4301 + 4305, rev. lines 13–16.

Lines 15–19 deal with the kingdom of Israel, referred to as Bit-Ḫumri. The Assyrian king claimed to have exiled the entire population of Israel. The claim is more likely an exaggeration as the text goes on to report Pekah's overthrow by his own subjects and Hoshea's appointment as king.[199]

According to the account, it was the Israelites who deposed Pekah. The anti-Assyrian Pekah had finally seized control of Samaria in 734 BCE, having been a rival king for almost a decade and a half. This was done through the defeat of the pro-Assyrian Menahem dynasty. It is possible that the appearance of Tiglath-pileser and the Assyrian forces in Syria-Palestine, beginning in 733 BCE, mobilized the pro-Assyrian faction of Israelite society. Defeated by the forces of Pekah but not entirely crushed and knowing the consequences of the nation's anti-Assyrian policy, they organized under the leadership of Hoshea for a rebellion against Pekah. While Tiglath-pileser was still in the region, sometime in 733–732 or 732–731 BCE, the revolt against Pekah was already underway. Tiglath-pileser recognized the leadership of Hoshea, appointed him as king, but left the Israelites to settle their civil strife as he moved on to deal with other rebellious states in the region, if in 733–732 BCE, or with rebellion in Babylonia, if in 732–731 BCE.

Verse 30 of 2 Kings 15 provides additional evidence concerning Hoshea's conspiracy against and overthrow of Pekah. The verse reads as follows: "Then Hoshea son of Elah made a conspiracy against Pekah son of Remaliah. He attacked and killed him,

---

[199] Irvine, *Syro-Ephraimitic Crisis*, 68.

and ruled in place of him." This verse confirms the Assyrian account, namely, that the Israelites themselves, not the Assyrians, were finally responsible for the removal of Pekah from the throne and his execution. The biblical account, in addition, points unequivocally to Hoshea's leading role in the overthrow of Pekah. When the revolt against Pekah began is, unfortunately, not indicated in the biblical text.

The rest of III R 10, 2 continues to detail the tribute that the Assyrian king received from Israel. On the evidence of the parallel text in ND 4301 + 4305, rev. lines 10–11, it is clear that Israel's tribute was paid to Tiglath-pileser at Sarrabanu, most likely after Hoshea had defeated Pekah and assumed kingship over Israel, probably in 731–730 BCE when Tiglath-pileser was in southern Babylonia.

The next section deals with Samsi queen of Arabia (lines 19–26), who was in all probability an active member of the anti-Assyrian coalition. It is surprising that this inscription does not mention the Assyrians' treatment of Hiram of Tyre. One can only speculate whether Tyre was mentioned in lines 1–4 together with the "cities on the Upper Sea."

L. ND 4301 + 4305

ND 4301 and ND 4305 are two adjoining fragments of a clay tablet found in 1955 at Nimrud. The inscription was first published by D. J. Wiseman in 1956.[200] The tablet, inscribed on both sides, is a summary inscription. Dividing lines mark each area covered in the inscription. The text appears to be organized geographically. The obverse of the surviving inscription begins with a record of Tiglath-pileser's campaigns in the northern regions of the Assyrian border, namely, Urartu (lines 1–8), Ulluba (lines 9–13), Tušḫan (lines 14–16), and Naʾiri (lines 17–23), before proceeding to his campaign in northern Syria, in particular against Bit-Agusi (lines 24–25). The reverse documents the campaigns of Tiglath-pileser in Syria-Palestine.[201] The following is a transliteration of lines 1–22 (reverse):

1) [. . . ^{URU}*ḫa-ta-*]*rik-ka a-di* ^{KUR}*s*[*a-ú-e* . . .]

---

[200]D. J. Wiseman, "A Fragmentary Inscription of Tiglath-pileser III from Nimrud," *Iraq* 18 (1956), 117–29.

[201]For the most recent study of the reverse side of ND 4301 + 4305, see Irvine, *Syro-Ephraimitic Crisis*, 56–62.

2) [. . . *a-na*] *mi-ṣir* ^{KUR}*aš-šur*^{KI} *ú-tir-ra* [. . .]

---

3) [. . . ^{KUR}É-]^{I}*ḫa-za-ʾa-i-li rap-šú a-na si-ḫir-šú* TA [. . .]

4) [. . . *ša pat-*]*ti*[202] ^{KUR}É-^{I}*ḫu-um-ri-a a-na mi-ṣir* ^{KUR}*aš-šur*^{KI} [*ú-tir-ra* . . .]

---

5) [. . . ^{I}*ḫi-*]*ri-mu* ^{KUR}*ṣur-ra-a-a ša it-ti* ^{I}*ra-ḫi-a-ni ša ku-na*[203] [. . .]

6) [. . . ^{URU}]*ma-ḫa-la-ab* URU *dan-nu-ti-šú a-di* URU.MEŠ-*ni* GAL.MEŠ *ak-šud šal-la-*[*ti* . . .]

7) [. . . *a-di*] *maḫ-ri-ia* DU-*ka-ma ú-na-áš-ši-qa* GÌR.II.MEŠ-*ia* 20GUN [. . .]

8) [. . .] *bir-me* ^{TÚG}GADA ^{LÚ}*šu-ut*-SAG.MEŠ ^{LÚ}ŠÌR.MEŠ ^{SAL}ŠÌR.MEŠ [. . .]

---

9) [. . . -]*a na-gi-*[*e* . . . *li*]-*me-ti-šú-nu a-*[*na* . . .]

10) [. . . ^{I}*a-ú-si-iʾ a-na* LUG]AL-*ú-ti* AŠ UGU-*šú-n*[*u áš-kun* . . .][204]

11) [. . .] *sar-ra-ba-ni*[205] *a-di maḫ-ri-ia* [. . .]

---

12) [. . .] 1 ME GUN KÙ.BABBAR *as-su-ḫa-am-ma a-*[. . .]

---

13) [. . .] *in-na-bi-it* ^{URU}*ḫa-az-zu-*[*tu* . . .]

14) [. . .] DÙ-*uš* AŠ *ki-rib* É.GAL *ša* ^{URU}*ḫa-az*[*-zu-tu* . . .]

15) [. . .]-*ḫu ul-tu* ^{KUR}*mu-uṣ-ri* [. . .]

16) [. . .] *a-na* É *ka-a-ri ša* ^{KUR}*ǎs-šur*^{KI} [. . .]

---

17) [. . .] AŠ ^{GIŠ}TUKUL *ú-šam-qit-ma gim-ri ki-*[. . .]

18) [. . .] *a-na la ma-ni* DINGIR.MEŠ [. . .]

19) [. . . *a*]*-šar ṣu-ma-me* GIM ^{SAL}EDIN.NA *taš-ku*[206]*-*[*na* . . .]

20) [. . . MURU]B_4 KARAŠ-*šá* AŠ IZ[I . . .]

21) [. . . ^{SAL}*a-n*]*a-qa-ti a-di* ^{ANŠE}*ba-ak*[*-ka-ri-ši-na* . . .]

22) [. . .] AŠ *muḫ-ḫi-šá áš-kun-ma* 10 LIM ^{LÚ}ÉRIN.MEŠ [. . .]

---

[202] Following Tadmor, "Southern Border of Aram," 116, n. 16.

[203] It is difficult to ascertain how the last two readable signs ought to be transliterated. Although Wiseman reads the signs as *ku-na*, he translates them as "Damascus" in parenthesis ("Fragmentary Inscription," 125, 123). Clearly, Rezin's place of origin cannot be read in the signs. One might read *ku-na* as the D stative of *kânum*, with an enclitic *ma* assimilated by the *n*. Thus, *ša ku-na* may be translated "who was made firm" or "who was supported."

[204] The line is restored on the basis of III R 10, 2:17–18, which reads: ^{I}*a-ú-si-iʾ* [*a-na* LUGAL-*ti*] AŠ UGU-*šú-nu áš-kun* (cf. Rost, *Keilschrifttexte*, 80). Cf. R. Borger and H. Tadmor, "Zwei Beiträge zur alttestamentliche Wissenschraft aufgrund der Inschriften des Tiglathpilesers III," *ZAW* 94 (1982), 246.

[205] Following Borger and Tadmor, "Zwei Beiträge," 246.

[206] So, correctly, Ephᶜal, *Ancient Arabs*, 35. Wiseman ("Fragmentary Inscription," 126, 129) reads the signs as UR.GI_7 (= *kalbu*).

[. . . Ḫata]rikka as far as Mt. S[aue . . . within] the territory of Assyria I brought back [. . .].

[. . .] the widespread [land of Bit-]Ḫazael in its entirety from [. . . which is on the bor]der of Bit-Ḫumri, into the territory of Assyria [I brought back . . .].

(5)[. . . Hi]ram of Tyre, who with Rezin who was supported [. . .] Maḫalab, his stronghold, together with great towns I captured. Spoil [. . . into] my presence he came and kissed my feet. 20 talents of [. . .] decorated [garments], linen garments, officials, singers, songstresses [. . .].

[. . .] district [. . .] their surrounding areas (10)[. . . Hoshea as ki]ng over them [I set . . .] Sarrabanu before me [. . .].

[. . .] 100 talents of silver I seized [. . .].

[. . .] he fled. Gaza [. . .] I made. Within the palace of Gaza (15)[. . .] from Egypt [. . .] for a trading-center of Assyria [. . .].

[. . .] with weapons I smote and like [. . .] numberless gods [. . .] an arid place, like a wild mare, she set [. . . (20)with]in her camp, by fire [. . .] female camels and their foals [. . .] over her I set and 10,000 soldiers [. . .].

Lines 1–2 are probably the continuation of the description of the Assyrian military action in northern Syria (begun in obverse, line 24), in association with the major campaign against Arpad in 743–739 BCE. The actions of Tiglath-pileser in Syria-Palestine in 734–731 BCE are reported in lines 3–22. Lines 3–4 deal with the Assyrian provincialization of the territory held by Bit-Ḫazael, after the capture of Damascus and the death of Rezin. The reference to Aram-Damascus as "the widespread land of Bit-Ḫazael in its entirety" differs from the reference to Aram-Damascus as simply KUR *Ša-imērišu* (Layard 72b + 73a, line 209; for Layard 72b + 73a, see above). The "land of Ša-imērišu" with its sixteen districts denotes the territory of Damascus proper. "The widespread land of Bit-Ḫazael in its entirety," on the other hand, refers to the entire territory controlled at the time by Rezin. This would have included, in addition to Damascus proper, "the way of the sea, the land beyond the Jordan, and Galilee of the nations" (Isa 8:23; see also the discussion of III R 10, 2).[207]

Lines 5–8 of ND 4301 + 4305 report on the Assyrian treatment of Tyre. Hiram is named as the king of Tyre. The text provides evidence that Hiram was an ally of Rezin (= Raḫianu). Tiglath-pileser's action against Hiram was significant. Maḫalab, Hiram's stronghold, and other important cities were captured by

---

[207]Irvine, "Southern Border of Syria."

the Assyrian army and booty was taken. Hiram apparently personally surrendered to Tiglath-pileser and paid tribute. Tyre, therefore, unlike Damascus, was not provincialized during this period.

Irvine dates this campaign against Tyre to either 733–732 or 732–731 BCE. This, Irvine argues, would explain Hiram's omission in the tribute list of 734–733 BCE in II R 67.[208] In all likelihood, the campaign occurred early in 733–732 BCE. This is indicated by the eponym chronicle, which notes that at the end of the year 733–732 BCE, the Assyrian army was already situated at Damascus (battling against the forces of Rezin). By subjugating Hiram early on, Tiglath-pileser was quickly dismantling the coalition in order to deal finally with Rezin.

Lines 9–11 appear to deal with Israel, assuming that the name of Hoshea is correctly restored. That Israel is presumably the next state dealt with in the text is supported by the sequence of Aram-Damascus, Tyre, and Israel in other texts of Tiglath-pileser.[209] Line 10 thus indicates that Tiglath-pileser recognized Hoshea as king over Israel. This event must have taken place during Tiglath-pileser's attack on Damascus in 733–732 or 732–731 BCE.[210] Line 11 notes Hoshea's (or his messengers') appearance before Tiglath-pileser at Sarrabanu, in southern Babylonia,[211] most likely bearing tribute. The Assyrian king is known to have campaigned in this area in 731–730 BCE (so *a-na* ^{URU}*šá-pi-ia* in the eponym chronicle) and again in 729–728 BCE (so Babylonian Chronicles, 1.i.19–23).[212] Hoshea's payment of tribute to the Assyrian king at Sarrabanu presumably took place after he gained control of Samaria and replaced Pekah as king.

Lines 13–16 note Tiglath-pileser's campaign against Gaza in 734–733 BCE, while lines 17–22 report the defeat of queen of the Arabs, probably in 733–732 or 732–731 BCE. These two states were also part of the anti-Assyrian coalition headed by Rezin. As a member of the coalition, Samsi, along with Rezin, Hiram, and

---

[208]*Ibid.*, 59. Contra Vogt ("Texte Tiglat-Pilesers," 348–51) and Asurmendi (*Guerra Syro-Efraimita*, 31), who date the campaign to 734 BCE.

[209]See the Iran stela and Layard 50a + 50b + 67a. So already noted by Asurmendi (*Guerra Siro-Efraimita*, 31, 36) and Irvine (*Syro-Ephraimitic Crisis*, 59).

[210]See Hayes and Kuan, "Final Years of Samaria," 154.

[211]While the exact location of Sarrabanu is unknown, most scholars agree that it lay somewhere in southern Mesopotamia. See Parpola, *Neo-Assyrian Toponyms*, 306.

[212]See Grayson, *ABC*, 72.

Pekah, probably did not submit and pay tribute in 734–733 BCE.[213]

Of central importance in lines 1–22 of ND 4301 + 4305 is the text's depiction of the political arrangements imposed by Tiglath-pileser over the anti-Assyrian states in Syria-Palestine following his 734–731 BCE campaign to the west. Moving in a north-south orientation, the text reports the following conditions established by the Assyrian ruler.

Ḫatarikka: It was provincialized and incorporated into the Assyrian empire (probably after the major campaign against Arpad in 743–739 BCE).

Bit-Ḫazael: The entire holdings of Rezin—"the widespread land of Bit-Ḫazael in its entirety"—were provincialized, including the sixteen districts of Damascus (Layard 72b + 73a, line 209) as well as other territory held by Rezin which bordered on the land of Bit-Ḫumri, including Transjordan down to the city of Gilead, Galilee, and the coastal plain (see Isa 8:23 and III R 10, 2, lines 5–7).

Tyre: Hiram, after being defeated, submitted to Tiglath-pileser and was allowed to remain on the throne after a heavy payment of indemnity.

Bit-Ḫumri: Hoshea was recognized as the new monarch over Bit-Ḫumri which now was limited to territory in Cisjordan south of Jezreel.

Gaza: Hanun, who had fled to Egypt, returned and was reestablished on the throne by Tiglath-pileser.

Arabia: Queen Samsi was defeated and made to pay indemnity but was allowed to remain on the throne under the supervision of a *qepu*-officer (see Layard 66, lines 216–217).

III. SYNOPSIS

From the above inscriptions of Tiglath-pileser III it is clear that he was present in the west as early as 743 BCE. The eponym chronicle for 743–742 BCE recorded that "in Arpad; a defeat of Urartu was inflicted," an event that apparently took place during

[213] Contra Irvine, *Syro-Ephraimitic Crisis*, 43. It is likely that Samsi had violated the oath sworn in the name of Šamaš (so Layard 72b + 73a, line 210) already in 734–733 BCE.

Tiglath-pileser's second regnal year. Further evidence for this comes from the king's annalistic text, Layard 71a + 71b + 72a, of his third *palû* (743–742 BCE), which alludes to a revolt of Anatolian and northern Syrian states that involved Sardurri of Urartu, Matiʾ-ilu of Arpad, Sulumal of Melid, Tarḫulara of Gurgum, and Kuštašpi of Kummuḫ. It is obvious that Urartian influence must have spread during the period of Assyrian weakness.[214] Although the Assyrian king claimed that it was a revolt against the Assyrian empire, it is more likely that these states were no longer under the influence or domination of the Assyrian empire. What Tiglath-pileser did then was to reclaim the territories that had once been under the subjugation of Assyria and to reassert Assyrian domination. That year, Sardurri, the Urartian king, was defeated in Kummuḫ (cf. II R 67).[215] Nevertheless, Arpad itself was able to withstand the Assyrian onslaught until its capture in 741–740 BCE, where the eponym entry of that year reads: "at (the same) city; after three years it was captured."[216] It was during this period (743–740 BCE) that Tiglath-pileser went down to Samaria to provide Menahem aid in maintaining his hold on the Israelite throne (cf. 2 Kgs 15:19–20). In the year 740–739 BCE, the Assyrian army remained in Arpad to carry out mop-up operations in the west. It is likely that it was in association with this mop-up operation that Tiglath-pileser dealt with Tutammû of Unqi (III R 9, 1).[217] Tutammû was defeated and his royal city, Kinalia (or Kullani),[218] captured. Unqi was most probably turned into a province, as Tiglath-pileser talks about "setting a governor over them" in III R 9, 1.[219] In all probability, it was at Arpad that the Assyrian king received the tribute of Anatolian and Syro-Palestinian rulers (so Layard 45b), including Rezin of Damascus, Tubail of Tyre, and most likely also Menahem of Israel.

---

[214]Grayson, "Ashur-dan II to Ashur-nirari V," 276–79; and *idem*, "Tiglath-pileser III to Sargon II," 74–77.

[215]See n. 5 above.

[216]So also Shea, "Menahem and Tiglath-pileser III," 45. Tadmor's argument against the reliablity of this notation is unintelligible ("Azriyau of Yaudi," 254).

[217]So Na'aman, "Sennacherib's 'Letter to God,'" 36–38.

[218]On the identification of Unqi, Kinalia, and Kullani as referring to a similar place, see, e.g., J. D. Ḥawkins, "Assyrians and Hittites," *Iraq* 36 (1974), 81–82; and Na'aman, "Sennacherib's 'Letter to God,'" 37, n. 51.

[219]See also Layard 65, l. 12, where the "province of the city of Ku-" to which Tiglath-pileser settled deportees of the Azriyau rebellion should most probably be reconstructed as Kunalia. Layard $69b_1$ likewise speaks of settling deportees in the city of Kunalia among other cities of Unqi.

In his seventh *palû*, 739–738 BCE, Tiglath-pileser turned his attention to Ulluba. It is quite certain that when the Assyrian army finally left Arpad, after being present from 743–739 BCE to deal with Ulluba, a rebellion broke out in Syria under the leadership of Azriyau. The Assyrian king imposed tribute upon the bloc of states that stayed away from the rebellion (so the Iran Stela), among whom were Rezin of Damascus, Menahem of Israel, Tubail the Tyre, and Sipatbail of Byblos. Ulluba was taken and provincialized.

In 738–737 BCE, Tiglath-pileser conducted a campaign to Syria to suppress the Azriyau rebellion. Nineteen districts of Hamath, and most probably also Hamath itself, participated in the rebellion. In addition, Kullani and other cities of Unqi were likely involved in the rebellion, for it was in that year that Kullani was recaptured (eponym chronicle) and repopulated with deportees of the districts of Hamath (Layard 65) and other tribal people (Layard $69b_1$). Hamath must have capitulated when Tiglath-pileser returned to suppress the rebellion, for in the tribute list of that year (Layard 50a + 50b + 67a) Enilu of Hamath was included among the eighteen rulers that paid tribute. As with the previous year, Damascus, Israel, Tyre, and Byblos were among the tributees. However, a change of ruler had taken place in Tyre when tribute was sent to the Assyrian king in that year, namely, Hiram had succeeded Tubail of the Tyrian throne.

Our analysis of the inscriptions of Tiglath-pileser III reveals also that the Assyrian king was involved in an effort to suppress a widespread anti-Assyrian rebellion in Syria-Palestine in 734–731 BCE.[220] Members of the coalition included Rezin of Aram-Damascus, Hiram of Tyre, Pekah of Israel, Samsi of Arabia, Mitinti of Ashkelon, and most probably also Hanun of Gaza. Although a number of these states had paid tribute to Assyria as late as 738–737 BCE, in all likelihood the anti-Assyrian movement was not a sudden initiative but was already in the making many years before. It has been noted in the previous chapter that with the accession of Rezin to the throne of Damascus, the Arameans once again sought to dominate affairs in Syria-Palestine, thereby

---

[220] Contra, most recently, R. Tomes, "The Reason for the Syro-Ephraimite War," *JSOT* 59 (1993), 55–71. Tomes argues that the inscriptions of Tiglath-pileser do not shed any light on the Syro-Ephraimitic crisis and that there is no evidence of an anti-Assyrian coalition during that time. He, therefore, concludes that "the Syro-Ephraimite war is much more likely to have been the result of local causes than part of an international plan to resist Assyria" (70).

opposing Assyrian control of the region. Pekah was already in league with Rezin during his reign as a rival king in Israel. Tyre joined the coalition in the last years of the reign of Jeroboam II when it broke the "covenant of brothers" with Israel (Amos 1:9). Zabibe queen of Arabia eventually joined the coalition. Nevertheless, the coalition was never a unified force in Syria-Palestine because Israel under Menahem and Judah under Ahaz refused to participate. The coalition was formed not only for political reasons but also for economic reasons. It was an attempt to deprive Assyria of unilateral control over trade in the area.[221] With a coalition that controlled the main trade routes, these states would be able to prevent Assyria from reaping the commercial benefits of the region. The tribute paid to Assyria in earlier years, as well as in 738–737 BCE (so Layard 50a + 50b + 67a), was more a token tribute to appease the Assyrians than a sign of their submission and loyalty. These states were content to pay token tribute as long as the Assyrians stayed away from direct interference and domination in the region. Hayes suggests that the "nominal tribute under the circumstances was a cheap way to buy time."[222] Over the years the Assyrians must have felt the effects of this trade deprivation and the growing anti-Assyrian sentiment of the region. The situation changed in 734–733 BCE, when Tiglath-pileser moved into southern Syria and Palestine in an attempt to suppress the anti-Assyrian elements in the region as well as to secure direct control of the important trade routes. In all probability, Aram-Damascus, Tyre, Israel, Gaza, and Arabia refused to pay tribute to Tiglath-pileser in open defiance of the Assyrian king when he appeared in Syria-Palestine in 733 BCE (so II R 67). Ahaz of Judah had remained loyal and became the first Judean king to offer tribute directly to an Assyrian king. Tiglath-pileser eventually dealt with the rebels one after another. Philistia appears to have been his first target, probably to block any assistance from Egypt. The eponym chronicle for the end of the year 734–733 BCE located the main Assyrian army in Philistia (*ana* ^{KUR}*pilišta*). ND 400 reports on the brief military action Tiglath-pileser took against the Phoenician coast on his way to Gaza to deal with Hanun. This was

---

[221] This enforced unilateral "trade exchange" had begun in the ninth century BCE. So Tadmor, "Assyria and the West," 36–40. See also I. M. Diakonoff, "Main Features of the Economy in the Monarchies of Ancient Western Asia," in *Proceedings of the Third International Conference of Economic History*, Munich, 1965 Congrès et Colloques X, 3 (Paris: Mouton, 1969), 28–29.

[222] Hayes in *HAIJ*, 325.

also an attempt to seize control of the Philistine ports and the overland trade routes in the region.[223]

After successfully dealing with the Philistine coast, Tiglath-pileser turned his attention to the other members of the coalition. Aharoni has noted that "Tiglath-pileser's strategy was to isolate Aram from her southern allies first before turning the full might of Assyria against Damascus itself."[224] Thus Tiglath-pileser must have spent several months dealing principally with Tyre, Israel, and Arabia.

Following the campaign against Gaza, it is likely that the Assyrian army moved northward along the Mediterranean coast to take action against Hiram of Tyre (ND 4301 + 4305, rev. lines 5–8). Several Tyrian cities and fortresses were captured. Hiram eventually capitulated and paid tribute.

It is likely that from Tyre, the Assyrian army moved east across the Galilee, at which time cities in the Galilee were captured and prisoners taken (Layard 29b, lines 231–234). It is possible that the Assyrian inscription is deliberately ambiguous regarding who had control of the Galilee.[225] The same is true of 2 Kgs 15:29. As we have suggested earlier, while the Galilean region was treated as distinct from the "sixteen districts of the land of Ša-imērišu/Bit-Ḫazael" (Layard 72b + 73a, line 209; Layard 29b, line 230), it was probably included in the Assyrian designation of the "widespread land of Bit-Ḫazael" (ND 4301 + 4305, line 3). We have argued on the basis of Isa 8:23 that this area was lost to the Arameans early in the reign of Rezin. Furthermore, when Pekah joined with Rezin, he was probably given jurisdiction over the Galilee. Therefore, if our analysis of Pekah's rival kingdom is correct, namely, that Pekah exercised control under Damascene oversight over not only Gilead but also the Galilee, then it is possible that he continued to assume control over the Galilee after usurping the throne in Samaria. However, since he probably began his rival rule as a puppet of Rezin, Aram-Damascus may have continued to lay claim over the territory.

From the Galilee, Tiglath-pileser moved directly against Israel (ND 4301 + 4305, rev. lines 9–11; III R 10, 2, lines 15–19; Layard

---

[223]Irvine, *Syro-Ephraimitic Crisis*, 70.

[224]Aharoni, *Land of the Bible*, 372.

[225]Irvine (*Syro-Ephraimitic Crisis*, 33–35) has recognized the ambiguity of the text but has proceeded to argue for Aramean control of the Galilee during the period. He has also noted the ambiguity in relation to 2 Kgs 15:29 (see above, pp. 168–71).

66, lines 17–18). It is likely that a pro-Assyrian and anti-Pekah movement under the leadership of Hoshea was already in the making, having been inaugurated by Tiglath-pileser's arrival in the region. Tiglath-pileser subsequently took some Israelite cities but never attacked Samaria. He also recognized Hoshea's claim to the Israelite throne and left the Israelites to deal with Pekah themselves.

The Assyrian army then moved toward Arabia to deal primarily with Samsi, queen of the Arabs (ND 4301 + 4305, rev. lines 17–22; ND 400, lines 24–27; III R 10, 2, lines 19–26; Layard 66, lines 3–8). Samsi's forces were defeated at Mt. Saqurri and she escaped to the desert "to save her life." She later returned and submitted to the Assyrian king, bringing tribute with her. She was left on the throne but a *qepu*-officer was appointed over her.

Having suppressed all the other members of the coalition, Tiglath-pileser then turned his full attention toward Rezin of Aram-Damascus. That Rezin was the leader of the coalition is clearly indicated in the Assyrian inscriptions. He was mentioned in the reports of the Assyrian action against other members of the coalition, like Hiram of Tyre (ND 4301 + 4305, rev. line 5) and Mitinti of Ashkelon (Layard 29b, line 236). Some Assyrian action against Aram-Damascus must have begun before the end of the year 733–732 BCE, since the eponym for that year recorded that the Assyrian army was stationed against Damascus (*ana* KUR*di-maška*). That the determinative KUR was used instead of URU is indicative that the Assyrian army was located somewhere in Aram-Damascus rather than at Damascus itself. The Assyrian texts speak of bringing "the widespread land of Bit-Ḫazael in its entirety within the border of Assyria" (ND 4301 + 4305, rev. lines 3–4; III R 10, 2, lines 5–8). The provincialization of Aram-Damascus was underway. The onslaught against Aram-Damascus must have lasted more than a year as the eponym chronicle for the following year 732–731 BCE continues to record the presence of the Assyrian army in the area (*ana* KUR*dimaška*).[226]

At the conclusion of this Syro-Palestinian campaign that lasted from 734 to 731 BCE, new Assyrian provinces were carved

[226] On the fall of Aram-Damascus, see especially Pitard, *Ancient Damascus*, 187–89.

out. These were Megiddo, Dor, Gilead, Hauran, Qarnini, Damascus, Manṣuate, and Subite.[227]

During the reign of Tiglath-pileser, two phases of relationship among Syro-Palestinian states in general, and among Aram-Damascus, Israel/Judah, and the Phoenicians in particular may be identified. We have noted, primarily on the basis of non-Assyrian texts, that in the late 750s BCE, following the death of Šamši-ilu, a new anti-Assyrian coalition was formed and headed by Rezin of Aram-Damascus. This coalition included, among others, Pekah, a rival king of Israel, Bit-Adini, Tyre, and the Philistine states.

Tiglath-pileser wasted no time in dealing with the coalition. A major campaign, undertaken by the Assyrian king in his second regnal year (743–742 BCE), lasted until 740–739 BCE. While the main target of the campaign appears to have been Arpad, other rebellious states were dealt with as well. This led to the collapse of the coalition momentarily. Syro-Palestinian states including Aram-Damascus, Tyre, and Israel apparently paid *maddattu* to the Assyrian king in 738–737 BCE (so Layard 50a + 50b + 67a). Israel paid *maddattu* because Menahem had remained loyal to Assyria. Menahem had earlier received Assyrian aid to hold on to his throne. Aram-Damascus and Tyre probably rendered token submission to the Assyrian king. With Pekah still functioning as a rival Israelite king and an ally to Rezin and Menahem remaining pro-Assyrian, no political nor commercial ties existed between Samaria and Damascus. Since Tyre had joined with Aram-Damascus, and Elath was under the control of Rezin, it is difficult to imagine that relations between Samaria and Tyre were good.

Not long after 738–737 BCE, the anti-Assyrian coalition began to gain momentum again. As soon as Pekah gained control of Samaria (in 734 BCE), the coalition launched an attack on Ahaz of Judah in order to force Judah to join them. It is clear from Assyrian inscriptions that open rebellion against Assyria was widespread. Members of the alliance included Aram-Damascus, Israel, Tyre, Gaza, Ashkelon, and Arabia. The entire coalition was dealt with during Tiglath-pileser's 734–731 BCE campaign.

---

[227]See Forrer, *Provinzeinteilung*, 62–63; A. Alt, "Das System der assyrischen Provinzen auf dem Boden des Reiches Israel," *ZDPV* 52 (1929), 220–42; Abel, *Géographie de la Palestine*, 2. 102–3.

CHAPTER FIVE

THE REIGN OF SHALMANESER V

I. INTRODUCTION

Tiglath-pileser III had a distinguished tenure as the king of Assyria. When he died, apparently while on campaign in the west in 726 BCE, he was succeeded by his son Shalmaneser V (726–722 BCE), who inherited a vast empire from him.

Shalmaneser's reign was not only short but also far less distinguished than that of his predecessor. His only achievement of any consequence was the capture of Samaria after a period of revolt. Two important issues related to the conquest of Samaria by Shalmaneser will be addressed in this chapter. (1) What was the course of events that led eventually to the fall of Samaria? (2) Who participated with Israel in the revolts of Samaria?

There are no royal Assyrian inscriptions available from the reign of Shalmaneser. Moreover, the eponym chronicle related to his reign is broken and nothing much can be made of it. As such, we are entirely dependent on non-Assyrian sources in an attempt to deal with the two issues mentioned.

II. ASSYRIAN (BABYLONIAN) SOURCES

A. The Eponym Chronicle

Regnal Year	*Dates*	*Reported Event*[1]
17	728–727 BCE	LUGAL ŠU ^{d}EN BAD^{bat} ^{URU}*di*-[. . .] the king took the hand of Bêl. The city of Di[. . .]
18	727–726 BCE	*a-na* ^{URU}[. . .]

[1]Eponym Canon C^{b} 3; A. Ungnad, "Eponymen," 432. Cf. G. Smith, "New Fragment," 331–32.

		[^{Id}SILIM.MA-*n*]*u*-MAŠ AŠ ^{GIŠ}[GU.ZA *it-tu-šib*] at [. . .][2] [Shalma]neser [ascended] the [throne].
1	726–725 BCE	*i*-[*na* KUR] i[n the land]
2	725–724 BCE	*a-na* [. . .][3] at [. . .]
3	724–723 BCE	*a-na* [. . .] at [. . .]
4	723–722 BCE	*a-na* [. . .] at [. . .]
5	722–721 BCE	*a-na* [. . .] at [. . .]

If the entry ^{URU}*di*-[. . .] for the year 728–727 BCE refers to the city of Damascus, then the Assyrians must have returned to Syria-Palestine after an absence of three years. If Damascus had fallen in 732–731 BCE, it must have rebelled again and had to be recaptured. Such a campaign against Damascus would have been undertaken by Tiglath-pileser, and at the end of his seventeenth regnal year (728–727 BCE) something was going on in Damascus. The notation, as we have argued earlier, probably refers to the capture of Damascus.

From the eponym chronicle, all that is known about the reign of Shalmaneser is that the Assyrian army was on campaign in his accession year, and in his second, third, and fourth regnal years. Unfortunately, against whom these campaigns were conducted cannot be determined from the eponym chronicle.

B. Babylonian Chronicle 1

The Babylonian Chronicle 1[4] encompasses the history of Babylonia from the reign of Nabū-naṣir (747–734 BCE) to the

[2]Luckenbill, following Olmstead, reads the line as "against Damascus" without indicating that the reading is a reconstruction (*ARAB*, 2. 437).

[3]For each of the years 725–724, 724–723, and 723–722 BCE, Luckenbill has reconstructed the notations to read "against [Samaria]" (*ARAB*, 2. 437). There is unfortunately no support for such reconstructions, except that the biblical text in 2 Kgs 17:5 mentions a three-year siege of Samaria.

[4]For the best publication and study of the Babylonian Chronicles, see Grayson, *ABC*. See also D. J. Wiseman, *Chronicles of the Chaldean Kings (626–556 B.C.) in the British Museum* (London: British Museum, 1956); and most recently J. A. Brinkman, "The Babylonian Chronicle Revisited," in *Lingering Over Words: Studies in Ancient Near East-*

reign of Šamaš-šumu-ukin (668–648 BCE). A copy of the text, BM 92502, was first published in 1887 by H. Winckler and J. N. Strassmaier.[5] The text begins with what is probably a fragmentary section on the interruption of the Akîtu festival.[6] The account of the accession of Tiglath-pileser III to the throne in Assyria marks the beginning of the first fully preserved section (i.1–5). Important for the present discussion is i.23–31, which covers the years 728–722 BCE. The following is Grayson's transliteration and translation of the text.[7]

23) ^{I}*Tukul-ti-ápil-*«AŠ»[8]*-é-šár-ra ina Bābìli*^{KI} *ina kússê ittašab*^{ab}

---

24) MU II *Tukul-ti-ápil-é-šár-ra ina* ^{ITI}*Ṭebēti šīmāti*^{MEŠ}

25) <x> MU^{MEŠ} *Tukul-ti-ápil-é-šár-ra šarru-ut* ^{KUR}*Akkadî*^{KI}

26) *u* ^{KUR}*Aš-šur īpuš*^{uš} II MU^{MEŠ} *ina libbi ina* ^{KUR}*Akkadî*^{KI} *īpuš*^{uš}

27) ^{ITI}*Ṭebētu* UD XXV *Šul-man-a-šá-red ina* ^{KUR}*Aš-šur*

28) <*u* ^{KUR}*Akkadî*>^{KI} *ina kússê ittašab*^{ab} ^{URU}*Šá-ma/ba-ra-'-in iḫ-te-pi*

---

29) MU V *Šul-man-a-šá-red ina* ^{ITI}*Ṭebēti šīmāti*^{MEŠ}

30) V MU^{MEŠ} *Šul-man-a-šá-red šarru-ut* ^{KUR}*Akkadî*^{KI} *u* ^{KUR}*Aš-šur īpuš*^{uš}

31) ^{ITI}*Ṭebēti* UD XII^{KÁM} *Šarru-kîn ina* ^{KUR}*Aš-šur ina kússê ittašab*^{ab}

23) Tiglath-pileser (III) ascended the throne in Babylon.

---

24) The second year: Tiglath-pileser (III) died in the month Tebet.
25) For <*eighteen*> years Tiglath-pileser (III) ruled Akkad
26) and Assyria. For two of these years he ruled in Akkad.
27) On the twenty-fifth day of the month Tebet Shalmaneser (V)
28) ascended the throne in Assyria <*and Akkad*>. He ravaged Samaria.[9]

---

ern Literature in Honor of William L. Moran (HSS 37; Atlanta: Scholars Press, 1990), 73–104.

[5]H. Winckler and J. N. Strassmaier, "The Babylonian Chronicle," *ZA* 2 (1887), 148–68. T. G. Pinches published a similar copy of the text in *JRAS* n.s. 19 (1887), 655–81.

[6]So Grayson, *ABC*, 14–15, 70.

[7]*Ibid.*, 72–73.

[8]Grayson notes that AŠ is a scribal error (*ABC*, 72).

[9]The arguments against identifying ^{URU}*Šá-ma/ba-ra-'-in* with Samaria that were raised by earlier scholars (e.g., H. Winckler, "Nachtrag," *ZA* 2 [1887], 351–52) can no longer be taken seriously. See Tadmor, "Campaigns of Sargon," 39–40; A. R. Millard, "Assyrian Royal Names in Biblical Hebrew," *JSS* 21 (1976), 7–8; B. E. J. H. Becking, *De Ondergang van Samaria: Historische, exegetische en theologische opmerkingen bij II Koningen 17* (diss.; Utrecht, 1985), 42; *idem*, *The Fall of Samaria: An Historical and Archaeological Study* (SHANE 2; Leiden: E. J. Brill, 1992), 23; S. Timm, "Die Eroberung Samarias aus assyrisch-babylonischer Sicht," *WO* 20–21 (1989–90), 64–66; N. Na'aman, "The Historical Background to the Conquest of Samaria (720 BC)," *Bib* 71 (1990), 215–16, n. 27.

29) The fifth year: Shalmaneser (V) died in the month Tebet.
30) For five years Shalmaneser (V) ruled Akkad and Assyria.
31) On the twelfth day of the month Tebet Sargon (II) ascended the throne in Assyria.

An important feature of the Babylonian Chronicles must be noted. Horizontal lines were used to set apart the reported events chronologically. Grayson speaks of the divisions as segments.[10] Line i.23 belongs to a section which is dated by the chronicles to the third year (729–728 BCE) of the Babylonian king, Nabu-mukîn-zēri. The chronicles reported that in that year, Tiglath-pileser III campaigned against Nabu-mukîn-zēri, defeated him, and ascended the throne in Babylon. The next section proceeds to report on events beginning with Tiglath-pileser's second regnal year (727–726 BCE) in Babylon, skipping those events of his first regnal year. The Assyrian king is reported to have died in the month Tebet after a reign of two years. He was succeeded by Shalmaneser V on the twenty-fifth day of Tebet. This section also notes that Shalmaneser ravaged Samaria. A new section reports on events beginning with the fifth regnal year (722–721 BCE) of Shalmaneser. This section notes that Shalmaneser died in the month Tebet after a reign of five years over Assyria and Babylonia. He was succeeded by Sargon II on the twelfth day of Tebet. Scholars have generally neglected the fact that the statement on the destruction of Samaria is separated from the statement about the fifth year of Shalmaneser's reign by a horizontal line. For example, S. Dalley states that "according to the Babylonian Chronicle, the capture of Samaria took place at the very end of Shalmaneser's reign."[11] On the contrary, the horizontal line indicates that the ravaging of Samaria occurred before the final year of his rule.[12] Although Na'aman has recognized the importance of these horizontal lines, he has unfortunately misinterpreted the evidence. He remarks that

> the text of the chronicle is organized throughout in a chronological order, with each and every event accurately dated within a specific year of the king of Babylonia and a traverse line marked to separate the years of reign. The

[10]Grayson, *ABC*, 15.

[11]Dalley, "Foreign Chariotry," 33.

[12]A. T. Olmstead noted that the capture of Samaria "is mentioned as the only event in Shalmaneser's reign, just before the account of his death and just after that of his accession. So far, then, as the Chronicle is concerned, we can only place it in his reign, that is, within the years 727–722" ("The Fall of Samaria," *AJSL* 21 [1904–5], 181).

> "ravaging" of Šamara'in is included within the accession year of Shalmaneser and should accordingly be assigned to that year.[13]

Other evidence from the chronicle does not bear out Na'aman's conclusion. An example may be cited from Chronicle 1.i.38–43:

---

38) The fifth year of Merodach-baladan (II): Humban-nikash (I), king of Elam, died.

39) For [twenty-six] years Humban-nikash (I) ruled Elam.

40) [Shutruk-Nahhu]nte (II), his sister's son, ascended the throne in Elam.

41) From the accession ye[ar of] Merodach-baladan (II) until the tenth year

42) [Assyria/Sargon (II)] was belligerent towards Merodach-baladan (II).

---

43) The tenth year: Merodach-baladan (II)

It is clear that lines 42 and 43 are separated chronologically by the horizontal line. Lines 38–42 belong to a section, which, although line 38 dates to the fifth year of Merodach-baladan, covers a period from the fifth through the ninth year. Similarly, although the notation about the destruction of Samaria is included in the section with the reference to the accession year of Shalmaneser, it cannot be concluded that the event took place during that year. In fact, lines 24–28 cover a period that includes the final year of Tiglath-pileser III (727–726 BCE), as well as the accession year (727–726 BCE) and the first four regnal years of Shalmaneser V (726–725 to 723–722 BCE). Therefore, only two conclusions may be drawn from the Babylonian Chronicle 1.i.24–29: Samaria was ravaged by Shalmaneser, and this event took place before his fifth year, that is, before 722–721 BCE.[14]

III. NON-CUNEIFORM SOURCES

A. Josephus's Antiquities *9.14.2 §§283–287*

In *Antiquities* 9.14.2 §§283–287, Josephus quotes Menander in describing Shalmaneser V's relationships with Phoenicia:

> And the king of Assyria came with an army and invaded Syria and all of Phoenicia. Now the name of the king is recorded in the Tyrian archives, for he marched upon Tyre in the reign of Elulaios. This is also attested by Menander, the author of a book of Annals and translator of the Tyrian archives into the Greek language, who has given the following account:

---

[13]Na'aman, "Conquest of Samaria," 210.

[14]So already Hayes and Kuan, "Final Years of Samaria," 158–59.

"And Elulaios, to whom they gave the name of Pyas,[15] reigned thirty-six years. This king, upon the revolt of the Kitieis (Cyprians), put out to sea and again reduced them to submission. During his reign Selampsas,[16] the king of Assyria, came with an army and invaded all Phoenicia and after making a treaty of peace with all (its cities), withdrew from the land. And Sidon and Arke and Old Tyre and many other cities also revolted from Tyre and surrendered to the king of Assyria. But, as the Tyrians for that reason would not submit to him, the king turned back again and attacked them after the Phoenicians had furnished him with sixty ships and eight hundred oarsmen. Against these the Tyrians sailed with twelve ships and, after dispersing the ships of their adversaries, took five hundred of their men prisoners. On that account, in fact, the price of everything went up in Tyre. But the king of Assyria, on retiring, placed guards at the river and the aqueducts to prevent the Tyrians from drawing water, and this they endured for five years, and drank from wells which they had dug." This, then, is what is written in the Tyrian archives concerning Salmanassēs, the king of Assyria (LCL translation).

The account reports on the events that led to the Assyrian siege of Tyre[17] by Shalmaneser V, lasting from 726–725 to 722–721 BCE. These events may be summarized as follows. During his accession year (Nisan 727–Nisan 726 BCE), Shalmaneser came with his army and invaded all Phoenicia, including Tyre, which must have been in revolt. After the Phoenician city-states made treaty arrangements with him, Shalmaneser withdrew from the region and returned to Assyria. (According to the eponym chronicle, the Assyrian army was "i[n the land]" during his first regnal year, Nisan 726–Nisan 725 BCE.) Thus, when Shalmaneser was

[15]The name Πύας or the variant Πύλας has created problems for interpreters. Some scholars suggested that Πύλας should be corrected to Λύλας, identical to Luli (so, e.g., J. Lévy, "Deux Noms Phéniciens altéréz chez Josèphe," *Mélanges Syriens offerts à Monsieur René Dussaud par ses amis et ses élèves*, II [Paris: Paul Geuthner, 1939], 545). Others have proposed that the name is the Greek for Pul, the other name of Tiglath-pileser III (so W. von Landau, "Die Belagerung von Tyrus durch Salmanassar bei Menander," *Beiträge zur Altertumskunde des Orients*, I [Leipzig: E. Pfeiffer, 1893], 14). Katzenstein, following von Landau, concludes that several words are missing from the opening quotation and suggests restoring the sentence as follows: "And Elulaios reigned (from the days of Tiglath-Pileser) to whom they gave the name Πύλας, thirty-six years" (*History of Tyre*, 221–22). Finally, S. Timm may be right in pointing out that the name may have derived from a Phoenician-Punic root פּלס, so that Πύλας may be taken as the Phoenician equivalent of Elulaios (*Die Dynastie Omri*, 217).

[16]G. Smith (*History of Sennacherib* [London: Williams & Norgate, 1878], 69–70) and Eduard Meyer (*Geschichte des Altertums*, II/2 [3d ed.; Basel: Benno Schwabe, 1953], 127) identify "Selampsas" with Sennacherib. The majority of scholars, however, identify him with Shalmaneser V, as first suggested by C. F. Lehmann (*Klio, Beiträge zur Alten Geschichte*, II [Leipzig: Dieterich'sche Verlagsbuchhandlung, 1902], 139–40), who was followed by Šanda (*Bucher der Könige*, 2. 212–13) and Katzenstein (*History of Tyre*, 224–26). This identification is supported by the Latin text, in which the name is written as "Salmanasar." Moreover, Josephus himself identifies "Selampsas" as "Salmanassēs" (*Ant.* 9.14.2 §287).

[17]Other than the eponym chronicle and the Babylonian Chronicles, only a fragment of a badly mutilated inscription (K 38345; cf. Luckenbill, *ARAB*, 1. §§828–30) is available from the reign of Shalmaneser V. As such one is totally dependent on Josephus's *Antiquities* for any knowledge of the Assyrian siege of Tyre.

back in Assyria, the Phoenician city-states revolted against Assyria again, most probably under the leadership of Tyre. However, many of the city-states that were subservient to Tyre recapitulated and surrendered to Assyria. Nevertheless, Tyre refused to submit to Assyria. With the help of the other Phoenician city-states, Shalmaneser took military action against it. (This probably occurred beginning in his second regnal year [Nisan 725–Nisan 724 BCE], in which according to the eponym chronicle a campaign was carried out. Although the location of the Assyrian army is no longer preserved in the eponym chronicle, it is more than likely that the west was involved.) Unable to subdue Tyre, Shalmaneser placed it under a siege that lasted for five years. (The siege would have been lifted with the death of Shalmaneser in Tebet 722/721 BCE.) On the basis of the Tyrian calendar, presumably a fall new year calendar, the siege would have begun in the year 726–725 BCE, that is, before the fall new year festival of 725 BCE, and lasted until after the fall new year festival in 722 BCE. The five years of the siege would have been 726–725, 725–724, 724–723, 723–722, and 722–721 BCE.

The Tyrian king that Shalmaneser dealt with is identified as Elulaios. This Tyrian king is mentioned in the annals of Sennacherib as "Luli."[18] According to Katzenstein, Elulaios ascended the throne in Tyre sometime between Tiglath-pileser's accession to the Babylonian throne after Nisan 729 BCE and his death in Tebet 727 BCE.[19] He based his argument on the identification of Πύας/Πύλας with Pul,[20] that is, Tiglath-pileser and on the assumption that Pul was his name when he took the throne in Babylon. The weakness of this dating rests on two counts. First, there is insufficient evidence to make the identification of Πύας/Πύλας with Tiglath-pileser. Second, the assumption that Pul was Tiglath-pileser's name as king of Babylonia is no longer valid.[21] Therefore, we do not know when exactly Elulaios ascended the throne in Tyre. We can only conclude from the above text that when Shalmaneser first campaigned against Phoenicia, probably in his accession year (727–726 BCE), Elulaios was already on the Tyrian throne. From an Assyrian inscription, it is evident that Hiram II was still on the throne in 733–732 BCE (ND

[18]Cf. Luckenbill, *ARAB*, 2. §239.

[19]Katzenstein, *History of Tyre*, 222.

[20]See n. 15 above.

[21]See, especially, Brinkman, *Political History*, 61–62. Cf. Grayson, "Tiglath-pileser III to Sargon II," 73.

4301 + 4305:rev. 5–8). However, from another text, K 3751:16, one gathers that Hiram had been succeeded by Mêtenna (Mattan). The text reads as follows:

> ^{LÚ}*šu-ut*-SAG-*ia* ^{LÚ}GAL.BI.LUL *a-na* ^{URU}*ṣur-ri aš-pur ša* ^{I}*me-e-te-en-na* ^{URU}*ṣur-ra-a-a* 1 ME 50 GUN KÙ.GI [. . .] *am-ḫur*
>
> My official, the rabšāqê, I sent to Tyre. From Mêtenna the Tyrian, 150 talents of gold [. . .] I received.

It is likely that Hiram II, after having submitted to Tiglath-pileser during the latter's campaign in Syria-Palestine in 734–731 BCE, had subsequently rebelled and withheld tribute. Tyre's rebellion was probably part of another regional revolt. The same text, II R 67, lines 14–15, reports that the same *rabšāqê* was dispatched by the Assyrian king to remove Uassurme of Tabalu from the throne and replace him with Hulli. The notation of the eponym chronicle for the year 728–727 BCE reads ^{URU}*di*-[. . .], referring undoubtedly to Damascus. Most probably, the rest of the line refers to the recapture of Damascus after the city had revolted.[22] The revolts in all these places most likely occurred simultaneously. During the visit of the *rabšāqê*, Mêtenna paid an enormous sum of tribute. The unparalleled amount was either the total amount of tribute that Tyre owed Assyria or more likely the amount that Mêtenna had to pay for Assyria's help in usurping the Tyrian throne, the same kind of help Menahem had received from Assyria over a century earlier. Mêtenna was probably succeeded by Elulaios the following year (727–726 BCE). If Mêtenna's submission was an indication of his pro-Assyrian stance, it was quickly reversed by the anti-Assyrian policy of Elulaios.

B. Second Kings 17:1–6; 18:9–12

Second Kings 17:1–6 and 18:9–12 narrate events of the last years of the northern kingdom of Israel. The DtrH began the account of Hoshea's reign by providing a synchronism with the twelfth year of Ahaz.[23] No matter how one deals with this synchronistic datum, extra-biblical evidence relating to the fall of Samaria requires that Hoshea's reign began in the late 730s.

---

[22]See chapter four, n. 6 above.

[23]Cf. 2 Kgs 15:30, where Hoshea was said to have begun his reign in the twentieth year of Jotham. On the complexity of these synchronistic data, see Thiele, *Mysterious Numbers*, 134–38; Hayes and Hooker, *New Chronology*, 64–65; Hughes, *Secrets of the Times*, 138–54.

Thiele, Hughes, and Barnes all date the beginning of Hoshea's reign to 732 BCE.[24] Hayes and Hooker, on the other hand, date Hoshea's accession to 731–730 BCE.[25] As expected, the DtrH offered an evaluation of Hoshea's reign with the standard phrase, "he did what was evil in the sight of YHWH," followed with a surprisingly qualified notation, "yet not like the kings of Israel who were before him." Although no reason is given for the modified criticism, Jones suggests that because of the turbulent political situation during his reign, Hoshea was not able to devote his attention to matters religious and so escaped the DtrH's more severe condemnation.[26] Jones's suggestion, however, cannot be sustained.

Verses 3–6 of 2 Kgs 17 narrate the chain of events that led to the capture of Samaria by the Assyrians and the deportation of its people. Beyond the general gist of the account, there is very little consensus regarding how these verses ought to be understood and interpreted.

First, a number of scholars hold that these verses refer to two different accounts of the same event. These two parallel accounts are traced back to two different sources, with vv. 3–4 deriving from northern archives and vv. 5–6 (plus 2 Kgs 18:9–11) from Judean archives.[27] This theory was based on the presumed difficulties involved in assuming that the Assyrian king conducted two or more campaigns against the northern kingdom, not confirmed by Assyrian sources, and that Samaria held out against the Assyrians after Hoshea had been captured.[28] There is nothing in the text, however, that would suggest different sources. Na'aman correctly notes that "there are no stylistic or linguistic differences between the two assumed sources."[29]

---

[24]Thiele, *Mysterious Numbers*, 134; Hughes, *Secrets of the Times*, 205; Barnes, *Chronology in the Divided Monarchy*, 154. So also Cogan and Tadmor, *II Kings*, 195.

[25]Hayes and Hooker, *New Chronology*, 64–65. Cf. Jones, *1 and 2 Kings*, 2. 545.

[26]Jones, *1 and 2 Kings*, 2. 546.

[27]This theory was first proposed by H. Winckler ("Beiträge zur Quellenscheidung der Königbücher," in his *Alttestamentliche Untersuchungen* [Leipzig: E. Pfeiffer, 1892], 16–25) and has found support in the works of M. Noth (*Überlieferungsgeschichtliche Studien* [2d ed.; Tübingen: J. C. B. Mohr, 1957], 78); W. F. Albright ("The Original Account of the Fall of Samaria in II Kings," *BASOR* 174 [1964], 66–67); and Gray, *I & II Kings*, 639. The theory is recently defended by Jones, *1 and 2 Kings*, 542–43, and Becking, *Fall of Samaria*, 47–53. Hobbs also speaks of vv. 3–4 and vv. 5–6 as referring to the same events, without postulating different sources (*2 Kings*, 226).

[28]So Jones, *1 and 2 Kings*, 2. 542.

[29]Na'aman, "Conquest of Samaria," 213.

Second, there are other scholars who see this account as a continuous sequential narrative but posit references to two different Assyrian kings. In an important study in 1958, H. Tadmor set forth his theory of the two conquests of Samaria. In his detailed analysis of the inscriptions of Sargon II, Tadmor demonstrated that Sargon conducted his first campaign in the west only in his second regnal year (720 BCE).[30] On that basis, Tadmor suggested that Samaria was conquered by Shalmaneser V in the late summer or early autumn of 722 BCE, after a siege that lasted approximately two years (724–722 BCE). This conquest of Samaria by Shalmaneser is noted in 2 Kgs 17:5–6a and the Babylonian Chronicle. Tadmor further posited that Hoshea had already been deported to Assyria when Samaria fell. When Sargon ascended the throne in Assyria, he was preoccupied with domestic strife. It was not until the second year of his reign that Sargon began to campaign in the west, where he subdued Yaubi'di of Hamath, suppressed the rebellion of the western provinces of Arpad, Ṣimirra, and Damascus, conquered Gaza, and defeated the *turtan* of Egypt. At the end of the campaign, Sargon returned to Samaria, deporting its people and rebuilding it as a new province of Samerina.[31]

In relation to the interpretation of 2 Kgs 17:3–6, what was implicit in Tadmor's study of Sargon is made explicit in the recent commentary he co-authored with M. Cogan, namely, that the text refers to two different Assyrian kings. The king referred to in verses 3–6aα is Shalmaneser V, while in verse 6aβ is Sargon II. Thus Cogan and Tadmor allege:

> MT reads as if the same king of Assyria besieged Samaria (v. 5), took it (6aα), and exiled Israel to Assyria (6aα–6b). Historically, however, this construing of the text cannot stand. Two kings of Assyria oversaw the events referred to in v. 6; Shalmaneser V captured Samaria; Sargon II exiled Israel.[32]

Tadmor's theory has been accepted by many scholars and has been recently defended, with minor variations, by B. Becking.[33]

---

[30]Tadmor, "Campaigns of Sargon," 33–36.

[31]*Ibid.*, 36–40. See also H. Tadmor, "The Chronology of the First Temple Period," in *The Age of the Monarchies: Political History*, ed. A. Malamat (WHJP 4/1; Jerusalem: Massada, 1979), 57–58.

[32]Cogan and Tadmor, *II Kings*, 197.

[33]Becking, *Fall of Samaria*. For a list of works that have adopted Tadmor's theory, see Becking, *Fall of Samaria*, 38, n. 78. In addition, see the works of Dalley, "Foreign Chariotry," 33–36; Na'aman, "Historical and Chronological Notes," 74; A. Laato, "New Viewpoints on the Chronology of the Kings of Judah and Israel," *ZAW* 98 (1986), 217–18;

Recently, N. Na'aman offered a new interpretation of the sources relating to the fall of Samaria. In his analysis of 2 Kgs 17:3–6, Na'aman concludes that the king of Assyria in vv. 3–4 is Shalmaneser, while the king in vv. 5–6 is Sargon. Accordingly, Na'aman reconstructs the sequence of events of this text as follows: (1) Hoshea's act of disobedience (v. 3) took place in conjunction with the political unrest and rebellion that broke out in the west in 727 BCE upon the death of Tiglath-pileser III and the accession of Shalmaneser V. The Assyrian king eventually sent his army to put down the revolt in the region, forcing the submission of rebellious kings and collecting their tribute. (2) In c. 724/723 BCE, Hoshea sent an embassy to Egypt and withheld his yearly tribute (v. 4). Shalmaneser responded by attacking Hoshea, arresting him, and deporting him to Assyria. (3) When Sargon II succeeded Shalmaneser, he was confronted with opposition at home. In his second regnal year (720 BCE), Sargon campaigned in the west. During this campaign, Samaria was besieged and conquered (vv. 5–6).[34]

Hypotheses that the account in 2 Kgs 17:3–6 refer to two different Assyrian kings are without textual support. It is clear that both Tadmor's interpretation and Na'aman's interpretation of the biblical text are influenced by their understanding and interpretation of extra-biblical sources. A straightforward reading of the biblical text suggests that the same Assyrian king—Shalmaneser V—is intended throughout. The biblical text must be interpreted on its own integrity and then *correlated* with extra-biblical sources.

On the basis of the biblical and non-biblical texts, the events of 2 Kgs 17:3–6 may be reconstructed as follows.

(1) In his accession year, Shalmaneser V completed a western campaign begun by Tiglath-pileser which involved the recapture of Damascus (so eponym chronicle). When Shalmaneser "campaigned against" (עלה על) Hoshea during this campaign, Hoshea submitted and paid tribute (v. 3).

H. Donner, *Geschichte des Volkes Israel und seiner Nachbarn in Grundzügen* (2 vols., Göttingen: Vandenhoeck & Ruprecht, 1987), 2. 314–15; Hayes and Hooker, *New Chronology*, 73.

[34]Na'aman, "Conquest of Samaria," 212–19. Na'aman alleges that "the three years of siege (v. 5b) and the date in v. 6a are both historical deductions by the Deuteronomistic Historian, who in his sources had found a datum that Samaria was besieged and conquered by the Assyrians three years *after* (emphasis his) its rebellion and the imprisonment of its king. He mistakenly interpreted the datum to mean that the city fell—after three years of siege—in Hoshea's last year, thus combining his last year with the fall of Samaria" (221).

(2) During his first regnal year (726–725 BCE), Shalmaneser remained "in the land" (so eponym chronicle). It was then that rebellion again broke out in the west; Hoshea participated in the revolt by sending representatives to Egypt[35] to enlist help and withheld his yearly tribute (v. 4a).

(3) Shalmaneser probably returned to the west in his second regnal year (725–724 BCE) to quell the rebellion. Samaria was attacked and Hoshea arrested and exiled (v. 4b). This virtually began the process of the provincialization of Samaria

(4) In all likelihood, Shalmaneser dealt with the northern kingdom again in his third regnal year (724–723 BCE). He invaded "all the land" before advancing against Samaria and placed it under a siege that lasted three years (v. 5).

(5) Shalmaneser captured Samaria during his fifth regnal year (722–721 BCE) and deported Israelites to other provinces of Assyria (v. 6).

Second Kings 18:9–11 confirms the dating of the sequence of events already suggested in 17:3–6. According to 2 Kgs 18:9 (cf. 17:5), the siege of Samaria began in the seventh year of Hoshea, which was also the fourth year of Hezekiah (724–723 BCE). Samaria was taken by the Assyrians in Hoshea's ninth year (722–721 BCE), after a siege of three years—that is, one full and parts of two additional regnal years (18:10; cf. 17:6aα). Following the capture of Samaria, Shalmaneser deported Israelites to other provinces of Assyria (18:11; cf. 17:6aβ).

C. Hosea 9:10–14

Hosea 9:10–14 is an oracle of comparisons. Drawing on tradition, Hosea begins by making a contrast between the Israel of the wilderness and the one at Baal-peor (v. 10).[36] Verses 11–14 then move on to speak of the impending fate of Ephraim. Again, it needs to be reiterated that the use of "Ephraim" in these verses is a correct reflection of the rump-state under the rule of Hoshea

---

[35] For a treatment of "So, the king of Egypt," see most recently D. L. Christensen, "The Identity of 'King So' in Egypt (2 Kings 17:4)," *VT* 39 (1989), 140–53; G. Ahlström, "Le «roi So» et la ruine d'Israël," *Svensk Exegetisk Årsbok* 54 (1989), 5–19; J. Day, "The Problem of 'So, king of Egypt' in 2 Kings xvii 4," *VT* 42 (1992), 289–301; and A. R. Green, "The Identity of King So of Egypt—An Alternative Interpretation," *JNES* 52 (1993), 99–108.

[36] J. L. Mays, *Hosea* (OTL; Philadelphia: Westminster, 1969), 132.

after Tiglath-pileser had provincialized the other regions once held by Israel.

Hosea 9:13 has presented translators and commentators alike with textual and interpretational problems. Jerome long ago noted: "Multum in hoc loco inter se discordant interpretes."[37] The MT of the verse reads as follows:

אֶפְרַיִם כַּאֲשֶׁר־רָאִיתִי לְצוֹר שְׁתוּלָה בְנָוֶה
וְאֶפְרַיִם לְהוֹצִיא אֶל־הֹרֵג בָּנָיו

On the basis of the MT, very different translations have been offered. The NJPSV translates as, "It shall go with Ephraim as I have seen it go with Tyre, which is planted in a meadow; Ephraim too must bring out his children to the slayers," adding that the meaning of the Hebrew text is uncertain. The NRSV translates as, "Once I saw Ephraim as a young palm planted in a lovely meadow, but now Ephraim must lead out his children for slaughter," similarly adding that the meaning of Hebrew text is uncertain. Andersen and Freedman in their Anchor Bible commentary translate as, "I saw Ephraim as in that place, by the Rival—[a fig tree] planted in a meadow—Ephraim indeed brought his children to the Slayer."[38]

The problem in translation is compounded by the Septuagint text which reads differently as follows:

Εφραιμ, ὃν τρόπον εἶδον, εἰς θήραν παρέστησαν τὰ τέκνα αὐτῶν, καὶ Εφραιμ τοῦ ἐξαγαγεῖν εἰς ἀποκέντησιν τὰ τέκνα αὐτῶν

Translating on the basis of the Greek text, the RSV, on the one hand, translates as, "Ephraim's sons, as I have seen, are destined for a prey; Ephraim must lead forth his sons to slaughter," while Wolff in his Hermeneia commentary, on the other hand, translates as, "Ephraim, as I see, has exposed his sons to the hunt. Now Ephraim must lead his sons to the butcher."[39]

In a recent article I have argued that the MT is the more original reading and should be translated, "Ephraim, just as I have seen Tyre planted in a pleasant place, so Ephraim must lead his children out to the slaughterer."[40]

---

[37]Jerome, *Commentariorum in Oseam Prophetam* in *Patrologiae cursus completus. Series Latina*, ed. J. P. Migne (Paris: J. P. Migne, 1865), 941.

[38]F. I. Andersen and D. N. Freedman, *Hosea* (AB 23A; Garden City, NY: Doubleday, 1980), 536.

[39]H. W. Wolff, *Hosea* (Hermeneia; Philadelphia: Fortress, 1982), 160–61.

[40]See Kuan, "Hosea 9:13," 103–8.

Although Wolff is wrong in his preference for the Septuagint reading over the Masoretic, he is nevertheless right in pointing to the political and military significance of the verse. He suggests that the event could refer either to Israel's involvement in the Syro-Ephraimitic alliance in 734–733 BCE or to Israel's change in allegiance from Assyria to Egypt after the death of Tiglath-pileser III, thus challenging Shalmaneser V in the years between 727 and 722 BCE.[41] Once we recognize, however, that what we have in this verse is evidently a comparison that Hosea seeks to make between Ephraim and Tyre, we can arrive nearer to a description of the events to which Hosea refers. The prophet declares that what was happening to Tyre would likewise befall Israel. In that period of history when Hosea was active as a prophet, there was a time when the fate of both nations ran almost parallel in their political relations with Assyria. Israel was put under siege by Shalmaneser V in 724–723 BCE, just two years after Tyre was besieged. Josephus's *Antiquities*, 9.14.2 §§283–287, provides an account of the events that led to the Assyrian siege of Tyre by Shalmaneser V that lasted from 726–725 to 722–721 BCE.[42] The similarities between Tyre and Israel are evident. They both revolted in Shalmaneser V's accession year (727–726 BCE) and became Assyrian vassals when the Assyrian king came to suppress the revolts in Syria-Palestine. Both nations revolted again when Shalmaneser was back in Assyria. Subsequently, when Shalmaneser returned to the west, first Tyre and then Samaria was placed under siege. In this situation, Ephraim sent its people out to defend Samaria against the Assyrian forces, just as the Tyrians had done. Against this historical context, we understand why the prophet Hosea proclaimed that just as had Tyre, so too Ephraim would bring out his children to the slaughterer.

IV. SYNOPSIS

Tiglath-pileser was on a western campaign to deal with a rebellion when he died and was succeeded by Shalmaneser V, who completed the campaign. While the eponym chronicle for 728–727 BCE refers most probably to Damascus, suggesting its involvement in the rebellion, by all indications the rebellion was more widespread. Israel and Tyre probably joined with their old

---

[41] Wolff, *Hosea*, 166.

[42] See above, pp. 199–202.

ally Aram-Damascus in the revolt. When Shalmaneser campaigned against Israel, Hoshea submitted and paid tribute (2 Kgs 17:3).

A rebellion broke out again in the west during Shalmaneser's first regnal year when the Assyrian king remained "in the land." Hoshea participated in the movement and sent representatives to Egypt to request assistance (2 Kgs 17:4a). Tyre must have been an active participant as well. In response to the revolt, Shalmaneser campaigned in the west again in 725–724 BCE. Samaria was attacked (Babylonian Chronicle 1.i.28) and Hoshea was arrested (2 Kgs 17:4b). With the arrest of Hoshea, Samaria was probably assigned provincial status. After suppressing Samaria, Shalmaneser moved against Tyre, placing it under siege (Hos 9:13; *Ant.* 9.14.2 §§285–286).

Revolt must have broken out again in Samaria and Ephraim in reaction to Shalmaneser's decree of provincialization. Shalmaneser was back to quell the rebellion in his third regnal year (724–723 BCE). The whole of Ephraim had to be attacked (2 Kgs 17:5a) before Samaria was put under siege (2 Kgs 17:5b; 18:9). At the end of a three-year siege, Samaria was captured by or surrendered to the Assyrians (722–721 BCE).

The series of revolts in which both Israel and Tyre participated suggests that some sort of mutual cooperation must have existed between the two states. The economic squeeze that the Assyrians placed on the Israelites and the Phoenicians must have been severe, leading to their repeated attempts to shake off the Assyrian yoke. Previous history in the region has shown that rebellions generally were staged not by individual states but through the cooperation and alliances of several states. Although Hoshea began his reign as a pro-Assyrian, he soon switched policy and became anti-Assyrian. Although Mêtenna of Tyre was forced to submit and pay a huge tribute to Assyria, his successor Luli most probably resisted Assyrian control of Phoenician commercial interest in the region (cf. ND 2715). This final period of cooperation between the Phoenicians and the Israelites must therefore be seen as a joint effort to deal with Assyrian domination in the region.

CONCLUSION

Among other things, this study has shown the importance of the Assyrian historical texts in any attempt to sketch the political and commercial relations of Syro-Palestinian states during the ninth and eighth centuries BCE. The empire of Assyria, in particular, had phenomenal influence over the politics and commerce in the region. Assyria's presence and influence, moreover, impacted relations between states directly. How each state related to Assyria determined how they related to one another. Israel's pro-Assyrian stance for a long period of its history, for example, established the direction of its relations with its immediate neighbors.

The foregoing study has uncovered nine phases in the political and commercial relations between Syro-Palestinian states generally and between Israel/Judah, Tyre/Sidon, and Aram-Damascus specifically.

Phase I: Before the 850s BCE, independent states related to one another as each state saw fit. Commercial and economic cooperation existed between states. Stronger states in the region were able to dominate weaker ones, but there was no "superpower" meddling in the affairs of the region. Israel, under the reign of Omri, must have had strong commercial relations with Tyre/Sidon as well as Aram-Damascus. Israel, in addition, was strong enough to dominate lesser states such as Judah and Moab. Without the interference and domination of a "superpower," this period, in particular, witnessed the relative wealth of Israel as a nation.

Phase II: With the Assyrians making inroads into the west beginning with the reign of Ashurnasirpal II, and with the more aggressive policy of Assyrian domination carried out by Shalmaneser III, this inter-state cooperation eventually turned into a military coalition. The coalition was organized to stop Assyria's intrusion into the region and its bid for control over regional commerce. The powerful coalition—headed by Adad-idri of Damascus and Irḫuleni of Hamath, and with the strong participation of Ahab of Israel—was able to oppose Shalmaneser's advance on at least four occasions (so the Monolith Inscription and the "Baghdad Text"). Tyre was likely to have been involved in the coalition in one form or another.

Phase III: A new phase in the relations of Syro-Palestinian states had developed by the eighteenth year of Shalmaneser's reign (841–840 BCE). The anti-Assyrian coalition in Syria-Palestine, which had successfully fended off Shalmaneser's attempts to penetrate beyond the Orontes River, had collapsed (so III R 5, 6, the Marble-Slab Inscription, and the Black Obelisk Inscription). Aram-Damascus, Tyre/Sidon, and Israel all responded differently to Shalmaneser on this campaign. Aram-Damascus under Hazael was in direct opposition to Assyria. Tyre under Ba^{c}al-^{c}azor II, in order to protect its commercial interests, opted for diplomatic co-operation with the Assyrians by means of giving "diplomatic gifts" to the Assyrian king. Jehu led Israel to submit politically to Assyria in order to win Assyrian support and protection in dealing with Aram-Damascus, as well as to secure his hold on the Israelite throne. With the collapse of this western coalition, the states in the region functioned more independently of one another. However, as Assyria's regional presence diminished in the decades following, Aram-Damascus set out to dominate the region. It is likely that Aram-Damascus controlled Elath during this period (cf. 2 Kgs 16:6), and as such, some ties, albeit commercial ones, probably existed between Aram-Damascus and Tyre.

Phase IV: After a period of domination by Aram-Damascus during the reign of Hazael, a new phase of political relations in Syria-Palestine is discernible, namely, the resurgence of a north Syrian-Anatolian coalition. The coalition consisted of sixteen states under the leadership of Ben-Hadad of Aram-Damascus and the king of Arpad (so the Zakkur stela), who is to be identified as Ataršumki (cf. Pazarcik Stela, obverse). The coalition mounted an attempt to force Zakkur, the king of Hamath and Lu^{c}aš, to join the alliance in order to create a strong united front against Assyria throughout eastern Anatolia and all of Syria. The attempt, however, was not successful. The failure was due in large part to a major campaign undertaken by Adad-nirari III in 805–802 BCE to crush the rebellion. This campaign resulted in the capture of Arpad (so the Sheikh Hammad Stela, the Scheil and Millard Fragment, and the Pazarcik Stela, obverse) and the weakening of Aram-Damascus's military strength (so the el-Rimah Stela, the Calah Slab, and the Saba$^{\supset}$a Stela).

During this phase, Israel under Jehoahaz remained hostile toward Aram-Damascus because of the latter's continued aggression toward Israel during the reign of Ben-Hadad (2 Kgs 13:3). Israel, as a loyal vassal of Assyria, received some relief from Aram-Damascus's aggression during Adad-nirari's 805–802 BCE campaign (2 Kgs 13:5). On the other hand, with Aram-Damascus continuing to control the trade routes, and in particular the seaport of Elath, Tyre probably had good relations with Aram-Damascus, at least commercially. There is no evidence—direct or indirect—to suggest that the relations between the Israelites and the Phoenicians were anything but strained.

Phase V: With the conclusion of Adad-nirari's 805–802 BCE campaign and the establishment of Šamši-ilu as the dominant Assyrian force in the west, a new phase in the politics of the region emerged. This phase of independent national actions, with some cooperation between states, lasted from the 800s to the 750s BCE. Šamši-ilu's presence in the west was a strong deterrent against anti-Assyrian activities. Rebellions were quickly put down (so Pazarcik Stela, reverse). With Assyria's dominating presence, pro-Assyrian states such as Israel and Judah were able to regain territorial holdings lost to Aram-Damascus at the height of its expansion. Joash of Israel was able to reclaim some territories from Ben-Hadad (2 Kgs 13:25; cf. 1 Kings 20 and 22:1–38). It was not, however, until early in the reign of Jeroboam II that Israel regained most, if not all, of its traditional territories, including all Galilee and Transjordan (cf. 2 Kgs 14:25, 28). Elath, the important seaport, was retaken from Aram-Damascus and restored to Judean control (2 Kgs 14:22). With Elath back in Israelite/Judean control, relations with Tyre were restored (cf. Amos 1:9).

Phase VI: When Rezin usurped the throne of Damascus, another phase of political and commercial relations in Syria-Palestine was introduced. This phase was made possible in part by the death of Šamši-ilu in the late 750s, which left a power vacuum in the west. This was the phase that witnessed the initial formation of a major anti-Assyrian coalition of Syro-Palestinian rulers headed by Rezin (cf. Amos 1). A rival state of Israel under Pekah; Bit-Adini, now under a local ruler; Tyre, which had broken its relations with Israel under Jeroboam II; and possibly also the Philistine cities of Gaza, Ashdod, Ashkelon, and Ekron were all participants in the coalition. Aggressive actions were taken by the coalition against Israel to recapture territory regained by Israel early in the reign of Jeroboam II (cf. Isa 8:23, 9:10–11a). Rezin likewise moved to retake the port of Elath and place it under Aramean control (2 Kgs 16:6). With Elath no longer under Israelite control, it is understandable that Tyre would choose to break off relations with Israel and join the coalition headed by Rezin.

Phase VII: When Tiglath-pileser III ascended the Assyrian throne, he soon organized a campaign to deal with the anti-Assyrian coalition. That campaign began in his second regnal year (743–742 BCE) and lasted until 740–739 BCE (so eponym chronicle). While the main target appears to have been Arpad, other rebellious states were dealt with as well. This led to a temporary collapse of the coalition. Syro-Palestinian states including Aram-Damascus, Tyre, and Israel were noted to have paid *maddattu* to the Assyrian king in 738–737 BCE (so Layard 50a + 50b + 67a). Israel paid *maddattu* because Menahem had remained loyal to Assyria. Menahem had earlier received Assyrian aid to hold on to his throne (2 Kgs 15:19–20). Aram-Damascus and Tyre probably rendered token submission to the Assyrian king. With Pekah still functioning as a rival Israelite king and an ally to Rezin and Menahem remaining pro-Assyrian, no political nor commercial ties existed between Samaria and Damascus. Since Tyre had joined with Aram-Damascus, and Elath was under the control of Rezin, it is difficult to suggest that relations between Samaria and Tyre were good.

Phase VIII: Not long after 738–737 BCE, the anti-Assyrian coalition began to resurface. As soon as Pekah gained control of Samaria (in 735–734 BCE), the coalition launched an attack on Ahaz of Judah in order to force Judah to join the coalition (Isa 7:1; 2 Kgs 16:5). It is clear from Assyrian inscriptions that open rebellion against Assyria was widespread. Members of the alliance included Aram-Damascus, Israel, Tyre, Gaza, Ashkelon, and Arabia. The entire coalition was dealt with during Tiglath-pileser's 734–731 BCE campaign (so ND 400, Layard 29b, Layard 72b + 72a, III R 10, 2, and ND 4301 + 4305).

Phase IX: In the early 720s BCE, another western rebellion broke out. Tiglath-pileser led a campaign to deal with the revolt in his last year of reign (727–726 BCE). Tiglath-pileser, however, died while campaigning and was succeeded by Shalmaneser V, who completed the campaign. While the eponym chronicle for 728–727 BCE refers most probably to Damascus, suggesting its involvement in the rebellion, by all indications the rebellion was more widespread. Israel and Tyre probably joined with their old ally in the revolt. When Shalmaneser campaigned against Israel, Hoshea submitted and paid tribute (2 Kgs 17:3).

A rebellion broke out again in the west during Shalmaneser's first regnal year when the Assyrian king remained "in the land." Hoshea participated in the movement and sent representatives to Egypt to request assistance (2 Kgs 17:4a). Tyre must have been an active participant as well. In response to the revolt, Shalmaneser campaigned in the west again in 725–724 BCE. Samaria was attacked (Babylonian Chronicle 1.i.28) and Hoshea arrested (2 Kgs 17:4b). With the arrest of Hoshea, Samaria was probably decreed provincial status. After suppressing Samaria, Shalmaneser moved against Tyre, placing it under siege (Hos 9:13; *Ant.* 9.14.2 §§285–286).

Revolt must have broken out again in Samaria and Ephraim in reaction to Shalmaneser's decree of provincialization. Shalmaneser was back to quell the rebellion in his third regnal year (724–723 BCE). The whole of Ephraim had to be attacked (2 Kgs 17:5a) before Samaria was put under siege (2 Kgs 17:5b; 18:9). After three years, Samaria fell to the Assyrians (722–721 BCE).

APPENDIX

MAJOR WESTERN COALITIONS IN THE NINTH AND EIGHTH CENTURIES BCE

Date	*Coalition*	*Leader(s)*	*Participating States*
850s	North Syrian-Anatolian	Bit-Adini (?)	Bit-Adini; Pattin; Carchemish; Samʾal; Que; Hiluk; Iasbuk
850s–840s	South Syrian-Palestinian (12 states)	Aram-Damascus; Hamath; Israel	Aram-Damascus; Hamath; Israel; Byblos; Egypt; Irqanata; Arwad; Usanata; Šianu; Arabia; Beth-Rehob; Ammon
800s	North Syrian-Anatolian (16 states)	Aram-Damascus; Arpad	Aram-Damascus; Arpad; Que; Umq; Gurgum; Samʾal; Melid; and others
750s	North Syrian	Arpad	Arpad; Hadrach; and others (?)
750s–740s	Syro-Palestinian	Aram-Damascus	Aram-Damascus; rival state of Israel; Bit-Adini; Tyre; Gaza; Ashdod; Ashkelon; Ekron
730s	Syro-Palestinian	Aram-Damascus	Aram-Damascus; Israel; Tyre; Gaza; Ashkelon; Arabia
720s	Syro-Palestinian	Israel (?)	Israel; Tyre; Damascus

BIBLIOGRAPHY

Abel, F. M. *Géographie de la Palestine.* 2 vols. Paris: J. Gabalda, 1933–38.

Aharoni, Y. "Beth-Haccherem." In *Archaeology and Old Testament Study*, 171–84. Ed. by D. W. Thomas. Oxford: Clarendon, 1967.

____. *The Land of the Bible: A Historical Geography.* 2d ed. Philadelphia: Westminster, 1979.

____. *The Archaeology of the Land of Israel from the Prehistoric Beginnings to the End of the First Temple Period.* Philadelphia: Westminster, 1982.

Ahlström, G. W. "King Jehu: A Prophet's Mistake." In *Scripture in History and Theology: Essays in Honor of J. Coert Rylaarsdam*, 47–69. Ed. by A. L. Merill and T. W. Overholt. Pittsburgh: Pickwick, 1977.

____. "The Battle of Ramoth-Gilead in 841 BCE." In *"Wünschet Jerusalem Frieden": Collected Communications to the XIIth Congress of the International Organization for the Study of the Old Testament, Jerusalem 1986*, 157–66. Ed. by M. Augustin and K.-D. Schunck. Beiträge zur Erforschung des Alten Testaments und des Antiken Judentums 13. Frankfurt am Main: Peter Lang, 1988.

____. "Le 'roi so' et la ruine d'Israël," *Svensk Exegetisk Årsbok* 54 (1989), 5–19.

____. *The History of Ancient Palestine from the Palaeolithic Period to Alexander's Conquest.* JSOTSup 146. Sheffield: JSOT, 1993.

Albright, W. F. "The Administrative Divisions of Israel and Judah," *JPOS* 5 (1925), 17–54.

____. "Bronze Age Mounds of Northern Palestine and the Hauran," *BASOR* 19 (1925), 5–19.

____. "Notes on Early Hebrew and Aramaic Epigraphy," *JPOS* 6 (1926), 75–102.

____. "New Light on the Early History of Phoenician Colonization," *BASOR* 83 (1941), 14–22.

____. "The Chronology of the Divided Monarchy," *BASOR* 100 (1945), 16–22.

____. "The Phoenician Inscription of the Tenth Century B.C. from Byblus," *JAOS* 67 (1947), 153–160.

____. "The Hebrew Expression for 'Making a Covenant' in Pre-Israelite Documents," *BASOR* 121 (1951), 21–22.

____. "The New Assyro-Tyrian Synchronism and the Chronology of Tyre," *Annuaire de l'Institut de Philologie et d'Historie Orientales et Slaves* 13 (1953) [*Mélanges Isidore Lévy* (Bruxelles, 1955)], 1–9.

____. "The Son of Tabeel (Isaiah 7:6)," *BASOR* 140 (1955), 34–35.

____. *The Archaeology of Palestine*. 4th ed. London: Penguin, 1960.

____. "The Role of the Canaanites in the History of Civilization." In *The Bible and the Ancient Near East*, 328–62. Ed. by G. E. Wright. London: Rutlege & Kegan Paul, 1961.

____. "The Original Account of the Fall of Samaria in II Kings," *BASOR* 174 (1964), 66–67.

____. *Yahweh and the Gods of Canaan: a Historical Analysis of Two Contrasting Faiths*. Jordan Lectures 1965. London: Athlone, 1968.

____. "Syria, the Philistines and Phoenicia." In *The Cambridge Ancient History*, II/2, 507–36. Ed. by I. E. S. Edwards *et al.* Cambridge: Cambridge University Press, 1975.

Alfrink, J. "L'expression שָׁכַב עִם אֲבוֹתָיו," *OTS* 2 (1943), 106–18.

Alt, A. "Das System der assyrischen Provinzen auf dem Boden des Reiches Israel," *ZDPV* 52 (1929), 220–42.

____. "Jesaja 8, 23-9, 6. Befreiungsnacht und Krönungstag." In *Festschrift Alfred Bertholet zum 80. Geburtstag gewidmet von Kollegen und Freuden*, 23–49. Ed. by W. Baumgartner *et al.* Tübingen: J. C. B. Mohr (Paul Siebeck), 1950.

____. "Die Rolle Samarias bei der Entstehung des Judentums." In his *Kleine Schriften* II, 316–37. Munich: C. H. Beck, 1953.

____. "Tiglathpilesers III. erster Feldzug nach Palästina." In his *Kleine Schriften* II, 150–62. Munich: C. H. Beck, 1953.

Amiran, R. *Ancient Pottery of the Holy Land from Its Beginnings in the Neolithic Period to the End of the Iron Age*. Jerusalem: Massada, 1969.

Andersen, F. I. and D. N. Freedman. *Hosea*. AB 24. Garden City, NY: Doubleday, 1980.

____. *Amos*. AB 24A. New York: Doubleday, 1989.

Anderson, W. P. *Sarepta I. The Late Bronze and Iron Age Strata of Area II, Y. The University Museum of the University of Pennsylvania Excavations at Sarafand, Lebanon*. Publications de l'Université Libanaise, Section des Études archéologiques 2. Beirut: Université Libanaise, 1988.

Ap-Thomas, D. R. "The Phoenicians." In *Peoples of Old Testament Times*, 259–86. Ed. by D. J. Wiseman. Oxford: Clarendon, 1973.

Arnold, P. M. "Beth-aven." In *The Anchor Bible Dictionary*, 1. 682. Ed. by D. N. Freedman. 6 vols. New York: Doubleday, 1992.

Astour, M. C. "The Origin of the Terms 'Canaan,' 'Phoenicia,' and 'Purple,'" *JNES* 24 (1965), 346–50.

____. "The Arena of Tiglath-pileser III's Campaign against Sarduri II (743 B.C.)," *Assur* 2/3 (1979), 69–91.

____. "841 B.C.: The First Assyrian Invasion of Israel," *JAOS* (1971), 383–89.

Asurmendi, J. M. *La Guerra Siro-Efraimita: Historia y Profestas*. Valencia: Institutión San Jerónimo, 1982.

Aubet-Semmler, M. E. *The Phoenicians and the West: Politics, Colonies and Trade*. Cambridge: Cambridge University Press, 1993.

Avigad, N. "The Ivory House Which Ahab Build." In *Eretz Shomron: The Thirtieth Archaeological Convention, September 1972*, 75–85. Ed. by J. Aviram. Jerusalem: Israel Exploration Society, 1973. [Hebrew]

Baramki, D. *Phoenicia and the Phoenicians*. Beirut: Khayats, 1961.

Barkay, G. "The Iron Age II-III." In *The Archaeology of Ancient Israel*, 302–73. Ed. by A. Ben-Tor. New Haven: Yale University Press, 1992.

Barnes, W. E. *The Second Book of Kings*. CBSC. Cambridge: Cambridge University Press, 1908.

Barnes, W. H. *Studies in the Chronology of the Divided Monarchy of Israel*. HSM 48. Atlanta: Scholars Press, 1991.

Barnett, R. D. "The Nimrud Ivories and the Art of the Phoenicians," *Iraq* 2 (1935), 185–99.

____. "Phoenician and Syrian Ivory Carving," *PEQ* 71 (1939), 4–19.

____. "Phoenicia and Ivory Trade," *Archeology* 9 (1956), 87–97.

____. *A Catalogue of the Nimrud Ivories with Other Examples of Ancient Near Eastern Ivories in the British Museum*. London: British Museum, 1957.

____. *Ancient Ivories in the Middle East and Adjacent Countries*. Qedem 14. Jerusalem: Hebrew University, 1982.

____. "Urartu." In *The Cambridge Ancient History*, III/1, 314–71. Ed. by J. Boardman *et al*. 2d ed. Cambridge: Cambridge University Press, 1982.

Barré, L. M. *The Rhetoric of Political Persuasion. The Narrative Artistry and Political Intentions of 2 Kings 9-11*. CBQMS 20. Washington, D.C.: Catholic Biblical Association of America, 1988.

Barth, H. *Die Jesaja-Worte in der Josiazeit. Israel und Assur als Thema einer productiven Neuinterpretation der Jesajaüberlieferung*. WMANT 48. Neukirchen-Vluyn: Neukirchener Verlag, 1977.

Barton, J. *Amos's Oracles against the Nations: A Study of Amos 1.3–2.5*. SOTSMS 6. Cambridge: Cambridge University Press, 1980.

Becking, B. E. J. H. *De Ondergang van Samaria: Historische, exegetische en theologische opmerkingen bij II Koningen 17*. Dissertation, Utrecht, 1985.

____. *The Fall of Samaria: An Historical and Archaeological Study*. SHANE 2. Leiden: E. J. Brill, 1992.

Begrich, J. "Der syrisch-ephraïmitische Krieg und seine weltpolitischen Zusammenhänge," *ZDMG* 83 (1927), 213–37.

____. *Die Chronologie der Könige von Israel und Juda*. Tübingen: J. C. B. Mohr (Paul Siebeck), 1929.

Benzinger, I. *Die Bücher der Könige*. KHC. Leipzig: J. C. B. Mohr (Paul Siebeck), 1899.

Ben-Zvi, E. "Tracing Prophetic Literature in the Book of Kings: The Case of II Kings 15,37," *ZAW* 102 (1990), 100–105.

Bikai, P. M. *The Pottery of Tyre*. Warminster: Aris & Phillips, 1978.

____. "Observations on Archaeological Evidence for the Trade between Israel and Tyre," *BASOR* 258 (1985), 71–72.

____. "The Late Phoenician Pottery Complex and Chronology," *BASOR* 229 (1978), 47–56.

____. "The Phoenician Imports." In *Excavations at Kition IV: The Non-Cypriote Pottery*, 23–36. Ed. by V. Karageorghis. Nicosia: Department of Antiquities of Cyprus, 1981.

____. *The Phoenician Pottery of Cyprus*. Nicosia: Leventis, 1987.

Billerbeck, A. and Delitzsch, F. "Die Palasttore Salmanassars III. aus Balawat." In *Beiträge zur Assyriologie und semitischen Sprachwissenschaft* IV/1. Leipzig: J. C. Hinrichs, 1908.

Birch, W. G. and Pinches, T. G. *The Bronze Ornaments of the Palace Gates of Balawat (Shalmaneser II, B.C. 859–825)*. 2 vols. London: Society of Biblical Archaeology, 1880–1902.

Biran, A. "Tel Dan," *BA* 37 (1974), 26–51.

____. "Tell Dan—Five Years Later," *BA* 43 (1980), 168–82.

____. "The Temenos at Dan." In *Harry M. Orlinsky Volume*, 15–43. Ed. by B. A. Levine and A. Malamat. ErIsr 16. Jerusalem: Israel Exploration Society, 1982. [Hebrew]

Black, J. A. "The New Year Ceremonies in Ancient Babylon: 'Taking Bel by the Hand' and Cultic Picnic," *Religion* 11 (1981), 39–59.

Bonnet, C. *Melqart*. Leuven: Peeters, 1988.

____. Lipiński, E., and Marchetti, P., eds. *Religio Phoenicia*. Studia Phoenicia 4. Namur: Société des Études Classiques, 1986.

Borger, R. *Die Inschriften Asarhaddons Königs von Assyrien*. AfO Beiheft 9. Osnabrück: Biblio-Verlag, 1967.

____. *Assyrischen-babylonische Zeilchenlist*. 2d ed. Neukirchen-Vluyn: Neukirchener Verlag, 1981.

____ and Tadmor, H. "Zwei Beiträge zur alttestamentliche Wissenschaft und aufgrund der Inschriften des Tiglathpilesers III," *ZAW* 94 (1982), 244–81.

Brandl, B. "A Proto-Aeolic Capital from Gezer," *IEJ* 34 (1984), 173–76.

Briend, J. "Jeroboam II sauveur d'Israël." In *Mélanges bibliques et orientaux en l'honneur de M. Henri Cazelles*, 41–49. Ed.

by A. Caquot and M. Delcor. AOAT 212. Neukirchen-Vluyn: Neukirchener Verlag, 1981.

Bright, J. *A History of Israel*. 3d ed. Philadelphia: Westminster, 1981.

Brinkman, J. A. *A Political History of Post-Kassite Babylonia, 1158-722 B.C.* AnOr 43. Rome: Pontifical Biblical Institute, 1968.

____. "Additional Texts from the Reigns of Shalmaneser III and Shamshi-Adad V," *JNES* 32 (1973), 40–46.

____. "A Further Note on the Date of the Battle of Qarqar and Neo-Assyrian Chronology," *JCS* 30 (1978), 173–75.

____. "Babylonia under the Assyrian Empire, 745–627 B.C." In *Power and Propaganda: A Symposium on Ancient Empires*, 223–50. Ed. by M. T. Larsen. Copenhagen: Akademisk Forlag, 1979.

____. "The Babylonian Chronicle Revisited." In *Lingering Over Words: Studies in Ancient Near Eastern Literature in Honor of William L. Moran*, 73–104. Ed. by T. Abusche, J. Huenergard, and P. Steinkeller. HSS 37. Atlanta: Scholars Press, 1990.

Briquel-Chatonnet, F. *Les relations entre les cités de la côte Phénicienne et les royaumes d'Israël et de Juda*. Studia Phoenicia 12. Leuven: Peeters, 1992.

Bron, F. and Lemaire, A. "Les inscriptions araméennes de Hazael," *RA* 83 (1989), 35–43.

Brown, J. P. *The Lebanon and Phoenicia: Ancient Texts Illustrating their Physical Geography and Native Industries I*. Beirut: American University of Beirut Centennial Publications, 1969.

Brown, W. P. "The So-called Refrain in Isaiah 5:25–30 and 9:7–10:4," *CBQ* 52 (1990), 432–43.

Buccellati, G. *Cities and Nations of Ancient Syria*. Rome: Istituto di Studi del Vicino Oriente, 1967.

Budge, E. A. W. *The Rise and Progress of Assyriology*. London: M. Hopkinson, 1925.

Bunnens, G. "Commerce et diplomatie phéniciens au temps de Hiram Ier de Tyr," *JESHO* 19 (1976), 1–31.

____. *L'expansion phénicienne en Méditerranée: Essai d'interprétation fondé sur une analyse des traditions littéraires*. Études de philologie, d'archéologie et d'histoire anciennes 17. Rome: Institut historique belge de Rome, 1979.

____. "Tyr et la mer." In *Redt Tyrus/Sauvons Tyr: Histoire phénicienne/Fenicische geschiedenis*, 7–21. Ed. by E. Gubel, E. Lipiński, and B. Servais-Soyez. Studia Phoenicia 1–2. Leuven: Katholieke Universiteit Leuven, 1983.

Burney, C. F. *Notes on the Hebrew Text of the Books of Kings*. Oxford: Clarendon, 1903.

Cameron, G. G. "The Annals of Shalmaneser III, King of Assyria," *Sumer* 6 (1950), 6–26.

Campbell, A. F. *Of Prophets and Kings: A Late Ninth-Century Document (1 Samuel–2 Kings)*. CBQMS 17. Washington, D.C.: Catholic Biblical Association of America, 1986.

Cantineau, J. "Remarques sur la stèle araméenne de Sefiré-Soudjin," *RA* 28 (1931), 167–78.

Carpenter, R. "The Phoenicians in the West," *AJA* 62 (1958), 35–53.

Cazelles, H. "Une nouvelle stèle d'Adad-nirari d'Assyrie et Joas d'Israël," *CRAIBL* (1969), 106–17.

Christensen, D. L. "The Identity of 'King So' in Egypt (2 Kings xvii 4)," *VT* 39 (1989), 140–53.

Clements, R. E. *Isaiah 1-39*. NCBC. Grand Rapids: Eerdmans, 1980.

Clifford, R. J. "Phoenician Religion," *BASOR* 279 (1990), 55–64.

Cody, A. "A New Inscription from Tell āl Rimaḥ and King Jehoash of Israel," *CBQ* 32 (1970), 325–40.

Cogan, M. "Tyre and Tiglath-pileser III: Chronological Notes," *JCS* 25 (1973), 96–99.

____ and Ephᶜal, I., eds. *Ah, Assyria . . . Studies in Assyrian History and Ancient Near Eastern Historiography Presented to Hayim Tadmor*. ScrHier 33. Jerusalem: Magnes, 1991.

____ and Tadmor, H. "Ahaz and Tiglath-pileser in the Book of Kings: Historiographic Considerations," *Bib* 60 (1979), 491–508.

____ and Tadmor, H. *II Kings*. AB 11. Garden City, NY: Doubleday, 1988.

Cohen, M. E. *The Cultic Calendars of the Ancient Near East*. Bethesda, MD: CDL, 1993.

Cohen, S. "The Political Background of the Words of Amos," *HUCA* 36 (1965), 153–60.

Contenau, G. "La cryptographie chez les Mésopotamiens." In *Mélanges bibliques rediges en l'honneur Andre Robert*, 17–21. Travaux de l'Institut Catholique de Paris 4. Paris: Bloud & Gay, 1957.

Cook, H. J. "Pekah," *VT* 14 (1964), 121–35.

Cooke, G. A. *A Text-Book of the North-Semitic Inscriptions*. Oxford: Clarendon, 1903.

Couroyer, B. "L'origine des Phéniciens," *RB* 80 (1973), 264–76.

Cross, F. M. "The Stela Dedicated to Melcarth by Ben-Hadad of Damascus," *BASOR* 205 (1972), 36–42.

____. *Canaanite Myth and Hebrew Epic*. Cambridge: Harvard University Press, 1973.

Crowfoot, J. W., Kenyon, K. M., and Sukenik, E. L. *Samaria-Sebaste I: The Buildings at Samaria*. London: Palestine Exploration Fund, 1942.

Crowfoot, J. W. and Crowfoot, G. M. *Samaria-Sebaste II: Early Ivories From Samaria*. London: Palestine Exploration Fund, 1938.

Crowfoot, J. W., Crowfoot, G. M., and Kenyon, K. M. *Samaria Sebaste III: The Objects From Samaria*. London: Palestine Exploration Fund, 1957.

Culican, W. *The First Merchant Venturers: The Ancient Levant in Industry and Commerce*. Library of the Early Civilizations. Ed. by S. Piggott. London: Thames and Hudson, 1966.

____. "Almuñécar, Assur and Phoenician Penetration of the Western Mediterranean," *Levant* 2 (1970), 28–36.

____. "Phoenicia and Phoenician Colonization." In *The Cambridge Ancient History*, III/2, 461–546. Ed. by J. Boardman *et al.* 2d ed. Cambridge: Cambridge University Press, 1991.

Curtis, J. "Balawat." In *Fifty Years of Mesopotamian Discovery: The Work of the British School of Archaeology in Iraq 1932–1982*, 113–19. Ed. by J. Curtis. London: British School of Archaeology in Iraq, 1986.

Dalley, S. "Foreign Chariotry and Calvary in the Armies of Tiglath-pileser III and Sargon II," *Iraq* 47 (1985), 31–38.

____. "Yahweh in Hamath in the 8th Century BC: Cuneiform Material and Historical Deductions," *VT* 40 (1990), 21–32.

Daniels, D. "Is There a 'Prophetic Lawsuit' Genre?" *ZAW* 99 (1987), 339–60.

Davies, G. I. *Megiddo*. Cambridge/Grand Rapids: Lutterworth/Eerdmans, 1986.

Day, J. "The Problem of 'So, king of Egypt' in 2 Kings xvii 4," *VT* 42 (1992), 289–301.

De Graeve, M.-C. *The Ships of the Ancient Near East (c. 2000–500 B.C.)*. Orientalia Lovaniensia Analecta 7. Leuven: Department Oriëntalistiek Leuven, 1981.

De Roche, M. "Yahweh's *Rîb* Against Israel: A Reassessment of the So-Called 'Prophetic Lawsuit' in the Preexilic Prophets," *JBL* 102 (1983), 563–74.

De Vries, S. J. *1 Kings*. WBC 12. Waco: Word, 1985.

Dearman, J. A., ed., *Studies in the Mesha Inscription and Moab*. Archaeology and Biblical Studies 2. Atlanta: Scholars Press, 1989.

____ and Miller, J. M. "The Melqart Stele and the Ben-Hadads of Damascus: Two Studies," *PEQ* 115 (1983), 95–101.

Delitzsch, F. *Assyrische Lesestücke*. 2d ed. Leipzig: J. C. Hinrichs, 1878.

____. *Biblical Commentary on the Prophecies of Isaiah*. 2 vols. 3d ed. New York: Funk & Wagnalls, 1889.

Dever, W. G. "Monumental Architecture in Ancient Israel in the Period of the United Monarchy," In *Studies in the Period of David and Solomon and Other Essays*, 269–306. Ed. by T. Ishida. Winona Lake, IN: Eisenbrauns, 1982.

____. "Qedah, Tell el-," In *The Anchor Bible Dictionary*, 5. 578–81. Ed. by D. N. Freedman. 6 vols. New York: Doubleday, 1992.

Diakonoff, I. M. "Main Features of the Economy in the Monarchies of Ancient Western Asia." In *Third International Conference of Economic History, Munich, 1965*. Congrès et Colloques 10/3. Ed. by D. E. C. Eversley. Paris: Mouton, 1969.

Dillman, A. *Der Buch Jesaja*. 5th ed. Leipzig: S. Hirzel, 1890.

Donbaz, V. "Two Neo-Assyrian Stelae in the Antakya and Kahramanmaraş Museums," *Annual Review of the Royal Inscriptions of Mesopotamia Project* 8 (1990), 5–24.

____ and Grayson, A. K. *Royal Inscriptions on Clay Cones from Ashur now in Istanbul*. Royal Inscriptions of Mesopotamia Supplements 1. Toronto: University of Toronto Press, 1984.

Donner, H. "Neue Quellen zur Geschichte des Staates Moab in der zweiten Haefte der 8. Jahrhundert v. Chr.," *MIO* 5 (1957), 155–84.

____. *Israel unter den Völkern. Die Stellung der klassischen Propheten des 8. Jahrhunderts v. Chr. zur Aussenpolitik der Könige von Israel und Juda*. VTSup 11. Leiden: E. J. Brill, 1964.

____. "Adadnirari III und die Vasallen des Westens." In *Archäologie und Alten Testament* (Festschrift K. Galling), 49–59. Ed. by A. Kuschke and E. Kutsch. Tübingen: J. C. B. Mohr (Paul Siebeck), 1970.

____. "The Separate States of Israel and Judah." In *Israelite and Judean History*, 381–434. Ed. by J. H. Hayes and J. M. Miller. Philadelphia: Westminster, 1977.

____. "Israel und Tyrus im Zeitalter Davids und Salomos. Zur gegenseitigen Abhängigkeit von Innen- und Aussenpolitik," *JNSL* 10 (1982), 43–52.

____."The Interdependence of Internal Affairs and Foreign Policy during Davidic-Solomonic Period (with Special Regard to the Phoenician Coast)." In *Studies in the Period of David and Solomon and Other Essays*, 205–14. Ed. by T. Ishida. Winona Lake, IN.: Eisenbrauns, 1982.

____. *Geschichte des Volkes Israel und seiner Nachbarn in Grundzügen*. 2 vols. Göttingen: Vandenhoeck & Ruprecht, 1984–87.

____ and Röllig, W. *Kanaanäische und Aramäishce Inschriften*. 3 vols. Wiesbaden: Otto Harrassowitz, 1969–73.

Dossin, G. "*BR G'YH* roi de *KTK*," *Muséon* 57 (1944), 147–55.

Doumet, J. *Étude sur la couleur pourpre ancienne*. Beirut: Imprimerie Catholique, 1980.

Driver, G. R. "Linguistic and Textual Problems: Isaiah I-XXXIX," *JTS* 38 (1937), 36–50.

____. "Isaianic Problems." In *Festschrift für Wilhelm Eilers*, 43–57. Ed. by G. Wiessner. Wiesbaden: Otto Harrasowitz, 1967.

Driver, S. R. *Notes on the Hebrew Text and the Topography of the Books of Samuel*. Oxford: Clarendon, 1913.

Du Plat Taylor, J. "The Cypriot and Syrian Pottery form Al Mina, Syria," *Iraq* 21 (1959), 87-88.

Dunand, M. "Stèle araméenne dédiée à Melqart," *Bulletin du Musée de Beyrouth* 3 (1939), 65–76.

____. "A propos de la stèle de Melqart du Musée d'Alep," *Bulletin du Musée de Beyrouth* 6 (1942–43), 41–45.

Dussaud, R. "La stèle araméenne de Zakir au Musée du Louvre," *Syria* 3 (1922), 175–76.

Eakin, F. E., Jr. "Yahwism and Baalism Before the Exile," *JBL* 84 (1965), 407–14.

Edelman, D. V. "Abel-meholah." In *The Anchor Bible Dictionary*, 1. 11–12. Ed. by D. N. Freedman. 6 vols. New York: Doubleday, 1992.

Elat, M. "The Campaigns of Shalmaneser III against Aram and Israel," *IEJ* 25 (1975), 25–35.

____. "The Economic Relations of the Neo-Assyrian Empire with Egypt," *JAOS* 98 (1978), 20–34.

____. "Tarshish and the Problem of Phoenician Colonisation in the Western Mediterranean," *OLP* 13 (1982), 55–69.

Elayi, J. "Baᵓliraᵓsi, Reshâ, Reshbaᵓl, étude de toponymie historique," *Syria* 58 (1981), 331–41.

Ellis, P. F. "1-2 Kings." In *The Jerome Biblical Commentary*, 1. 179–209. Ed. by R. E. Brown *et al.* 2 vols. Eaglewood Cliffs, NJ: Prentice Hall, 1968.

Emerton, J. A. "Some Linguistic and Historical Problems in Isaiah VIII 23," *JSS* 14 (1969), 151–75.

Ephᶜal, I. "Assyrian Dominion in Palestine." In *The Age of the Monarchies: Political History*, 276–89. Ed. by A. Malamat. WHJP 4/1. Jerusalam: Massada, 1979.

____. *The Ancient Arabs: Nomads on the Borders of the Fertile Cresent 9th-5th Centuries B.C.* Jerusalem/Leiden: Magnes/E. J. Brill, 1982.

____. "'The Samarian(s)' in the Assyrian Sources." In *Ah, Assyria . . . Studies in Assyrian History and Ancient Near Eastern Historiography Presented to Hayim Tadmor*, 36–45. Ed. by M. Cogan and I. Ephᶜal. ScrHier 33. Jerusalem: Magnes, 1991.

____ and Naveh, J. "Hazael's Booty Inscription," *IEJ* 39 (1989), 192–200.

Fales, F. M., ed. *Assyrian Royal Inscriptions: New Horizons in Literary, Ideological, and Historical Analysis*. Rome: Istituto per l'Oriente Centro per le Antichità e la Storia dell'Arte Vicino Oriente, 1981.

Fensham, F. C. "The Treaty between the Israelites and Tyrians." In *Congress Volume: Rome, 1968*, 71–87. Ed. by G. W. Anderson *et al.* VTSup 17. Leiden: E. J. Brill, 1969.

____. "The Treaty between Solomon and Hiram and the Alalakh Tablets," *JBL* 79 (1960), 59–60.

Fishbane, M. "The Treaty Background of Amos I.11 and Related Matters," *JBL* 89 (1970), 313–18.

Fitzmyer, J. A. *The Aramaic Inscriptions of Sefire*. Rome: Pontifical Biblical Institute, 1967.

____ and Kaufman, S. A. *An Aramaic Bibliography, Part I: Old, Official, and Biblical Aramaic*. Baltimore: Johns Hopkins University Press, 1992.

Fleming, W. B. *The History of Tyre*. Columbia University Oriental Studies 10. New York: Ams, 1966 [reprint of 1915].

Flinder, A. "Is This Solomon's Seaport?" *BARev* 15/4 (1989), 30–43.

Ford, M. "The Contradictory Records of Sargon II of Assyria and the Meaning of *palû*," *JCS* 22 (1969), 83–84.

Forrer, E. *Zur Chronologie der neuassyrischen Zeit*. MVAG 20/3. Leipzig: J. C. Hinrichs, 1916.

____. *Die Provinzeinteilung des assyrischen Reiches*. Leipzig: J. C. Hinrichs, 1920.

Frankenstein, S. "The Phoenicians in the Far West: A Function of the Neo-Assyrian Imperialism." In *Power and Propaganda: A Symposium on Ancient Empires*, 263–94. Ed. by M. T. Larsen. Copenhagen: Akademisk Forlag, 1979.

Fricke, K. D. *Das Zweite Buch von den Königen*. BAT 12/11. Stuttgart: Calwer, 1972.

Friedrich, J. *Phönizisch-Punische Grammatik*. AnOr 32. Rome: Pontificum Institutum Biblicum, 1951.

Gadd, C. J. *The Stones of Assyria: The Surviving Remains of Assyrian Sculpture, Their Recovery and Their Original Positions*. London: Chatto and Windus, 1936.

____. "Inscribed Prisms of Sargon II from Nimrud," *Iraq* 16 (1954), 173–201.

Galling, K., ed. *Textbuch zur Geschichte Israels*. 3d ed. Tübingen: J. C. Mohr (Paul Siebeck), 1979.

Garbini, G. *History and Ideology in Ancient*. New York: Crossroads, 1988.

Garelli, P. "Nouveau coup d'œil sur Muṣur." In *Hommages à André Dupont-Sommer*, 37–48. Ed. by A. Caquot and M. Philonenko. Paris: Librairie Adrien Maisonneuve, 1971.

____. "The Achievement of Tiglath-pileser III: Novelty or Continuity?" In *Ah, Assyria . . . Studies in Assyrian History and Ancient Near Eastern Historiography Presented to Hayim Tadmor*, 46–64. Ed. by M. Cogan and I. Eph^cal. ScrHier 33. Jerusalem: Magnes, 1991.

Gelb, I. J. *et al. The Assyrian Dictionary of the Oriental Institute of the University of Chicago*. Chicago: Oriental Institute, 1955–.

Geller, M. J. "2 Kings XV.25," *VT* (1976), 374–77.

Gemser, B. "The *rîb*- or Controversy-Pattern in Hebrew Mentality." In *Wisdom in Israel and the Ancient Near East: Essays Presented to H. H. Rowley*, 120–37. Ed. by M. Noth and D. W. Thomas. VTSup 3. Leiden: E. J. Brill, 1955.

Genge, H. *Stele neuassyrischen Könige, Teil I, Die Keilinscriften*. Dissertation, Freiburg im Breisgau, 1965.

Gerstenberger, E. "Covenant and Commandment," *JBL* 84 (1965), 38–51.

Geus, C. H. J. de. "Het israelitische Palmette- of Volutenkapiteel," *Phoenix* 27 (1981), 34–45.

____. "The Material Culture of Israel and Phoenicia." In *Phoenicia and the Bible*, 11–16. Ed. by E. Lipiński. Studia Phoenicia 11. Leuven: Peeters, 1991.

Geva, S. "Archaeological Evidence for the Trade between Israel and Tyre?" *BASOR* 248 (1982), 69–72.

Gibson, J. C. L. *Textbook of Syrian Semitic Inscriptions*. 3 vols. Oxford: Clarendon, 1971–82.

Ginsberg, H. L. "An Unrecognized Allusion to Kings Pekah and Hoshea of Israel." In *Benjamin Mazar Volume*, 61*–65*. Ed. by M. Avi-Yonah *et al.* ErIsr 5. Jerusalem: Israel Exploration Society, 1958.

Goedicke, H. "The End of 'So, King of Egypt,'" *BASOR* 171 (1963), 64–66.

Gooding, D. W. "Text-sequence and Translation-revision in 3 Reigns 9,10–10,33," *VT* 19 (1969), 448–63.

Gordon, C. H. "Damascus in Assyrian Sources," *IEJ* 2 (1952), 174–75.

____. *Ugaritic Textbook*. AnOr 38. Rome: Pontifical Biblical Institute, 1965.

Gray, J. *I & II Kings*. 2d ed. OTL. Philadelphia: Westminster, 1970.

Grayson, A. K. "Chronicles and the Akītu Festival." In *Actes de la XVIIe Rencontre Assyriologique Internationale*, 160–70. Ed. by A. Finet. Ham-sur-Heure: Comité belge de recherches en Mesopotamia, 1970.

____. *Assyrian Royal Inscriptions*. 2 vols. Wiesbaden: Otto Harrassowitz, 1972–76.

____. *Assyrian and Babylonian Chronicles*. Texts from Cuneiform Sources 5. Locust Valley, NY: J. J. Augustin, 1975.

____. "Studies in Neo-Assyrian History: The Ninth Century B.C.," *BO* 33 (1976), 134–45.

____. "Histories and Historians of the Ancient Near East: Assyria and Babylonia," *Or* 49 (1980), 140–94.

____. "Assyria: Ashur-dan II to Ashur-nirari V (934–745 B.C.)." In *The Cambridge Ancient History*, III/1, 238–81. Ed. by J. Boardman *et al.* 2d ed. Cambridge: Cambridge University, 1982.

____. "Akkadian Treaties of the Seventh Century B.C.," *JCS* 39 (1987), 127–60.

____. "Assyria: Tiglath-pileser III to Sargon II (744–705 B.C.)," *The Cambridge Ancient History*, III/2, 71–102. Ed. by J. Boardman *et al.* 2d ed. Cambridge: Cambridge University Press, 1991.

____. "Mesopotamia, History of (Assyria)." In *Anchor Bible Dictionary*, 4. 741–43. Ed. by D. N. Freedman. 6 vols. New York: Doubleday, 1992.

Green, A. R. "Sua and Jehu: The Boundaries of Shalmaneser's Conquest," *PEQ* 111 (1979), 35–39.

____. "David's Relations with Hiram: Bibilical and Josephan Evidence for Tyrian Chronology." In *The Word of the Lord Shall Go Forth: Essays in Honor of David Noel Freedmand in Celebration of His Sixtieth Birthday*, 373–97. Ed. by C. L. Meyers and M. O'Connor. Winona Lake, IN: Eisenbrauns, 1983.

____. "The Identity of King So of Egypt—An Alternative Interpretation," *JNES* 52 (1993), 99–108.

Greenfield, J. C. "Scripture and Inscription: The Literary and Rhetorical Element in Some Early Phoenician Inscriptions." In *Near Eastern Studies in Honor of W. F. Albright*, 253–68. Ed. by H. Goedicke. Baltimore: Johns Hopkins, 1971.

Gubel, E. *et al. Les Phéniciens et le monde méditerranéen*. Brussels: Générale de Banque, 1986.

____ and Lipiński, E., eds. *Phoenicia and Its Neighbours*. Studia Phoenicia 3. Leuven: Peeters, 1985.

_____. Lipiński, E., and Servais-Soyez, B., eds. *Redt Tyrus/Sauvons Tyr: Histoire phénicienne/Fenicische geschiedenis*. Studia Phoenicia 1–2. Leuven: Katholieke Universiteit Leuven, 1983.

Gunneweg, A. H. J. *Geschichte Israels bis Bar Kochba*. Stuttgart: W. Kohlhammer, 1972.

Gurney, O. R. and Finkelstein, J. J. *The Sultantepe Tablets* I. London: British Museum of Archaeology at Ankara, 1957.

____ and Hulin, P. *The Sultantepe Tablets* II. London: British Museum of Archaeology at Ankara, 1964.

Gutschmid, A. von. *Kleine Schriften* IV. Leipzig: B. G. Teubner, 1893.

Hachmann, R., ed. *Frühe Phöniker im Libanon*. Mainz am Rhein: P. von Zabern, 1983.

Hallo, W. W. "From Qarqar to Carchemish: Assyria and Israel in the Light of New Discoveries." *BA* 23 (1960), 34–61.

Halpern, B. "Yaua, Son of Omri, Yet Again," *BASOR* 265 (1987), 81–85.

Hanson, R. S. *Tyrian Influence in the Upper Galilee*. Cambridge, MA: ASOR, 1980.

Haran, M. "The Rise and Decline of the Empire of Jeroboam ben Joash," *VT* 17 (1967), 266–97.

____. "Observations on the Historical Background of Am. 1.2–2.6," *IEJ* 18 (1968), 202–12.

Harden, D. *The Phoenicians*. 3d ed. Ancient Peoples and Places 26. Harmondsworth: Penguin, 1980.

Harper, R. F. *Assyrian and Babylonian Letters Belonging to the Kouyunjik Collection(s) of the British Museum*. Chicago: University of Chicago Press, 1892–1914.

Harris, Z. S. *A Grammar of the Phoenician Language*. AOS 8. New Haven: American Oriental Society, 1936.

____. *Development of the Canaanite Dialects: An Investigation in Linguistic History*. AOS 16. New Haven: American Oriental Society, 1939.

Harvey, J. "Le 'Rîb-Pattern,' réquitsitoire prophetiqué sur la rupture de l'alliance," *Bib* 43 (1962), 172–96.

Hawkins, J. D. "Assyrians and Hittites," *Iraq* 36 (1974), 67–83.

____. "Von Kummuh nach Kommagene," *AW* 6 (1975), 8–9.

____. "The Neo-Hittite States in Syria and Anatolia," In *The Cambridge Ancient History*, III/1, 372–441. Ed. by J. Boardman *et al.* 2d ed. Cambridge: Cambridge University, 1982.

____. "The Hittite Name of Til Barsip: Evidence from a New Hieroglyphic Fragment from Tell Ahmar," *AnSt* 33 (1983), 131–36.

Hayes, J. H. *Amos, the Eighth-Century Prophet: His Times and Preaching*. Nashville: Abingdon, 1988.

____ and Hooker, P. K. *A New Chronology for the Kings of Israel and Judah and Its Implications for Biblical History and Literature.* Atlanta: John Knox, 1988.

____ and Irvine, S. A. *Isaiah, the Eighth-Century Prophet: His Times and Preaching*. Nashville: Abingdon, 1987.

____ and Kuan, J. K. "The Final Years of Samaria (730–720 BC)," *Bib* 72 (1991), 153–81.

____ and Miller, J. M., eds. *Israelite and Judean History*. Philadelphia: Westminster, 1977.

Haydn, W. H. "Azariah of Judah and Tiglath-Pileser III," *JBL* 26 (1909), 182–88.

Henige, D. "Comparative Chronology and the Ancient Near East: The Case for Symbiosis," *BASOR* 261 (1986), 57–68.

Herm, G. *The Phoenicians: The Purple Empire of the Ancient World*. New York: William Morrow & Co., 1975.

Herrmann, S. *A History of Israel in Old Testament Times*. Philadelphia: Fortress, 1975.

Hertzberg, H. W. *I and II Samuel*. OTL. Philadelphia: Westminster, 1964.

Hillers, D. R. *Covenant: The History of a Biblical Idea*. Baltimore: Johns Hopkins, 1969.

Hitti, P. K. *Lebanon in History: From the Earliest Times to the Present*. 3d ed. London: Macmillan, 1967.

Hobbs, T. R. *2 Kings*. WBC 13. Waco: Word, 1985.

Hoftijzer, J. "Une Lettre du roi de Tyr," *UF* 11 (1980), 383–88.

Hölbl, G. *Ägyptisches Kulturgut in phönikischen und punischen Sardinien.* Leiden: E. J. Brill, 1986.

Hölscher, C. G. "Marsyas." In *Real-Encyclopedie der classischen Altertumswissenschaft*, XIV/2. cols 1986. Ed. by Pauly-Wissowa-Kroll-Mittelhaus. Stuttgart: J. B. Metzlersche, 1930.

Hommel, F. *Geschichte Babyloniens und Assyriens*. Berlin: G. Grote, 1885.

Honeyman, A. M. "The Phoenician Inscriptions of the Cyprus Musuem," *Iraq* 6 (1939), 104–8.

____. "An Unnoticed Euphemism in Isaiah IX 19–20?" *VT* 1 (1951), 221–23.

Honigmann, E. "Historische Topographie von Nordsyrien Altertum," *ZDPV* 46 (1923), 149–92; *ZDPV* 47 (1924), 1–64.

____. "Massyas." In *Real-Encyclopedie der classischen Altertumswissenschaft*, XIV/2. cols 2165–66. Ed. by Pauly-Wissowa-Kroll-Mittelhaus. Stuttgart: J. B. Metzlersche, 1930.

____. "Ba^{c}albek." In *Reallexikon der Assyriologie*, 1. 327–28. Ed. by E. Ebeling and B. Meissner. Berlin: Walter de Gruyter, 1928–.

Huffmon, H. B. "The Covenant Lawsuit in the Prophets," *JBL* 78 (1959), 285–95.

Hughes, J. *Secrets of the Times: Myth and History in Biblical Chronology*. JSOTSup 66. Sheffield: JSOT, 1990.

Hulin, P. "The Inscriptions on the Carved Throne-Base of Shalmaneser III," *Iraq* 25 (1963), 48–69.

Ikeda, Y. "Royal Cities and Fortified Cities," *Iraq* 41 (1979), 75–87.

____. "Solomon's Trade in Horses and Chariots in Its International Setting." In *Studies in the Period of David and Solomon and Other Essays*, 215–38. Ed. by T. Ishida. Winona Lake, Ind.: Eisenbrauns, 1982.

____. "The Neo-Hittite Kingdom Masuwari and the Arameans of Bit-Adini," *Oriento* 32 (1989), 1–13. [Japanese]

____. "Once Again *KTK* in the Sefire Inscriptions." In *Avraham Malamat Volume*, 104*–8*. Ed. by S. Aḥituv and B. A. Levine. ErIsr 24. Jerusalem: Israel Exploration Society, 1993.

Irvine, S. A. *Isaiah, Ahaz, and the Syro-Ephraimitic Crisis*. SBLDS 123. Atlanta: Scholars Press, 1990.

____. "The Southern Border of Syria Reconstructed," *CBQ* 56 (1994) 21–41.

Ishida, T. *The Royal Dynasties in Ancient Israel: A Study on the Formation and Development of Royal-Dynastic Ideology.* BZAW 142. Berlin: Walter de Gruyter, 1977.

Istituto per la Civiltà Fenicia e Punica. *Atti del I Congresso Internationale di Studi Fenici e Punici, Roma 1979.* 3 vols. Rome: Consiglio Nationale delle Richerche, 1983.

Jankowska, N. B. "Some Problems of the Economy of the Assyrian Empire." In *Ancient Mesopotamia: Socio-Economic History*, 253–76. Ed. by I. M. Diakonoff. Moscow: "Nauka" Publishing House, 1969.

Jepsen, A. "Israel und Damaskus," *AfO* 14 (1941–45), 153–72.

____. *Die Quellen des Königsbuches.* Halle: Max Niemeyer, 1956.

____. "Ein neuer Fixpunkt für die Chronologie der israelitischen Könige?," *VT* 20 (1970), 359–61.

Jeremias, F. *Tyrus bis zur Zeit Nebuchadnezars.* Leipzig: B. G. Teubner, 1891.

Jerome, *Commentariorum in Oseam Prophetam.* In *Patrologiae cursus completus. Series Latina.* Ed. by J. P. Migne. Paris: J. P. Migne, 1865.

Jidejian, N. *Byblos Through the Ages.* Beirut: Dar el-Mashreq, 1968.

____. *Sidon Through the Ages.* Beirut: Dar el-Mashreq, 1971.

____. *Tyre Through the Ages.* Beirut: Dar el-Mashreq, 1969.

Jones, G. H. *1 and 2 Kings.* 2 vols. NCBC. Grand Rapids: Eerdmans, 1984.

Josephus. *Against Apion.* LCL. London: William Heinemann, 1926.

____. *Jewish Antiquities*, Books V–VIII. LCL. London: William Heinemann, 1934, 1966.

Kaiser, O. *Isaiah 1-12.* 2d ed. OTL. Philadelphia: Westminster, 1983.

____, ed. *Texte aus dem Umwelt des Alten Testaments.* Gütersloh: Gerd Mohn, 1982–.

Kallai-Kleinmann, Z. "Notes on the Topography of Benjamin," *IEJ* 6 (1956), 180–87.

Kallner-Amiran, D. H. "A Revised Earthquake Catalogue of Palestine," *IEJ* 1 (1950–51), 223–46; *IEJ* 2 (1952), 48–65.

Kantor, H. J. "Syro-Palestinian Ivories," *JNES* 15 (1956), 153–74.

Kapelrud, A. S. *Central Ideas in Amos*. Oslo: Aschehoug & Co., 1956.

Kaplan, J. "The Identification of Abel Beth Maacah and Janoah," *IEJ* 28 (1978), 159–60.

Katzenstein, H. J. "Who Were the Parents of Athaliah?" *IEJ* 5 (1955), 194-97.

____. "Is There Any Synchronism between the Reigns of Hiram and Solomon?" *JNES* 24 (1965), 116–17.

____. *The History of Tyre from the Beginning of the Second Millenium B.C.E. until the Fall of the Neo-Babylonian Empire in 586 B.C.E.* Jerusalem: Schocken Institute for Jewish Research, 1973.

Kellner, H.-J. *Urartu. Ein wiederentdeckter Rivale Assyriens*. Prähistorische Staatssammlung München, Museum für Vor- und Frühgeschichte, Ausstellungskataloge 2. Munich: Buchdruckwerkstätte Pichlmayr, 1976.

Kenrick, J. *Phoenicia*. London: B. Fellows, 1855.

Kenyon, K. M. *Amorites and Canaanite*. Schweich Lectures 1963. London: Oxford University Press, 1966.

____. *Archeology in the Holy Land*. 2d ed. London: Ernest Benn, 1965.

____. *Royal Cities of the Old Testament*. New York: Schocken, 1971.

Kenyon, K. M. and Moorey, P. R. S. *The Bible and Recent Archaeology*. Rev. ed. Atlanta: John Knox, 1987.

Kessler, K. "Die Anzahl der assyrischen Provinzen des Jahres 738 v. Chr. in Nordsyrien," *WO* 8 (1975), 49–63.

Kestemont, G. "Le commerce phénicien et l'expansion assyrienne du IXe–VIIIe s.," *OrAnt* 11 (1972), 137–44.

____. "Tyr et les Assyriens." In *Redt Tyrus/Sauvons Tyr: Histoire phénicienne/Fenicische geschiedenis*, 53–78. Ed. by E. Gubel, E. Lipiński, and B. Servais-Soyez. Studia Phoenicia 1–2. Leuven: Katholieke Universiteit Leuven, 1983.

____. "Les Phéniciens en Syrie du Nord." In *Phoenicia and Its Neighbours*, 135–61. Ed. by E. Gubel and E. Lipiński. Studia Phoenicia 3. Leuven: Peeters, 1985.

Khalifeh, I. A. *Sarepta II. The Late Bronze and Iron Age Strata of Area II, X. The University Museum of the University of Pennsylvania Excavations at Sarafand, Lebanon*. Publications de l'Université Libanaise, Section des Études archéologiques 2. Beirut: Université Libanaise, 1988.

King, L. W. *The Bronze Reliefs from the Gates of Shalmaneser, King of Assyria B.C. 860-825*. London: British Museum, 1915.

King, P. J. *Amos, Hosea, Micah—An Archaeological Commentary*. Philadelphia: Westminster, 1988.

____. "The Eighth, the Greatest of Centuries?," *JBL* 108 (1989), 3–10.

Kinnier-Wilson, J. V. "The Kurbaʾil Statue of Shalmaneser III," *Iraq* 24 (1962), 90–115.

Kittle, R. *Die Bücher der Könige*. HKAT 1/5. Göttingen: Vandenhoeck & Ruprecht, 1900.

Klein, J. "Akitu." In *The Anchor Bible Dictionary*, 1. 138–40. Ed. by D. N. Freedman. 6 vols. New York: Doubleday, 1992.

Klengel, H. *Geschichte Syriens im 2. Jahrtausend v.u.Z.* 3 vols. Deutsche Akademie der Wissenschaften zu Berlin, Institut für Orientforschung 40. Berlin: Akademie Verlag, 1965–70.

____. *Syria, 3000 to 300 B.C.: A Handbook of Political History*. Berlin: Akademie Verlag, 1992.

Knauf, E. A. "King Solomon's Copper Mine." In *Phonicia and the Bible*, 167–86. Ed. by E. Lipiński. Studia Phoenicia 11. Leuven: Peeters, 1991.

Knott, J. B. *The Jehu Dynasty: An Assessment Based Upon Ancient Near Eastern Literature and Archeology*. Dissertation, Emory University, 1971.

Koehler, L. and Baumgartner, W. *Hebräisches und Aramäisches Lexicon zum Alten Testamentum*. 3d ed. Leiden: E. J. Brill, 1967–83.

Kraeling, E. G. H. *Aram and Israel*. New York: Columbia University Press, 1918.

Krauss, R. "Sôʾ, König von Ägypten, ein Deutungsvorschlag," *BN* 11 (1980), 29–31.

Kuan, J. K. "Third Kingdoms 5.1 and Israelite-Tyrian Relations During the Reign of Solomon," *JSOT* 46 (1990), 31–46.

____. "Hosea 9:13 and Josephus's *Antiquities* IX, 277–287," *PEQ* 123 (1991), 103–108.

____. "Was Omri a Phoenician?" In *History and Interpretation: Essays in Honour of John H. Hayes*, 231–44. Ed. by M. P. Graham, W. P. Brown, and J. K. Kuan. JSOTSup 173. Sheffield: JSOT, 1993.

Kugler, F. X. *Sternkunde und Sterndienst in Babylon* 11/2. Münster in Westfalen: Aschendorff, 1912.

Kupper, J. R. "Northern Mesopotamia and Syria." In *The Cambridge Ancient History*, II/1, 1–41. Ed. by I. E. S. Edwards *et al.* Cambridge: Cambridge University Press, 1973.

Laato, A. "New Viewpoints on the Chronology of the Kings of Judah and Israel," *ZAW* 98 (1968), 217-18.

Laessøe, J. "Building Inscriptions from Fort Shalmaneser, Nimrud," *Iraq* 21 (1959), 38–41.

____. "A Statue of Shalmaneser III, from Nimrud," *Iraq* 21 (1959), 147–57.

Lance, H. D. *The Old Testament and the Archaeologist*. Guides to Biblical Scholarship. Philadelphia: Fortress, 1981.

Landau, W. F. von. "Die Belagerung von Tyrus durch Salamassar bie Menander." In his *Beiträge zur Altertumskunde des Orients I*, 5–16. Leipzig: E. Pfeiffer, 1893.

____. "Die Bedeutung der Phönizier im Völkerleben," In *Ex Oriente Lux*, 1. 159–202. Ed. by H. Winckler. 2 vols. Leipzig: E. Pfeiffer, 1905.

Landsberger, B. *Sam'al: Studien zur Entdeckung der Ruinenstaette Karatepe*. Ankara: Türkischen Historischen Gesellschaft, 1948.

Lane, W. R. *A Handbook of Phoenician Inscriptions*. Dissertation, Johns Hopkins University, 1962.

Laughlin, J. C. H. "The Remarkable Discoveries at Tel Dan," *BAR* 7/5 (1981), 20–37.

Layard, A. H. *Inscriptions in the Cuneiform Character from Assyrian Monuments*. London: Harrison and Son, 1851.

Lederer, C. *Die biblische Zeitrechnung vom Auszuge aus Ägypten bis zum Beginne der babylonischen Gefangenschaft*. Speier: F. Kleeberger, 1888.

Lehmann, C. F. *Klio, Beiträge zur Alten Geschichte* II. Leipzig: Dieterich, 1902.

Lemaire, A. "Le pays d'Eden et le Bît-Adini," *Syria* 58 (1981), 313–30.

____. "Le stèle araméenne de Bar-Hadad," *Or* 53 (1984), 337–49.

____. "Les Phéniciens et le commerce entre la Mer Rouge et la Mer Méditerranée." In *Phoenicia and the East Mediterranean in the First Millennium B.C.*, 49–60. Ed. by E. Lipiński. Studia Phoenicia 5. Leuven: Peeters, 1987.

____. "Hazaël de Damas, roi d'Aram." In *Marchands, diplomates et empereurs, Etudes sur la civilisation mésopotamienne offertes à P. Garelli*, 91–108. Ed. by D. Charpin and F. Joannes. Paris: Editions Recherche sur les civilisations, 1991.

____. "Joas de Samarie, Barhadad de Damas, Zakkur de Hamat. La Syrie-Palestine vers 800 av. J.-C." In *Avraham Malamat Volume*, 148*–57*. Ed. by S. Aḥituv and B. A. Levine. ErIsr 24. Jerusalem: Israel Exploration Society, 1993.

____ and Durand, J.-M. *Les Inscriptions Araméennes de Sfiré et l'Assyrie de Shamshi-ilu*. Hautes Études Orientales 20. Genéve/Paris: Droz, 1984.

Levine, L. D. *Contributions to the Historical Geography of the Zagros in the Neo-Assyrian Period*. Dissertation, University of Pennsylvania, 1969.

____. *Two Neo-Assyrian Stelae from Iran*. Toronto: Royal Ontario Museum, 1972.

____. "Menahem and Tiglath-Pileser: A New Synchronism," *BASOR* 206 (1972), 40–42.

____. "East-West Trade in the Late Iron Age: A View from the Zagros." In *Le plateau iranien et l'Asie centrale des origines à la conquête islamique*, 171–86. Colloques internationaux du Centre national de la recherche scientifique 567. Paris: Editions du Centre national de la recherche scientifique, 1976.

Lewy, J. "Studies in the Historic Geography of the Ancient Near East," *Or* 21 (1952), 1–12, 265–92, 393–425.

Limburg, J. "The Root ריב and the Prophetic Lawsuit Speeches," *JBL* 88 (1969), 291–304.

Lipiński, E. "Le Ben-Hadad II de la Bible et l'histoire." In *Proceedings of the Fifth World Congress of Jewish Studies*, 1. 157–73. Ed. by P. Peli. Jerusalem: R. H. Hacohen, 1969.

____. "Ba^{c}li-Ma^{c}zer II and the Chronology of Tyre," *RSO* 45 (1970), 59–65.

____. "The Assyrian Campaign to Manuate, in 796 B.C., and the Zakir Stela," *AION* 31 (1971), 393–99.

____. "ᶜAttar-hapeš, the Forefather of Bar-Hadad II," *AION* 31 (1971), 101–4.

____. "Note de topographie historique: Baᶜli-Raᵓši et Raᵓšu-Qudšu," *RB* 78 (1971), 84–92.

____. "An Assyro-Israelite Alliance in 842/841 B.C.E.?" In *Proceedings of the Sixth World Congress of Jewish Studies*, 1. 273–78. Ed. by A. Shinan. 3 vols. Jerusalem: Jerusalem Academic Press, 1975–77.

____. "Aram et Israël du Xᵉ au VIIIᵉ siècle av. n. e.," *Acta Antiqua* 27 (1979), 49–102.

____. ed. *Phoenicia and the East Mediterranean in the First Millennium B.C.* Studia Phoenicia 5. Leuven: Peeters, 1987.

____. "Jéroboam II et la Syrie." In *Storia e Tradizioni di Israele: Scritti in onore di J. Alberto Soggin*, 171–76. Ed. by D. Garrone and F. Israel. Brescia: Paideia, 1991.

Liver, J. "The Chronology of Tyre at the Beginning of the First Millennium B.C.," *IEJ* 3 (1953), 113–120.

Long, B. O. *1 Kings; with an Introduction to Historical Literature*. FOTL 9. Grand Rapids: Eerdmans, 1984.

Lubetski, M. "Ezion-geber." In *The Anchor Bible Dictionary*, 2. 723–26. Ed. by D. N. Freedman. 6 vols. New York: Doubleday, 1992.

Lucas, L. *Geschichte der Stadt Tyrus zur Zeit der Kreuzzüge*. Marburg: J. Hamel, 1895.

Luckenbill, D. D. *The Annals of Sennacherib*. Chicago: University of Chicago Press, 1924.

____. "Azariah of Judah," *AJSL* 41 (1925), 217–32.

____. *Ancient Records of Assyria and Babylonia*. 2 vols. Chicago: University of Chicago Press, 1926–27.

Mahmud M. and Black, J. "Recent Work in the Nabu Temple, Nimrud," *Sumer* 44 (1985–86), 135–55.

Malamat, A. "Amos 1:5 in the Light of the Til-Barsip Inscriptions," *BASOR* 129 (1953), 25–26.

____. "Aspects of the Foreign Policies of David and Solomon," *JNES* 22 (1963), 1–17.

____. "On the Akkadian Transcription of the Name of King Joash," *BASOR* 204 (1971), 37–39.

____. "A New Proposal for the Identification of KTK in the Sefire Inscriptions." In *M. Razin Volume: Census Lists and Ge-*

nealogies and Their Historical Implications, 7–11. Ed. by S. Bendor. Haifa: University of Haifa, 1976. [Hebrew]

____. "A Political Look at the Kingdom of David and Solomon and Its Relations with Egypt." In *Studies in the Period of David and Solomon and Other Essays*, 189–204. Ed. by T. Ishida. Winona Lake, IN: Eisenbrauns, 1982.

Mallowan, M. E. L. *Nimrud and Its Remains*. 2 vols. London: Collins, 1966.

____. "Samaria and Calah Nimrud: Conjunctions in History and Archaeology." In *Archaeology in the Levant: Essays for Kathleen Kenyon*, 155–63. Ed. by R. Moorey and P. Parr. Warminster: Aris & Phillips, 1978.

Marcus, M. "Geography as an Organizing Principle in the Imperial Art of Shalmaneser III," *Iraq* 49 (1987), 77–90.

Margalith, O. "A Note on *šālîšîm*," *VT* 42 (1992), 266.

Markoe, G. E. "The Emergence of Phoenician Art," *BASOR* 279 (1990), 13–26.

Martin, W. J. *Tribut und Tributleistungen bei den Assyrern*. StudOr 8/1. Helsinki: Societas Orientalis Fennica, 1936.

Massa, A. *The Phoenicians*. Geneva: Minerva, 1977.

Matthews, S. W. "The Phoenicians. Sea Lords of Antiquity," *National Geographic* 146 (1974), 149–89.

Mays, J. L. *Hosea*. OTL. Philadelphia: Westminster, 1969.

____. *Micah*. OTL. Philadelphia: Westminster, 1976.

Mazar, A. *Archaeology of the Land of the Bible, 10,000–586 B.C.E.* ABRL. New York: Doubleday, 1990.

Mazar, B. "The Tobiads," *IEJ* (1957), 236–37.

____. "Geshur and Maacah," *JBL* 80 (1961), 16–28.

____. "The Aramean Empire and Its Relations with Israel," *BA* 25 (1962), 98–120.

____. "The Philistines and the Rise of Israel and Tyre," *Proceedings of the Israel Academy of Sciences and Humanities* 7/1 (1967), 1–22.

____. "The House of Omri." In *Yigael Yadin Memorial Volume*, 215–19. Ed. by A. Ben Tor, J. C. Greenfield, and A. Malamat. ErIsr 20. Jerusalem: Israel Exploration Society, 1989.

McCarter, P. K. "'Yaw, Son of Omri': A Philological Note on Israelite Chronology," *BASOR* 216 (1974), 5–7.

McKenzie, S. L. *The Trouble With Kings: The Composition of the Book of Kings in the Deuteronomistic History*. VTSup 42. Leiden: E. J. Brill, 1991.

Mendels, D. *The Land of Israel as a Political Concept in Hasmonean Literature: Recourse to History in Second Century B.C. Claims to the Holy Land.* Texte und Studien zum Antiken Judentum 15. Tübingen: J. C. B. Mohr (Paul Siebeck), 1987.

Meshel, Z. "On the Problem of Tell el-Kheleifeh, Elath and Ezion-Geber." In *Nelson Glueck Memorial Volume*, 49–56. Ed. by B. Mazar. ErIsr 12. Jerusalem: Israel Exploration Society, 1975.

Messerschmidt, L. *Keilschrifttexte aus Assur historischen Inhalts.* Abhandlungen der deutschen Orient-Gesellschaft, ser. E, I/1. Leipzig: J. C. Hinrichs, 1911.

Meyer, E. *Geschischte des Altertums* II/2. 3d ed. Basel: Benno Schwabe, 1953.

Michel, E. "Die Assur-Texte Salmanassar III. (858-824)," *WO* 1 (1947–52), 5–20, 57–71, 205–22, 255–71, 385–96, 454–75; *WO* 2 (1954–59), 27–45, 137–57, 221–33, 408–15; *WO* 3 (1964), 146–55; *WO* 4 (1967–68), 29–37.

Millard, A. R. "Adad-nirari III, Aram, and Arpad," *PEQ* 105 (1973), 161–64.

____. "Assyrian Royal Names in Biblical Hebrew," *JSS* 21 (1976), 7–8.

____."Eden, Bit Adini and Beth Eden." In *Avraham Malamat Volume*, 173*–77*. Ed. by S. Aḥituv and B. A. Levine. ErIsr 24. Jerusalem: Israel Exploration Society, 1993.

____ and Tadmor, H. "Adad-nirari III in Syria: Another Stele Fragment and the Dates of His Campaigns," *Iraq* 35 (1973), 57–64.

Miller, J. M. *The Omride Dynasty in the Light of Recent Literary and Archaeological Research.* Dissertation, Emory University, 1964.

____."The Elisha Cycle and the Accounts of the Omride Wars," *JBL* 85 (1966), 441–54.

____. "The Fall of the House of Ahab," *VT* 17 (1967), 307–24.

____. "The Rest of the Acts of Jehoahaz (I Kings 20; 22:1–38)," *ZAW* 80 (1968), 337–42.

____. "So Tibni Died," *VT* 18 (1968), 392–94.

____ and Hayes, J. H. *A History of Ancient Israel and Judah*. Philadelphia: Westminster, 1986.

Minokami, Y. *Die Revolution des Jehu*. GTA 38. Göttingen: Vandenhoeck & Ruprecht, 1989.

Mitchell, T. C. "Israel and Judah until the Revolt of Jehu (931–841 B.C.)." In *The Cambridge Ancient History*, III/1, 442–87. Ed. by J. Boardman *et al.* 2d ed. Cambridge: Cambridge University Press, 1982.

____. "Israel and Judah from Jehu until the Period of Assyrian Domination." In *The Cambridge Ancient History*, III/1, 488–510. Ed. by J. Boardman *et al.* 2d ed. Cambridge: Cambridge University Press, 1982.

____. "Israel and Judah from the Coming of Assyrian Domination until the Fall of Samaria, and the Struggle for Independence." In *The Cambridge Ancient History*, III/2, 322–70. Ed. by J. Boardman *et al.* 2d ed. Cambridge: Cambridge University Press, 1991.

Montgomery, J. A. "Archival Data in the Book of Kings," *JBL* 53 (1934), 46–52.

____. *A Critical and Exegetical Commentary on the Books of Kings*. Ed. by H. S. Gehman. ICC. Edinburgh: T & T Clark, 1951.

Moran, W. L. "The Ancient Near Eastern Background of the Love of God in Deuteronomy," *CBQ* 25 (1963), 77–87.

____. "A Note on the Treaty Terminology of the Sefîre Stelas," *JNES* 22 (1963), 173–76.

Morgenstern, J. "Chronological Data of the Dynasty of Omri," *JBL* 59 (1940), 385–96.

Moscati, S. *The World of the Phoenicians*. London: Weidenfeld & Nicolson, 1968.

____ *et al. The Phoenicians*. New York/Milan: Abbeville/Bompiani, 1988.

Moshe, E. "The Impact of Tribute and Booty on Countries and Peoples within the Assyrian Empire." In *Vorträge gehalten auf der 28. Rencontre Assyriologique Internationale in Wien 6.–10. Juli 1981*, 244–51. Ed. by H. Hirsch. AfO Beiheft 19. Horn: Berger, 1982.

Movers, F. C. *Die Phönizier*. 4 vols. Bonn: E. Weber, 1841–56.

Muhly, J. D. "Phoenicia and the Phoenicians." In *Biblical Archaeology Today: Proceedings of the International Congress on Biblical Archaeology, Jerusalem, April 1984*, 177–91, 226–37. Ed. by J. Amitai. Jerusalem: Israel Exploration Society, 1985.

Na'aman, N. "Sennacherib's 'Letter to God' on His Campaign to Judah," *BASOR* 214 (1974), 25–38.

____. "Two Notes on the Monolith Inscription of Shalmaneser III from Kurkh," *Tel Aviv* 3 (1976), 89–106.

____. "Looking for KTK," *WO* 9 (1978), 220–39.

____. "Historical and Chronological Notes on the Kingdoms of Israel and Judah in the Eighth Century B.C.," *VT* 36 (1986), 71–92.

____." Beth-aven, Bethel and Early Israelite Sanctuaries," *ZDPV* 103 (1987), 13–21.

____. "The Historical Background to the Conquest of Samaria (720 BC)," *Bib* 71 (1990), 206–225.

____. "Forced Participation in Alliances in the Course of the Assyrian Campaigns to the West." In *Ah, Assyria . . . Studies in Assyrian History and Ancient Near Eastern Historiography Presented to Hayim Tadmor*, 80–98. Ed. by M. Cogan and I. Eph^{c}al. ScrHier 33. Jerusalem: Magnes, 1991.

____. "Azariah of Judah and Jeroboam II of Israel," *VT* 43 (1993), 227–34.

Napier, B. D. "The Omrides of Jezreel," *VT* 9 (1959), 366–78.

Naveh, J. *Early History of the Alphabet: An Introduction to West Semitic Epigraphy and Palaeography*. Leiden: E. J. Brill, 1982.

Negbi, O. "Evidence for Early Phoenician Communities on the Eastern Mediterranean Islands," *Levant* 14 (1982), 179–82.

Negev, A., ed. *Archaeological Encyclopedia of the Holy Land*. 3d ed. New York: Prentice Hall, 1990.

Noth, M. "Beiträge zur Geschichte des Ostjordanlandes, 1. Das Land Gilead als Siedlungsgebiet israelitischer Sippen," *PJ* 37 (1941), 69–71.

____. *Überlieferungsgeschichtliche Studien*. 2d ed. Tübingen: J. C. B. Mohr (Paul Siebeck), 1957.

____. "Gilead und Gad," *ZDPV* 75 (1959), 35–40.

____. *The History of Israel*. 2d ed. New York: Harper & Row, 1960.

____. *Könige I: I Könige 1-16*. BKAT 9/1. Neukirchen-Vluyn: Neukirchener Verlag, 1968.

____. *The Deuteronomistic History*. 2d ed. JSOTSup 15. Sheffield: JSOT, 1981.

____. *The Chronicler's History*. JSOTSup 50. Sheffield: JSOT, 1987.

Oates, D. "The Excavations at Nimrud (Kalhu), 1961," *Iraq* 24 (1962), 16–17.

____. "The Excavations at Tell al Rimah," *Iraq* 30 (1968), 115–38.

Oates, J. "Balawat: Recent Excavations and a New Gate." In *Essays on Near Eastern Art and Archaeology in Honor of Charles Kyrle Wilkinson*, 40–47. Ed. by P. Harper and H. Pittman. New York: Metropolitan Museum of Art, 1983.

Oded, B. "Observations on Methods of Assyrian Rule in Transjordania after the Palestinian Campaign of Tiglath-pileser III," *JNES* 29 (1970), 177–86.

____. "The Campaigns of Adad-Nirari III into Syria and Palestine." In *Studies in the History of the Jewish People and the Land of Israel* 2. 25–34. Ed. by B. Oded. 2 vols. Haifa: University of Haifa, 1970–72. [Hebrew]

____. "The Historical Background of the Syro-Ephraimitic War Reconsidered," *CBQ* 34 (1972), 153–65.

____. "The Phoenician Cities and the Assyrian Empire in the Time of Tiglath-pileser III," *ZDPV* 90 (1974), 38–49.

____. "Neighbors on the West." In *The Age of the Monarchies: Political History*, 222–46. Ed. by A. Malamat. WHJP 4/1. Jerusalem: Massada, 1979.

Olmstead, A. T. "The Fall of Samaria," *AJSL* 21 (1904–5), 179–82.

____. "The Assyrian Chronicle," *JAOS* 34 (1915), 344–68.

____. *Assyrian Historiography: A Source Study*. Columbia, MO: University of Missouri, 1916.

____. "Shalmaneser III and the Establishment of the Assyrian Power," *JAOS* 41 (1921), 345–82.

____. *History of Assyria*. New York/London: C. Scribner's Sons, 1923.

____. *History of Syria and Palestine*. New York/London: C. Scribner's Sons, 1931.

Oppenheim, A. L. *Ancient Mesopotamia: Portrait of a Dead Civilization*. Chicago: University of Chicago Press, 1964.

____. "Neo-Assyrian and Neo-Babylonian Empires." In *The Symbolic Instrument in Early Times*, 111–44. Ed. by H. Lasswell, D. Lerner, and H. Speier. Propaganda and Communication in World History 1. Honolulu: East-West Center, 1979.

Oren, E. *et al.* "A Phoenician Commercial Center on the Egyptian Border," *Qadmoniot* 19 (1986), 83–91. [Hebrew]

Ottosson, M. "The Prophet Elijah's Visit to Zarephath." In *In the Shelter of Elyon: Essays on Palestinian Life and Literature in Honor of G. W. Ahlström*, 185–98. Ed. by W. Barrick and J. Spencer. JSOTSup 31. Sheffield: JSOT, 1984.

Otzen, B. "Israel Under the Assyrians." In *Power and Propaganda: A Symposium on Ancient Empires*, 251–61. Ed. by M. T. Larsen. Copenhagen: Akademisk Forlag, 1979.

Page, S. "A Stela of Adad-nirari III and Nergal-ereš from Tell al Rimah," *Iraq* 30 (1968), 139–53.

____. "Adad-nirari III and Semiramis: the Stela of Saba'a and Rimah," *Or* 38 (1969), 457–58.

____. "Joash and Samaria in a New Stela Excavated at Tell al-Rimah, Iraq," *VT* 19 (1969), 483–84.

Pallis, S. A. *The Babylonian Akîtu Festival*. Copenhagen: A. F. Høst & Sons, 1926.

Parker, S. "Jezebel's Reception of Jehu," *Maarav* 1 (1978–79), 67–78.

Parpola, S. *Neo-Assyrian Toponyms*. AOAT 6. Neukirchen-Vluyn: Neukirchener Verlag, 1970.

____. "Neo-Assyrian Treaties from the Royal Archives of Nineveh," *JCS* 39 (1987), 161–87.

____. ed. *The Correspondence of Sargon II, Part I: Letters From Assyria and the West*. SAA 1. Helsinki: Helsinki University Press, 1987.

____ and Watanabe, K. *Neo-Assyrian Treaties and Loyalty Oaths*. SAA 2. Helsinki: Helsinki University Press, 1988.

Parrot, A., Chéhab, M. H., and Moscati, S. *Die Phönizier*. Munich: Beck, 1977.

Paul, S. M. "Amos 1:3-2:3: A Concatenous Literary Pattern," *JBL* 90 (1971), 397-403.

____. *Amos*. Hermeneia. Philadelphia: Fortress, 1991.

Peckham, B. "Israel and Phoenicia." In *Magnalia Dei: The Mighty Acts of God, Essays on the Bible and Archaeology in Memory of G. Ernest Wright*, 224–48. Ed. by F. M. Cross, W. E. Lemke, and P. D. Miller, Jr. Garden City, NY: Doubleday, 1976.

____. "Phoenicia and the Religion of Israel: The Epigraphic Evidence." In *Ancient Israelite Religion: Essays in honor of Frank Moore Cross*, 79–99. Ed. by P. D. Miller, Jr., P. D. Hanson, and S. D. McBride. Philadelphia: Fortress, 1987.

Peñuela, J. M. "Las inscripciones de Salmanasar III," *Sefarad* 3 (1943), 251–60.

Pietschmann, R. *Geschichte der Phönizier*. Berlin: G. Grote, 1889.

Pinches, T. G. "The Bronze Gates Discovered by Mr. Rassam at Balawat," *TSBA* 7 (1880–82), 83–118.

____. "The Babylonian Chronicle," *JRAS* n.s. 19 (1887), 655–81.

Piotrovsky, B. B. *The Ancient Civilization of Urartu*. London/New York: Cresset/Cowles, 1969.

Pitard, W. T. *Ancient Damascus: A Historical Study of the Syrian City-State from Earliest Times until its Fall to the Assyrians in 732 B.C.E.* Winona Lake, IN: Eisenbrauns, 1987.

____. "The Identity of the Bir-Hadad of the Melqart Stela," *BASOR* 272 (1988), 3–21.

____. "Rezin." In *The Anchor Bible Dictionary*, 4. 708–9. Ed. by D. N. Freedman. 6 vols. New York: Doubleday, 1992.

Poebel, A. "The Assyrian King List from Khorsabad," *JNES* 1 (1942), 247–306, 460–92; *JNES* 2 (1943), 56–90.

Poidebard, A. *Un grand port dispartu-Tyr*. Paris: Paul Geuthner, 1939.

Postgate, J. N. *Neo-Assyrian Grants and Decrees*. Studia Pohl, ser. major 1. Rome: Biblical Institute, 1969.

____. *Taxation and Conscription in the Assyrian Empire*. Studia Pohl, ser. major 3. Rome: Biblical Institute, 1974.

____. "The Economic Structure of the Assyrian Empire." In *Power and Propaganda: A Symposium on Ancient Empires*, 193–221. Ed. by M. T. Larsen. Copenhagen: Akademisk Forlag, 1979.

Pratico, G. D. "Nelson Glueck's 1938–1940 Excavations at Tell el-Kheleifeh: A Reappraisal," *BASOR* 259 (1985), 1–32.

Priest, J. R. "The Covenant of Brothers," *JBL* 84 (1965), 400–406.

Pritchard, J. B., ed. *Ancient Near Eastern Texts Relating to the Old Testament*. 3d ed. Princeton: Princeton University Press, 1969.

____. *The Ancient Near Eastern in Pictures Relating to the Old Testament*. 2d ed. Princeton: Princeton University Press, 1969.

____. "The Phoenicians in Their Homeland," *Expedition* 14/1 (1971), 14–23.

____. "The Phoenician City of Sarepta," *Archaeology* 24 (1971), 61–63.

____. "Sarepta in History and Tradition." In *Understanding the Sacred Text*, 101–14. Ed. by J. Reusmann. Valley Forge, PA: Judson, 1972.

____. *Sarepta: A Preliminary Report on the Iron Age: Excavations of the University Museum of the University of Pennsylvania, 1970–1972*. Philadelphia: University Museum, University of Pennsylvania, 1975.

____. *Recovering Sarepta, A Phoenician City*. Princeton: Princeton University Press, 1978.

____. *Sarepta IV. The Objects from Area II, X. The University Museum of the University of Pennsylvania Excavations at Sarafand, Lebanon*. Publications de l'Université Libanaise, Section des Etudes Archéologiques 2. Beirut: Université Libanaise, 1988.

Procksch, O. *Jesaia I*. KAT 9. Leipzig: A. Deichert, 1930.

Puech, É. "Athalie, fille d'Achab et la chronologie des rois d'Israël et Juda," *Salamanticensis* 28 (1981), 117–36.

____. "La Stèle de Bar-Hadad à Melqart et les Rois d'Arpad," *RB* 99 (1992), 311–34.

Rahmani, L. Y. "A Votive Stele with Proto-Aeolic Capital," *IEJ* 32 (1982), 199–202.

Rasmussen, N. *Salmanasser den II's Indskrifter*. Kjobenhavn: Nielsen and Lydiches, 1897.

Rassam, H. "Excavations and Discoveries in Assyria," *TSBA* 7 (1880–82), 37–58.

____. *Asshur and the Land of Nimrod*. Cincinnati/New York: Curts and Jennings/Eaton and Mains, 1897.

Rawlinson, G. *Cuneiform Inscriptions of Western Asia*. 5 vols. London: British Museum, 1861–1909.

____. *History of Phoenicia*. London: Longmans, 1889.

Reade, J. E. "The Palace of Tiglath-pileser III," *Iraq* 30 (1968), 69–73.

____. "The Neo-Assyrian Court and Army: Evidence from the Sculptures," *Iraq* 34 (1972), 87–112.

____. "Assyrian Campaigns, 840–811 B.C., and the Babylonian Frontier," *ZA* 68 (1978), 251–60.

Redford, D. B. *Egypt, Canaan, and Israel in Ancient Times*. Princeton: Princeton University Press, 1992.

Reinhold, G. G. G. "The Bir-Hadad Stele and the Biblical Kings of Aram," *AUSS* 24 (1986), 115–26.

____. *Die Beziehungen Altisraels zu den aramäischen Staaten in der israelitisch-judäischen Königszeit*. Europäische Hochschulschriften 23. Frankfurt am Main: Peter Lang, 1989.

Renan, E. *Mission de Phénicie*. 2 vols. Paris: Imprimerie Impériale, 1864.

Rignell, L. G. "Das Immanuelszeichen. Einige Gesichtspunkte zu Jes 7," *ST* 11 (1957), 99–119.

Robinson, H. and F. Horst. *Die Zwölf Kleinen Propheten*. HAT 1/14. Tübingen: J. C. B. Mohr (Paul Siebeck), 1938.

Röllig, W. "Die Phönizier des Mutterlandes zur Zeit der Kolonisierung," *Phönizier im Westen*, 15–30. Ed. by H.-G. Niemeyer. Madrider Beiträge 8. Mainz am Rhein: Philipp von Zabern, 1982.

____. "On the Origin of the Phoenicians," *Berytus* 31 (1983), 79–83.

Rösel, H. "Studien zur Topographie der Kriege in den Büchern Josua und Richter," *ZDPV* 91 (1975), 159–90; *ZDPV* 92 (1976), 10–46.

Rost, P. *Die Keilschrifttexte Tiglat-Pilesers III. nach den Papierabklatschen und Originalen den Britischen Museums*. 2 vols. Leipzig: E. Pfeiffer, 1893.

Rudolph, W. "Die angefochtenen Völkersprüche in Amos 1 und 2." In *Schalom. Studien ze Glaube und Geschichte Israels, A. Jepsen zum 70. Gerburtstagdargebracht*, 45–49. Ed. by K.-H. Bernhardt. AzTh 1/46. Stuttgart: Calwer, 1971.

Russell, H. F. "Shalmaneser's Campaign to Urartu in 856 B.C. and the Historical Geography of Eastern Anatolia According to the Assyrian Sources," *AnSt* 34 (1984), 171–201.

Sader, H. S. "Quel était l'ancien nom de Hama-sur-l'Oronte?," *Berytus* 34 (1986), 129–34.

____. *Les États araméens de Syrie: Depuis leur fondation jusqu'à leur transformation en provinces assyriennes*. Beiruter Texte und Studien 36. Beirut: Franz Steiner, 1987.

Safar, F. "A Further Text of Shalmaneser III. From Assur," *Sumer* 7 (1951), 3–21.

Saggs, H. W. F. "The Nimrud Letters, 1952–Part II: Relations with the West," *Iraq* 17 (1955), 126–60.

____. "The Nimrud Letters, 1952–Part IV: The Urartian Frontier," *Iraq* 20 (1955), 182–212.

____. *The Greatness that was Babylon: A Sketch of the Ancient Civilization of the Tigris-Euphrates Valley*. New York: Hawthorn, 1962.

____. *The Might That Was Assyria*. London: Sidgwick & Jackson, 1984.

____. *The Greatness that was Babylon: A Survey of the Ancient Civilization of the Tigris-Euphrates Valley*. Rev. ed. London: Sidgwick & Jackson, 1988.

Šanda, A. *Die Bücher der Könige*. 2 vols. EHAT 9. Münster: Aschendorff, 1911–12.

Scheil, V. "Notules, XXXV. Fragment d'une inscription de Salmanasar, fils d'Aššurnaṣirpal," *RA* 14 (1917), 159–60.

Schley, D. G. "1 Kings 10:26–29: A Reconsideration," *JBL* 106 (1987), 595–601.

____. "The *šālišîm*: Officers or Special Three-man Squads?," *VT* 40 (1990), 321–26.

Schneider, T. J. *A New Analysis of the Royal Annals of Shalmaneser III*. Dissertation, University of Pennsylvania, 1991.

____. *Form and Context in the Royal Inscriptions of Shalmaneser III*. Occasional Papers of the Institute for Antiquity and Christianity 26. Claremont: Institute for Antiquity and Christianity, 1993.

Schoville, K. N. "A Note on the Oracles of Amos Against Gaza, Tyre, and Edom." In *Studies on Prophecy: A Collection of Twelve Papers*, 55–63. Ed. by G. W. Anderson *et al.* VTSup 26. Leiden: E. J. Brill, 1974.

Schrader, E. *Die Keilinschriften und das Alte Testament*. Giessen: J. Ricker, 1872.

____. *Keilinschriftliche Bibliothek*. 2 vols. Berlin: H. Reuther, 1889–90.

Schramm, W. "War Semiramis assyrische Regentin?," *Historia* 21 (1972), 513–21.

____. *Einleitung in die assyrischen Königsinschriften. Zweiter Teil: 934–722 v. Chr.* Handbuch der Orientalistik I/5. Leiden/Köln: E. J. Brill, 1973.

Schroeder, O. *Keilschrifttexte aus Assur historischen Inhalts*. Abhandlungen der deutschen Orient-Gesellschaft, ser. E, II/2. Leipzig: J. C. Hinrichs, 1922.

Segert, S. *A Grammar of Phoenician and Punic*. München: C. H. Beck, 1976.

Seux, M. J. *Épithètes Royales Akkadiennes et Sumériennes*. Paris: Letouzey et Anê, 1967.

Seyrig, H. "Antiquities Syriennes: Sur une Pretendue ere Tyrienne les Trouvailles," *Syria* 34 (1957), 93–98.

Shanks, H. "Ancient Ivory: The Story of Wealth, Decadence and Beauty," *BARev* 11/5 (1985), 40–53.

Sharon, I. "Phoenician and Greek Ashlar Construction Technique at Tel Dor, Israel," *BASOR* 267 (1987), 21–42.

Shavit, Y. "Hebrews and Phoenicians: An Ancient Historical Image and its Usage," *Studies in Zionism* 5/2 (1984), 157–80.

Shaw, C. S. *The Speeches of Micah: A Rhetorical-Historical Analysis*. Dissertation, Emory University, 1990.

Shea, W. H. "A Note on the Date of the Battle of Qarqar," *JCS* 29 (1977), 240–42.

____. "Adad-nirari III and Jehoash of Israel," *JCS* 30 (1978), 101–14.

____. "Menahem and Tiglathpileser III," *JNES* 37 (1978), 43–49.

____. "The Kings of the Melqart Stela," *Maarav* 1 (1978–79), 159–76.

Shenkel, J. D. *Chronology and Recensional Development in the Greek Text of Kings*. HSM 1. Cambridge: Harvard University Press, 1968.

Shiloh, Y. *Foreign Influences on the Masonry of Palestine in the Tenth–Ninth Centuries B.C.* Dissertation, Hebrew University, 1974. [Hebrew]

____. "New Proto-Aeolic Capitals Found in Israel," *BASOR* 222 (1976), 67–77.

____. "The Proto-Aeolic Capital. The Israelite 'Timorah' (Palmette) Capital," *PEQ* 109 (1977), 39–52.

____. *The Proto-Aeolic Capital and Israelite Ashlar Masonry*. Qedem 11. Jerusalem: Hebrew University, 1979.

Smit, E. J. "The Philistines in the Eighth Century B.C.," *Old Testament Essays* 2 (1989), 61–72.

Smith, C. C. "Jehu and the Black Obelisk of Shalmaneser III." In *Scripture in History and Theology: Essays in Honor of J. Coert Rylaarsdam*, 71–105. Ed. by A.L. Merill and T. W. Overholt. Pittsburgh: Pickwick, 1977.

Smith, G. "On a New Fragment of the Assyrian Canon Belonging to the Reigns of Tiglath-pileser and Shalmaneser," *TSBA* 2 (1873), 321–32.

____. *The Assyrian Eponym Canon*. London: S. Bagster & Sons, 1875.

____. *History of Sennacherib*. London: Williams & Northgate, 1887.

Smith, H. P. *A Critical and Exegetical Commentary on the Books of Samuel*. ICC. New York: Charles Scribner's Sons, 1904.

Soggin, J. A. "Ein ausserbiblisches Zeugnis für die Chronologie des Jĕhôʾāš/Jôʾāš, König von Israel," *VT* 20 (1970), 366–68.

____. *A History of Israel: From the Beginnings to the Bar Kochba Revolt, AD 135*. London: SCM, 1984.

Spanuth, J. *Die Phönizier*. Osnabrück: Zeller, 1985.

Steck, O. H. *Überlieferung und Zeitgeschichte in den Elia-Erzählungen*. WMANT 26. Neukirchen-Vluyn: Neukirchener Verlag, 1968.

Stern, E. "Excavations at Tell Mevorach and the Late Phoenician Elements in the Architecture of Palestine," *BASOR* 225 (1977), 17–27.

____. *Excavations at Tel Mevorakh (1973–1976). Part One: From the Iron Age to the Roman Period*. Qedem 9. Jerusalem: Hebrew University, 1978.

____. "A Favissa of a Phoenician Sanctuary from Tel Dor," *JJS* 33 (1982), 35–54.

____. *The Material Culture of the Land of the Bible in the Persian Period 538–332 B.C.* Jerusalem: Israel Exploration Society, 1982.

____. "Two Phoenician Glass Seals From Tel Dor," *JANESCU* 16–17 (1984/85), 213–16.

____. "The Excavations at Tel Dor—A Canaanite-Phoenician Port City on the Carmel Coast," *Qadmoniot* 20 (1987), 66–81. [Hebrew]

Stieglitz, R. R. "The Geopolitics of the Phoenician Littoral in the Early Iron Age," *BASOR* 279 (1990), 9–12.

Strange, J. "Joram, King of Israel and Judah," *VT* 25 (1975), 191–201.

Tadmor, H. "The Campaigns of Sargon II of Assur: A Chronological-Historical Study," *JCS* 12 (1958), 22–40, 77–100.

____. "Azriyau of Yaudi." In *Studies in the Bible*, 232–71. Ed. by C. Rabin. ScrHier 8. Jerusalem: Magnes, 1961.

____. "Que and Muṣri," *IEJ* 11 (1961), 143–50.

____. "The Southern Border of Aram," *IEJ* 12 (1962), 114–22.

____."The Assyrian Campaigns to Philistia." In *Military History of the Land of Israel in Biblical Times*, 261–85. Ed. by J. Liver. Tel Aviv: Israel Defense Forces Publication House, 1964. [Hebrew]

____. "Philistia under Assyrian Rule," *BA* 29 (1966), 86–102.

____. "Introductory Remarks to a New Edition of the Annals of Tiglath-Pileser III," *Proceedings of the Israel Academy of Sciences and Humanities* 2/9 (1967), 168–87.

____. "A Note on the Saba'a Stele of Adad-nirari III," *IEJ* 19 (1969), 46–48.

____. "La stèle d'Adad-Nirari III de Tell el Rimah," *Qadmoniot* 2 (1969), 135–36.

____. "The Historical Inscriptions of Adad-nirari III," *Iraq* 35 (1973), 141–50.

____. "Assyria and the West: The Ninth Century and its Aftermath." In *Unity and Diversity: Essays in the History, Literature and Religion of the Ancient Near East*, 36–48. Ed. by H. Goedicke and J. J. M. Roberts. Baltimore: Johns Hopkins University, 1975.

____.. "Observations on Assyrian Historiography." In *Essays on the Ancient Near East in Memory of Jacob Joel Finkelstein*, 209–13. Ed. by M. de J. Ellis. Hamden: Archon, 1977.

____. "The Chronology of the First Temple Period." In *The Age of the Monarchies: Political History*, 44–60. Ed. by A. Malamat. WHJP 4/1. Jerusalam: Massada, 1979.

____. "'Rashpuna'—A Case of Epigraphic Error." In *Nahman Avigad Volume*, 180–82. Ed. by B. Mazar and Y. Yadin. ErIsr 18. Jerusalem: Israel Exploration Society, 1985. [Hebrew]

____. *The Inscriptions of Tiglath-Pileser III*. Jerusalem: Israel Academy of Sciences and Humanities, forthcoming.

____ and Cogan, M. "Ahaz and Tiglath-Pileser in the Book of Kings: Historiographical Considerations," *Bib* 60 (1979), 491–508.

____ and Weinfeld, M., eds. *History, Historiography and Interpretation: Studies in Biblical and Cuneiform Literatures*. Jerusalem: Magnes, 1983.

Tasyürek, O. A. "A Rock Relief of Shalmaneser III on the Euphrates," *Iraq* 41 (1979), 47–53.

Tappy, R. E. *The Archaeology of Israelite Samaria, Volume I: Early Iron Age through the Ninth Century*. HSS 44. Atlanta: Scholars Press, 1992.

Thiele E. R. "The Chronology of the Kings of Judah and Israel," *JNES* 3 (1944), 137–86.

____. "Corengencies and Overlapping Reigns Among the Hebrew Kings," *JBL* 93 (1974), 194–98.

____. "An Additional Chronological Note on 'Yaw, Son of Omri,'" *BASOR* 222 (1976), 19–23.

____. *The Mysterious Numbers of the Hebrew Kings: A Reconstruction of the Chronology of the Kingdoms of Israel and Judah*. 3d ed. Grand Rapids: Zondervan, 1984. [First edition, 1951]

Thierry, G. J. "Gebal, Byblos, Bible: Paper," *VT* 1 (1951), 130–31.

Thomas, D. W., ed. *Documents from Old Testament Times*. New York: Harper and Row, 1961.

Thomas, W. "The root אָהֵב; 'love' in Hebrew," *ZAW* 57 (1939), 57–64.

Thompson, J. A. "The Significance of the Verb *Love* in the David-Jonathan Narratives in 1 Samuel," *VT* 24 (1974), 334–38.

Thompson, M. E. W. *Situation and Theology: Old Testament Interpretations of the Syro-Ephraimite War*. Sheffield: Almond, 1982.

Thureau-Dangin, F. *et al. Arslan Tash*. 2 vols. Bibliothéque Archéologique et Historique 16. Paris: Paul Geuthner, 1931.

____. and Dunand, M. *Til-Barsib*. Bibliothéque Archéologique et Historique 23. Paris: Paul Geuthner, 1936.

Timm, S. "Die territoriale Ausdehnung des Staates Israel zur Zeit der Omriden," *ZDPV* 96 (1980), 20–40.

____. *Die Dynastie Omri: Quellen und Untersuchungen zur Geschichte Israels im 9. Jahrhundert vor Christus*. FRLANT 124. Göttingen: Vandenhoeck & Ruprecht, 1982.

____. "Die Eroberung Samarias aus assyrisch-babylonischer Sicht," *WO* 20–21 (1989–90), 62–82.

Tomes, R. "The Reason for the Syro-Ephraimitic War," *JSOT* 59 (1993), 55–71.

Toorn, K. van der. "The Babylonian New Year Festival: New Insights from the Cuneiform Text and Their Bearing on Old Testament Study." In *Congress Volume: Leuven, 1989*, 331–39. Ed. by J. A. Emerton. VTSup 43. Leiden: E. J. Brill, 1991.

Trebolle-Barrera, J. C. *Salomon y Jeroboan: Historia de la recensión y redacción de I Reyes 2–12, 14*. Salamanca: Universidad Pontificia, 1980.

____. *Jehú y Joás. Texto y composición literaria de Reyes 9–11*. Institucion San Jeromino 17. Valencia: (s. n.), 1984.

Unger, E. *Zum Bronzetor von Balawat*. Leipzig: Eduard Pfeiffer, 1913.

____. *Relief-stele Adadniraris III. aus Saba'a und Semiramis*. Publicationen der Kaiserlich osmanischen Museen 2. Constantinople: A. Ihsan, 1916.

____. *Die Reliefs Tiglat-pilesars III. aus Nimrud*. Publications des Musées d'Antiquités de Stamboul 5. Constantinople: A. Ihsan, 1917.

____. *Die Reliefs Tiglat-pilesars III. aus Arslan Tash*. Publications des Musées d'Antiquités de Stamboul 7. Constantinople: A. Ihsan, 1925.

Unger, M. F. *Israel and the Arameans of Damascus*. Grand Rapids: Zondervan, 1957.

Ungnad, A. "Jaua mâr Humrî," *OLZ* 9 (1906), col. 224–26.

____. "Eponymen." In *Reallexikon der Assyriologie*, 2. 412–57. Ed. by E. Ebeling and B. Meissner. Berlin: Walter de Gruyter, 1928–.

Ussishkin, D. "Was Bit-Adini a Neo-Hittite or Aramean State?," *Or* 40 (1971), 431–37.

Van Beek, G. and Van Beek, O. "Canaanite-Phoenician Architecture: The Development and Distribution of Two Styles." In *Y. Aharoni Memorial Volume*, 70*–77*. Ed. by B. Mazar. ErIsr 15. Jerusalem: Israel Exploration Society, 1981.

Van Seters, J. "Histories and Historians of the Ancient Near East: The Israelites," *Or* 50 (1981), 137–95.

Vanel, A. "Ṭâbeʾél en Is. VII 6 et le roi Tubail de Tyr." In *Studies on Prophecy: A Collection of Twelve Papers*, 17–24. Ed. by G. W. Anderson *et al.* VTSup 26. Leiden: E. J. Brill, 1974.

Vaux, R. de. "La Chronologie de Hazael et de Benhadad III, Rois de Damas," *RB* 43 (1934), 512–18.

____. *Ancient Israel: Its Life and Institutions*. New York: McGraw Hill, 1961.

____. "La Phénicie et les Peuples de la Mer," *Mélanges de l'Université Saint-Joseph* 45 (1969), 479–98.

Vincent, L. H. "Les Fouilles de Byblos," *RB* 34 (1925), 161–93.

____. *Fertile Soil: A Political History Under the Divided Monarchy*. New York: American Press, 1957.

Vogt, E. "Die Texte Tiglat-Pilesers III. über die Eroberung Palästina," *Bib* 45 (1964), 348–54.

Waltke, B. K. and M. O'Connor. *An Introduction to Biblical Hebrew Syntax*. Winona Lake, IN: Eisenbrauns, 1990.

Ward, J. M. *Hosea: A Theological Commentary*. New York: Harper and Row, 1966.

Ward, W. A., ed. *The Role of the Phoenicians in the Interaction of Mediterranean Civilizations*. Beirut: American University of Beirut Centennial Publications, 1968.

Watson, W. G. E. "David Ousts the City Rulers of Jebus," *VT* 20 (1970), 501–2.

Weidner, E. F. "Die Annalen des Königs Aššurbêlkala von Assyrien," *AfO* 6 (1930–31), 75–93.

____. "Der Staatsvertrag Aššurnirâris VI. von Assyrien mit Matiʾilu von Bît-Agusi," *AfO* 8 (1932–33), 17–34.

____. "Die assyrischen Eponymen," *AfO* 13 (1939–40), 308–18.

Weinfeld, M. *Deuteronomy and the Deuteronomic School*. Oxford: Clarendon, 1972.

Weippert, H. *Palästina in vorhellenistischer Zeit*. Handbuch der Archäologie 2/1. München: C. H. Beck, 1988.

Weippert, M. "*Jau(a) mār Ḫumrî*—Joram oder Jehu von Israel?" *VT* 28 (1978), 113–18.

____. "Menahem von Israel und seine Zeitgenossen in einer Steleninscrift des assyrischen Königs Tiglathpileser III. aus dem Iran," *ZDPV* 89 (1973), 26–53.

Wellhausen, J. *Die Composition des Hextaeuch und der historischen Bücher des Alten Testaments*. 4th ed. Berlin: Walter de Gruyter, 1963.

White, H. "The Question of Narrative in Contemporary Historical Theory," *History and Theory* 23 (1984), 1–33.

Whitley, C. F. "The Deuteronomic Presentation of the House of Omri," *VT* 2 (1952), 137–52.

____. "The Language and Exegesis of Isaiah 8:16–23," *ZAW* 90 (1978), 41–42.

Wildberger, H. *Jesaga 1-12*. 2nd ed. BKAT 10/2. Neukirchen-Vluyn: Neukirchener Verlag, 1980.

____. *Isaiah 1–12: A Commentary*. Continental Commentaries. Minneapolis: Fortress, 1990.

Williams, R. J. *Hebrew Syntax: An Outline*. 2d ed. Toronto: University of Toronto Press, 1976.

Winckler, H. "Nachtrag," *ZA* 2 (1887), 351–52.

____. *Die Keilinschrifttexte Sargons I*. Leipzig: E. Pfeiffer, 1889.

____. "Das syrische Land Yaudi und der angebliche Azarja von Juda," *Altorientalische Forschungen* 1 (1983), 1–23.

____. "Beiträge zur Quellenscheidung der Königbuücher." In his *Alttestamentliche Untersuchungen*, 16–25. Leipzig: E. Pfeiffer, 1892.

____ and Strassmaier, J. N. "The Babylonian Chronicle," *ZA* (1887), 148–68.

Winter, I. J. "Phoenician and North Syrian Ivory Carving in Historical Context: Questions of Style and Distribution," *Iraq* 38 (1976), 1–22.

Wiseman, D. J. "Two Historical Inscriptions from Nimrud," *Iraq* 13 (1951), 21–28.

____. "A Fragmentary Inscription of Tiglath-pileser III from Nimrud," *Iraq* 18 (1956), 117–29.

____. *Chronicles of the Chaldean Kings (626-556 B. C.) in the British Museum*. London: British Museum, 1956.

____. "Historical Records of Assyria and Babylonia." In *Documents from Old Testament Times*, 46–83. Ed. by D. W. Thomas. London: Thomas Nelson and Sons, 1958.

____. "Fragments of Historical Texts from Nimrud," *Iraq* 26 (1964), 118.

____. ed. *Peoples of Old Testament Times*. Oxford: Clarendon, 1973.

Wolff, H. W. *Hosea: A Commentary on the Book of the Prophet Hosea*. Hermeneia. Philadelphia: Fortress, 1974.

Würthwein, E. *Die Bücher der Könige*. 2 vols. ATD 11. Göttingen: Vandenhoeck & Ruprecht, 1977–84.

Yadin, Y. "Excavations at Hazor, 1957," *IEJ* 8 (1958), 1–14.

____. *Hazor II: An Account of the Second Season of Excavations, 1956*. Jerusalem: Magnes: 1960.

____. "New Light on Solomon's Megiddo," *BA* 23 (1960), 62–68.

____. *The Art of Warfare in Biblical Lands in the Light of Archaeological Discovery*. London: Weidenfeld and Nicolson, 1963.

____. "Megiddo of the Kings of Israel," *BA* 33 (1970), 66–96.

____. *Hazor: The Head of All Those Kingdoms*. Schweich Lectures, 1970. London: Oxford University Press, 1972.

____. "'The House of Baal' in Samaria and Judah." In *Eretz Shomron: The Thirtieth Archaeological Convention, September 1972*, 52–66. Ed. by J. Aviram. Jerusalem: Israel Exploration Society, 1973. [Hebrew]

____. *Hazor: The Rediscovery of a Great Citadel of the Bible*. New York: Random House, 1975.

Yeivin, S. "Did the Kingdom of Israel have a Maritime Policy?" *JQR* 50 (1959–60), 193–228.

Young, G. D. *The Historical Background of Phoenician Expansion into the Mediterranean in the Early First Millennium B.C.* Dissertation, Brandeis, 1969.

Zadok, R. "Phoenicians, Philistines, and Moabites in Mesopotamia," *BASOR* 230 (1978), 57–65.

____. "On the Historical Background of the Sefire Treaty," *AION* 44 (1984), 529–38.

Zevit, Z. "Phoenician Inscription and Biblical Covenant Theology," *IEJ* 27 (1977), 110–18.

Zimansky, P. E. *Ecology and Empire: The Structure of the Urartian State*. SAOC 41. Chicago: Oriental Institute, 1985.

Zorn, J. F. "Elath." In *The Anchor Bible Dictionary*, 2. 429–30. Ed. by D. N. Freedman. 6 vols. New York: Doubleday, 1992.

GEOGRAPHICAL NAME INDEX

Abdadana, 82
Abel-beth-maacah, 122, 169, 170, 178–80
Abil el-Qamḥ, 170
Abila, 74
Acco, 122, 170
Achzib, 122
Adad, 79
Adinnu, 30
Africa, 103, 125, 132
Aḫsana, 70
ᶜAin el-Qudeirât, 170
Akkad, 12, 195–96
Aleppo (*see* Ḫalman)
Allabria, 82
Amanus, Mt., 20, 49
ᶜAmmana, 33
Ammon, 31–34, 39, 101, 162
Amurru, 79–80, 82–83, 140
Anat, 79, 86
Anatolia, 33, 77, 80, 83–84, 91–93, 100, 105, 108–9, 135, 146, 148, 152, 154, 156–57, 162–63, 186–87, 210
Andiu, 82
Antakya, 75
Aparasu, 49
Aphek, 35, 37
Apku, 86
Aqabah, Gulf of, 68, 132
Arabah, Sea of, 121–22
Arabia, 31, 34, 39, 103, 125, 132, 140, 147–48, 155–57, 162–63, 168, 172–74, 177, 182, 186, 188–92, 212
Aram, Greater, 132, 147–48
Aram-Damascus, 1–3, 6, 20–22, 28, 32, 34–40, 46–47, 49, 52–59, 61, 63, 66–68, 70–71, 75, 79–81, 83, 86–87, 91–93, 100–106, 109, 111, 115–16, 119, 122–25, 128–34, 135–36, 140, 144, 148, 151, 157–59, 161–63, 165–69, 171–73, 175, 178–81, 184–85, 188–92, 207, 209–12
Aras Valley, 108–9
Araziaš, 82
Argana, 30
Arne, 49
Arnon Valley, 70
Aroer, 70
Arpad, 16–17, 72–75, 77–78, 88–89, 91–101, 104–5, 109–10, 114, 120–21, 136–39, 141–42, 144, 151, 184, 186–87, 192, 202, 210, 212
Arqa, 177
Arrapḫa, 113
Arslan Tash, 130
ʾArsuf, 179
Aruma, 168–69
Arwad, 5, 31, 34, 39–40, 44, 79, 162–63, 165–66

Ashdod, 134, 167, 211
Ashkelon, 134, 162, 167–68, 171, 188, 191–92, 211–12
Aššur, 7, 11, 15–16, 30, 47, 61, 113–14, 120, 148
Aššur-uttir-aṣbat (*see* Pitru)
Assyria, 1–3, 5–7, 9, 11–13, 15–18, 20, 22, 24–26, 28, 32–35, 39–40, 44, 46–47, 50–51, 53–55, 57–61, 64–67, 70–71, 73–75, 77–80, 82–83, 86–88, 90–93, 95, 97–101, 103–5, 107–12, 114, 116, 119–21, 123–24, 127, 129, 133, 135, 138, 142–46, 150–51, 156–57, 163–66, 168–71, 174–75, 177–78, 181–82, 184–92, 193–204, 206–7, 209–13
Aštamaku, 26, 49
Atuna/Tuna, 140, 147, 155, 157, 162
Aven, Valley of, 111, 129–30
ᶜAzāz (*see* Ḫazazi)

Baal-peor, 204
Baalbek, 74
Babylon, 9, 12–14, 70, 83, 195–96, 199
Babylonia, 22, 70, 83, 94, 181–82, 185, 194, 196, 199
Balâwât, 22, 25
Baᶜli, 72, 74, 94, 99, 104
Baᶜli-raᵓsi, 52, 55, 62, 74, 94
Baᶜli-ṣapuna, 74
Baliḫ River, 30, 32
Barga, 30
Bashan, 71, 178, 180
Beqaᶜ Valley, 55, 75, 105, 130
Beth-Arbel, 56
Beth-Aven, 129
Beth-Eden (*see also* Bit-Adini), 110–11, 129–30
Beth-Rehob, 32, 34, 39
Beth-shean, 180
Bit-Adini, 5, 27–28, 30–32, 52, 66, 109–10, 112, 130, 133, 167, 192, 211
Bit-Agusi, 30, 32, 50, 52, 92, 110, 182
Bit-Amukkanu, 12
Bit-Dakuri, 30, 52
Bit-Ḫazael, 168–69, 178, 184, 186, 190–91
Bit-Ḫumri (*see also* Israel), 27, 45, 52, 61, 63, 65, 82–83, 126, 168–69, 175, 177–78, 181, 184, 186
Bit-Ruḫub (*see* Beth-Rehob)
Bit-Zeri, 9–11
Brook of Egypt, 164–65
Byblos, 5, 31, 33–34, 39–40, 44–45, 63–64, 140, 147–48, 155, 157, 162–63, 177, 188

Calah (*see also* Nimrud), 45, 107, 114, 135
Calneh (*see* Kullani)
Carchemish, 25, 30–32, 49–50, 139–40, 147, 155, 162
Cedar Mountain, 19–20, 112, 114
Chaldea, 70, 83
Chinneroth, 122

Cisjordan, 186
Cyprus, 43

Damascus, 6, 21, 35, 52, 54–57, 59, 64, 71, 83–84, 86–87, 91–98, 100, 103–5, 112, 115, 119, 121–25, 128, 130–33, 136–38, 140, 163, 173, 178, 181, 184–88, 190–91, 194, 200, 202–3, 206, 209, 211–12
Dan, 37, 122
Danabu, 19–20, 64
Dead Sea, 122
Der, 19, 70, 72–73
Dor, 191
Dūr-Adad-nirari, 79
Dūr-Aššur, 79
Dūr-EN-KUR-Sangari, 79
Dūr-Inanna, 79
Dūr-Marduk, 79
Dūr-Nergal-ereš, 79
Dūr-Šar-rukku, 7

Edom, 39–40, 46–47, 82–83, 101–104, 162
Egypt, 1, 31, 33–34, 39–40, 46, 61, 66, 142–43, 161, 164–66, 174, 177, 184, 186, 189, 202–204, 206–207, 213
Ekron, 134, 167, 211
Elam, 197
Elath, 102–103, 106, 124–25, 131–34, 192, 210–12
Ellipi, 82
Ephesus, 41, 62
Ephraim, 126–27, 159, 180, 204–207, 213
Euphrates River, 5–6, 28, 30–32, 49, 52, 63, 82, 86, 88, 91, 98, 101, 107

Fertile Crescent, 148

Gabari, 30, 32
Galʾaza, 178–79
Galilee, 116, 118–19, 122–23, 127–28, 131–33, 168–71, 178, 180–81, 184, 186, 190, 211
Gannanati, 113
Gath, 71, 102
Gaʾuni, 110
Gaza, 134, 162, 164–67, 177, 181, 184–86, 188–90, 192, 202, 211–12
Gilead, 38, 70–71, 118, 122, 128, 132, 169–70, 178–81, 186, 190–91
Gilzau, 31
Gilzanu, 62, 64–65
Gizilbunda, 82
Golan, 178, 180
Gurgum, 30, 32, 50, 90–92, 109, 115, 138–40, 142, 147, 155–57, 162, 186
Guzana, 13, 15, 72, 113

Ḫadara, 128, 172
Hadrach (*see also* Ḫatarikka), 16–17, 92–93, 100–101, 119, 149
Hakkāri Mountains, 151
Ḫalman, 30, 32
Hamath, 6, 26, 28, 30–32, 34, 39, 49, 53–55, 58, 61, 66, 75, 77–78, 91–93, 99–101, 104–5, 109, 119, 121–24, 140, 148–51, 156–57, 162, 188, 202, 209–10
Hannathon, 169

Ḫarḫar, 82
Harran, 77, 91
Ḫatarikka (*see also* Hadrach), 16–17, 113–14, 119–20, 150, 177–78, 184, 186
Ḫatti/Ḫattu, 14, 30, 76–77, 79–80, 82–84, 86–88, 101, 108–9, 140, 147–48, 156
Hauran, 52, 54, 178, 191
Ḫazazi, 72–74, 99, 101, 104
Hazor, 37, 122–23, 129, 169–70
Ḫinatuna, 168–69
Ḫindanu, 86, 107
Ḥorvat Qedesh (*see* Khirbet Qedîsh)
Ḫubišna (*see* Ḫušemna)
Ḫubuškia, 72–73
Huleh Valley, 170
Ḫušemna, 140, 147, 155–56, 162

Iaraqu, Mt., 49
Iatbiti, 168–69
Ijon, 122, 169
Imērišu (*see* Aram-Damascus)
Ionia, 43
Iran, 108, 146, 151
Irmaia, 172
Irqanata, 31, 33–34, 39
Israel, 1–3, 6, 28, 34–40, 42–47, 51, 55–61, 65–68, 70–71, 75, 81, 87, 93–98, 101, 103–6, 111, 116, 118–19, 121–34, 135, 143–46, 148–49, 158, 162–70, 173, 175, 178, 180–82, 185, 187–92, 193, 200–202, 204–7, 209–13
Ištunda, 140, 147, 155–56, 162
Itu'a/Itu'u, 73, 112–13

Jabbok River, 179–80
Janoah, 169–70
Janua, 169
Jerusalem, 100–102, 116, 143, 158
Jezreel, 34, 60, 122, 186
Jezreel Valley, 122, 180
Jordan River, 70, 116, 122, 127–29, 132, 180, 184
Jotbah, 169
Judah, 1–3, 35, 37, 39–41, 44, 47, 51, 55, 60–61, 70–71, 95–96, 99, 101–3, 121–29, 133, 149, 158–63, 169, 189, 191–92, 201, 209, 211–12

Kadesh, 170
Kadesh-barnea, 170
Kaldu (*see* Chaldea)
Kar-Aššur-naṣir-apli, 86
Kar-Shalmaneser (*see also* Til-Barsip), 28, 30, 45, 109
Kar-Sin, 79
Kaska, 140, 147, 155, 162–63
Kašpuna, 165–66, 179–80
Kedesh, 169–70
Khirbet Jefat, 169
Khirbet Jel^{c}ad, 179–80
Khirbet Niha, 170
Khirbet Rume, 169
Khirbet Qedîsh, 170
Khirbet Yanum, 170
Kinalia (*see* Kullani)

Kirruri, 12
Kiš, 9–11
Kiski, 73
KTK, 110, 121
Kulkhai, 108
Kullani, 135, 137–38, 156, 187–88
Kummuḫ, 9, 30, 32, 90–92, 109, 115, 138–42, 147, 151, 155, 157, 162–63, 187
Kunalia, 187
Kurkh, 27
Kuruṣṣa, 172
Kutha, 83

Lakê, 79, 86
Lebanon, 5, 52, 74, 105, 114, 122, 178
Lebanon, Mt., 61, 79, 179
Levant, 34
Luᶜaš, 91, 93, 100, 104–5, 119, 210
Lušia, 72

Madai, 72–73, 82, 113, 137
Maḫalab, 184
Malaḫu, 19–20, 64
Mannai, 20, 69, 72, 95, 97, 148
Manṣuate, 72, 75, 94–96, 98, 100, 105, 191
Marad, 113
Marê, 86
Marj ᶜAyun, 170
Marqasa, 9–10
Marum, 168–69
Masyat, 75
Medeibiyeh, 44
Media, 108, 150–51
Mediterranean Sea, 27, 43, 74, 94, 98
Mediterranean Seaboard, 33, 95, 135, 142, 166, 190
Megiddo, 37, 123, 170, 179, 191
Melid, 19, 30, 32, 91, 109, 138, 140, 142, 147, 155, 162, 186
Merom, 169
Mesopotamia, 1, 74, 108, 185
Mesu, 82
Metuna, 172
Moab, 37, 39–40, 44, 4647, 101, 103, 162, 209
Mukhmas, 129
Munna, 82
Muški, 109
Muṣri (in Anatolia), 33
Muṣri (*see* Egypt)

Nablus, 170
Naḫlasi, 77
Naᵓiri, 24, 79–80, 82, 153, 182
Nâl, Mt., 137
Namri, 19, 72, 82, 109, 112–14, 136, 148
Naphtali, 116, 119, 122, 132, 169–70
Naṣibina, 135
Nimrud, 22, 51, 63, 81, 161, 164, 176, 182
Nineveh, 30, 49, 73

Orontes River, 5–6, 31–32, 53, 66–67, 75, 77, 210
Orontes Valley, 55

Palestine, 1–2, 6, 26, 32–33, 35, 40, 42, 46–47, 50–51, 53, 56, 63, 66, 70, 80, 83–84, 92, 95–96,

98, 101–5, 107–9, 111–12, 123, 125, 128–30, 133, 135–36, 138, 140, 142, 145–46, 148, 151–52, 154, 156–58, 162–64, 167, 171, 174–76, 178, 181–82, 184, 186, 188–89, 191–92, 194, 200, 206, 209–11
Paqiraḫubuna, 88, 91
Parsua, 82
Pattin (*see* Unqi)
Persian Gulf, 74
Philistia, 70–71, 82–83, 101–4, 132–34, 137–38, 163–66, 189, 192, 211
Phoenicia, 1–3, 6, 24–28, 33, 39–46, 60–61, 64, 66, 75, 93, 103–4, 106, 122, 124–25, 130–32, 136, 152, 164, 166, 189, 191, 197–99, 207
Pitru, 30, 32, 86

Qana/Khirbet Qana, 167
Qarnini/Qarnaim, 178, 191
Qarqar, 27–28, 31–32, 35, 44, 46, 57, 66
Qatni, 79, 86
Qedar, 147–48
Qiryat Shemona, 170
Que, 19, 31, 33, 91, 139–40, 147, 155, 157, 162–63

Ramoth-gilead, 36, 38, 55–57, 178–79
Raṣappa, 79, 86, 94, 107
Rās en-Nāqūra (*see* Baᶜli-raʾsi)
Ras Shamra, 74
Rašpuna, 177, 179–80
Red Sea, 103, 125
Riʾraba, 177
Rishpon, 179
Riʾsiṣu, 177
Rumah, 169

Sabaʾ, Mt., 174
Sagur River, 30
Saḫlala, 30
Ša-imērišu (*see* Aram-Damascus)
Samaʾl, 31, 91, 140, 147, 155, 157, 162
Samandag, 75
Samaria, 2, 35, 37, 41–43, 57, 79–81, 116, 123, 125–28, 140, 147, 152, 155, 159, 162–63, 169, 174–75, 181, 185, 187, 190, 192, 193–97, 201–4, 206–7, 212–13
Samerina (*see* Samaria)
Saniru, Mt., 52
Šapiya, 137
Saqurri, Mt., 174, 177, 191
Sarepta, 42
Sarrabanu, 182, 184–85
Saue, Mt., 177, 184
Sharon, Plain of, 180
Sheikh Hammad, 87
Šianu, 31, 33–34, 39, 177
Sidon, 5–6, 24–28, 40–41, 44–47, 51–53, 55, 59–64, 67, 79–83, 101, 103–4, 122, 152, 198, 209–10
Siluna, Mt., 82
Ṣimirra, 165, 177–78, 202
Singibutu, 148
Sinjar hills, 84
Sirqu, 86
Subite, 191
Suḫi, 79, 86
Suweinit Valley, 129

Syria, 1–2, 6, 17, 20, 23–24, 26–28, 31–35, 38–40, 42, 44, 46–47, 50–51, 53, 56, 63, 66, 70–71, 73–74, 77, 80–81, 83, 91–96, 98, 100–105, 107–12, 118–21, 123–25, 128, 130, 133, 135–36, 138, 140, 142, 144–46, 148, 151–53, 156–59, 162–64, 171, 174–76, 178, 181–82, 184, 186–89, 191–92, 194, 197, 200, 206, 209–12

Tabalu, 19, 140, 144, 147, 155, 157, 162, 200
Tabel, 160
Tel Aviv, 179
Tell Abu Sifre, 180
Tell Abu Ṣuṣ, 180
Tell ed-Dibbîn, 169
Tell el-Bedeiwijeh, 169
Tell el-Khirbeh, 169
Tell el-Qedaḥ, 170
Tell el-Rimah, 78
Tell Maryam, 129
Tell Nebi Mind, 170
Tell Qadis/Tel Qedesh, 170
Tell Refād (*see* Arpad)
Tigris River, 30, 151
Til Abil, 170
Til-Barsip (*see also* Kar-Shalmaneser), 28, 45, 75, 83, 109–10, 130
Til-ša-Turaḫi, 30
Tille, 69
Transjordan, 38, 57, 67, 103, 122, 125, 127–29, 131–33, 144, 160, 178, 180, 186, 211
Tuḫana, 140, 147, 155, 162
Turkey, 75
Tušḫan, 12–13, 182
Tyre, 5–6, 23–28, 40–42, 44–47, 51–53, 55, 57, 59–64, 66–68, 79–83, 101, 103–4, 106, 122, 130–34, 135, 139–40, 144, 146–48, 150–53, 155–57, 160–63, 165–67, 182, 184–92, 197–200, 205–7, 209–13

Ugarit, 33, 42
Ulluba, 19, 137, 148, 151–52, 182, 187–88
Umq, 91
Unqi, 19, 30, 31, 50, 151, 154, 187–88
Urartu, 19, 24, 108, 112–13, 136–38, 142, 182, 186–87
Usanata, 31, 33–34, 39
Usnu, 177

Van, Lake, 5, 108

Wadi es-Suweinit, 129
Wadi Qelt, 129

Yanuḥ, 170
Yarmuk River, 180
Yaʾudi/Yʾdy-Samʾal, 59, 149
Yiron/Yarun, 167

Zab River, Greater, 151
Zabanni, 86
Zagros mountains, 5
Zamaḫu, 79
Zarate, 69
Zebulun, 116, 119, 132
Zimarra, 177

PERSONAL NAME INDEX

Adad, 30–31, 77, 79, 85–86, 91
Adad-idri, 6, 28, 31–32, 34, 37, 49–50, 53–54, 56, 58, 66, 69, 209
Adad-nirari III, 2, 8–9, 42, 70–75, 77–83, 85–91, 93–101, 103–6, 107–9, 115, 129, 133, 144, 210–11
Adramu/Arame, 30, 49–50, 77, 89, 91, 100
Adunu-baʾil, 31
Ahab, 6, 31, 34–41, 43, 45, 60–61, 66, 123, 209
Ahaz/Jehoahaz, 100, 116, 128, 131, 158, 161–64, 189, 192, 200, 212
Ahaziah (of Israel), 52, 56
Ahaziah (of Judah), 55, 60
Ahuni, 31
Amaziah, 124
Amos, 129–31, 167
Anu, 79, 85
Argishti I, 108
Asa, 122
Ashur-dan III, 2, 16, 75, 107, 109, 113, 119–20
Ashur-nirari V, 2, 9, 16–17, 75, 107, 109, 114, 120–21, 136
Ashurbanipal, 7, 10
Ashurnasirpal II, 5, 9, 24–25, 28, 44, 66, 209
Aššur, 7, 10–11, 31, 77, 82–83, 86, 88, 91, 165
Aššur-bêl-kala, 97
Aššur-bēlu-kaʾʾin, 28, 45
Aššur-daʾʾin-apli, 70
Astarte, 41
Ataršumki, 42, 77, 88–89, 91–93, 100–101, 105, 210
Athaliah, 39, 96, 99
Ayanur, 160
Azariah (*see* Uzziah)
Azriyau, 149–50, 156, 187–88

Baal, 41–42
Baʿal-ʿazor II (*see also* Baʿli-ma-AN-zēr), 51, 57, 61–62, 210
Baalšamayn, 92
Baʿli-ma-AN-zēr (*see* Baʿal-ʿazor II), 27, 45, 55, 60–62
Bar-gaʾyah, 110, 121
Bar-guš (*see also* Ataršumki), 92, 110
Bar-Hadad (of the Melqart Stela), 42, 100
Bar-Hadad/Ben-Hadad I, 122
Bar-Hadad/Ben-Hadad II (son of Adad-idri), 54
Bar-Hadad/Ben-Hadad III (son of Hazael; *see also* Mariʾ), 35, 37–38, 81,

91, 100, 104–5, 130–31, 133, 210–11
Barrakab, 59
Bêl, 9, 12–14, 83, 137, 193
Bēl-abūa, 18
Bēl-ḫarrān-bēlu-uṣur, 13, 15, 108
Bēl-tarṣi-iluma, 107
Ber, 77
Bur-sagale, 8, 15

Dadi-il, 147, 155, 163
Dagan-bēlu-nāṣir, 5
David, 57, 123
Dayān-Aššur, 27–28, 30–31, 64
Dūr-Aššur, 13

Ekur, 82
Elah, 181
Elijah, 41, 57
Elisha, 37, 57
Elulaios (*see also* Luli), 197–200
Enilu, 148–49, 155–56, 162, 188
Esarhaddon, 7, 10
Ešarra, 82
Ethbaal I, 40–41, 61
Ethbaal II, 152, 160

Giammu, 30
Gindibuʾ, 31

Ḫadiānu, 109, 115–16, 119, 125, 132
Hanun, 162, 164–67, 177, 186, 188–89
Hazael, 19–21, 38, 52–56, 59, 63–64, 67–68, 70–71, 81, 92–93, 95, 100–103, 105, 123–24, 128, 130, 132, 210
Hezekiah, 144, 149, 204
Hiram I, 131
Hiram II, 146, 148, 150, 154–57, 160, 163, 182, 184–86, 188, 190–91, 200
Hosea, 56, 58, 126–27, 204, 206
Hoshea, 118, 125, 175, 177, 181–82, 184–86, 190, 200–204, 207, 213
Hulli, 144, 200
Humban-nikash, 197

Idibiʾilu, 168, 174–75
Iluma-lēʾi, 18
Irḫuleni, 6, 26, 28, 30–32, 34, 37, 49–50, 53, 58, 66, 209
Isaiah, 158–60
Ishtar, 86
Ittobaal (*see* Ethbaal)

Jehoahaz (of Israel), 37–38, 94, 96–97, 99, 101, 104–5, 123, 211
Jehoash/Joash (of Israel), 37–38, 75, 79, 81, 87, 93–99, 104, 121–24, 133, 211
Jehoash/Joash (of Judah), 71, 96, 102
Jehoram/Joram (of Judah and Israel), 38–39, 51–52, 55–58, 60
Jehoshaphat, 35, 39–40, 51
Jehu, 6, 25, 27–28, 36–38, 45, 52–53, 55–65, 67, 70–71, 96, 101, 103–4, 131, 144, 210

Jeroboam II, 1, 103, 118, 121–25, 127–29, 131–34, 163, 169, 188, 211–12
Jezebel, 40–41, 60–61, 67
Josephus, 41, 62, 197–98, 206
Jotham, 128, 132, 158, 200

Kaušmalaka, 162
Kilamuwa, 59
Kundaspi, 30
Kuštašpi, 139, 141–42, 147, 151, 155, 157, 162, 187

Lalli, 30
Lipḫur-ilu, 12–13
Luli (*see also* Elulaios), 198–99, 207

Marduk, 14, 86, 91
Mariʾ (*see also* Bar-Hadad III), 79, 81, 83, 86–87, 144
Matiʾ-ilu, 17, 110, 120–21, 141–42, 186
Matinu-baʾil, 31
Matanbiʾil, 162
Mattan (*see* Mêtenna)
Menahem, 59, 118, 125–27, 140, 143–47, 151–52, 155–56, 181, 187–89, 192, 200, 212
Menander, 41, 62, 197
Merodach-baladan, 197
Mêtenna, 144, 200, 207
Mitinti, 162, 168, 171, 188, 191
Mutakkil-Aššur, 16

Naboth, 38, 58
Nabû, 83
Nabû-bēlu-uṣur, 7–8, 12
Nabu-mukin-zeri, 12
Nabū-naṣir, 194
Nebuchadnezzar, 13–14, 143
Nergal, 31, 83
Nergal-ilāya, 77
Nergal-ereš, 79–80, 86, 94, 107
Nergal-naṣir, 135

Omri, 28, 42, 52, 66, 124, 209

Palalam, 91
Panammu, 59, 147, 155, 162
Pekah, 57, 111, 116, 118, 125–29, 131–33, 144, 158–59, 161, 163, 166–69, 175, 177–78, 181–82, 185, 188, 190–92, 211–12
Pekahiah, 125–27
Phelles, 41
Pisiris, 147, 155, 163
Pul (*see* Tiglath-pileser III)

Qalparuda/Qalparunda, 30, 49–50, 91

Raḫianu (*see* Rezin)
Rakabel, 59
Raᶜyān/Raqyān (*see* Rezin)
Remaliah, 125–26, 158–59, 181
Rezin, 102–3, 111, 119, 125, 128–34, 139, 141–42, 151, 157–58, 160–61, 163, 167–69, 171–73, 175, 178, 183–88, 190–92, 211–12
Rukibtu, 168, 171

Salamanu, 162
Šamaš, 86, 91, 172–73, 185
Šamaš-nūri, 5
Šamaš-ilāya, 18
Šamaš-šumu-ukin, 7, 194
Sammu-rāmat (*see* Semiramis)
Samsi, 163, 172–75, 177, 182, 185–86, 188, 191
Šamši-Adad I, 23
Šamši-Adad V, 21, 69–70, 77, 79, 86–91, 101, 115
Šamši-ilu, 2, 75, 77, 90, 99–100, 108–112, 114–16, 119–21, 123–25, 128–30, 133, 192, 211
Sangara, 25, 30, 49
Sanipu, 162
Sardurri II, 109, 136, 142, 186–87
Sargon II, 2, 7–10, 13, 21, 35, 97, 141, 149, 196–97, 202–3
Saul, 57, 133
Semiramis, 73, 91, 97, 99, 108
Sennacherib, 9–10, 144, 149, 152–53, 198–99
Shalmaneser III, 2, 5–6, 8–9, 17–18, 20–22, 24–28, 31–34, 36, 38–39, 41, 44–47, 49–51, 53–67, 69–70, 74, 77, 79, 86–87, 89, 91–92, 109–10, 119, 209–10
Shalmaneser IV, 2, 8, 10, 18, 75, 89–90, 107, 109, 112, 114–16, 119
Shalmaneser V, 2, 9, 13, 15, 56, 118, 138, 193–99, 202–4, 206–7, 212–13
Shutruk-Nahhunte, 197
Sin, 77, 91
Sipittibiʾil/Sipatbail, 147, 155, 162, 188
Solomon, 43, 123, 131
Sûa, 62, 64–65
Sulumal, 142, 147, 155, 162, 186

Ṭāb-bēlu, 18
Tabeʾal/Tabeʾel (*see also* Tubail), 153, 159–61
Taklāk-ana-šarri, 47
Tarḫulara, 139, 142, 147, 155–57, 162, 186
Tiglath-pileser I, 23, 62
Tiglath-pileser III, 2, 8–9, 12–15, 21, 23, 59, 100, 109, 111–12, 114, 118, 120, 125, 127–28, 131, 135–36, 138–53, 156–57, 160–64, 166–67, 169–71, 173, 175, 178, 180–82, 184–92, 193–200, 203, 205–6, 212
Tubail, 146–48, 150–53, 156–57, 160–61, 187–88
Tuḫamme, 147, 155–56, 162
Tukulti-ninurta II, 80
Tutammû, 151, 187

Uassurme, 147, 155, 162, 200
Ulūlāyu, 15
Urballa, 147, 155, 157, 162
Urik/Urikki, 139, 147, 155, 157, 162
Urimmi/Uirimi, 147, 155–56, 163
Ušḫiti, 147, 155, 157, 162
Ušpilulume, 90–91, 115
Uzziah, 124–25, 129, 149, 158, 169

Yaubiʾdi, 202
YHWH, 70, 106, 123, 132, 201
Zabibe, 147, 155–57, 188
Zakkur, 77–78, 91–93, 100, 104–5, 210

SCRIPTURE INDEX

Genesis
50:11 180

Exodus
8:11 117
8:28 117
9:34 117
10:1 117
16:34 116
18:22 117

Numbers
1:19 116
33:49 180

Deuteronomy
4:43 179

Joshua
20:8 179
21:38 179

Judges
7:22 180
10:17 179
11:33 180
12:7 179

Ruth
2:1 145

1 Samuel
6:5 117
9:1 145

2 Samuel
19:44 117
20:14 180
20:15 180

1 Kings
4:12 180
4:13 179
9:13 131
11:28 145
12:4 117
12:9 117
12:10 117
12:14 117
14:25 143
15:17 143
15:20 .... 122, 180
16:31 40–41
16:32 41
19:15–18 58
20 ....35–38, 104, 133, 211
20:1 143
20:2 38
20:4 37
20:13 38
20:14 38
20:15 37
20:22 143
20:23–25 37
20:26 37
20:32–33 131
20:34 .... 35, 38
21 .... 38, 122
22 .... 38, 58, 104
22:1–38 ....35–38, 133, 211

22:1–40 36
22:3 .... 38, 179
22:4 40
22:20 38
22:40 38
22:45 39
22:48 40

2 Kings
1:1 37
3:5 37
5:1 145
6:24 143
8:7–15 54
8:28 179
8:29 179
8:28–29 .... 38, 55–57
9–10 57
9:1 .... 38, 179
9:4 38
9:7–10a 57
9:7a 57
9:7b 57
9:8–9 57
9:10a 57
9:13 56
9:14 .... 38, 57, 179
9:14–15a 56
9:14–16 57
9:14–26 122
9:14b 56
9:14b–15a 55–57
9:15a 57
9:15b 56
9:16aα 57
9:16aβ 57
9:17–24 60
9:25–26 57
9:27 60
9:27b–29 57
9:30–33 67
9:30–37 60
9:36–37 57
9:36a 57
9:36b 57
9:37 57
10:1–17 61
10:1a 57
10:10–17 57
10:18–28 57
10:29–36 57
10:32 128
10:32–33 .... 38, 57, 67, 70, 101
10:36 56
12:17–18 71
12:17a 102
12:17b–18 102
12:18 143
13 37
13:3 .... 105, 211
13:5 .... 94, 106, 123, 211
13:12 95
13:17 37
13:22–25 95
13:25 .... 38, 101, 104, 133, 211
14:8–14 .... 95, 124
14:16 124
14:19–20 124
14:22 .... 124, 133, 211
14:25 .... 121–22, 133, 211
14:28 .... 121–23, 133, 211
15:2 129
15:10 30
15:19 143
15:19–20 .... 59, 143, 187 212
15:20a 145
15:22 146
15:25 126
15:27 126
15:27–31 169
15:29 .... 118, 143, 169–71,

180, 190
15:30 ....175, 181, 200
15:32 126
15:37 ....128, 157
16:1...............................126
16:5.......................158, 212
16:6........102, 131, 134, 158
210, 212
16:6a.............................102
16:6b 102
17:1–6............................200
17:3........143, 203, 207, 213
17:3–4....................201, 203
17:3–6........................201–4
17:3–6aα.........................202
17:4a..............204, 207, 213
17:4b 204, 207, 213
17:5.......................194, 204
17:5a.....................207, 213
17:5b 207, 213
17:5–6....................201, 203
17:5–6a..........................202
17:6...............................204
17:6aα............................204
17:6aβ....................202, 204
18:9........143, 204, 207, 213
18:9–11 ....201, 204
18:9–12 200
18:10 204
18:11 204
18:13 143
18:25 143
23:29 143
24:14 145
25:1...............................143
25:4...............................159
25:8...............................143
25:25 143

1 Chronicles
5:17...............................122
6:65...............................179

2 Chronicles
10:4 117
10:9 117
10:10..............................117
10:14..............................117
16:4 180
22:6 179
25:19..............................117
32:1 159

Ezra
4:7.................................160

Nehemiah
5:15 118

Isaiah
6:10 117
7:1 ....158–59, 212
7:6.................................153
7:1–9......................158, 164
7:2–9..............................159
7:5–6..............................159
7:10–17..........................159
8:21–22..........................116
8:21–9:6.........................116
8:22b..............................116
8:23 .... 116–18, 123, 132,
134, 184, 186, 190, 212
8:23aα........................... 116
8:23aβ–9:6 116
9:10–11a 132, 134, 212
9:12 167
23:9 117
47:6 117

Jeremiah
30:19..............................117
39:2 159

Lamentations
3:7.................................117

Ezekiel
22:7 ... 117
26:10 ... 159
30:16 ... 159

Hosea
1:4–5 ... 58
1:5 ... 132
2:1–3 ... 175
4 ... 127
5 ... 127
5:5 ... 127
5:8 ... 129
5:13 ... 143
6:8 ... 179
8 ... 127
9:10 ... 204
9:10–14 ... 204
9:11–14 ... 204
9:13 ... 116, 205, 207, 213
10 ... 127
10:13–15 ... 56
12:12 ... 179

Amos
1 ... 132–33, 157, 211
1:1 ... 129
1:3–5 ... 128, 167
1:3–8 ... 133
1:5 ... 110–12, 129–30
1:6–8 ... 167
1:9 ... 133, 188, 211
1:9–10 ... 167
1:15 ... 103
2:1 ... 103
2:3 ... 103
6:13 ... 132
6:13–14 ... 127

Jonah
1:5 ... 117

Habakkuk
2:6 ... 117

Zechariah
7:11 ... 117
14:4–5 ... 129

AUTHOR INDEX

Abel, F. M., 179, 191
Aharoni, Y., 44, 167–70, 180, 190
Ahlström, G. W., 31, 56, 101, 122, 204
Albright, W. F., 44, 125, 149, 152, 160, 180, 201
Alt, A., 117–18, 165–66, 179, 191
Andersen, F. I., 111, 130, 205
Arnold, P. M., 129
Astour, M. C., 55–56
Asurmendi, J. M., 162, 185

Barnes, W. E., 123
Barnes, W. H., 41, 201
Barnett, R. D., 108–9, 151
Barré, L. M., 55, 57–58
Barth, H., 116–18
Barton, J., 130
Becking, B. E. J. H., 195, 201–2
Begrich, J., 94, 128, 175, 179
Ben-Zvi, E., 128
Benzinger, I., 55
Billerbeck, A., 22, 31, 50
Biran, A., 37
Birch, W. G., 25
Black, J. A., 13, 14, 22
Boling, R. G., 179
Borger, R., 30, 146, 153, 183
Briend, J., 106
Bright, J., 36, 94, 124, 127
Brinkman, J. A., 12, 74, 94,
Briquel-Chatonnet, F., 1, 30–31, 35, 40, 53, 68, 73, 94, 130–31, 152
Budge, E. A. W., 138
Burney, C. F., 123

Cameron, G. G., 22, 27, 31, 34, 47–48
Campbell, A. F., 55, 58
Cantineau, J., 121
Cazelles, H., 74
Christensen, D. L., 204
Clements, R. E., 116, 158
Cody, A., 97–99
Cogan, M., 58, 102, 127–28, 141, 144–46, 148–50, 154, 156, 158, 167, 169–70, 179, 201–2
Cohen, M. E., 13, 14
Cohen, S., 131
Contenau, G., 121
Cook, H. J., 126–27
Cross, F. M., 33
Crowfoot, J. W., 37, 43–44
Culican, W., 33

Dalley, S., 35, 196, 202
Day, J., 204
Dearman, J. A., 39, 101
Delitzsch, F., 8, 12–13, 22, 31, 50, 137, 158
Dever, W. G., 170
Diakonoff, I. M., 189
Dillman, A., 158
Donbaz, V., 76, 87–88, 90, 108–9, 115

Donner, H., 78, 94, 158, 160, 170, 202
Dossin, G., 121
Driver, G. R., 116–18, 159
Dunand, M., 76, 108–9, 130
Durand, J.-M., 110, 121

Edelman, D. V., 180
Elat, M., 34, 46, 65
Emerton, J. A., 117–18
Eph^{c}al, I., 68, 101, 147, 162–63, 165, 168–69, 171, 173–77, 183

Finkelstein, J. J., 19, 69
Fishbane, M., 130
Fitzmyer, J. A., 42, 91
Ford, M., 21
Forrer, E., 9, 169, 175, 179, 191
Freedman, D. N., 111, 130, 205
Fricke, K. D., 124

Gadd, C. J., 35
Garelli, P., 33
Genge, H., 85
Gerstenberger, E., 130–31
Geus, C. J. H. de, 44
Gibson, J. C. L., 91
Ginsberg, H. L., 116–18
Gray, J., 55–56, 102, 123, 128, 169–70, 180, 201
Grayson, A. K., 5–6, 12–14, 16, 50, 66, 70, 76, 97, 107–9, 135, 151, 185, 187, 194–96, 199
Green, A. R., 204
Gurney, O. R., 19, 69

Haran, M., 124, 128, 130
Hawkins, J. D., 75–77, 80, 92, 100, 108–9, 111, 140, 187
Haydn, W. H., 149
Hayes, J. H., 35, 51, 58, 99, 104, 111, 122, 124–25, 127–29, 131, 142, 145, 158, 169, 185, 189, 197, 200–201, 203
Harris, Z. S., 152
Hobbs, T. R., 102, 124, 143–46, 170, 201
Hölscher, C. G., 75
Hommel, F., 176, 178
Honigmann, E., 74–75
Hooker, P. K., 51, 58, 99, 104, 127, 129, 142, 169, 200–201, 203
Horst, F., 131
Hughes, J., 53, 98–99, 125–26, 149–50, 163, 200–201
Hulin, P., 19, 69

Irvine, S. A., 102, 116–19, 128, 132, 137, 158–59, 161–66, 168–71, 173, 175–76, 179–82, 184–85, 189–90

Jankowska, N. B., 26
Jepsen, A., 36, 54, 71, 94–95, 104
Jerome, 205
Jones, G. H., 40, 102, 145, 201

Kaiser, O., 116–17, 132–33, 158
Kallai-Kleinmann, Z., 129
Kallner-Amiran, D. H., 129
Kapelrud, A. S., 131

Kaplan, J., 170
Katzenstein, H. J., 24–25, 27, 41, 46, 62, 68, 146, 152, 198–99
Kaufman, S. A., 42, 91
Kellner, H.-J., 108
Kenyon, K. M., 37, 42
Kessler, K., 178
Kestemont, G., 40
King, L. W., 22–25
King, P. J., 129
Kinnier-Wilson, J. V., 62
Klein, J., 13
Klengel, H., 33
Kraeling, E. G. H., 91, 160
Kuan, J. K., xi, 35, 116, 185, 197, 205
Kugler, F. X., 135

Laato, A., 202
Laessøe, J., 63
Landau, W. von, 198
Landsberger, B., 139
Laughlin, J. C. H., 37
Layard, A. H., 63, 138–39, 154–56, 167, 171, 176
Lederer, C., 126
Lehmann, C. F., 198
Lemaire, A., 110, 121
Levine, L. D., 108, 146, 148, 150–51, 153
Lévy, J., 198
Lipiński, E., 54–55, 58, 75, 94, 121
Lubetski, M., 102
Luckenbill, D. D., 5, 8, 18, 22, 63, 84, 149, 152–53, 161, 194, 198–99

Mahmud, M., 22
Malamat, A., 110–11
Margalith, O., 126
Mays, J. L., 204
Mazar, A., 42–44
Mazar, B., 47, 71, 160
McCarter, P. K., 52, 62
McKenzie, S. L., 36, 55, 57–58
Mendels, D., 1
Messerschmidt, L., 53
Meyer, E., 198
Michel, E., 20, 22–25, 31, 45, 47–51, 53, 61–63
Millard, A. R., 10, 74–75, 81, 87–89, 95, 101, 195
Miller, J. M., 36, 39, 43, 51, 54, 56, 95, 101, 104
Minokami, Y., 57
Montgomery, J. A., 55, 102
Morgenstern, J., 36
Moshe, E., 23

Na'aman, N., 10–11, 33–35, 129, 149–50, 187, 195, 197, 201–3
Naveh, J., 68, 101
Noth, M., 36, 55, 57, 179, 201

O'Connor, M., 116, 145–46
Oates, D., 107
Oded, B., 40, 128, 141, 160
Olmstead, A. T., 7, 9, 18, 25, 135, 194, 196
Oppenheimer, A. L., 7–9, 63, 149

Page, S., 73, 78, 80, 95, 97
Pallis, S. A., 11, 13
Parpola, S., 7, 17, 30, 33, 40, 52, 59, 74, 120–21, 185
Pinches, T. G., 25
Piotrovsky, B. B., 108

Pitard, W. T., 1, 19–21, 31–33, 35–36, 42, 53–56, 64, 70–71, 74, 81, 92–95, 98, 100–101, 104, 123–25, 128, 131, 139, 141, 152–53, 160, 191
Poebel, A., 7, 9, 74, 97
Poidebard, A., 42
Postgate, J. N., 23, 107
Priest, J., 130–31
Pritchard, J. B., 42
Procksch, O., 132
Puech, É, 42, 100

Rawlinson, H. C., 8, 27, 34, 51, 81, 138, 148, 153, 161, 176, 180
Rasmussen, N., 28
Rassam, H., 87
Reade, J. E., 19–22, 64, 130
Redford, D. B., 23, 34, 61
Reinhold, G. G. G., 1, 32
Rignell, L. G., 160
Robinson, T. H., 131
Rösel, H., 180
Rost, P., 128, 139, 141, 146, 153–54, 156–57, 161, 167, 171–74, 176–80, 183

Sader, H. S., 51, 94, 125
Safar, F., 27, 31, 34, 45, 50, 61
Saggs, H. W. F., 5, 7–9, 11, 13, 70, 107–8, 112, 135, 160
Šanda, A., 144, 198
Scheil, V., 88–89
Schley, D., 126
Schneider, T. J., 2
Schoville, K. N., 130
Schrader, E., 28, 30, 73, 149, 179
Schramm, W., 73, 107
Segert, S., 152
Seux, M. J., 84
Sharon, I., 43–44
Shea, W. H., 96–99, 141, 152, 187
Shiloh, Y., 43
Smith, C. C., 23, 59, 62, 65
Smith, G., 7, 12–13, 137, 148, 153–55, 161, 176, 180, 193, 198
Soggin, J. A., 94–95
Steck, O. H., 55
Strange, J., 51
Strassmaier, J. N., 195
Sukenik, E. L., 37

Tadmor, H., 2, 6–7, 9–11, 16, 21, 24, 30, 32–33, 52–54, 58, 73–75, 80–82, 84–85, 87–88, 95, 97, 101–2, 107, 127–28, 136, 138–39, 141–42, 144–45, 148–50, 153–54, 156–58, 167, 169–71, 173–74, 178–81, 183, 187, 189, 195, 201–3
Tappy, R. E., 37, 42
Thiele, E. R., 95, 99, 125, 127, 149–50, 156, 169, 200–201
Thomas, D. W., 63
Thureau-Dangin, F., 68, 76, 108–9, 130
Timm, S., 1, 41, 55, 195, 198
Tomes, R., 188
Toorn, K. van der, 13–14
Trebolle-Barrera, J. C., 55

Unger, E., 25, 84–85, 97
Unger, M. F., 36, 123
Ungnad, A., 5, 7–8, 12–13, 16, 18–19, 31, 64, 69, 72, 75, 77, 112, 136–37, 153, 193

Van Beek, G., 43
Van Beek, O., 43
Vanel, A., 153, 160
Vaux, R. de, 74, 145
Vincent, L. H., 152
Vogelstein, M., 126
Vogt, E., 165, 185

Waltke, B. K., 116, 145–46
Watanabe, K., 7, 17, 59, 120–21
Watson, W. G. E., 111
Weidner, E. F., 7–8, 97
Weippert, M., 52, 141, 146–47, 162–63
Wellhausen, J., 57
Whitley, C. F., 36, 104, 118
Wildberger, H., 116–17, 132, 158–59
Winckler, H., 97, 149, 195, 201
Wiseman, D. J., 80, 164–65, 174, 176, 182–83, 194
Wolff, H. W., 205–6
Würthwein, E., 102

Yadin, Y., 37, 129, 170

Zimansky, P. E., 108
Zorn, J. F., 102

www.ingramcontent.com/pod-product-compliance
Lightning Source LLC
Chambersburg PA
CBHW071236230426
43668CB00011B/1459
9781498281430